The Best Towns in America

The Best Towns in America

A Where-to-Go Guide for a Better Life

Hugh Bayless

Mesa, Arizona
San Diego
Ashland, Oregon

Houghton Mifflin Company Boston 1983

Library of Congress Cataloging in Publication Data

Bayless, Hugh.
The best towns in America.

Bibliography: p.
1. United States—Description and travel—1981–
—Guide-books. 2. Cities and towns—United States—
Guide-books. I. Title
E158.B37 1983 917.3'04927 83-8483
ISBN 0-395-34391-7
ISBN 0-395-34833-1 (pbk.)

Printed in the United States of America

V 10 9 8 7 6 5 4 3 2 1

To everyone who is searching
for a better place to live

Acknowledgments

This book, like most books, represents a personal viewpoint, a statement of my own observations and opinions. However, the specialized nature of this volume, a compilation of both years of personal experience and an unwieldy mass of unsorted data, made the writing of this book a project as well as a statement. The data shaped the statement. It did not alter the personal viewpoint.

So many people were helpful, providing the varied information I needed, that it is impossible to thank each and every one here. They know who they are and they know I am grateful.

At Houghton Mifflin, Robie Macauley was just what an editor should be. He believed in my book, supported me when I needed support, and left me alone the rest of the time. His assistant, Larry Kessenich, perhaps deserves the most credit of all — he pulled my manuscript out of the pile and made Robie read it. And of course my deep appreciation goes to Clay Morgan, the impressively knowledgeable and keenly alert copy editor, whose infinite patience and attention to detail gave the final polish to the rough edges of my manuscript.

Finally, there is one person without whose help this book would not be finished today — my wife Kitty, who kept me going when I wondered if I could ever again face my typewriter, offering encouragement at the right moments, never faltering in her faith in me and the book I was writing.

Contents

Preface

This book is written for you, if you've ever asked, "Is there anywhere I could live that is better than the zoo I am living in now?" There *are* better places. That's what this book is all about. Where they are and how to get there.

Approximately 5 million people move from one state to another each year. Unfortunately, many of them move without knowing what they are moving to, except that it is just "somewhere else." There is no need to make such a move blindly, without knowledge.

For many years, until I retired in 1977, I was the city manager of Carmel-by-the-Sea, California's renowned resort village. Since retiring, I have spent most of my time traveling around the United States with my wife, studying my favorite subject — small towns.

Ours is a wonderful country, the most wonderful in the world. It is filled with marvelous people. Wherever we went, we talked to people, listened to their opinions, learned about their likes and dislikes, and found out why they lived in their own towns or why they wanted to leave their own big cities.

I came to Carmel, on the Monterey Peninsula, many years ago because it offered everything discussed in this book — a quiet small-town atmosphere, safety, lack of long commutes, good schools, friendly people. With the growth in population and the influx of tourists, it has changed somewhat, but it is still one of the most beautiful places on earth. It is still a tourist haven with shops to cater to every taste.

Every reader will wonder why such a "perfect meeting of land and sea" should be left out of this book. The answer is simple. The Monterey Peninsula has never had much to offer in the way of jobs for newcomers. I was fortunate to find what I was looking for when I arrived. Another problem is the cost of housing. Few places in the nation have housing prices equal to those of Carmel, where an 800-

square-foot frame house on a 4000-square-foot lot with no view sells for $225,000. I wish I could recommend this area today as I could have twenty-five years ago. I can't.

There are still good places to live. Over the years, my wife and I have visited thousands of cities and towns in almost every state. We found some towns that we loved and some that were dull, dreary, and uninteresting. A few towns were really outstanding, ones we would enjoy living in ourselves.

We found places once settled by particular ethnic groups that have remained pockets of foreign culture and even foreign language — places where French, Spanish, Czech, or German is still heard as often as English. These are the places where we discovered hams still being smoked over wood fires, whole milk that was half thick yellow cream, freshly ground corn, rye and wheat flours being used in bakeries that still made bread with fresh eggs and whole milk.

Our travels confirmed that the quality of life in big cities is still declining, just as reported in the recent study completed by the prestigious Brookings Institution. Government at all levels has been trying one expensive program after another, wasting our tax dollars in ineffective attempts to cure or at least slow urban blight. Increasingly cities are unable to cope with the very basics of police protection, waste disposal, and education. Cities suffer from growing unemployment, an increase in violent crime, higher municipal debt, higher taxes, and falling per capita income.

That is why so many have chosen to live somewhere else, in small cities and towns, places that are not infected with the creeping blight of our big population centers.

Whenever we visited the larger cities and the more densely populated centers, we met people who asked the same questions, over and over again — where to go and how to get there. When we visited the towns selected in this book, the people never asked these questions. They didn't need to. They already had what the city dwellers were seeking.

In this book, I share with you all that I learned about the good places to live. There has been no attempt to "rate" these good towns. They are all different. Each is good in its own way.

Finally, because of the constant stories, television specials, and newspaper articles about the terrible condition of today's economy, I talked to people in each of these towns just before this book went to press. I am delighted to report that the economies of these best towns are still healthy, that the good life is still there.

Here they are. Pick your own best town in America.

The Best Towns in America

Best Size and Location

For generations, Americans have been bombarded with propaganda that repeated the message, "Bigger is better!" It just isn't so.

Hundreds of our larger cities are suffering "serious financial difficulties," meaning they're broke. Urban decay is continuing, not improving. The shift of population away from cities is not diminishing. Some of our most loved and most frequently visited cities, including Atlanta, Boston, Philadelphia, St. Louis, and New York, are suffering the most from the decline affecting all cities.

While officials in these cities protest the reports of their cities' decline, the fact remains that not only has New York City defaulted on redeeming its municipal bonds but so have Philadelphia, San Francisco, Chicago, Pittsburgh, Dallas, Little Rock, Detroit, Atlanta, New Orleans, Charleston, Memphis, and hundreds of other cities.

It is not only obvious and publicized factors that make big cities different and less desirable than their smaller counterparts. City environments have higher summer temperatures (because the buildings and pavements trap rather than reflect the sunlight), increased air pollution (because of the concentration of automobiles and industries), and increased flooding (because paved areas cannot absorb and retain water as earth does in rural areas). In general, towns offer greater safety, lower crime rates, cleaner air, lower taxes, fresher foods, and more time to enjoy life.

In the golden years between 1900 and 1930 the United States abounded with good towns. It was hard to find a semirural town that did not offer its residents a good life. Then came the Depression, the Dust Bowl, the migration west, the acceleration of a shift from rural America to the industrialized cities, the decline of the small farm, and the proliferation of agribusiness. Small towns died, cities grew — some with dignity, others like cancers on the green countryside.

During and after World War II, most American cities experienced an unexpectedly rapid aging and physical decay, resulting in an exodus of middle-class residents to new suburbs. With this exodus came an erosion of the cities' tax bases, making it increasingly difficult for them to cope with rising social problems.

It is possible that these trends may eventually be reversed, but not in the immediate or foreseeable future. While government is making great efforts and spending huge sums to reverse the deterioration of the cities, even the most optimistic experts agree that it will take a minimum of twenty years to effect any significant changes in urban patterns.

There is, however, an alternative to accepting big-city life or waiting twenty years for it to change for the better. A different kind of life exists in some of the smaller towns and cities of America. Businesses are finding them more hospitable than big cities, with lower taxes and better facilities. People are finding that they offer a new richness in life.

My wife and I met Mike in a small resort town on the Texas coast. Barefoot, wearing faded worn jeans and a T-shirt, he looked like a native — lean, tanned, and healthy, with sun wrinkles at the corners of his gray eyes. But his speech wasn't Texan. Over a cup of coffee, we got his story.

A year before, his doctor in Cleveland had told him to take a vacation — or else. He'd packed a bag with a few clothes and his assorted pills and medicines and flown down to Texas to spend some time fishing.

In Cleveland he had been a success. After getting his master's degree in economics, he had gone to work for a leading financial firm. His rise up the corporate ladder was meteoric. At thirty-four he was a vice-president of the company, drawing a huge salary and living like a king. His future was assured.

With success had come the pressures of executive work and city living. He fought traffic twice a day to and from the office. He struggled to maintain his corporate image. He couldn't spare the time to do the things he enjoyed, because everything was too far away, too time-consuming — long drives through heavy traffic were necessary to play golf, go fishing, or take the family on a picnic.

He had married Elaine during their senior year in college. She was a great wife, bright, energetic, understanding. Their two children grew older, started school, were doing well. Everything should have been wonderful — only it wasn't.

"That's why I came down here for that vacation a year ago. Things weren't wonderful at all. I realized I was paying a terribly high price for success. Sure, I made a lot of money, but we always spent it as fast as it came in — parties and country clubs, a big home in the right neighborhood, the latest fashions and the biggest cars. I thought I was doing great because I never had time to sit down and think about it.

"I found myself snarling at the other drivers on the roads and at the secretaries in the office. I never had a chance to talk with Elaine or play with the children. I had a big, hard, painful knot in the middle of my gut that wouldn't go away. I'd get home from work, gulp three or four martinis, and then fight with my wife just to work off my daily collection of frustrations and anger." He shook his head. "I wonder why Elaine put up with me for so long.

"I came down here to spend a month relaxing, but after a couple of weeks I didn't need my pills anymore. That was when I knew I couldn't go back to the way I had been living. At the end of the month, I called the president of the company and told him I was resigning. Then I called Elaine and told her to pack up and bring the kids down here."

He grinned across the table at us. "I didn't think she would, but she had been ready to get out of the rat race for a long time. She locked up the house and brought the kids down for a look. When she saw how much I had improved in just one month, she didn't need any other persuasion.

"The whole family had a vacation for another month. We got to know each other for the first time in years, and we got to know our neighbors too. It was a wonderful new experience for us, and the kids loved the fishing, hunting shells on the beaches, getting to know the local children."

They went back to Cleveland, just long enough to pack up the things they really needed and put the house on the market. Then they came back to stay. It was pretty frightening — to walk away from everything they had worked so hard for.

"But we came back here, found a place to live, and I began looking around for something to do besides just fishing and sleeping." He laughed softly. "I never thought I'd graduate from executive to janitor, but I discovered that there was nobody doing housecleaning for all the rich people who have vacation homes down here. And there are a lot of them."

Mike bought an old van, hired some housewives who wanted to make some extra money, and started cleaning expensive homes after parties and at the end of vacations. Before long the business was on a regular schedule throughout the year. One customer led to another, and now he has all the work he can handle. He has a fleet of six vans and about twenty part-time employees.

"My family and I eat well, we don't owe anybody anything, I enjoy the work, and I like having Elaine helping me — she keeps the books and schedules the crews. And with all that, we still have time to go fishing, spend time together, take the kids to the beach." He sipped his cooling coffee. "I'll never make the money here that I was making in Cleveland, but I already have much more of the things that really matter."

He slapped his hard, flat stomach. "You'd never guess I was thirty pounds overweight when I got here. I got rid of the fat, brought my blood pressure down to normal, forgot all about psychiatrists, my bellyache vanished, and most important of all, I began to learn about living.

"Go back? Never! There is nothing in the world that could drag us back to what we left behind — not after finding the kind of life we enjoy here."

The stories go on and on, in one town after another. The service-station owner was a stockbroker in New York City, the clerk selling fishing tackle once sold jewelry in one of Chicago's finest stores, the man operating the Laundromat used to build cars in Detroit. Their stories are all different but their thinking is the same. They have traded the pressures of city life for the comfort, quiet, and security of small-town living.

Since we keep talking about towns, perhaps we should try to define one. Socrates said that the right size for a "city" was 5000 people. Of course he was counting only those who were not slaves. In his time, slaves were not considered people. If we counted both slaves and freemen, his ideal town might have contained 10,000 people altogether.

In a world in which the normal method of getting from one place to another is walking, any town becomes difficult to live and work in when it grows beyond a mile or two in diameter. Larger than that, a town tends to break into clusters or neighborhoods, each retaining most of the characteristics of a small town. Prior to 1900, most cities were like that. London is still that way today.

With the coming of the automobile and today's personal mobility, all of the rules changed. It was no longer necessary to live within easy walking distance of work. People found that they could live in the suburbs, work in a city center, and shop wherever the best buys were to be found. Suburbs grew and flourished, central-city areas became more industrialized, and the neighborhood grocery gave way to the suburban supermarket.

As the revolution in transportation began to concentrate industries into clusters in the growing cities, taxation policies encouraged the growth of slums. Landlords were penalized with higher taxes for each improvement made to a rental property, so they stopped even trying to maintain standards. This deterioration of older residential areas encouraged those who could afford it to move away from the city itself to new suburban housing developments.

As expanding cities grew and engulfed the new suburbs, and as the population shifted from the city centers to the fringes, most cities became less and less desirable as places in which to live, work, and play. More and more time was needed for the long commute from home to job. Specialized recreational areas developed apart from both home and office. City services declined and crime increased on the streets and in the homes.

While there is no sharp dividing line between "too big" and "the right size," we did find many reasons to draw the line at 100,000 people. Above that figure, a community begins to take on too many of the attributes of a big city.

At the lower end, we found that towns with less than 25,000 population were usually too small to have stable and independent economies, adequate schools and cultural opportunities, and good medical facilities.

The best towns described in this book, then, for the most part fall within the population range of 25,000 to 100,000.

The Bureau of the Census has established what they call "Standard Metropolitan Statistical Areas," or SMSAs for short. These are areas that have a central city of at least 50,000 population, or urbanized areas consisting of one or more towns with 50,000 population collectively in a county or area with a total population of at least 100,000. The boundaries of these SMSAs coincide with county lines and do not indicate population boundaries. The Standard Metropolitan Statistical Areas map (page 6) indicates clearly where the heaviest concentrations of population are located.

While there is some overlap (some of our best towns are big enough to qualify as small SMSAs), in general anything large enough to be a SMSA is too large to be a desirable place to live.

Size, however, is not the only criterion for establishing a "best

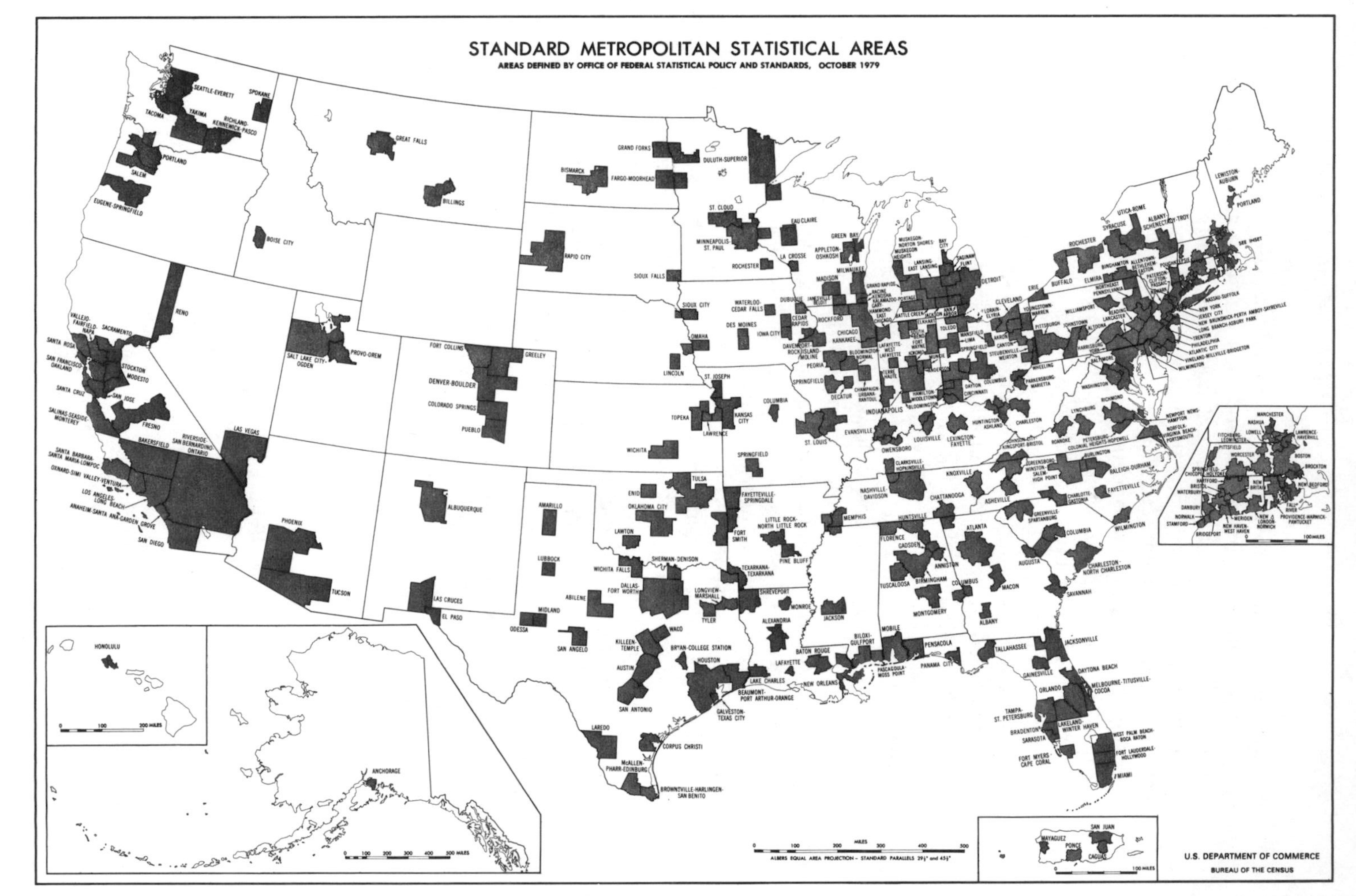

STANDARD METROPOLITAN STATISTICAL AREAS
AREAS DEFINED BY OFFICE OF FEDERAL STATISTICAL POLICY AND STANDARDS, OCTOBER 1979
SEATTLE-EVERETT
TACOMA
SPOKANE
YAKIMA
RICHLAND-KENNEWICK-PASCO
PORTLAND
SALEM
EUGENE-SPRINGFIELD
GREAT FALLS
BILLINGS
BOISE CITY
RENO
SACRAMENTO
VALLEJO-FAIRFIELD-NAPA
SANTA ROSA
SAN FRANCISCO-OAKLAND
STOCKTON
MODESTO
SANTA CRUZ
SAN JOSE
SALINAS-SEASIDE-MONTEREY
FRESNO
BAKERSFIELD
RIVERSIDE-SAN BERNARDINO-ONTARIO
LAS VEGAS
SANTA BARBARA-SANTA MARIA-LOMPOC
OXNARD-SIMI VALLEY-VENTURA
LOS ANGELES-LONG BEACH
ANAHEIM-SANTA ANA-GARDEN GROVE
SAN DIEGO
SALT LAKE CITY-OGDEN
PROVO-OREM
PHOENIX
TUCSON
FORT COLLINS
GREELEY
DENVER-BOULDER
COLORADO SPRINGS
PUEBLO
ALBUQUERQUE
LAS CRUCES
EL PASO
GRAND FORKS
BISMARCK
FARGO-MOORHEAD
RAPID CITY
SIOUX FALLS
SIOUX CITY
OMAHA
LINCOLN
DULUTH-SUPERIOR
ST. CLOUD
MINNEAPOLIS-ST. PAUL
ROCHESTER
EAU CLAIRE
LA CROSSE
WATERLOO-CEDAR FALLS
DUBUQUE
CEDAR RAPIDS
DES MOINES
IOWA CITY
DAVENPORT-ROCK ISLAND-MOLINE
ST. JOSEPH
TOPEKA
KANSAS CITY
LAWRENCE
COLUMBIA
WICHITA
SPRINGFIELD
ST. LOUIS
AMARILLO
LUBBOCK
MIDLAND
ODESSA
ABILENE
SAN ANGELO
ENID
TULSA
OKLAHOMA CITY
LAWTON
WICHITA FALLS
SHERMAN-DENISON
DALLAS-FORT WORTH
LONGVIEW-MARSHALL
TYLER
WACO
KILLEEN-TEMPLE
BRYAN-COLLEGE STATION
AUSTIN
HOUSTON
SAN ANTONIO
LAREDO
CORPUS CHRISTI
McALLEN-PHARR-EDINBURG
BROWNSVILLE-HARLINGEN-SAN BENITO
BEAUMONT-PORT ARTHUR-ORANGE
GALVESTON-TEXAS CITY
LAKE CHARLES
FAYETTEVILLE-SPRINGDALE
FORT SMITH
LITTLE ROCK-NORTH LITTLE ROCK
PINE BLUFF
TEXARKANA-TEXARKANA
SHREVEPORT
MONROE
ALEXANDRIA
LAFAYETTE
BATON ROUGE
NEW ORLEANS
JACKSON
BILOXI-GULFPORT
PASCAGOULA-MOSS POINT
MOBILE
PENSACOLA
PANAMA CITY
MEMPHIS
NASHVILLE-DAVIDSON
CLARKSVILLE-HOPKINSVILLE
HUNTSVILLE
FLORENCE
GADSDEN
ANNISTON
TUSCALOOSA
BIRMINGHAM
MONTGOMERY
COLUMBUS
ATLANTA
MACON
ALBANY
AUGUSTA
COLUMBIA
SAVANNAH
CHARLESTON-NORTH CHARLESTON
TALLAHASSEE
JACKSONVILLE
GAINESVILLE
DAYTONA BEACH
ORLANDO
MELBOURNE-TITUSVILLE-COCOA
TAMPA-ST. PETERSBURG
LAKELAND-WINTER HAVEN
BRADENTON
SARASOTA
FORT MYERS-CAPE CORAL
WEST PALM BEACH-BOCA RATON
FORT LAUDERDALE-HOLLYWOOD
MIAMI
CHATTANOOGA
KNOXVILLE
ASHEVILLE
JOHNSON CITY-KINGSPORT-BRISTOL
GREENVILLE-SPARTANBURG
CHARLOTTE-GASTONIA
GREENSBORO-WINSTON-SALEM-HIGH POINT
RALEIGH-DURHAM
FAYETTEVILLE
WILMINGTON
BURLINGTON
ROANOKE
LYNCHBURG
PETERSBURG-COLONIAL HEIGHTS-HOPEWELL
RICHMOND
NEWPORT NEWS-HAMPTON
NORFOLK-VIRGINIA BEACH-PORTSMOUTH
WASHINGTON
CHARLESTON
HUNTINGTON-ASHLAND
LEXINGTON-FAYETTE
LOUISVILLE
OWENSBORO
EVANSVILLE
INDIANAPOLIS
BLOOMINGTON
TERRE HAUTE
LAFAYETTE-WEST LAFAYETTE
CHAMPAIGN-URBANA-RANTOUL
DECATUR
SPRINGFIELD
PEORIA
BLOOMINGTON-NORMAL
KANKAKEE
CHICAGO
ROCKFORD
MADISON
MILWAUKEE
GREEN BAY
APPLETON-OSHKOSH
DETROIT
FLINT
SAGINAW
BAY CITY
LANSING-EAST LANSING
MUSKEGON-NORTON SHORES-MUSKEGON HEIGHTS
GRAND RAPIDS
TOLEDO
CLEVELAND
LORAIN-ELYRIA
AKRON
CANTON
YOUNGSTOWN-WARREN
ERIE
PITTSBURGH
WHEELING
STEUBENVILLE-WEIRTON
PARKERSBURG-MARIETTA
COLUMBUS
DAYTON
CINCINNATI
HAMILTON-MIDDLETOWN
BUFFALO
ROCHESTER
SYRACUSE
UTICA-ROME
ALBANY-SCHENECTADY-TROY
BINGHAMTON
ELMIRA
WILLIAMSPORT
JOHNSTOWN
ALTOONA
HARRISBURG
YORK
LANCASTER
READING
ALLENTOWN-BETHLEHEM-EASTON
NORTHEAST PENNSYLVANIA
BALTIMORE
NEW YORK
JERSEY CITY
NASSAU-SUFFOLK
NEW BRUNSWICK-PERTH AMBOY-SAYREVILLE
LONG BRANCH-ASBURY PARK
TRENTON
PHILADELPHIA
ATLANTIC CITY
VINELAND-MILLVILLE-BRIDGETON
WILMINGTON
LEWISTON-AUBURN
PORTLAND
SEE INSET
MANCHESTER
NASHUA
LOWELL
LAWRENCE-HAVERHILL
FITCHBURG-LEOMINSTER
PITTSFIELD
WORCESTER
BOSTON
BROCKTON
SPRINGFIELD-CHICOPEE-HOLYOKE
HARTFORD
BRISTOL
NEW BRITAIN
WATERBURY
DANBURY
NORWALK
STAMFORD
BRIDGEPORT
NEW HAVEN-WEST HAVEN
MERIDEN
NEW LONDON-NORWICH
PROVIDENCE-WARWICK-PAWTUCKET
FALL RIVER
NEW BEDFORD
HONOLULU
ANCHORAGE
SAN JUAN
MAYAGUEZ
PONCE
CAGUAS
ALBERS EQUAL AREA PROJECTION - STANDARD PARALLELS 29½° and 45½°
U.S. DEPARTMENT OF COMMERCE
BUREAU OF THE CENSUS

town." Realtors say that the three most important factors in considering a home are location, location, and location. The location of a town determines its climate, its exposure to manmade and natural hazards, and the cultural, educational, and recreational opportunities available to the residents.

Whole sections of the country were excluded from consideration in this book for various reasons. The beautiful New England area, for example, was excluded because of its present economically depressed status, the acid rain fallout from eastern industry, and the high cost of energy that makes living so expensive there.

Other areas were left out because of their proximity to primary military targets, ground water pollution, nearby radioactive and chemical waste dumps, and various other undesirable features of today's world.

A town near a big city acquires some of the big city's problems, such as increased crime, air pollution, and heavy traffic. That is why none of the towns selected in this book are closer than about fifty miles from any large population center.

Natural hazards are not equally distributed across the nation. These will be discussed in greater detail later, but it should be noted that they were kept very much in mind when we were selecting our best towns. No towns that we selected are in areas of extreme natural hazard.

But there is more to location than avoiding hazards.

Many people fail to realize that there are great legislative and governmental differences between the states, with each state enacting separate laws and developing separate policies.

Take welfare, for example. California ranks highest in welfare payments (aid to families with dependent children), as given in the Social Security Administration's current report. At the low end of the scale are Mississippi and Texas. Obviously, any family relocating in order to take advantage of welfare would be far better off in California than in Mississippi.

While it is highly unlikely that any reader will decide to relocate on the basis of welfare payments, there are many other differences between states that may affect the selection of a new hometown. For example, gun-control laws vary widely from state to state under the overall Federal Firearms Law. While I do not propose to get involved in the pros and cons of firearm regulation, it is worth noting that regulations range from those of the District of Columbia, where the ownership and carrying of handguns are prohibited and rifles and shotguns may only be bought or sold through licensed dealers, to those of Louisiana, which does not require a permit for the purchase of rifles, shotguns, or handguns.

While the regulation of firearms is certainly not of interest to everyone, for those who *are* interested, information on each state can be obtained from:

NRA Institute for Legislative Action
1600 Rhode Island Avenue NW
Washington, DC 20036

The purchase of a home is usually the greatest and most important financial transaction of any family. Since each state has the power to enact legislation to regulate land use, and every state has to some extent delegated to local government the authority to exercise local regulation, land-use laws and regulations vary widely from place to place. These regulations can have a profound effect on how land is used and on its future value to the owner.

California's now-famous Coastal Plan regulates land use within the Coastal Zone (which is more or less between the high-tide line and the top of the coastal mountain range). While well-intentioned, this plan has prevented many property owners from building on, or otherwise using, their own properties. Many lawsuits are now before the courts to decide in such cases whether the "public good" overrides individual property rights.

In most states, there are many agencies with varying responsibilities affecting or involving land use. At the last count, California had seventeen such state agencies, though there may be more today, making it the most restrictive of all states in regard to the utilization of private land for private purposes.

Other states, including Vermont, Maine, Oregon, Florida, and Wyoming, have statewide land-use programs. The first three listed have central permit-issuing agencies, while Florida regulates only in state-designated areas of critical state concern and in housing and other developments that have regional impact. Almost all states, including Florida, have delegated planning authority to local governments while retaining some sort of regional advisory control.

Another means of regulating land use is the "land use–value tax assessment law," which provides for lower tax assessment of land used for "desirable" things and higher assessment for those things not considered desirable by the current regulators. Most states use this method of regulation to some degree.

Still another form of control is through deed restriction, whereby the seller of land himself imposes many of the restrictions usually covered by zoning laws. This has been the traditional method of land-use control in most of Texas.

Before buying property, therefore, check the local zoning regulations *and* any restrictions in the deed to that particular property. Seldom will zoning affect land used for a home, though it may affect the size, bulk, setbacks, and other features involved in any improvements or additions made to the home. But if it is proposed that a home also include some sort of business, make sure that such use is permitted before you complete the purchase.

All states have laws regulating the use of water and providing for the protection of water resources. Even though there are federal laws that deal with water pollution, state laws may be more stringent and extensive. Some states, such as New York, regulate the discharge of wastes underground as well as on the surface. Generally, these regulations do not have any effect on the average homeowner, beyond protecting his water supplies, but rural land can be seriously affected. If buying a rural home or farm, be sure to check on water rights and water resource controls before buying.

Each state has its own air pollution regulations, though none have gone as far as England, where in some areas the burning of wood in open fireplaces is now prohibited. Regulations are continually being changed in each state, though the main thrust appears to be directed toward the reduction of automobile emissions.

Solid-waste management — dealing with the disposal of garbage and other wastes — also varies from state to state. The federal government administers an overall program under which states and local governments enact their own laws. The impact on homeowners is moderate — largely through prohibiting the burning or burying of garbage at home and controlling the further disposal of toxic wastes that might pollute local environments.

Controls on noise pollution are being enacted almost everywhere. For the average homeowner, the primary effect of this sort of regulation is to determine local airport location and use. Beyond avoiding the purchase of a home in the landing pattern or immediate vicinity of an airport, there is little the buyer of a home need consider in this area.

Power-plant siting, particularly the siting of nuclear facilities, is also a matter of federal, state, and local land-use control. No town described in this book is close to any existing or projected nuclear power plant. Under present regulations, ample local notice of any new proposal must be made, and all affected citizens have an opportunity to be heard if they so desire.

Taxes also vary from state to state. Local tax rates will be specified later in the discussion of each individual town, but it is worth remembering that the total annual taxation per capita varies greatly from state to state, with Delaware leading with $866.75 per capita taxes in 1980, and New Hampshire at the bottom with a per capita tax of $290.44. The national average is $606.88. A convenient source of current information on state-by-state taxation is *The World Almanac.*

To sum up the criteria for determining the best location and size for a town: A good town has between 25,000 and 100,000 people living in it, is at least fifty miles from any large population center, has moderate taxes and acceptable regulations, and is not close to any known hazards, as defined in the following pages.

Best Towns Are Safe

Nowhere in the world is perfectly safe. On the other hand, there are some places that are much safer than others. Hazards like the automobile are with us wherever we live. Other hazards, such as crime, vary with location.

It is an unfortunate fact of life that crime is increasing everywhere — in metropolitan areas, in rural communities, in big cities and small towns. The FBI Crime Index Total chart shows this in detail. In ten years, crime nationwide has increased about 50%.

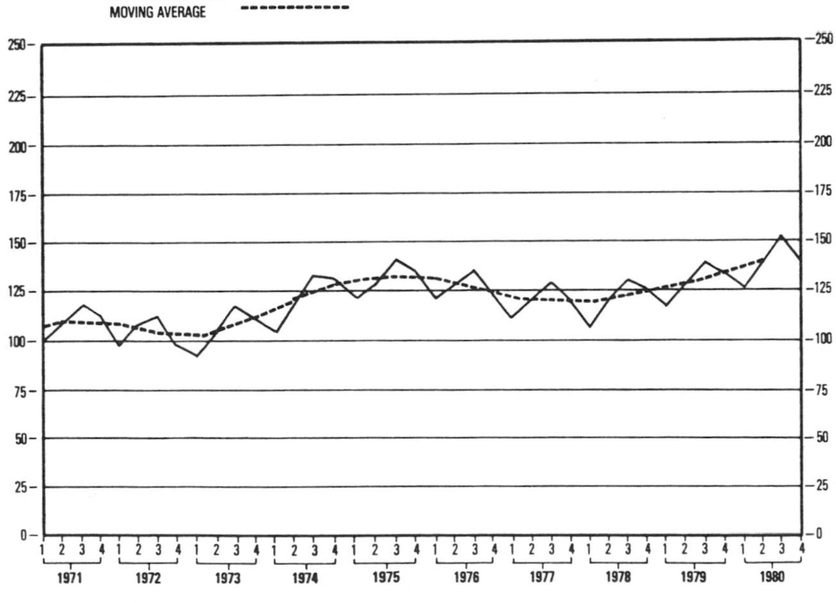

*THE FIRST QUARTER OF 1971 IS EQUATED TO 100 AND IS USED AS A BASE PERIOD.

The only good news in this bleak record is that the amount of crime in rural areas and small towns is roughly one-third that of metropolitan centers. The FBI divides crime into eight categories. The Area Crime Rate table shows these categories and compares metropolitan and rural areas.

AREA CRIME RATE, 1980

[Rate per 100,000 inhabitants]

Offense	Total United States	Metropolitan area	Rural area	Other cities
Crime Index total	5,899.9	6,757.6	2,290.4	5,395.8
Modified Crime Index total				
Violent	580.8	702.1	182.4	353.1
Property	5,319.1	6,055.5	2,108.0	5,042.7
Murder	10.2	11.5	7.5	5.8
Forcible rape	36.4	43.4	15.5	20.6
Robbery	243.5	319.0	22.5	64.6
Aggravated assault	290.6	328.3	136.9	262.0
Burglary	1,668.2	1,911.8	830.2	1,263.3
Larceny-theft	3,156.3	3,534.9	1,143.9	3,519.1
Motor vehicle theft	494.6	608.8	133.9	260.3
Arson				

Towns adjacent to big cities tend to have somewhat more crime than small towns that are more isolated. This is one of the reasons that none of our best towns is much closer than 50 miles from any large population center. As a rule, towns chosen in this book are limited to those with an FBI Crime Index of less than 100 crimes per thousand of population. The crime rate in many of these towns is far below that figure.

Some areas of the country are subject to weather hazards such as tornadoes and hurricanes. Despite modern warning systems, such storms are still potentially hazardous and should be considered when you pick a new home.

Tornadoes are perhaps the most destructive of all storms, with strong winds, heavy rain, hail, lightning, and a severe pressure drop within the funnel. They can occur at any time but are most frequent between 2 P.M. and 7 P.M. from April through June. They have been reported in every state but are most frequent in the area shown on the Tornado map (page 14).

Hurricanes are the most intense stages of storms called tropical cyclones. When the winds of a tropical cyclone are less than 39 miles per hour, the storm is called a tropical depression. With winds from 39 to 74 miles per hour, they are called tropical storms. When winds exceed 74 miles per hour, these storms earn the title of hurricanes. Hurricanes hit the United States mainly along the Atlantic and Gulf coasts, and sometimes strike Southern California as well. On the average, four tropical cyclones reach the mainland of the United States each year, and two of these are hurricanes.

A large part of the damage and more than three-fourths of the loss of life from hurricanes have been caused by storm tides or storm surge. This occurs when the high winds flood coastal areas with seas 15 or more feet higher than normal high tides. The areas subject to hurricane hazard are shown on the Hurricane map (page 14). Hurricanes, tornadoes, and cyclones are events that grow out of the intersection of climate and physical geography. These matters are discussed in detail in the Appendix.

Not all potential dangers are generated by nature. Man himself has created entirely too many for his own good. If our nation became involved in a total, all-out nuclear war, nowhere on the face of the globe would be safe. However, should armed conflict include "limited nuclear war," as the news commentators glibly call it, some places might be safer than others.

We know where the primary military targets are — places like Omaha, Nebraska, with its huge SAC (Strategic Air Command) headquarters, and Bremerton, Washington, with its Trident nuclear submarine base. We know that in *any* nuclear war, those places will not be safe. For that reason, there is no best town closer than fifty miles to any known primary military target. Using presently available government information, I have plotted the locations of the major nuclear targets on the Nuclear Targets map (page 15).

In addition to nuclear weapons, we are also having to learn to live with nuclear power plants. This book is not the place for a discussion of the benefits and costs of nuclear power. From the standpoint of a good place to live, nuclear power plants do pose a potential hazard. We need only remember Three Mile Island, near Harrisburg, Pennsylvania, to know that there are better places to live than next door to an operational nuclear power plant. That is why most of the towns mentioned in this book are no closer than 40 or 50 miles from any such facility.

Love Canal, in the northeastern corner of Niagra Falls, New York, made headlines when it was discovered that a housing development

TORNADO MAP

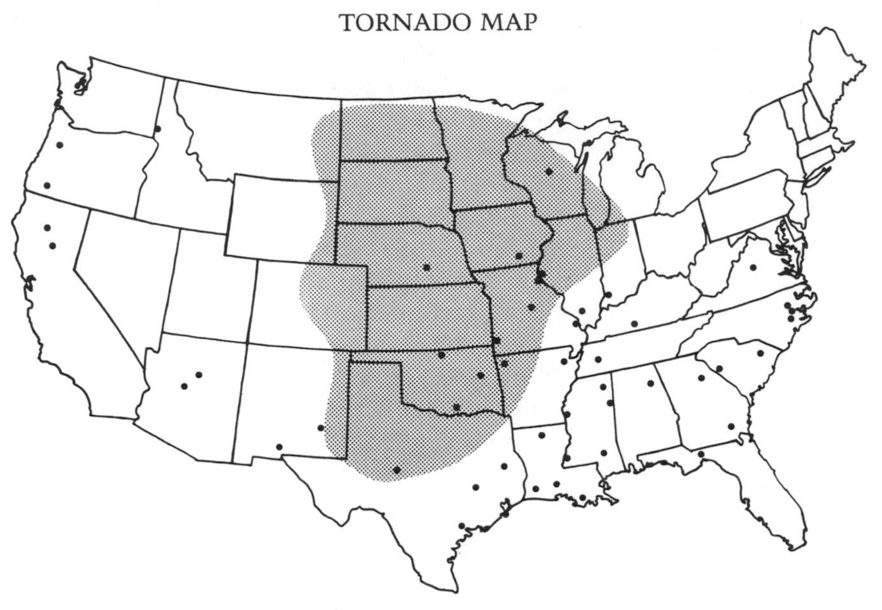

HURRICANE MAP

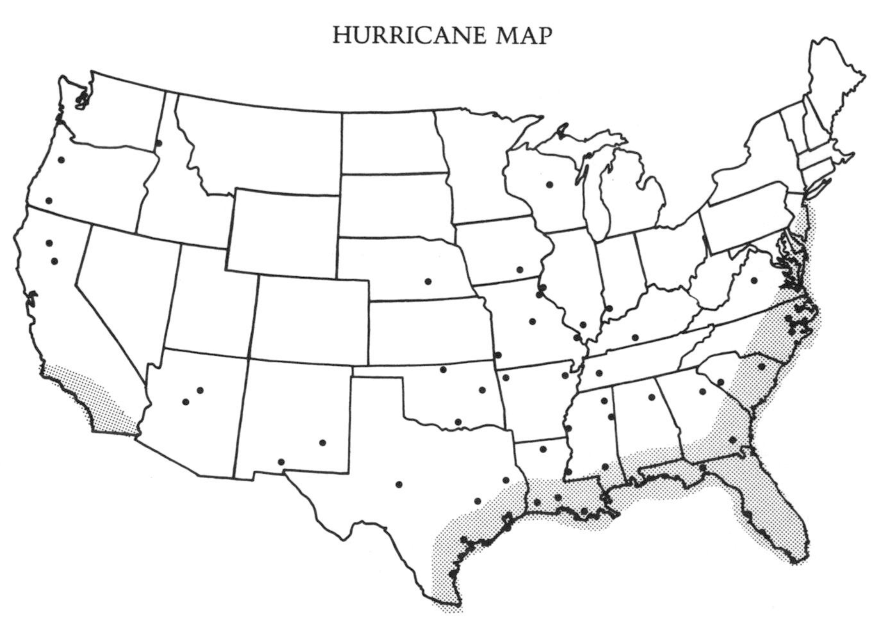

NUCLEAR TARGETS

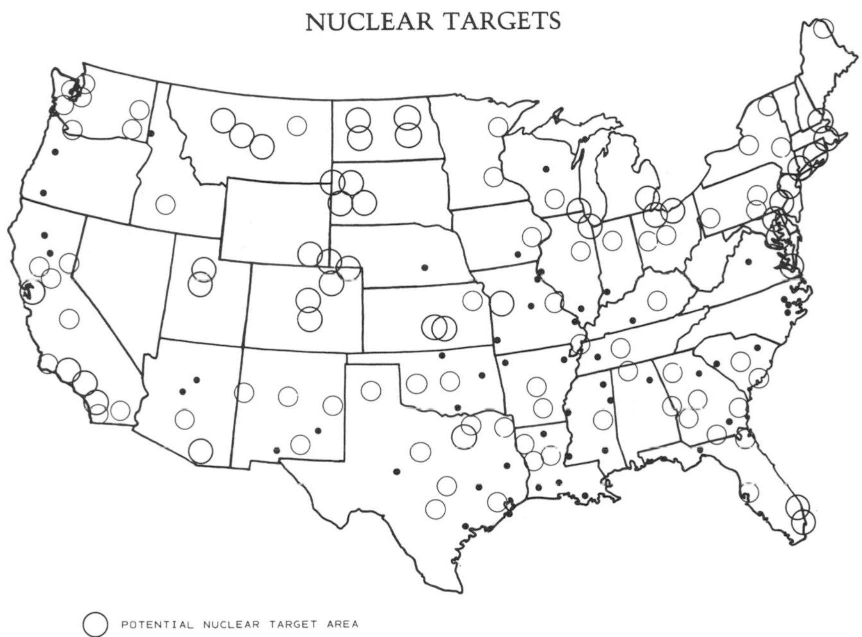

had been built at the site of a dump of some 20,000 tons of very hazardous chemical wastes. Other potentially dangerous wastes have been dumped in many spots across the nation. Probably not all of these locations are known today, but none of our best towns are near any known site.

Some readers may wonder why no Colorado towns are included in this book. After all, Colorado is famed for its magnificent scenery, clear skies, and clear water. Unfortunately, it also has huge dumps of radioactive wastes — tailings left behind from the radium mines of an earlier era. These mounds of tailings, still radioactive, have sometimes become foundations for subdivisions, residences, shopping centers, and schools. That is why one specialist in nuclear medicine, at the Lawrence Radiation Laboratory, affiliated with the University of California at Berkeley, has suggested that the entire state of Colorado be declared a disaster area, and that is why no Colorado towns are listed in this book.

While not all nuclear power plants and chemical and other waste sites pose immediate hazards, the potential is there and is sufficiently serious to justify avoiding them when selecting a place to live. The locations of presently known sites of nuclear power

POTENTIAL POLLUTION

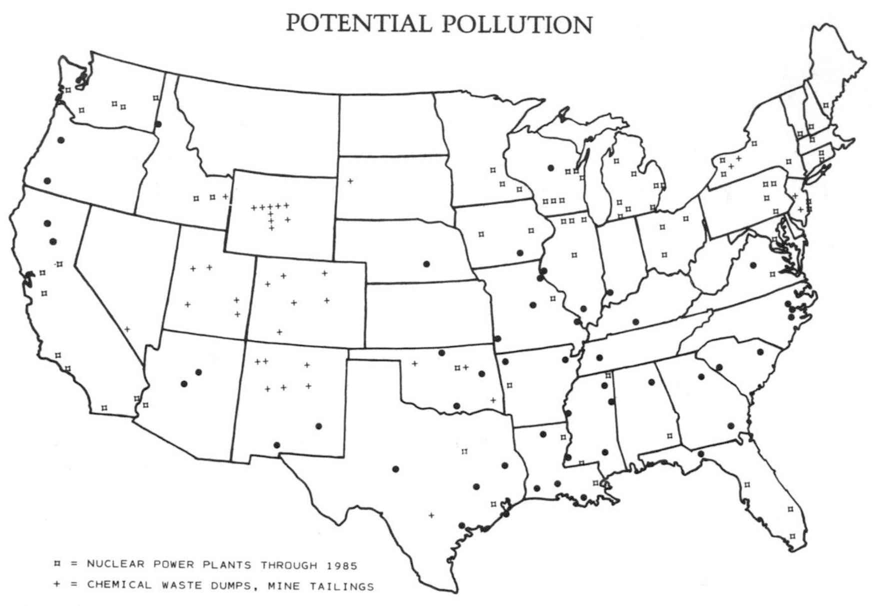

SEISMIC RISK MAP

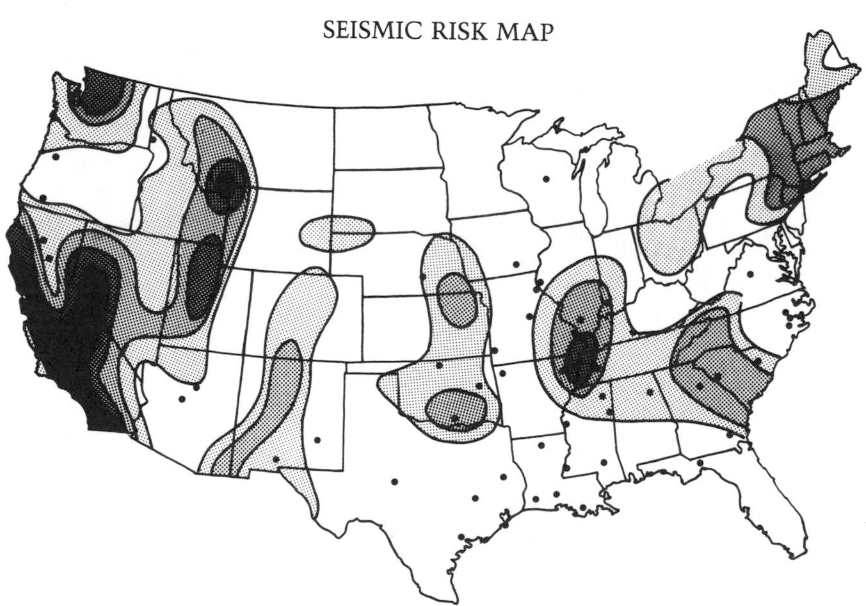

Prepared for the Applied Technology Council. Areas of highest risk are darkest. Areas of virtually no risk are white.

plants and hazardous waste dumps are shown on the Potential Pollution map (opposite).

Another potential hazard comes from the earth itself — earthquakes. While scientists are still seeking ways to predict earthquakes, they are already able to give us some indication of what areas carry the greatest risk. The Seismic Risk map (opposite) shows these areas of risk. Some of the towns chosen for this book are in areas of some seismic risk, but I have tried to avoid the areas of highest risk.

Floods are another natural hazard, but flood-control projects have largely tamed our major rivers, reducing the dangers of flooding and providing water-sports facilities in the process. No town listed in this book is in an area subject to recurrent flood hazard, though anyone moving into a new town is urged to investigate possible local flooding before buying a home.

Forest fires, once a terrible danger to small towns in wooded areas, are now better controlled than ever before. Our forestry services have developed techniques that have greatly reduced the dangers to life and property for families living in such areas. However, there is still some danger, and anyone considering establishing a home in a forested area should be aware of the higher risk.

Given the many potential hazards, it would seem impossible to find anywhere to live that is reasonably safe. Fortunately, there are still some good places. While nowhere is completely safe, there are many places where safety is great and hazards are distant. All of our best towns are reasonably safe — much more so than the big cities, and appreciably more so than many other towns.

The Measure of a Best Town

There is much more to consider than size, location, and present or potential hazards when choosing a good town to live in. In our description of each town, we cover, in the following order, all of these subjects:

- Population
- Elevation above sea level
- Location
- Climate
- History
- Economy and employment
- Taxes
- Shopping facilities
- Residential properties
- Safety, including potential hazards, police and fire protection, and Fire Insurance Rating
- Education, including higher education
- Medical facilities, with information on hospitals and doctors
- Cultural facilities and activities
- Recreational opportunities in the area
- Town government and how it is organized
- Water, its quality and supply
- Energy and energy costs
- Television facilities available
- Newspapers, both the local daily paper and others
- For further information, where to write and whom to ask

Climate

Climate is what happens over the long term. Weather is what happens from day to day. The three most perfect climates in the world are said to be in Hawaii, Kenya, and Mexico's Lake Chapala region. Perth (Australia), Capetown (South Africa), and San Diego (California) have to rank right at the top as well. Few of us can, or even wish to, move to those places. But we do have a very wide variety of climates available to us across the continental United States.

Climate has a tremendous effect on us: on the way we live, the way we spend our time, the way we feel, and the things we spend our money on. In hot climates we save on winter fuel only to pay for summer air conditioning. Some of us are comfortable at average temperatures in the low 60s. Others are only happy when the thermometer climbs above 80°F.

High, dry desert country is supposed to be perfect for people with respiratory problems, yet some people develop bronchitis or sinusitis in such a climate — and get rid of the problem when they return to a low, moist coastal climate.

People living in the Gulf Coast region cannot indulge in winter sports without taking a long and expensive trip. Residents of Colorado, on the other hand, have to go just as far to find deep-sea fishing. In Milwaukee, residents shovel snow off the sidewalks in winter. In Houston, people spend nine months each year cutting grass that never stops growing in the hot, humid climate.

City dwellers live for the most part in manmade miniclimates. They go from air-conditioned apartments to air-conditioned subways to reach air-conditioned offices or factories. At lunchtime, they brave the elements long enough to go to air-conditioned restaurants. Because the tendency in towns is to live much closer to nature, to accept changes in the daily weather as they come, it is important to think seriously about the climate that is the most comfortable or suitable for a desired way of life.

Because climate is so important, we include a fairly complete description of the local climate when discussing each town. In addition, the Appendix provides more information about how climate is created and how, in turn, it generates our daily weather.

Rainfall and the growing season matter little in cities but are of paramount importance in rural areas for those who plan to be gardeners. Both are covered in the sections on climate. And our description of each town gives the "heating degree days" and "cooling degree days" per year. In general, these provide some indication of the relative costs of heating or cooling a home in a particular area. These concepts are discussed in detail on page 393. "Heating degree days" are units for measuring the heating required for a given location, while "cooling degree days" are a measure of summer air conditioning needed for comfort. With equal energy prices, it will cost less to heat and cool a home in Medford, Oregon, with 4800 heating degree days and 800 cooling degree days per year, than it would cost for the same home in a town such as Grand Island, Nebraska, with 6530 heating degree days and 1000 cooling degree days each year.

History

History is surprisingly important in determining what sort of a place a town is today. For example, it is history that makes the Bayou Country of Louisiana, with its French-Acadian culture, so unique. This is an area that was first occupied by the Indians, visited and claimed by the Spanish, later explored and claimed by the French, and contested by the two countries until ceded to Spain in 1762. It was then re-ceded to France as French-speaking settlers arrived from Acadia in French Canada. Today this wooded, watery country reflects all of this history with a culture that is a blend of its French, Spanish, and later English-American heritage.

Economy and Employment

The economy of a town is built on its history. The direction of its early development determines whether a town becomes a "one-crop town" or one with a solid, diversified economy. For this reason, the brief history of each town listed is followed by a summary of its present economic situation.

The most stable towns are those with the broadest and most varied economic base: a mixture of business, trade, agriculture, education, and tourism. All of the best towns have many or all of these factors in a sound and stable mixture. Some otherwise very nice towns were not chosen as best towns because they are single-crop or single-industry towns. For instance, in the lumber towns of Oregon the local economy can change from prosperity to depression if the demand for the single product falls off or a crop fails.

Business and industry have been looking at towns for several decades. Most of the towns chosen in this book have been attracting new industries from big cities, companies that found many advantages in relocating away from metropolitan areas. New industries not only benefit from moving to towns, they also enlarge the economic bases of these towns in return.

In looking at each town, I list the major employers and indicate what they produce. Anyone considering relocating to one of these towns will have a good indication of whether or not it is likely to offer employment in various special fields.

Employment opportunities change constantly in any community, but these best towns generally have more varied types of work than the average. When available, the address of the local state employment office has been provided for each town. Also, the chamber of commerce can provide addresses of employment agencies. But the best source of current information on job opportunities will be the local newspaper.

Taxes

Taxes have a considerable effect on the cost of living in any location. Sales and income taxes vary from state to state. Residential property taxes vary from town to town. Information on taxes in each of our best towns is provided. The local chamber of commerce will usually be able to provide information on any changes in tax rates that have occurred since this book was written.

Shopping

Shopping is a necessary part of today's living, and retail and wholesale trade are important aspects of each town's economic base. All of the towns described in this book have adequate shopping facilities for the everyday needs of the residents. Major national and regional chains are represented, along with local specialty shops. However, there are times when residents have unusual needs that cannot be met locally — the special wedding dress or the part needed to finish restoration of the antique car. In the description for each town, mention is made of the nearest metropolitan shopping area or city where local residents normally look for unusual or special items. In most cases these cities are near enough to permit one-day shopping trips.

Residential Properties

Information on residential properties changes almost daily. The material in this book was current when it went to press, but undoubtedly it will have changed since then. Nevertheless, a town with low-cost housing today will probably have low-cost housing tomorrow. If housing is scarce and expensive now, it will most likely continue to be scarce and expensive in the future.

Up-to-date information on housing is easy to obtain. The first source is the chamber of commerce of the town you are interested in. They always have lists of local realtors available for anyone who asks. The second important source of information is the local newspaper. Subscribe for a month and read the ads. Write or telephone some of the realtors about the homes they advertise. Ask what else they may have in your price range, whether for rent or purchase.

Safety

For each town we give crime statistics, and point out any known nearby hazards and any recurrent dangers such as tornadoes or hurricanes. And whenever the information is available, the Fire Insurance Rating for each town is given. This is determined by insurance underwriters on the basis of their anticipated risk. The lower the assigned class, the better the rating. The rating is reflected in fire insurance premiums, and a homeowner in a town with a Class 5 rating will pay less for insurance than a homeowner with an equivalent home in a town with a Class 6 rating.

Education

Education is obviously important to families with children and to adults who want to continue their studies. What is not so obvious is that an institution of higher learning in a community is much more than a place to study. A college or university is always one of the town's largest employers, and one of the greatest stabilizing influences on a town's economy. For that reason, many of the best towns are also college or university towns.

Medical Facilities

Medical facilities are available in every town chosen, and the local hospitals and the number of local medical personnel are listed. For those who may need specialized service or treatment, the location of the nearest big-city facilities is also provided.

Cultural Activities

The center of a town's activities is often the local college or university. Most colleges have fine-arts departments that sponsor various concerts and other programs throughout the year, and these are usually open to the public as well as to students. Many colleges have excellent theaters and invite community participation in dramatic and musical productions.

For every town listed, information on the local library facilities is provided. University libraries are usually open to local residents throughout the school year and form a valuable supplement to the public library system.

A remarkable number of towns and cities have their own symphony orchestras, little theaters, civic opera associations, and other cultural activities. In many towns, the old tradition of local residents producing local entertainment is still followed, whereas in big cities, more and more people expect government to provide everything from cradle to grave, including amusement. In towns, residents are much more inclined to get together, decide what they would like to have, and then go ahead and producc it for themselves.

Recreation

Recreation is particularly important in towns, where more time is usually available than in big metropolitan centers. Most towns offer a wide variety of outdoor activities not readily available to city dwellers. Every town has golf courses, tennis courts, playgrounds for children, and parks for everyone. In addition, most towns have nearby state and national parks with facilities for hiking, swimming, boating, water skiing, and many other outdoor activities.

In many towns it is possible to go fishing, swimming, or strolling beside a nearby lake in the hours between the end of work and sundown, hours that city dwellers spend commuting between home and work. That is why we go into so much detail about what is available to local residents. In cities, recreation is a vacation project. In towns, it is a way of life.

Government

Government in a big city is something we live with, often resentfully. It is never something we feel we can do anything about, except on election days when we mark our ballots and hope. Towns are different. Every resident is much closer to local government. Some residents *are* local government. Anybody can be a part of local government, and everyone can have a voice in how it is run.

The way a town's government is organized has quite a lot to do with the way the town functions and how efficient and effective the local government is in providing necessary services. All town governments are not the same.

Most big cities and some towns are organized according to the Mayor-Council system, in which the voters select a mayor who is the chief executive and manager of the city. He supervises and directs the city departments in their day-by-day operations. The elected city council is the legislative head of the city, and the mayor usually sits as the chairman of the council when it is in session. The council makes the local laws and establishes local government policy. The Mayor-Council system is an old one in our country and has both advantages and disadvantages. As an elected executive, the mayor is presumably responsive to the voters, perhaps more so than someone who is appointed. On the other hand, the mayor is often not a professional manager, and some mayors have badly mismanaged their towns during their time in office.

Equally ancient is the Commissioner system, in which each member of the city council serves as the commissioner of a department. In other words, each department head is an elected official. The mayor in such a system is the same chief executive as in the Mayor-Council system. The Commissioner system has been outlawed in some states, such as California, because of many past abuses and the obvious inefficiency of confusing electability with effectiveness in office. A person might be able to function well as a member of an elected city council, shaping the laws and policies of the town to accommodate the desires of the voters, yet be totally incompetent at directing the activities of the police, fire, or public-works departments, where specialized knowledge and training are essential.

The Commissioner system is still in use in some states and is in effect in a few of our best towns. The fact that a town can succeed while operating under this system does not make it a good system. It only indicates that the town is remarkably stable and sound.

The Council-Manager system is well established and growing in most states. Under this system, the elected city council employs a professional manager to supervise the everyday operations of the town. The council is responsible to the people, and the manager is responsible to the council. The department heads, in turn, are responsible to, and report to, the city manager. This is the most businesslike system of local government and the one least susceptible to abuse. Fortunately, a great many of our best towns operate under this system.

Water

Having water piped into our homes is so commonplace today that we seldom think about where it comes from, whether the supply is adequate, what the quality is, or what we can expect in the future. Whenever the information is available for a town, we provide data on the water, such as its hardness, acidity, or alkalinity, and whether it is fluoridated. The water quality is satisfactory for every town listed in this book.

Many parts of the nation have water supply problems, or will in the future. In some areas so much water has been drawn from the ancient underground aquifers that the water table has fallen drastically and problems are developing. In coastal areas, such problems may include salt-water intrusion. In other areas, it may simply mean a present or future shortage.

Florida's peninsula has a water problem despite a more than adequate rainfall. The soil is so shallow that it cannot retain the rainfall, which simply runs off into rivers and lakes and then into the Atlantic or the Gulf of Mexico. Other areas, which have traditionally drawn water supplies from lakes and rivers, are increasingly finding their sources polluted by agricultural runoff or industrial wastes dumped into the streams that feed downstream water sources.

While water pollution and water shortages are not problems in any of the best towns listed in this book, they have been factors in the omission of some otherwise nice towns.

Good clean pure water can have various characteristics. It can be hard or soft, alkaline or acid. We all know that soft water is great for washing clothes and hard water isn't. Those of us who have lived with hard water know that it makes nasty rings in bathtubs and sinks, leaves a residue in the bottom of the teakettle, and builds up deposits that choke steam irons and water pipes. But hard water sometimes carries with it certain minerals that are beneficial, such as the fluorides that appear naturally in some water supplies in areas where tooth decay is virtually unknown.

Generally, water hardness is caused by calcium carbonate dissolved in the water, though it can also be due to other minerals, including iron. In areas with hard water, water-softening equipment can be installed to remove all or most of the minerals — which will add to the cost of living in that particular area.

Alkalinity in water usually develops in underground water sources where the water has passed through limestone or other alkaline strata. Both hardness and alkalinity occur in underground water supplies.

Water softness is merely the absence of dissolved minerals. Soft water is always surface water that has not had an opportunity to absorb minerals on its journey from the source to the home faucet.

Surface water comes initially from precipitation, either as rain or as subsequently melting snow. It is during precipitation that water picks up acidity, if it does at all. Most acidity comes from sulfuric-acid vapors in the air, generated by man from the burning of coal or fuel oil or from automobile exhausts. Rain or snow washes this acid out of the air and carries it along in the water as it moves from source to destination.

Acid rain has reached such serious proportions in the northeastern states that some lakes and streams can no longer support fish and other aquatic life. None of our best towns are in areas of acid rain or highly acid water supplies.

Pure rainwater in totally unpolluted areas is neutral, neither acid nor alkaline, and completely soft.

Energy

Energy is of increasing concern to everyone as the costs of electricity, oil, and natural gas continue to rise. For each chosen town we provide information on the average cost per month of utilities. Given the frequent, continuing, and sometimes severe increases in utility rates, all utility costs provided in this book will probably be out of date before publication. However, if a town's utility costs are shown to be low, they should continue to be low in comparison to those of other towns. In cold climates, the costs will be highest in the winter. In hot climates, summer air conditioning will account for a large portion of annual utility costs. In all areas an assured supply of energy is essential.

Energy-efficient homes are still scarce and hard to find, though often it is possible to improve the efficiency of an existing home by adding insulation and taking other measures. When considering any home for purchase, or even for extended lease, it is important to learn what the utility costs have been in the past. Some older homes are so badly insulated that utility costs can be astronomical unless extensive work is done.

Television

Television is the major source of current news and leisure-time entertainment in most homes. For that reason, television facilities for each listed town are described. Most towns have cable systems to supplement whatever stations may be received on home antennas. Some towns have better coverage than others. We report on what we have learned about television in each community.

Newspapers

Newspapers are one of the primary sources of information on any community. Want ads concerning jobs and real estate are obvious reasons for reading the local newspaper before visiting a town or considering it seriously as a new home. Beyond that, reading the newspaper for a few weeks gives a prospective resident a much better picture of the community than could be obtained in any way short of living there. Some newspapers will send a sample copy free, though most ask a dollar or two to cover the cost of mailing. All newspapers will mail a one-month's subscription for a moderate charge. Write and inquire about the cost, then subscribe and read the paper.

In many small communities, the local newspaper is just that and little more. It reports the local news and weather and carries local advertising, but lacks broader coverage of national and international events. In those towns, many residents subscribe to a newspaper from a nearby big city — sometimes the daily edition, sometimes only the Sunday edition. Thus we list for each town the other newspapers available locally.

For Further Information

For further information, the primary source is the local chamber of commerce. Most chambers of commerce are helpful and respond quickly to inquiries. A few, pinched for funds, respond with brief notes asking for money to cover the cost of mailing their materials. In any case, one of the first steps in finding out more about any town is to write the local chamber of commerce. The chamber of commerce address is given for each town listed in the book.

Sometimes there are other sources of local information, such as a historical society or a "welcome" office, and these are listed as well. In addition, every state has a tourist board or equivalent office, and we provide the address of each. It is always worth writing a letter or postcard to ask for information on the area near the town of primary interest. Normally all such material is free.

Other offices are sometimes listed, such as state park and recreation offices, hunting and fishing departments, and local government employment offices. When we feel any such office has useful information, we provide the address.

Finally, one of the most valuable sources of information on any community is the telephone directory. Just reading the yellow pages can tell you more about a town than several days of visiting. From the directory you can learn what the residents buy and what they do. The telephone directory for any town in the United States can usually be obtained through your local telephone office. So far, they are free for the asking. Make the directory one of the first items you get when doing research on any town of serious interest.

*

There is a wealth of information in the following pages about the best towns in America. If one or more seem to be your own best town, make use of the additional material that is available for the asking. Learn as much about your selected town as possible before going to look at it.

Here they are, the best towns in America! Each town is unique. Each has its own advantages and drawbacks. The information is here. Read about them and make up your own mind. Pick *your own* best town. Whatever your needs or desires, there is a best town for you.

Enjoy your journey!

The Best Towns

Ardmore, Oklahoma

POPULATION: 23,465 within the city limits
43,528 in Carter County
76,580 within a 30-mile radius

ELEVATION: 872 feet above sea level

Ardmore, the county seat of Carter County, is located in the south-central part of Oklahoma amid gently rolling crop and pasture land. Fifteen miles to the north are the Arbuckle Mountains, and 20 miles to the south is the famous Red River, which forms the southern boundary of Oklahoma. Oklahoma City is 113 miles to the north and Dallas is 113 miles to the south.

Ardmore is a commercial, processing, and shopping center for a rich farm area that produces varied crops, poultry, livestock, oil, and asphalt. It is northeast of the huge Lake Texoma recreational area, which has boating, fishing, and water sports.

Climate

The south-central portion of Oklahoma around Ardmore has a subhumid continental-type climate characteristic of the southeastern edge of the Great Plains. The area is primarily influenced by the warm, moist air from the Gulf of Mexico.

Summers are long and warm, with temperatures in the 90s from June into September. There are about 98 days per year with temperatures of 90°F and above, and 2250 cooling degree days per year. The summer temperatures are somewhat moderated by relatively low humidity and good prevailing southerly winds, with occasional moderate showers.

Winters are mild and short, with the first frost usually coming in the first week of November and the last frost the first week of April, with 230 frost-free days between. Snowfall is light, seldom more than 4 inches per year, and snow seldom stays on the ground more than a few hours. There are, on the average, only three days per year when the temperature fails to rise above freezing, and less than one day per year when the temperature drops to zero or below. Winters bring occasional northers, when the winds shift to the north, bringing arctic air and an abrupt drop in temperature. Northers seldom last more than a few days.

Ardmore's 37-inch annual rainfall is well distributed, though there are heavier rains in spring that coincide favorably with the long growing season and provide adequate moisture for the stock-farming period and enough subsoil reserves for the lighter rains of summer, when crops are maturing.

In winter, the relative humidity averages approximately 61% in the afternoons and around 79% at night. In summer, the humidity averages about 47% in the afternoons and 83% at night.

Prevailing winds are southerly, except during January and February when north winds predominate. Winds range from about 10 miles per hour in summer to 15 miles per hour in March and April.

While tornadoes have occasionally hit Carter County, only one has hit Ardmore in 87 years, making it an area of relatively low risk for residents.

History

Like many another western town, Ardmore owes its beginnings to the railroad. In 1887, the Santa Fe railroad pushed its tracks northward across the rolling hills of southern Oklahoma, and Ardmore was born on July 28, 1887, when the first Santa Fe train puffed into the tent city that was to become Ardmore. The site had been chosen by railroad officials, who named the town after Ardmore, Pennsylvania. The railroad brought in the lumber and building supplies used to replace the original tent city.

With the Santa Fe connecting Ardmore to the rest of the world, it quickly became the major trading center and largest city in the Indian Territory. Pioneers swarmed in to claim the rich lands, and farmers from as much as 100 miles away came to Ardmore to sell their products and buy needed supplies.

By the 1890s, Ardmore was the largest inland cotton market in the world. Cotton ginning and coal and asphalt mining were Ardmore's primary industries in the early days. By 1895, up to 60,000 bales of cotton were passing through the local cotton gins and compresses each season.

Disaster struck in 1895, when the "Great Fire" reduced more than 85 businesses and residences to ashes and threatened the life of the infant community. But the early residents united and from these ashes began building today's Ardmore.

Economy and Employment

Ardmore is still served by the Santa Fe line, but the Frisco railway line and six truck lines have been added since the early days. It is still a center for a prospering agricultural area, but it has grown to become much more. Ardmore has a widely diversified industrial base, with manufacturers employing more than 3000 in various jobs involving asbestos products, beverages, plastics, printing, monuments, food seasonings, neon signs, meat packing, clothing, saddles, and asphalt products.

Major employers include: Ardmore Manufacturing (men's slacks, 100 employees); Stromberg Carlson Corp. (communications equipment, 250); Uniroyal (tires, 2000); SEMCO (oil tanks, 350); and Total Pet Co. (pet products, 250).

In addition to industry and manufacturing, there are many opportunities in retail, wholesale, and service businesses.

Taxes

The state income tax ranges from 0.5% on the first $2000 of taxable income to 6% on incomes above $15,000. The combined state and local sales tax is 5%. Local property taxes on a home selling for $65,000 would run about $650 per year.

Shopping

Ardmore's stores include many national and regional chains and can meet all of the normal shopping needs for residents. For greater variety one can go to Oklahoma City, two hours to the north, or Dallas, two hours to the south.

Residential Properties

Construction appears to have kept up with need in Ardmore, and houses and condominiums are available for purchase. A few typical listings are:

> ASSUME LOAN on this 3-bedroom brick home with fireplace, built-in kitchen, central heat and air for only $41,500.
>
> TWO ACRES with this 4-bedroom, 2½-bath home with formal living and dining rooms, den with fireplace, 2-car garage, and assumable loan. $76,000.
>
> ENERGY EFFICIENT brick home with 3 bedrooms, 1½ baths, tiled entry, fireplace, large lot, assumable loan. $49,500.
>
> CENTRAL HEAT and air in this 2000-square-foot 4-bedroom home with lots of storage and an upstairs hideaway. Low-interest loan. $49,900.
>
> BARGAIN OF THE MONTH. 3-bedroom, central heat and air. Built-in kitchen. $32,500.

Rentals are scarce at the present time. The apartments that are available usually have a waiting list. One-bedroom apartments rent for $200 to $350 per month and a two-bedroom apartment or condo will cost $350 to $450 per month.

Safety

The FBI Crime Index rating is 62 crimes per thousand of population per year. The police department has 34 employees and 11 vehicles. Fire protection is provided by a department with 45 full-time employees. The Fire Insurance Rating is Class 6. There are no nearby manmade hazards or military targets.

Education

The local public school system provides six elementary, one middle, one junior high, and one senior high school. An indication of the quality of local education is the fact that 63% of Ardmore's high school graduates go on to college.

The Southern Oklahoma Area Vo-Tech School, located two miles outside of town, offers career and skills training for about 1000 students each year.

The Ardmore Higher Education Center, the only one of its kind in the nation, is a post-secondary educational institution at which local residents can work toward college degrees.

Within a 100-mile radius of Ardmore are 21 institutions of higher learning, including Southeastern Oklahoma State University at Durant, 53 miles to the east, which offers college courses through the masters' level, and the University of Oklahoma at Norman, 81 miles north, which offers a wide range of undergraduate and graduate courses leading to bachelors', masters', and doctoral degrees.

Medical Facilities

Ardmore has two hospitals, the Seventh-Day Adventist Hospital and the Memorial Hospital of Southern Oklahoma, together offering a total of 253 beds for acute-care patients. In addition, there are six nursing homes with a total of 414 beds available. There are 38 physicians and 12 dentists to provide health care to the community from nine clinics.

While the medical facilities in Ardmore are excellent, Oklahoma City, 113 miles to the north, and Dallas, 113 miles to the south, offer some of the finest medical care in the world.

Cultural Activities

Numerous cultural programs, exhibits, and classes are offered through the Charles B. Goddard Center for Visual and Performing Arts. There is an active little-theater group.

The Ardmore Public Library serves the community with 58,484 volumes, and the Chickasaw Library System has an additional 74,791 volumes.

Recreation

Eleven city parks totalling 160 acres, one 9-hole and two 18-hole golf courses, 12 tennis courts, 7 baseball and softball fields, and an indoor coliseum provide a wide range of recreational opportunities for the community. In addition, there are frequent rodeos and fairs, art shows, and well-attended school sporting events.

Three nearby lakes offer boating, swimming, and water-skiing, as well as camping facilities and fishing. Nearby one can hunt small game, quail, and doves.

Dornick Hills Golf and Country Club offers its members an 18-hole golf course and swimming, tennis, and dining facilities.

Government

Ardmore operates under the Council-Manager system of local government.

Water

A 19.5-million-gallons-per-day water plant supplies Ardmore from local wells. The maximum delivery of the plant is more than adequate for projected population growth through the year 2000 and beyond. The local tap water is neutral, soft, and not fluoridated.

Energy

Electricity is provided by the Oklahoma Gas & Electric Company, and comes largely from gas-fired generating plants. In view of the large Texas and Oklahoma natural-gas fields, the supply should be adequate for a long time to come. Natural gas is supplied by the Oklahoma Natural Gas Company, and there seems to be plenty for the foreseeable future.

At present, utility costs average $85 to $90 per month for the average two-bedroom home.

Television

The local cable system provides television coverage on 11 channels.

Newspapers

The local newspaper is:

The Daily Ardmoreite
Ardmore, OK 73401

Write to find out about a trial subscription and ask about a free sample copy.

The *Oklahoma City Oklahoman* and the *Dallas News* are also available locally.

For Further Information

Ardmore Chamber of Commerce
P.O. Box 2585
Ardmore, OK 73401

Ask for their package of information for newcomers.

Tourism Promotion Division
500 Will Rogers Memorial Office Building
2401 N. Lincoln Blvd.
Oklahoma City, OK 73105

Ask for tourist information on southern Oklahoma.

Athens, Georgia

POPULATION: 49,600 within the city limits
71,900 in Clarke County

ELEVATION: 775 feet above sea level

Athens, the county seat of Clarke County, is located in northeast Georgia on the Oconee River, 70 miles east-northeast of Atlanta. It is primarily a cotton center and a shopping center for the surrounding farming area, and in addition is an area of increasing industrial development. It is also a center of education, home of the University of Georgia and a growing vocational-technical school.

An old town, Athens is noted for its fine old antebellum homes. It is in an area of rolling hills, open fields, and thick woods — the Classic South of Georgia.

Climate

The climate of Georgia is determined by a mixture of influences — the Gulf of Mexico to the south, the Atlantic Ocean to the east, and the altitude of the area. Athens is in the Piedmont region, which lies between the flat coastal plain area to the south and the mountainous Blue Ridge area to the northwest. The sandy loam and clay make the soil of this area ideal for cotton, corn, small grains, and many other crops.

Summers are long and warm, with 57 days of temperatures 90°F and above and 1500 cooling degree days per year, though the average daily maximum temperatures do not exceed 88°F throughout the summer.

Winters are generally mild, with average temperatures seldom dropping below freezing, though there are about 49 days per year with temperatures 32°F and below. Snowfall is light, generally not more than 2 inches per year. The first frost in fall does not arrive before the second week in November, and the last frost in spring usually comes before the last week of March, giving a period of 244 frost-free days per year. There are about 2950 heating degree days per year.

Throughout the year, Athens receives about 60% of possible sunshine. Precipitation is ample, about 51 inches per year, and is fairly evenly spread throughout the year, though there is usually more rain from December through April than during the summer months. The rains assure an adequate water supply — some 900 million gallons per square mile per year, and 20 million gallons per capita.

Winds are usually moderate, coming from the north-northwest in the winter and from the south and southwest in the summer.

Tornadoes have occurred in all months in Georgia, though they are more likely in the western part of the state. Tropical hurricanes from the Gulf of Mexico seldom carry much energy as far inland as Athens, though they can dump considerable rain on the area.

History

Sometime before 1785, a tiny settlement started at Cedar Shoals, where the old Cherokee Indian trading trail crossed the Oconee River. In 1785 an academic committee selected a high hill nearby as the site for a future university and named it Athens, after the great classical center in Greece. This settlement was incorporated as a city in 1806, becoming the home of the nation's first state-chartered university.

As the years passed, the role of Athens as a cultural and educational center increased. Beautiful Federal and Greek Revival homes, surrounded by magnolia-shaded formal gardens, encircled the growing campus. Life was unhurried and gracious. The Civil War briefly interrupted the good life in Athens, but shortly afterward the "Classic City" resumed its position in the cultural life of the state.

With the growth of the university, Athens began to develop industries, including one of the first paper mills, a brick works, and the oldest textile mill south of the Potomac.

Economy and Employment

As the largest town in northeastern Georgia, Athens is the major shopping and trading center for a large agricultural area where cotton, livestock, corn, hay, poultry, and truck crops are produced.

Industries include mining, construction, cotton processing, stockyards, grist mills, lumber mills, textiles, and garments.

Among the larger employers are: Westinghouse (makers of transformers, 1215 employees); General Time Corp. (electric clocks, 1125); Reliance Electric (electric motors, 813); Central Soya (poultry processors, 800); Gold Kist (poultry, 530); Chicopee Manufacturing Corp. (cotton fabrics, 528); Wilkins Industries, Inc. (women's and men's jeans, 500); DuPont (synthetic yarns, 412); Thomas Textile Co. (children's clothing, 363); and Kendall Co. (nonwoven textiles, 304). The University of Georgia, the City of Athens, and Clarke County are all important local employers.

Growth in Athens has been steady and employment has been stable.

Taxes

There is a combined state and local sales tax of 4%. The state income tax ranges from 1% on the first $1000 to 6% on incomes over $10,000, with a $3,000 exemption for heads of households.

Local property taxes are based on an assessment of 40% of current market value. For instance, a home selling for $65,000 would be assessed at $26,000, and with the tax rate of $3.19 per $100, the annual tax would be about $830.

Shopping

Athens serves as the shopping center for all the farming area within a 25-mile radius, and the result is good facilities for local residents. Most major retail chains are represented, plus a number of regional and local stores. For more extensive shopping, Atlanta is 70 miles to the west.

Residential Properties

Homes are available for rent and purchase. A few typical listings of homes for sale are:

> NEW HOME with 2 bedrooms and 1 bath downstairs, completely finished, plus unfinished upstairs area studded in for 2 more bedrooms and 1 more bath. Nice wooded lot, only $5000 down, with special financing. Only $49,000.
>
> GOOD INVESTMENT. 3-bedroom ranch home for starter home or rental. $29,900.
>
> POULTRY FARM netting $13,000 per year with lovely 3-bedroom, 1½-bath brick ranch home on 5.6 acres with 1-acre lake. 7¼% loan assumable. $94,500.
>
> WALK TO SCHOOLS AND SHOPPING from this 4-bedroom 2-bath home with large family room, fireplace, separate living room and dining room. 2200 square feet of living space for $65,750.

Rentals are scarce, since the economy is prospering, but with patience one can find one-bedroom apartments renting for $125 to $250 per month and two-bedroom apartments or condos for $175 to $400 per month.

Safety

The FBI Crime Index rating is 104 crimes per thousand of population per year, which is at the upper limit of what is considered acceptable in this book. Police protection is provided by five different law-enforcement agencies: the City of Athens Police, the Clarke County Police, the Clarke County Sheriff's Department, the Georgia State Patrol, and the University of Georgia Police.

Fire protection is provided by a department with five fire stations, 21 pieces of equipment, and 105 firemen. The county contracts with the city to provide fire protection to the unincorporated areas. The Fire Insurance Rating is Class 3.

Education

The Clarke County school district administers the public schools both in Athens and in the unincorporated areas, providing nine elementary, four middle, and two high schools. There are several private schools, including Athens Academy and Athens Christian School, both covering kindergarten through the twelfth grade, a Montessori school, a school for the mentally retarded, and a Catholic school. There is also a vocational-technical school.

Higher education is available locally at the University of Georgia, a four-year institution with some 22,000 students and a broad curriculum through the doctoral level.

Medical Facilities
There are two hospitals in Athens, with a total of 433 beds. These are supplemented by the University Health Center, the Clarke County Health Department, and a U.S. Navy Corps School health service.

There are 95 physicians and 22 dentists in Athens, and for more extensive health care, Atlanta is only 70 miles away.

Cultural Activities
Library facilities available to the local residents include the Athens Regional Library, with over 200,000 volumes, and the University of Georgia library, with nearly two million volumes. In addition, there are three specialized governmental libraries.

Cultural activities in the area include the Resident Theater Company, a professional and dinner theater, summer stock, musicals, and mime. Many of these groups perform in the University Fine Arts Building, a center seating 450.

Atlanta offers many cultural attractions throughout the year, including ballet, contemporary dance, pop and symphony concerts, theater, and many world-famous guest artists and performers. Local residents frequently drive the 70 miles to attend these performances.

Recreation
Athens has two country clubs, each with an 18-hole golf course. There is also a public 9-hole course, and the university has an 18-hole course for its faculty, alumni, and students.

There are 15 tennis courts, 16 parks, and 5 swimming pools open to the public, plus similar private facilities at the country clubs.

Watson Mill Bridge State Park offers picnicking, fishing, camping, hiking trails, and canoeing. Sandy Creek Lake, 5 miles from town, has swimming, fishing, camping, water-skiing, motorboating, and picnicking facilities. Forty miles to the northwest is Lake Sidney Lanier, a huge manmade lake with boating, fishing, swimming, and other recreational opportunities.

Seasonal events include major college sports at the university; the Athens Arts Festival, in the spring; a Christmas tour of homes; the Oconee Raft Race, in the spring; the Dean Tate Road Race, also in the spring; the Downtown 5000 Road Race, in the fall; and the Marigold Festival, in the summer.

Athens abounds in scenic attractions, including antebellum homes, the Old Mill, the Botanical Gardens, and Sandy Creek Nature Center.

Government

Athens is governed by the Mayor-Council system, with an elected mayor and 10 councilmen representing the city's five wards.

Water

The water for Athens comes from the Middle Oconee and North Oconee rivers and Sandy Creek. The water-plant capacity is roughly twice present peak demand, providing more than ample reserve for the foreseeable future. The tap water is slightly alkaline but soft and fluoridated.

Energy

Electric power supply in Athens is part of the state's modern, integrated electrical system, and coal comprises 88% of the fuel supply in the generating plants. Electricity is supplied by Georgia Power Company, which has offices at 1001 Prince Avenue. No deposit is required for new homeowners.

Natural gas is available through the Georgia Natural Gas Company, located at 1190 Prince Avenue.

Utilities in Athens cost $85 to $100 per month for the average home, depending upon insulation and user demands.

Television

There are three Atlanta television stations and a local university educational television station that can be received on home antenna systems. In addition, there is a local cable system offering 12-channel coverage to subscribers.

Newspapers

The local daily newspaper is:

The Athens Banner-Herald
1 Press Place
Athens, GA 30603

There is also a weekly newpaper, the *Athens Observer*, and the university has its own student newspaper. The Atlanta newspapers are available locally.

For Further Information

Athens Area Chamber of Commerce
Box 948
Athens, GA 30603

Georgia Department of Industry & Trade
P.O. Box 1776
Atlanta, GA 30301

Bowling Green, Kentucky

POPULATION: 38,887 within the city limits
65,300 in Warren County

ELEVATION: 509 feet above sea level

Bowling Green, the county seat of Warren County, is an old town, established in 1797. It is located on the Barren River in southwestern Kentucky, 61 miles north of Nashville, Tennessee, and 111 miles south-southwest of Louisville. A shopping and trade center for an 11-county area of southwestern Kentucky, it is active in agriculture and light industry.

Mammoth Cave National Park is 30 miles to the northeast and Barren River Lake is 30 miles to the southeast. The countryside is level to gently rolling, with many wooded areas between the open fields.

Climate

Bowling Green has a climate that is typical of the mild central temperate zone, with four pronounced seasons. Summers are short and warm. In June through August, temperatures range from the 80s to 90s in the daytime, though summer nights generally cool down to the 60s. There are only about 45 days per year with temperatures of 90°F and above, and summers have only 1500 cooling degree days.

Winters are brief and mild, with daytime highs in the 40s and lows in the upper 20s to mid 30s from December through February. This period has about 80 days with temperatures of 32°F and below, bringing some 4000 heating degree days. The first frost arrives during the last week of October, and the frost is over by mid-April. Snowfall seldom exceeds 8 to 10 inches, mostly in December through February, and snow seldom stays on the ground for long.

Spring and fall are beautiful, with warm days and cool nights.

Bowling Green receives about 80% of possible sunshine throughout the year. Annual humidity ranges from 81% in early mornings to a low 56% in late afternoons. Precipitation is about 48 inches per year, fairly evenly divided throughout the year. Winds are westerly in winter and southerly in summer.

Tornadoes occur at the rate of about one per year somewhere in the state, making the hazard low for any particular area.

History

In 1790, a pioneer settler named Robert Moore was scouting for a settlement location and found a site he liked on the banks of Barren River not far from Ewing's Ford. He claimed the land and dedicated 2 acres for future public buildings. Today that land is Fountain Square Park.

In 1796 — four years after Kentucky was admitted as the fifteenth state of the new Union — Warren County was formed. In 1798, Bowling Green was chartered as a town. It was named after the central green that was used for the popular sport of lawn bowling.

By 1830, Bowling Green was a flourishing agricultural community. Because river transportation was the major means of moving freight, Bowling Green became an important river port, and it remained so until the completion of the Louisville and Nashville railroad in 1859, when it became an important rail and water crossroads and transfer point.

During Civil War days, Bowling Green was the capital of Kentucky, and it remained so until 1862 when the Union troops moved in. The town remained under martial law until 1865. After the Civil War, the area continued to prosper and grow.

After a lapse during World War I, an oil boom brought prosperity again to Bowling Green. The present industrial growth began during World War II and has continued ever since.

Economy and Employment

Agriculture is still an important part of the local economy, with some 350,000 acres of farmland in the area. Warren County leads the state in the production of beef cattle, and poultry and dairy products are also produced in abundance. Tobacco is a major crop, and Bowling Green is an important tobacco marketing center. Other crops include strawberries, apples, and peaches.

The greatest growth, however, has been in industry and manufacturing. Plentiful natural resources, such as coal, limestone, rock, asphalt, petroleum, natural gas, sand, clay, and gravel, have attracted industry since World War II. Local industries include garment manufacturing, milk production, auto parts, woodworking, laundry equipment, meat packing, bedding, and electronic controls. As the nearest town of any size to Mammoth Cave National Park, Bowling Green has also become an important tourist center.

Employment has remained high and unemployment low because of the broad economic base of the community. Among the larger employers in the area are: Western Kentucky University; Holley Carburetor Division of Colt Industries (automotive carburetors, 2000 employees); Cutler-Hammer, Inc. (electrical controls and switches, 835); Detrex Chemical Industries (parts-cleaning equipment, 180); Dibrell-Kentucky, Inc. (tobacco, 200 to 500); FMC Corporation's Crane & Excavator Division (534); Firestone Textiles (tire cord fabric, 712); Koehring Atomaster (portable oil-fired space heaters, 448); and Union Underwear (men's and boys' underwear, 1315).

Smaller companies employ workers in the production of shipping containers, liniment, soft drinks, bakery goods, air compressors, furniture, boxes, fertilizers, and storm doors.

For current employment information, write:

Kentucky Unemployment Division
803 Chestnut Street
Bowling Green, KY 42101

Taxes

Kentucky has a 5% sales tax, and the state income tax ranges from 2% on the first $3000 to 6% on incomes over $8000. Bowling Green levies a 3% tax on utilities, including electric, gas, water, sewer, and telephone services.

The residential property tax rate is $1.30 per $100 of assessed value inside the city limits and $0.55 per $100 in the county. The tax on a $65,000 home would be about $845 per year.

Shopping

Because Bowling Green has a large university student body and serves an 11-county trade and shopping area, its stores are more than adequate for most needs. Many major chain stores are represented in the downtown business and shopping area and in the five suburban shopping centers, and there are numerous local and regional stores.

For those who feel the need to shop for items not available in Bowling Green's stores, Nashville, Tennessee, which has a population of 850,000, is only 61 miles south on I-65.

Residential Properties

Bowling Green has a broad spectrum of homes to choose from. A few typical examples are:

COUNTRY KITCHEN in this 3-bedroom, 2-bath home with family room with fireplace, living room, on 1½ acres. $44,500.

COUNTRY HOME on 20 acres with central heat and air, 3 bedrooms, 1½ baths, double garage, in excellent condition. $69,500.

NICE 2-bedroom starter home with 2 acres and garden, deck, butane furnace, well water fed by spring. $28,500.

MAGNIFICENT old 5-bedroom home with separate living room, dining room, parlor, 4 fireplaces, 3 baths, gas heat, trees, and class. $55,000.

SECLUDED 3000-square-foot home 20 minutes from center of town with 65 acres — 14 in crop land, balance in pasture. $130,000 with only 10% down and owner financing.

Homes and apartments are available for rent. One-bedroom apartments currently rent for about $150 to $275 per month, and two-bedroom apartments or condos rent for $195 to $395. The local board of realtors will send you a free copy of the magazine *Homes* if you write them at:

Bowling Green Board of Realtors
440½ East Main Street
Bowling Green, KY 42101

Safety

The FBI Crime Index rates Bowling Green at 73 crimes per thousand of population per year. There are no manmade hazards closer than the nuclear power plant just northwest of Nashville, Tennessee, about 50 miles from Bowling Green.

Police protection is provided by the local police department, which has 76 employees and 30 vehicles.

Fire protection is provided by a department with four stations, 80 employees, and 12 vehicles, and the county areas are protected by seven rural stations. The Fire Insurance Rating for Bowling Green is Class 4.

Education

Within the city limits, public education is provided by a school district with six elementary, one junior high, and one senior high school. In the areas outside the city limits, the county school system provides elementary and junior high schools and another high school.

Bowling Green State Vocational Technical School offers training in a variety of technical and vocational subjects, with 26 programs ranging from Auto Body Repair and Civil Technology to Electronics and Health Occupations. Bowling Green Business College is a private college offering secretarial and business training. Community Education offers residents programs in art, music, adult education, and leisure-time pursuits.

Western Kentucky University serves more than 13,500 students. The undergraduate division provides four-year programs leading to bachelor of arts, bachelor of fine arts, bachelor of science, bachelor of science in nursing, and bachelor of music degrees. Thirty-six associate degree programs are also available. The graduate school offers masters' degrees in a wide range of fields.

Medical Facilities

Bowling Green–Warren County Hospital is a full-service community hospital with 298 beds. Greenview Hospital has 157 beds and is expanding. It also provides an unusual 24-hour outpatient service.

Several nursing homes in the area offer medical services and extended care to supplement the hospital services.

The Bowling Green–Warren County Health Department provides a broad range of public services, including testing for disease, giving inoculations, and administering hearing and vision tests.

There are two mental-health centers and a 23-doctor clinic near the center of town. Other clinics are located near the two hospitals.

Cultural Activities

Much of the cultural activity in Bowling Green revolves around the university, which has a tradition of providing cultural and intellectual resources for the area. Its Kentucky Building houses a museum and the university library. Hardin Planetarium is one of the 26 largest in the nation and gives regular shows for the public.

The university's Fine Arts Festival has become one of the foremost cultural attractions in the state. A lecture series brings prominent speakers from all over the country. Plays performed by the theater department are open to the public.

The university library is open to the public and houses a collection of over 750,000 volumes. The newly renovated Bowling Green–Warren County Library, which has over 76,000 volumes, offers an art gallery, a children's story hour, and film showings.

To the north of Bowling Green is Horse Cave Theater, a professional repertory theater located in the Old Thomas Opera House, built in 1911. Other cultural activities are available both in Louisville, 111 miles to the north, and in Nashville, 61 miles to the south.

Recreation

Bowling Green offers many opportunities for the active sportsman and for the spectator. Every winter, thousands gather at Western Kentucky University to watch football and basketball. Beech Bend International Raceway is the home of the NHRA Sportsnationals as well as many other auto racing events.

Golfers can choose from four courses within the city. Indian Hills and Bowling Green country clubs both have 18-hole courses, while the Municipal Park and Hobson Grove offer 9-hole courses.

Boating, fishing, swimming, and other water sports are readily available on the many lakes and streams in the area. Shanty Hollow, a 175-acre lake well stocked with a variety of fish, is fourteen miles north of town. Also within easy driving distance are Barren River Reservoir, Nolin Reservoir, Lake Malone, Lake Cumberland, Barkley Lake, Dale Hollow, and Kentucky Lake. The Barren River Reservoir State Park offers boating, fishing, swimming, horseback riding, camping, and cabins. A lodge provides restaurant facilities for residents and visitors. Bass, crappie, bluegill, and catfish abound in the Barren, Green, and Gasper rivers, and the many creeks are also stocked with fish.

There is a local bowling alley, and a skating rink. The local recreation system provides facilities at 15 parks for tennis, baseball, basketball, horseshoes, and picnicking. Eight of the parks have supervised playgrounds for children.

Government

Bowling Green operates under the Council-Manager form of government, with a mayor, four commissioners, and a full-time city manager.

Water

The Municipal Utilities Department provides water that is slightly alkaline, soft, and fluoridated. Because of the many rivers and lakes in the area, water is plentiful and the supply assured.

Energy

Electricity is furnished by the Municipal Utilities Department within the city limits, and through a county cooperative in the unincorporated areas. Gas is provided by Western Kentucky Gas.

Information on the current rates for utilities may be obtained by writing the chamber of commerce. Utility costs average between $75 and $100 per month for a two- to three-bedroom home, including water, sewer, electricity, and gas bills.

Television

There are a local ABC television station, an educational station, and a local cable system. Four channels from Nashville are also available locally on home antenna systems.

Newspapers

The local daily newspaper is:

The Daily News
Bowling Green, KY 42101

The *Nashville Tennessean* and the *Louisville Courier-Journal* are also available locally.

For Further Information

Bowling Green–Warren County Chamber of Commerce
P.O. Box 51
Bowling Green, KY 42101

Kentucky Department of Public Information
Capitol Annex
Frankfort, KY 40601

Bryan, Texas

POPULATION: 44,265 within the city limits
93,588 within the Bryan–College Station area

ELEVATION: 367 feet above sea level

Bryan and College Station are virtually a single community today. Bryan was originally an agricultural community, while College Station grew up around Texas A & M University.

Bryan–College Station is located in east-central Texas, in Brazos County, 95 miles northwest of Houston, 90 miles southeast of Waco, and 165 miles south of Dallas. The area is flat to gently rolling, with ample water supply for both agriculture and industry.

The university, which has over 31,000 students, forms a large and important part of the population and greatly affects the life of the community.

Climate

Since Bryan is located in the coastal plain of Texas, the climate is predominately controlled by the warm moist air from the Gulf of Mexico. Summers are long and hot, and winters are short and mild, except for an occasional norther that brings in arctic air.

The long summers bring some 2900 cooling degree days per year, with 105 days of temperatures 90°F and higher. These normally occur from June through September. Minimum temperatures in the summer average above 70°F through June, July, and August.

Winters are mild, with maximum temperatures in the 60s and minimums in the 40s the norm from December through February, though extreme lows of −5°F to −21°F have been recorded from December through March. Such cold is unusual: There are no more than 10 days per year with frost, and none at all in some years, giving Bryan an average frost-free period of 305 days per year. Snowfall is almost unknown, and when it has happened, it has rarely stayed on the ground more than an hour or two. There are 1475 heating degree days per year.

Rainfall is ample, at 38.75 inches per year, and is fairly evenly spread throughout the year, with slightly more rainfall from April to June, and most months averaging around 3 inches. The annual precipitation of 650 million gallons per square mile assures an adequate water supply year-round. Combined with the warm, moist air from the Gulf of Mexico, it produces an average humidity of 70% throughout the year.

While there are only 6 to 8 days per month with rain, the high incidence of large, puffy, white cumulus clouds reduces the sunshine falling on Bryan to 62% of possible sunshine.

History

The area that is now Brazos County was part of the territory granted to Moses Austin by Spain in 1821 and colonized by his son Stephen F. Austin, for whom the capital city of Texas was later named. When Texas became a republic in 1836 the present county limits were drawn, and Boonville, three miles east of Bryan, was established as the county seat. But Boonville did not grow the way Bryan did, and in 1866 the county seat was moved to its present location in Bryan.

The original economy of the area was based on agriculture, but when the citizens of the county donated 2000 acres of land and $50,000 in 1871 to attract the proposed Texas A & M University, the economic base broadened.

Economy and Employment

With no large population center nearer than Houston or Waco, Bryan–College Station is the economic center of a seven-county area. There are ample energy resources in the vicinity, with over 100 oil and gas wells plus nearby surface lignite coal deposits.

Within the past 10 years Bryan has grown 32% and College Station 110% — so fast that city officials are becoming concerned and are looking for ways to control growth. But given the very low unemployment rate, it seems unlikely that much will be done in the near future to develop controls.

Today's economy is based on a large retail trade that serves a wide area, and on diverse industries such as cotton-gin manufacturing, printing and publishing, cattle, poultry, corn, cotton, aluminum windows, and concrete blocks.

The largest employer in the area is Texas A & M University. Manufacturers include: Alenco (aluminum products, with 850 employees); Butler Manufacturing Co. (building materials, 375); ARC Division of Kaneb (electronic terminals, 325); Babcock & Wilcox (oil-well tubing, 250); and International Shoe (rubber heels and soles, 150).

For information on current job opportunities, write:

Texas Employment Commission
801 East 29th St.
Bryan, TX 78801

Taxes

Texas has no state income tax, and the combined city and state sales tax is 5%. The property tax on a home selling for $65,000 runs about $1450 per year at current rates.

Shopping

Bryan and College Station, which now form an almost continuous community, provide a large downtown business and shopping area strung along the highway that connected Houston and Waco before the freeway bypassed the towns. Bryan's downtown shopping center is 10 blocks long and 5 blocks wide. Both Bryan and College Station have several suburban and neighborhood shopping centers.

Most of the major regional chain stores are represented locally, but for a wider choice many residents drive to Houston, where some of the world's finest stores are now located.

Residential Properties

Rapid growth in the area has so far been matched by considerable residential construction. Homes can be found in older, close-in locations, or farther away in new subdivisions. Prices range accordingly. Examples are:

PERFECT FOR A YOUNG FAMILY. 3-bedroom, 1-bath home on large lot in nearby Hearne with hardwood floors and central heat. $32,500.

TOWNHOME conveniently located close to schools, shopping and hospitals in quiet neighborhood. 2-bedroom condominium has ample storage and includes washer, dryer and refrigerator at $41,500.

JUST BUILT in beautiful subdivision, this 3-bedroom 2-bath home with double garage is on a corner lot with trees and lawn. $54,900.

OLDER 2-bedroom stone house on wooded lot close in and near stores and schools. $24,500.

Rentals are plentiful, with one-bedroom apartments available for $145 to $320 per month and two-bedroom apartments or condos for $225 to $420 per month.

Safety

The FBI Crime Index rating is only 74 crimes per thousand of population per year. Bryan has 51 full-time policemen and College Station has 68. Their separate but cooperating fire departments have 54 and 60 members, respectively. Together, they have 18 pieces of modern firefighting equipment.

There are no known natural hazards nearby, and the closest manmade potential hazards are over 90 miles away — at Austin (Bergstrom Air Force Base) and at Temple (Fort Hood).

Education

Bryan and College Station are in separate school districts. Both have new high schools. Together they serve close to 13,000 students. Bryan provides special education for physically and mentally handicapped children, and College Station provides special programs for the learning disabled, homebound, and others. Both schools districts offer vocational education in a variety of subjects.

In addition to the public school system, there is Allen Academy, formerly Allen Military Academy, a college preparatory school in Bryan with approximately 290 students, most of whom go directly into Texas A & M. There is also a Catholic parochial school with 260 students in grades one through eight, and St. Michael's

Academy, an Episcopal school, offers a nondenominational college preparatory program to 150 students.

At the college level, Blinn College, in Bryan, offers both two- and four-year programs in the fields of law enforcement, tire technology, real estate, and medication. And Texas A & M University, which has over 31,000 students, is a land and sea grant institution of national importance.

Medical Facilities
There are three hospitals in the area with a combined total of 231 beds. Over 60 physicians and more than 30 dentists serve the area. For more extensive medical service, Houston is two hours' drive to the southeast.

Cultural Activities
Texas A & M is the cultural center of the community, sponsoring annual musicals, appearances by popular entertainers, and operatic, symphonic, and other programs.

The public library serves the community with over 77,000 volumes, and the library resources at the university are also available to local residents.

Recreation
The Texas World Speedway attracts visitors from near and far for many types of auto racing.

Brazos County Park features 50 acres of nature trails and picnic facilities, and has a rodeo arena and a covered livestock show area.

The Bryan–College Station park systems include some 40 parks, 16 of which offer playground equipment, 5 swimming pools, 2 public golf courses, and 19 tennis courts. There is also a private 18-hole golf course, plus 2 outdoor theaters, 2 lakes, bowling alleys, youth centers, and facilities for softball, basketball, and volleyball.

Hunting and fishing are readily available throughout most of the year at the nearby Brazos River and in the surrounding area.

Government
Both Bryan and College Station have Council-Manager governments, each with an elected mayor and six council members.

Water
Owing to an annual rainfall of nearly 40 inches, there is a plentiful supply of water. Local tap water is very soft and fluoridated.

Energy
With 100 oil and gas wells in the vicinity and two power plants under construction nearby, the power needs of the area appear to be taken care of for the foreseeable future. Gas is supplied by the Lone Star Gas Company, while electricity is supplied by the municipal departments of Bryan and College Station. At present, utility costs for an average two-bedroom home are about $90 per month.

Television
There are two cable television systems in the area and two regular network stations. A local public television station is also in operation.

Newspapers
The daily newspaper is:

The Eagle
Bryan, TX 77801

Also, there is a weekly newspaper that has a useful real-estate review section. It is:

The Press
Bryan, TX 77801

The *Houston Post*, the *Houston Chronicle*, the *Dallas News*, and the *Dallas Times Herald* are available locally.

For Further Information

The Bryan–College Station Chamber of Commerce
P.O. Box 726
Bryan, TX 77801

Tourist Development Agency
P.O. Box 12008, Capitol Station
Austin, TX 78711

In addition, the following office will provide a current list of the top 25 manufacturers in the Brazos Valley:

Brazos County Industrial Foundation, Inc.
2700 Texas Avenue
Bryan, TX 77801

Cape Girardeau, Missouri

POPULATION: 34,318 within the city limits
50,500 within the overall trade area of the city

ELEVATION: 350 to 500 feet above sea level

Cape Girardeau (pronounced ji-rar'doe) is located on the eastern border of Missouri, on the Mississippi River some 115 miles south of St. Louis and 160 miles north of Memphis. It is a focal point for commercial, educational, medical, industrial, and cultural services for a 10-county area, as well as a regional industrial and trade center.

Topography in the area varies from flat lowlands to the south to rolling hills and picturesque valleys to the north and west, with the Mississippi River forming the eastern border of the town. Several creeks pass through Cape Girardeau, including Cape LaCroix Creek, which runs diagonally from northwest to southeast.

The hilly western and northern sections of Cape Girardeau have evolved primarily as residential areas, while the flat southern section has developed industry and farming.

Climate

The climate of Cape Girardeau is essentially continental, with frequent changes in weather, both from day to day and from season to season. Eastern Missouri is in the path of cold air moving down from Canada, warm, moist air coming up from the Gulf of Mexico, and dry air blowing in from the west.

Summers are warm to hot, with normal maximum temperatures ranging from 70°F in April and October to the high 80s and low 90s in May through September. There are about 64 days per year with temperatures of 90°F and above.

Winters are short and vary from mild to cold, with normal daily ranges from the high 40s to the low 30s from December through February. Minimum temperatures have reached as low as −12°F in January. The last frost is usually in the first week of April, and the first frost of fall comes at the end of October, with about 210 days between frosts and 70 days with temperatures 32°F and below.

Precipitation averages around 43 inches per year, more or less evenly divided throughout the year, with slightly more rain falling in March through June. The number of days with precipitation each month ranges from 8 in October and November to 12 in March through May, giving the area about 65% of possible sunshine per year.

Winds are moderate and variable from westerly to southerly throughout most of the year, except during storms. Snowfall averages around 12 inches per year, falling mostly in December through March, and snow seldom stays on the ground for long.

History

The name of the town is derived from an early trading post established by Jean B. Girardot, an ex-ensign in the French marines. Other than contributing his name, Girardot had little or nothing to do with the development of the present town. Rather, it was Louis Lorimer, who settled on the present site in 1792, who was responsible for founding the town. In 1793 the settlement was recognized by the Spanish authorities as an independent post on the Mississippi.

The village of Cape Girardeau was included in the 1803 purchase of the Louisiana Territory from France. Five years later it was incorporated as a city.

In the 1830s, Cape Girardeau began a remarkable expansion,

mainly the result of the steamboat traffic on the Mississippi, which lasted until the coming of the railroads after the Civil War. Union soldiers occupied the town during the Civil War and erected four forts to protect themselves from the Confederate army. Only one minor engagement took place in the area, and the war generally bypassed the town.

From an early trading post, Cape Girardeau developed into an important trading center, as French, German, and Yankee settlers moved in and cultivated the rich farmland in the area.

Economy and Employment

While Cape Girardeau is still an important trading center for a large agricultural area, industry has been steadily increasing in importance since International Shoe Company opened a plant in 1907 and the Marquette Company began operations in 1910. Today there are over 75 manufacturing concerns in Cape Girardeau.

Local industry includes the manufacturing of such items as plastic sheets, men's shoes, furniture, cement, diapers, leather jackets, and electrical products.

Nonmanufacturing business includes transportation, meat and frozen-food products, general construction, utilities, retail and wholesale stores, and public services.

Unemployment has remained lower than the national average. Major employers in the area include: Procter & Gamble (disposable diapers, 1350 employees); Southeast Missouri State University (900); St. Francis Medical Center (900); Superior Electric (electrical products, 750); Florsheim shoes (600); Sam Tanksley Trucking (650); Thorngate, Ltd. (apparel, 400); Southeast Missouri Hospital (680); and Missouri Utilities (225).

Taxes

The state of Missouri has modest taxes, with a personal income tax rate that ranges from 1.5% to 6% of taxable income earned within the state. The combined state, county, and city sales taxes add up to a moderate 4⅝%.

Real estate taxes on residential property are $5.45 per $100 of assessed value, which is based on 30% of true market value. Thus, a residence selling for $65,000 would be taxed at approximately $1063 per year.

Shopping

As the trading center for a large agricultural area, Cape Girardeau is well supplied with a wide variety of retail outlets. In addition to the central business and shopping district, there is the large Town-Plaza Shopping Center, which has over 30 stores. Many national chain stores are represented, including Sears, Ward's, Woolworth, K-Mart, IGA, Walgreen, Kroger, Gallenkamps, Firestone, Western Auto, Radio Shack, and 7-Eleven.

For more sophisticated shopping, St. Louis is 115 miles to the north and Memphis is 160 miles to the south.

Residential Properties

Building in Cape Girardeau has kept up with demand, with the result that an adequate supply of housing is available. Examples of currently available properties are:

> TRADITIONAL CHARM with 4 bedrooms, 2 baths, lovely screened front porch, newly remodeled kitchen, on a dead-end street. $46,900.
>
> VIEW OF GOLF COURSE from this 3-bedroom, 2-bath brick ranch-style home with over 2000 square feet of living space. Financing below going rates at $78,900.
>
> OWNER FINANCING on this 2-bedroom home with fenced yard and new carpeting, large garden, workshop, utility room and garage. $31,900.

Rentals are plentiful, with one-bedroom apartments renting for $110 to $180 per month and two-bedroom apartments or condos renting for $235 to $400.

In addition to ads in the local newspaper, there is a little monthly magazine called *Tipoff* that carries many real estate ads in addition to a calendar of events and useful local information. The address is given under the heading of *Newspapers* in this section.

Safety

The FBI Crime Index rating is a moderate 66 crimes per thousand of population per year, largely because of the efforts of the fine police service provided by a department with 50 full-time paid officers and a 53-member police reserve.

The fire department has 55 full-time members and operates four stations.

The nearest potential manmade hazard is a nuclear-weapons storage site some 50 miles to the east, near Paducah.

Education

Six elementary schools, one seventh-grade center, and one junior and one senior high school serve 4500 area students. In addition, there is Cape Girardeau Vocational-Technical School, which has 580 daytime students and over 3500 adults attending evening classes that cover a wide range of technical and vocational subjects. Other schools include several parochial schools, a school for retarded children, a beauty school, a Montessori school, a business college, and several religious academies.

Community needs for higher education are met by Southeast Missouri State University. Students can select from over 100 areas of study in the university's six colleges. In addition, masters' programs are now available in many areas, including business, English, history, education, art, biology, chemistry, music, physical education, and physics.

Medical Facilities

Southeast Missouri Hospital, with a 77-member medical staff and 290 beds, provides full hospital facilities for the area. The St. Francis Medical Center, with 252 beds and over 100 physicians on the staff, offers a comprehensive range of medical services, including a 24-hour emergency medical center with a heliport to serve a four-state area.

Doctors' Park, a 51-acre complex, is the most comprehensive health-service center between St. Louis and Memphis, with 60 specialists providing services in general medicine, internal medicine, urology, obstetrics, gynecology, oral surgery, radiology, and many other fields of medicine.

There are also 10 nursing homes and many independent physicians and dentists in the area.

Cultural Activities

Much of the cultural life of the community focuses on Southeast Missouri State University, which provides excellent facilities for the university theater, the Community Concert Association, and the Artist and Lecture Series. Many kinds of musical and dance performances are presented at the university, as well as art exhibitions, experimental theater, and summer repertory.

Throughout the year, there are Municipal Band concerts, the Community Concert Series, and children's theater.

The Cape Girardeau Public Library serves as the library resource center for a wide region and has over 80,000 volumes. The university library of almost 500,000 volumes is also open to the public during the school year.

Recreation
There are 16 parks, totaling 422 acres of land, that offer playground facilities, swimming, tennis, baseball, fishing, and covered shelters for picnicking. In winter, a fishing pond is used for ice skating. The centrally located Capaha Park has a band pavilion where summer concerts are given, as well as three baseball fields, one of which is lighted for night games.

Cape Girardeau also has a bowling alley; two 18-hole golf courses, one public and one private; a golf driving range; four indoor theaters and one outdoor theater; a roller rink; and several tennis courts. Two racquet clubs offer tennis, handball, and racquetball.

For the sportsman, shooting ranges are available at the SEMO Trap Range and the Cape Bootheel Archer Club. For hunters there are game reserves at Horseshoe Lake, 18 miles from town; at Duck Creek, 35 miles away; and at Union County Refuge, 12 miles northeast of town. Camping, fishing, and boating facilities are plentiful in the area.

Good fishing abounds close to town at Lyerla Lake, on streams feeding into the Mississippi, at Lake Girardeau, and in the Mississippi River itself.

Government
Cape Girardeau is governed by a Council-Manager team, with a five-member city council that appoints the city manager to serve as the administrative head of the local government. The mayor is elected from within the council by the members themselves.

Water
The local tap water is neutral, hard, and fluoridated. It is supplied by the Missouri Utilities Company, which also provides the community with electricity and gas. It is an investor-owned utility serving all or part of 25 counties in southeastern and central Missouri. Water is drawn from deep wells capable of producing some 4.5 million gallons daily.

Energy
The Missouri Utilities Company provides electric and gas service under regulation of the Missouri Public Service Commission, which sets the rates and determines the rules and regulations.

Ample electric energy is available to meet present and future needs. It is supplied through interconnected ties with Union Electric and from a gas turbine generator located south of town that supplements during peaking and emergency loads. Natural gas comes from Texas through several pipeline companies, and the supply is ample for present and future needs.

Water, electricity, and gas rates can be obtained by dropping a line to:

Missouri Utilities Company
400 Broadway
Cape Girardeau, MO 63701

Television

There is a local CBS station, and other stations at Paducah, Kentucky, and Harrisburg, Illinois, are within easy pickup range on home antenna systems. A local cable television system is also being installed, and it should be in service by the time this book is published.

Newspapers

The local daily newspaper is:

The Southeast Missourian
Cape Girardeau, MO 63701

A monthly freebie called *Tipoff* carries a great deal of useful information, including real estate ads and a calendar of local events. Its address is:

Tipoff Magazine
P.O. Box 816
Cape Girardeau, MO 63701

The *St. Louis Globe-Democrat* and the *St. Louis Post-Dispatch* are also available locally.

For Further Information

Cape Girardeau Chamber of Commerce
P.O. Box 98
Cape Girardeau, MO 63701

Division of Tourism
Department of Consumer Affairs
308 East High St.
Jefferson City, MO 65101

Carbondale, Illinois

POPULATION: 26,144 within the city limits
57,400 in Jackson County

ELEVATION: 415 feet above sea level

Carbondale is a coal-mining and farming center in southern Illinois, located about 100 miles southeast of St. Louis. It is the gateway to the Shawnee National Forest and to Crab Orchard Lake, the state's largest manmade body of water.

Carbondale is an important trade and educational center, the home of Southern Illinois University. It is also an important railroad junction and has a variety of light industries. The surrounding farming region produces fruits and truck vegetables, many of which find their way to local tables.

Climate

Southern Illinois is midway between the Continental Divide and the Atlantic Ocean and some 500 miles north of the Gulf of Mexico. The climate is typically continental, with cold winters, warm summers, and frequent short-term fluctuations in temperature, humidity, cloudiness, and wind direction. The excellent soil and the well-distributed annual precipitation of 43 inches favor a very high standard of agricultural production.

With no protection from nearby mountain ranges, the area experiences the full sweep of the winds that are constantly bringing in the weather of other areas. Southeast and easterly winds bring mild, wet weather. Southerly winds are warm and showery. Westerly winds are dry and bring moderate temperatures. Winds from the north and northwest are also dry but cooler.

Storm systems move through the state most frequently during the winter and spring months and bring the greatest cloudiness during these seasons. Summers are sunny with intermittent thunderstorms, and autumns vary between pleasant, dry Indian-summer days and cooler, wetter spells.

Normal temperatures in winter range from lows in the 30s to highs in the 40s from December through February and into March, though lows can drop as far as −14°F. Snow averages about 12 inches a year, usually occurring from December through March. The last frost in spring is usually in the first week of April, and the first frost in fall comes in late October, allowing a 210-day frost-free growing period. Winters usually have about 70 days with temperatures of 32°F and below, with about 4000 heating degree days per year.

Summer temperatures range from lows in the 50s and 60s to highs in the upper 80s and low 90s, with about 64 days per year with temperatures of 90°F and above. Extreme high temperatures in June through September can climb as high as 106°F for brief periods. There are about 1750 cooling degree days per year.

Precipitation is well distributed throughout the year and provides a total of 773 million gallons per square mile per year for the area, which drains into the Mississippi River to the west. There is about 65% of possible sunshine each year.

History

Carbondale began as a railroad town, and for many years its economy depended on the Illinois Central railroad, which located its division headquarters there. This continued until 1900, when Ayer-

Lord Corporation (now Koppers Company) opened a 600-employee wood-treating plant. About the same time, coal mines became important in southern Illinois, and this increased the traffic on the railroad.

In 1870, a small teachers' college was started in town. It had little influence on the community until 1917. With the advent of war, however, people in the area began accepting the idea of higher education. By 1947 the college had obtained full university status and the name was changed to the present one of Southern Illinois University. The university has since been the prime motivating force in the city's economy and is the center of higher education and culture for all of southern Illinois.

Economy and Employment

Today there are three industrial parks in the Carbondale area to accommodate manufacturing and business. The economy is growing, with a wide variety of manufacturing industries in such diverse fields as clothing, electronics, foundries, radiators, shoes, signs, and concrete products.

The university and local schools form the largest sector of employment, employing about 40% of the total labor force. A new federal office building will bring additional jobs to the area. Other employers include: Tuck Industries (pressure-sensitive tapes, 450 employees); Koppers Co. (wood preservatives and wood products, 65); Southern Illinoisan (publishing and printing, 160); and Interstyle, Inc. (women's sportswear, 173).

Taxes

Illinois has a flat 2.5% income tax on all net income above the $1000-per-person exemption. There is a 5% combined state and local sales tax.

Property taxes are based on 33.3% of market value and vary by district, but total taxes will average about $975 per year on a home that sells for $65,000.

Shopping

As a local trade and shopping center as well as the home of a large university population, Carbondale has good shopping facilities in both its downtown and suburban areas. Normal needs can be filled quite easily at local shops. For more extensive shopping, St. Louis is about 100 miles to the northwest.

Residential Properties

Many houses and apartments are available for rent, with prices ranging from $95 per month for a one-bedroom efficiency apartment to $525 per month for a four-bedroom home.

There is also a good selection of homes for sale. Here are some typical listings:

NICE STARTER HOME with 2 bedrooms, living room, dining room, kitchen with appliances, $19,900.

LOVELY HOME with outdoor barbecue, large patio, 3 bedrooms, and beamed ceilings. $48,500.

COUNTRY PRIVACY with city conveniences in this 3-bedroom tri-level home on a full tree-covered acre at only $60,000.

SWIM IN POOL and picnic in your own patio in this 3-bedroom home with large family room, fireplace, and choice location. $35,000.

Rentals are available, with one-bedroom apartments renting for $150 to $265 per month and two-bedroom condos or apartments renting for $175 to $385.

Safety

There are no natural hazards near Carbondale, and the nearest manmade potential hazard is the nuclear power plant at Paducah, Kentucky, about 60 miles to the southeast.

The FBI Crime Index rating is 68 crimes per thousand of population per year. The police department employs 50 full-time officers and operates 16 vehicles in providing protection to Carbondale.

Fire protection is provided by 32 full-time firefighters. Equipment includes one aerial truck, six pumpers, one service vehicle, two administrative cars, and one boat. The city's Fire Insurance Rating is Class 7.

Education

The local schools are operated under a dual system, with separate high schools and elementary schools. The high school operates a vocational center with programs to prepare students for technical careers.

Southern Illinois University serves some 23,000 students as a multipurpose institution. It offers undergraduate and graduate studies in the schools of agriculture, business administration, education, communications and fine arts, engineering and technology, human resources, liberal arts, and science. It also provides a wide variety of continuing-education courses for adults in the area.

Medical Facilities

Carbondale is the health-care center for southern Illinois. Memorial Hospital, with 140 beds and 97 full-time physicians, has a trauma center and operates a direct helicopter service to St. Louis. The Carbondale Clinic has 30 physicians and clinicians specializing in 11 different medical fields.

For more extensive health care, St. Louis is 100 miles to the northwest and can provide some of the finest medical care in the country.

Cultural Activities

The university forms the nucleus of most of the cultural activity of the region, offering regular concerts, plays, art exhibits, and lectures.

The Carbondale Public Library has about 60,000 volumes, and the university library has some 1,500,000 printed volumes and more than 1,600,000 microtext units. The university's Morris Library is one of the largest open-shelf academic libraries under one roof in the nation. It is also a depository for federal, state, and United Nations documents.

Recreation

The Carbondale area has a local park district that provides playgrounds, athletic programs, arts and crafts classes, day camps for children, and community-center programs. The YMCA offers many programs for all ages.

There are four state parks nearby, and over two dozen lakes for swimmers, boaters, and fishermen, plus the 43,000-acre Shawnee National Forest, which is open for hunting, camping, picnicking, and hiking.

Crab Orchard Wildlife Refuge is a few minutes' drive to the east and provides areas for camping, swimming, picnicking, boating, and boat launching. Five marinas and eight youth camps are also located within its boundaries.

There are two public golf courses, plus a private course at the local country club.

Government

Carbondale operates under the Council-Manager form of government, with an elected mayor and four council members who hire the full-time city manager.

Water

The water system is municipally owned and has a capacity well in excess of present peak demand. The local tap water is alkaline and soft.

Energy

Electricity is provided by the Egyptian Electric Cooperative Association, and the Central Illinois Public Service Company provides both electric and gas service.

At present, utility costs average about $90 per month for a two-bedroom home.

Television

The university operates two television stations, both affiliated with PBS. Local reception of the stations in Harrisburg, Illinois, Paducah, Kentucky, and Cape Girardeau, Missouri, is possible, providing full coverage of all three major networks. There is also a local cable television system, which provides coverage of St. Louis stations.

Newspapers

The local daily newspaper is:

The Southern Illinoisan
710 N. Illinois St.
Carbondale, IL 62901

The *St. Louis Globe-Democrat* and the *St. Louis Post-Dispatch* are both available locally.

For Further Information

Greater Carbondale Area Chamber of Commerce
217 W. Walnut St.
Carbondale, IL 62901

Division of Tourism
222 S. College St.
Springfield, IL 62706

Charlottesville, Virginia

POPULATION: 39,804 within the city limits
55,518 in Albemarle County

ELEVATION: 480 feet above sea level

Charlottesville is located in central Virginia, about 70 miles west of Richmond, in an immense bowl on the eastern slope of the foothills of the Blue Ridge Mountains. Overlooking the town is Monticello, now a national shrine and originally the home of Thomas Jefferson, who supervised its design and construction.

An old and historic town, Charlottesville has kept up with progress and change while preserving its heritage. Today it is a farm and shopping center, with quality horses and beef cattle raised in the surrounding area. Business and industry are growing. Charlottesville is the home of the prestigious University of Virginia.

Climate

Virginia is in the zone of the prevailing westerlies — winds that move from west to east; in or near the mean path of winter storm tracks; and in the mean path of tropical, moist air coming from the southwest Atlantic and Gulf of Mexico throughout much of the summer and early fall seasons.

Winters are moderate, with about 18 inches of snow each season, which seldom causes any damage, though wide variations from this average can occur. There are usually about 3900 heating degree days each winter and about 75 days with temperatures of 32°F and below, resulting in a frost-free growing season of about 210 days. From December through February, nighttime temperatures generally drop below freezing and daytime temperatures are in the 40s and 50s.

Summers are long and warm, with average daily highs in the mid-80s and lows in the 60s from June through mid-September. There are about 40 days per year with temperatures of 90°F and above, and about 1000 cooling degree days per season.

Precipitation is about 44 inches per year, fairly well distributed throughout the year, with slightly heavier rainfall in the summer months. Summers are generally humid, and the annual average humidity ranges from 83% at night to 53% in the afternoons. Thunderstorms occur on the average of 40 per year, and about 85% of these occur from May to September.

Only about four tornadoes are reported in Virginia each year, and these seldom cause much damage, though a series of tornadoes in 1929 caused severe damage. Hurricanes have affected Virginia for as long as records of the weather have been kept, but most have decreased in intensity before reaching the state, and Charlottesville is located far enough from the coast that the effects are not severe.

Northeasters — storms that develop in the Atlantic — sometimes move northward along the Virginia coast and bring heavy rain and high winds, though again Charlottesville is far enough inland to miss the full force of these storms.

History

In Colonial days, Charlottesville — named after the wife of King George III of England — was situated on a main trail running from the Tidewater region of the Virginia coast to the frontier area in the west. Peter Jefferson, the father of Thomas, settled here in 1737. Seven years later Albemarle County was created, and in 1761, the county seat was established in Charlottesville. However, Charlottesville was not incorporated as a city until 1880.

During the American Revolution, Colonel Tarleton raided the town in an attempt to capture Thomas Jefferson, who had escaped westward with other revolutionaries after the fall of Richmond.

The Central Virginia railroad reached the town in 1848, ending the use of the nearby Rivanna River for trade and commerce.

Economy and Employment

For many years, Charlottesville has been the trade and shopping center for a large farming area. The raising of livestock is an important part of the economy, and Albemarle County has over 200,000 acres of private farmlands.

The University of Virginia has made a major contribution to the local economy ever since it was founded in 1819. Today it has over 16,000 students, and their purchases compose an important part of local business.

Manufacturing has grown in recent years and is well diversified, with industries producing such items as electronic equipment, nylon and acetate, frozen foods, and office-record equipment. In addition, Charlottesville has a large law-book publishing firm, many research and industrial offices, and a broad range of retail and wholesale stores.

Natural resources in the area include a commercial forest and an abundant supply of granite, soapstone, and slate.

The largest single employer is the university, which employs over 9000. The federal government employs over 700, many of whom work at the army's Foreign Science and Technology Center.

Over 10,000 people are employed in manufacturing. Major employers include: Acme Visible Records (files and forms, 814 employees); General Electric (industrial controls, 1100); Frank Ix and Sons (synthetic fabrics, 530); Michie Company (legal publications, 430); Morton Frozen Foods (frozen prepared foods, over 1300 employees in their corporate offices in Charlottesville and in their plant in nearby Crozet); Ovenair, Inc. (crystal oscillators and ovens, 138); Pepsi-Cola (beverages, 125); Sperry Marine Systems (marine navigational equipment, 925); Stromberg-Carlson (telecommunications equipment, 1280); Teledyne Avionics (aircraft instruments and flight-control systems, 200); Uniroyal (tire cord fabrics, 310); and Badger-Powhatan (fire extinguishers and ladders, 183).

For current job information, write:

Virginia Employment Commission
400 Preston Ave.
Charlottesville, VA 22902

Taxes

There is a 4% sales tax in Charlottesville. State income tax ranges from 2% on incomes under $3000 to almost 10% on incomes over $12,000.

Local property taxes are based on 100% of full market value and run $1.13 per $100 of assessed value inside the city limits and $0.67 per $100 in the unincorporated areas of the county. Thus a $65,000 home inside the city limits would pay approximately $735 in taxes per year, and the same home in the county would pay approximately $435.

Certain residents over 65 years of age can obtain special property-tax rates upon application to the tax assessor.

Shopping

There is an excellent downtown shopping area, along with a number of surburban centers. Because of the large number of tourists passing through town and regular shopping by the residents of a large surrounding area, Charlottesville has a great diversity of stores and offers a wide variety of choices for shoppers.

For even wider choices, Richmond is 70 miles to the southeast and Washington, D.C., is a little over 100 miles to the northeast.

Residential Properties

The average market value of homes in the Charlottesville area is in the $60,000 range, though this may change with fluctuations in the economy. A few typical listings at the time of writing are:

> ATTRACTIVE TOWNHOUSE with good location near Fashion Mall with 3 bedrooms, living room, dining area, family room with fireplace off kitchen, storm windows, excellent insulation, gas heating and cooking. Energy efficient. $58,500.
>
> QUALITY in this 3-bedroom, 1½-bath ranch home with formal dining room, eat-in kitchen, family room, wood stove, gas heat. Recently remodeled and redecorated. $72,400.
>
> 1873 VICTORIAN on 4 acres, about 20 minutes southwest of town, 3 bedrooms, 2 baths, study, dining room, many fireplaces, gazebo, separate workshop. Owner financing. $118,500.
>
> NEAR UNIVERSITY. 4-bedroom, 1-bath brick home with living room, fireplace, eat-in kitchen, enclosed back porch, gas heat. $69,500.

Rentals are plentiful in Charlottesville. One-bedroom apartments can be rented for $225 to $350 per month and two-bedroom apartments or condos rent for $300 to $475 per month. A note to the chamber of commerce will bring you a current list of realtors, any of whom will be glad to help you find the right place to live.

Safety

The FBI Crime Index rating is 96 crimes per thousand of population per year. There are no nearby manmade hazards. The nearest potential hazard is the nuclear power plant 30 miles east on the Pamunkey River at Mineral. It should be noted, however, that the Environmental Protection Agency has found signs of acid rain across all of central Virginia. The Fire Insurance Rating is Class 3.

Education

Both Charlottesville and Albemarle County have excellent public school systems, with a pupil/teacher ratio of 15:1 in the county and 19:1 in the city. In addition, there are a number of accredited private schools for students of all ages from nursery school through high school.

Higher education is amply represented in Charlottesville by two technical-vocational schools, a junior college, and the University of Virginia. There is an Institute of Textile Technology, and the Charlottesville-Albemarle Technical Education Center offers many vocational-technical courses for students attending local high schools and for adults desiring to learn skilled trades.

Piedmont Virginia Community College is a two-year state institution primarily serving local residents. It offers an occupational-technical program, university and parallel-college transfer courses, general studies, adult education, special training, and developmental programs.

The University of Virginia, located in Charlottesville, is known as Mr. Jefferson's University. With neoclassical buildings, white porticoes, and impressive vistas, it is considered one of the most beautiful universities in the nation. Noted for its schools of law and medicine, it offers undergraduate programs and graduate studies leading to masters' and doctoral degrees in the arts and sciences.

Medical Facilities

There are two modern hospitals in Charlottesville. The University of Virginia Hospital has 672 beds and serves the university medical school. Martha Jefferson Hospital has 221 beds, and the Towers convalescent hospital provides another 128 beds.

Cultural Activities

Much of the cultural life of the community is centered on the university. In addition, Charlottesville has many art galleries, the Bayly Art Museum, and a chapter of the Virginia Museum of Fine Arts. Instruction in music, art, dance, and crafts is available locally. The university music club offers concerts regularly throughout the year.

The Heritage Repertory Company is central Virginia's only resident professional theater company. It performs a full season of American plays each year. Other theater groups include the Community Children's Theater; the Albemarle Players; the Virginia Players of the university; and the Four County Players, a group serving Albemarle, Greene, Louisa, and Orange counties.

On the campus of the university, the Alderman Library has a fine rare-book collection and over 2 million volumes in its regular book collection. The Jefferson-Madison Regional Library serves the community with nearly 200,000 volumes.

Recreation

The city of Charlottesville has a modern recreational program with a full-time staff and offers 20 parks and playgrounds with facilities that include four swimming pools, six wading pools, picnic grounds, tennis courts, golf courses, and ballparks.

Albemarle County also has a number of recreational facilities, including four county-owned lakes and several private lakes, all of which offer fishing, swimming, and boating. Nearby is Shenandoah National Park for hiking, picnicking, and mountain climbing.

The coast — the Chesapeake Bay and beyond that the Atlantic Ocean — is two hours away and offers most water-related sports, from sailing in the bay to deep-sea fishing out of many of the coastal towns. Virginia Beach is approximately three hours away.

Government

Charlottesville operates under the Council-Manager form of government. Albemarle County has a board of supervisors and a county executive, an arrangement similar to the Council-Manager system used in cities.

Water

The city and county are both supplied water by the Rivanna Water and Sewer Authority, which owns and operates five filter plants and three reservoirs. The local tap water is very soft and is fluoridated.

Energy

Electric power for the area is furnished by Virginia Electric and Power Company from a combination of fossil-fuel and nuclear-power plants.

Natural gas is supplied locally by a municipal gas system within the city limits and by the Virginia Pipe Line Company in the unincorporated areas. Bottled gas and fuel oil are also available locally.

Utility costs for an average two-to-three-bedroom home run about $100 to $125 per month.

Television

There is a local NBC affiliate station, and the television stations in Richmond, Washington, D.C., Lynchburg, and Harrisonburg can all be received locally on home antenna systems. In addition, there are three cable television systems providing full-channel coverage.

Newspapers

The local daily newspaper is:

The Daily Progress
413 E. Market St.
Charlottesville, VA 22902

The *Washington Post*, the *Washington Star*, the *Richmond Times-Dispatch*, and three weekly newspapers are also available locally.

For Further Information

Charlottesville and Albemarle County
Chamber of Commerce
P.O. Box 1564
Charlottesville, VA 22902

Virginia State Travel Service
6 North Sixth St.
Richmond, VA 23219

Chico, California

POPULATION: 26,431 within the city limits
134,200 in Butte County

ELEVATION: 190 feet above sea level

Chico lies about 80 miles north of Sacramento in the central Sacramento Valley of California, at the western foot of the Sierra Nevada mountain range. It is a trade and shopping center for a large farming area, and the home of California State University at Chico.

Chico offers an interesting mixture of the old and the new. There are contemporary shops and malls, a flourishing artisans' community where craftsmen practice their trades using the skills of an earlier period, gourmet restaurants with old-fashioned hospitality, turn-of-the-century homes, tree-lined streets, and a beautiful university campus with ivy-covered buildings.

As their chamber of commerce puts it, "In Chico, you will discover a city that remembers its heritage and has lovingly preserved its yesterdays in today."

Climate

California is a state of many climates, despite the fact that some people wrongly assume the climate and smog of Los Angeles are typical of the whole state.

Northern California has two primary mountain chains running parallel to the coast: the Coast Range near the ocean, and the Sierra Nevada, which more or less separates California from Nevada. While the coastal strip of land west of the Coast Range is cool and frequently foggy, the central Sacramento Valley, lying between the two mountain ranges, is much more continental in climate, with warmer summers, colder winters, greater daily and seasonal temperature ranges, and generally lower humidities.

Summer is a dry period, with the semipermanent Pacific high moving northward during the warm months. In winter, this high moves southward and permits Pacific storms to move into and across the state, producing rain at low elevations and snow in the mountains.

Chico's climate is moderate, with warm summers and wet, cool winters. During the summer months, the daily maximum temperature reaches or exceeds 90°F, though the low humidity makes the heat more bearable than in many other locations. In winter, the average daily minimum hovers around the mid-30s. The last spring frost comes around February 23, and the first winter frost generally arrives around the end of November. The area has about 3000 heating degree days per year and some 1500 cooling degree days each summer.

Winds are generally moderate, mostly from the south, the result of westerlies blowing in through the break in the Coast Range at San Francisco Bay and swinging north up the central valley.

Precipitation averages 25.75 inches a year, with most of it falling during the coldest months. Only about 3% of the year's total falls during June through September. Thunderstorms, hail, snow, and sleet are almost unknown.

During a typical year, Chico will have 219 clear days, 57 partly cloudy days, and 89 cloudy days. Sunshine averages 50% during the winter months and up to 95% during the summer and fall.

History

Gold first brought settlers to the Chico area, but the rich green land encouraged many of the gold-seekers to stay. Chico was founded by General John Bidwell, one of the members of the first overland wagon train to reach California.

General Bidwell used his earnings from the gold fields to establish his 28,000-acre Rancho Del Arroyo in 1849. With his wife, Annie, he carefully planned the new community springing up beside the great ranch, and the Bidwells' influence is still evident today in the 2400-acre Bidwell Park and in the ornate Victorian Bidwell Mansion, now preserved as a state historical park.

From those beginnings, and under the careful guidance of the Bidwells, Chico grew to become the agricultural and social capital of the northern part of the state.

Economy and Employment

Chico's economy is based on a comfortable mix of agriculture, trade, service, and education, with very little industry in the area as yet. It is a regional service and retail trade center, and these activities account for 50% of the total employment. Government and education provide another 27% of local employment, and agriculture between 5% and 10%, depending on the season.

The largest single employer is California State University–Chico, with 1800 employees, followed closely by the many retail businesses in North Valley Plaza Mall, which collectively employ over 1400 people. Other major nonmanufacturing employers are: Chico Unified School District (700 employees); Butte Community College (675); N. T. Enloe Memorial Hospital (530); Pacific Telephone (426); Chico Community Hospital (320); Pacific Gas & Electric (175); and the *Chico Enterprise Record* (the daily newspaper, 140).

Manufacturing covers a wide range of products, with 52 firms in the area, the largest of which are: Continental Nut Company (nuts, 600 employees); Diamond International (wood products, 435); Rexnord, Inc. (conveyor systems, 175); California Almonds (nuts, 160); Sierra Pacific Industries (wood moldings, 100); Jessup Door Co. (doors and door stock, 100); Knudsen & Sons (fruit juices, 50); and Poly Plastics (laminated plastics, 49).

For current job information, write to:

Employment Development Department
109 Parmac Road
Chico, CA 95926

Taxes

There is a 6% state and local sales tax, and California's income tax ranges from 1% on the first $2630 to 11% on incomes over $20,450, with a 2% surtax on unearned income over $15,000. This makes California's taxes among the highest in the nation.

Property taxes in California are limited by Proposition 13 to 1% per year of true market value. Thus a home selling for $65,000 would be taxed at $650 per year.

In addition to the property tax, the city of Chico levies a utility tax that is equal to 5% of the user's yearly utility bill, so that if a homeowner pays $200 per month for utilities, the tax will be $120 per year.

Shopping

Because Chico is a trade and shopping center for a prosperous agricultural area, and the home of a large university, it offers a wide variety of shopping facilities. The downtown shopping area, at Broadway and Main streets, is supplemented by large surburban shopping centers.

While most needs can be taken care of locally, San Francisco, 174 miles to the south, is a shopper's paradise.

Residential Properties

Given the growing demand for housing for faculty and employees of the university, plus the normal growth of the area, housing is not as plentiful or cheap as in some other parts of the country. Because of the high interest rates of today, however, many people are anxious to sell and will offer "creative financing" to help the buyer. A few typical listings are:

A GOOD ADDRESS with 3 bedrooms and 1 bath, good assumable loan. $50,000.

LOVELY 3-bedroom 2-bath home with family room and leisure pool, near park, great financing. $99,500.

DESPERATE SELLER must sell 3-bedroom 2-bath, 1340-square-foot multi-level home. Assume existing loan and owner will carry 2nd with as little as $2500 down. $77,500.

COMFORTABLE 3-bedroom home on one acre in the pines. Large deck to enjoy the view of the valley. Paved road. $79,500.

Rentals are plentiful, with one-bedroom apartments available at $200 to $265 per month and two-bedroom condos and apartments renting for $235 to $385 per month. There are also many mobile homes available for purchase or rent at varying prices.

Safety

There are no natural hazards nearby, except for the ever-present earthquake hazard that threatens all of California to some extent, though Chico is not on a major fault line. The nearest manmade potential hazard is a nuclear power plant near Sacramento, about 100 miles to the south.

The FBI Crime Index rating is 94 crimes per thousand of population per year. The police department provides 24-hour patrol service and an active crime-prevention and home-security program.

The fire department is equipped and trained for the protection of urban areas, and Chico has a Class 3 Fire Insurance Rating.

Education

The California public schools vary in quality, but Chico's are rated high. At the elementary level, there are 14 schools, with 30 pupils per teacher on the average. Chico has 2 junior high schools and 1 senior high school. The system offers a complete range of courses and a full sports program. An adult education program provides instruction to over 2300 adults each year.

Butte Community College is located in the foothills between Chico, Oroville, and Paradise, just a few miles from Chico. It has 8000 students and offers two-year career-oriented programs to local resident students plus academic courses in preparation for transfer to four-year institutions. Its curriculum includes criminal justice and paramedic training.

California State University–Chico was established in 1817 as a Normal School on land donated by General John Bidwell. It is the second oldest university in the California state system. Today, it is a five-year institution with an enrollment of over 12,000. Bachelors' and masters' degrees can be earned in more than 10 fields, including business, education, nursing, communications, science, engineering, agriculture, humanities, and social sciences.

Medical Facilities

Chico has two general hospitals, the Chico Community Hospital, with 135 beds, and the N. T. Enloe Memorial Hospital, with 117 beds. In addition, there are 95 physicians and 46 dentists to serve the community.

For medical care and treatment beyond the capacities of the local hospitals and physicians, the University of California Medical Center in San Francisco offers some of the finest and most modern medical care available in the world. San Francisco is only a three- to four-hour drive to the south.

Cultural Activities

In addition to its educational function, California State University–Chico serves as a major cultural and entertainment center for the community, where local residents can attend dance productions, musical concerts, drama, athletic events, and films. The on-campus facilities are also used by local groups for meetings, banquets, conventions, and special events.

Also active in Chico are the Community Concert Association and the Symphony Orchestra. Facilities available for theatrical productions, concerts, lectures, and other events include the Harlan M. Davis Theater at California State University–Chico, which seats 500, and the Robert C. Laxon Auditorium, which seats 1400.

Readers are served by three libraries, the largest of which is the university library with 412,000 volumes.

Recreation

Chico is located in the center of an immense playground area that includes the Sacramento River and its valley to the west and the High Sierras to the east, with hundreds of lakes and waterways in between. Two snow-cooled mountain streams, the Big Chico and Little Chico creeks, cut through the center of town.

Bidwell Park, with 2400 acres, is the third-largest city park in the world and includes an 18-hole golf course, an archery range, a rifle range, a riding ring, two large developed swimming areas with bathhouse facilities, plus children's playgrounds and hundreds of picnic and barbecue facilities.

The Chico area has a total of 7 playgrounds, 2 bowling alleys, 3 golf courses, a roller-skating rink, 46 tennis courts, 4 swimming pools, 5 lighted baseball fields, 1 lighted football field, and 9 racquetball courts.

Hunters and fishermen have access to the many streams, lakes, and forests within a few hours' drive, and the Sacramento River delta area, to the south, offers opportunities for many kinds of boating, from sailing to houseboating.

Government

California has two forms of city government. The larger cities have "city charters" granted by the state and operate under elected mayors who function as the chief executives and administrative officers for their cities. Smaller cities and towns operate under the general laws of the state. Chico is one of the latter class and has an elected city council and a city manager hired by the council to manage the everyday affairs of the town.

Water
The local water supply is provided by California Water Service Company from local wells. The tap water is alkaline, soft, and not fluoridated.

Energy
Pacific Gas and Electric Company supplies both gas and electricity to Chico. Electricity is generated in a variety of stations, including hydroelectric plants in the Sierra Nevada, nuclear reactors near Sacramento, Eureka, and San Francisco, and several gas- and oil-fired steam-generating plants. Electricity rates are controlled by the state. Current rates can be obtained by writing:

Pacific Gas & Electric Co.
340 Salem St.
Chico, CA 95927

Gas is drawn from central and southern California gas wells.

Television
Four television channels can be received with home antenna systems, and there is a cable television system that provides full coverage for subscribers.

Newspapers
The daily newspaper is:

The Chico Enterprise Record
P.O. Box 9
Chico, CA 95927

There is also a weekly newspaper, the *Chico News & Review*, which primarily reports local news. The *San Francisco Chronicle-Examiner* is also available locally.

For Further Information

Chico Visitor & Convention Bureau
P.O. Box 3303
Chico, CA 95927

Distribution Center
Department of Parks & Recreation
P.O. Box 2390
Sacramento, CA 95811

For $1.00 the Distribution Center will send you "Guide to the California Park System." It is well worth the price.

Columbus, Mississippi

POPULATION: 27,370 within the city limits
44,600 within the immediate area
54,100 within Lowndes County

ELEVATION: 367 feet above sea level

Columbus sits on a 125-foot-high bluff overlooking the Tombigbee River in northeastern Mississippi near the Alabama state line. It has been a trading town ever since it began, and is still a busy trade, industrial, and shipping center for a farming and dairy region that raises cotton, corn, and livestock.

The population of the 30-mile radius around Columbus is over 160,000, most of whom turn to Columbus for trade and shopping, since there are no big cities nearby. Birmingham, Alabama, the closest, is 117 miles to the east. Jackson, Mississippi, is 147 miles to the southwest, and Memphis, Tennessee, is 166 miles to the northwest.

The countryside around Columbus is flat to slightly rolling, laced with waterways and spotted with lakes and ponds.

Climate

In Columbus, the prevailing southerly winds provide a moist, semitropical climate that brings frequent afternoon thundershowers. When the pressure distribution changes to bring westerly or northerly winds, periods of drier weather interrupt the generally warm, moist conditions.

Summers are long and warm to hot, with normal maximum temperatures exceeding 90°F from June into September, providing some 70 days per year with temperatures of 90°F or above. Summers brings an average of 2300 cooling degree days.

Winters are generally mild, though the area is alternately subjected to warm tropical air and cold continental air. Cold spells seldom last over 3 or 4 days. The ground rarely freezes. There are only about 53 days per year with temperatures of 32°F and below. The first frost generally arrives during the first week in November, and the last spring frost occurs by the last week in March, providing 230 days of growing season. Winters bring approximately 2500 heating degree days per year.

Precipitation averages 52 inches per year, with the greatest rainfall occurring in November through March. September and October are the driest months. Summers bring frequent rains, in the form of thundershowers, from June through early September. Snow seldom exceeds 3 inches per year and only remains on the ground for a short time. Humidity is about 72% throughout the year, and there is about 60% of possible sunshine annually.

While Mississippi is subject to hurricanes from the Gulf of Mexico, these storms are usually greatly weakened by the time they reach as far north as Columbus. Tornadoes can occur anywhere in the state, though seriously damaging ones are infrequent.

Overall, the climate is moderate, without extremes of either heat or cold, and outdoor activities are generally possible throughout the year. The growing season is long, and cold spells are short. Rainfall is plentiful, but so is sunshine.

History

Located at the juncture of three rivers — the Tombigbee, the Buttahatchie, and the Luxapalila — Columbus is the place mentioned earliest in the historical records of Mississippi. Hernando de Soto crossed the Tombigbee here in 1540. John Pitchlyn operated a trading post on the Tombigbee, near the site of Columbus, as early as the 1780s.

The town began in 1816 with the arrival of a group of some 20 pioneers. In the beginning, it was only a small trading post with the uninspired name of Possum Town. Then, during the years 1817–1820, the Military Road was established from Nashville to New Orleans, crossing the Tombigbee at Columbus.

The city of Columbus was formally organized and named in 1821. From then on, it became a city of "firsts." That same year, the first free public school in Mississippi, Franklin Academy, opened in Columbus. In 1822, the area's first steamboat, the *Cotton Plant,* landed in Columbus.

The First Columbus National Bank, opened in 1852, is the oldest bank in Mississippi operating under an original charter. And the world's first state-supported college for women, the Mississippi University for Women, founded in 1884, is still an important local educational institution.

Economy and Employment

Having started out as a trading post, Columbus has developed a healthy and diversified economy based on retail trade, industry, education, agriculture, and transportation. Today there are over 50 plants in and around Columbus providing some $85 million in local payrolls each year. Six firms have recently built in the new 200-acre Columbus-Lowndes Industrial Park. Thirteen miles south of Columbus, Weyerhauser Company operates a paper mill that cost over $775 million to build.

To take advantage of the Tennessee-Tombigbee Waterway, the city of Columbus has purchased more than 250 acres and over one mile of water frontage for an industrial park. Another 1000-acre industrial park is being built near the airport.

Farming is an important part of the local economy, with more than $10 million in sales of farm products annually. Dairying and cattle raising are important, with some of the finest Aberdeen Anguses, Polled Herefords, and Santa Gertrudis cattle grazing on local farms.

Major employers in the area include: AMBAC Industries (automotive electrical equipment, 1200 employees); Baldor Electric Co. (large electric motors, 250); Columbus Air Force Base (pilot training, 531 civilian employees); General Tire & Rubber Co. (vinyl fabric and wall coverings, 625); Johnson-Tombigbee Furniture (furniture, 613); and Mississippi University for Women (450).

With the opening of the Tennessee-Tombigbee Waterway as a navigable waterway to the Gulf of Mexico, the various water-related businesses can be expected to grow rapidly and to need many more trained employees.

Taxes

There is a state sales tax of 5%, and the state income tax ranges from 3% to 4%. There is no city or county sales or income tax.

Property tax rates are $1.555 inside the city limits and $1.031 outside, per $100 of actual market value. Thus the tax on a $65,000 residence will run about $1010 per year inside the city limits and $670 outside.

Shopping

With no nearby large cities, Columbus has had to develop good shopping facilities for the large area it serves. There is a 13-block shopping area in downtown Columbus, supplemented by three large surburban shopping centers. Major national stores such as Sears, J. C. Penney, Woolco, Gibson, K-Mart, Walgreen, Rexall, A&P, and Kroger are represented. There are also numerous local and regional stores in all retail categories.

All day-to-day needs can easily be met by local shopping, but for greater variety, Birmingham is two hours' drive to the east.

Residential Properties

Homes can be found in a wide range of prices and qualities. A few typical listings are:

> SPOTLESS 3-bedroom home with large dining room, pine floor, and well-established landscaping. Priced to sell at $55,000.
>
> NICE AND CLEAN 2-bedroom home with an existing loan at 8½% and total payments of only $146 per month. Asking $27,500.
>
> IMMACULATE 3 bedrooms and 2 baths with fireplace and screened patio with 8½% assumable VA loan and monthly payments of only $360. Sale price $59,900.
>
> PRIVACY ON A HILLTOP with 4 bedrooms, 2½ baths, large kitchen plus pantry, separate dining room and separate living room. $106,900.

Rentals are plentiful at present, with one-bedroom apartments renting for $185 to $250 per month and two-bedroom apartments or condos for $275 to $375. On request, the chamber of commerce will send a list of realtors, all of whom will be happy to send current listings. In addition, the local newspaper ads are an easy way to learn the state of the local real estate market.

Safety

The FBI Crime Index rating is 80 crimes per thousand of population per year. The police department has 62 employees and 38 patrol cars. The fire department has 58 full-time personnel supplemented by five volunteer companies, and operates eight pump trucks and one aerial service truck. The Fire Insurance Rating is Class 6.

There are no known nearby manmade hazards. While Columbus Air Force Base is only 9 miles to the north of town, it is a training base and not likely to be a target in the event of war.

Tornadoes do strike this general area, but the chance of any particular spot being hit is rather small.

Education

Both the Columbus and Lowndes County public school systems offer comprehensive education from grades one through twelve, plus two vocational schools. In addition, there are one parochial school and two private schools, as well as three private schools for kindergarten and the beginning grades.

Mississippi University for Women, located in Columbus, is a liberal arts college and vocational training school for women, with a student body of 2550.

East Mississippi Junior College has an extension school 10 miles west of Columbus and offers training in nursing, welding, refrigeration and air conditioning, electrical technology, secretarial skills, and many other fields, including riverboat-crew training.

Mississippi State University is located 24 miles to the west and provides a broad four-year curriculum. The University of Mississippi is 90 miles to the north and offers a four-year curriculum and graduate studies in many areas.

Medical Facilities

There are three local hospitals providing a total of 367 beds to serve the community. There are 43 physicians, 17 dentists, 2 orthodontists, and 1 oral surgeon in the area.

Modern medical-support facilities, operated by physicians in private practice, include a urology clinic, a radiology clinic with nuclear equipment and a CAT scanner, and a pathology lab that has two locations. There is a regional mental-health complex, and psychiatric care is available at the local hospitals.

Cultural Activities

The Columbus–Lowndes County Public Library has some 95,000 volumes and features a local history and genealogy room plus a modern reference section.

The Civic Arts Council sponsors a variety of lectures, theatrical performances, musicals, and other special events. The Little Theater Group offers residents a chance to appreciate and participate in several stage productions each year.

The Mississippi University for Women also produces several theatrical performances annually, and often enlists support from local citizens. The University Artist Lecture Series brings world-renowned performers and stage personalities to the area.

For those interested in architecture, there are some 100 antebellum homes in Columbus, many of which are open to the public.

Recreation

Because of the mild climate, outdoor recreation is available almost all year. Lake Lowndes State Park, one of the most beautiful parks in Mississippi, offers campsites, picnic grounds, and various water sports on Lake Lowndes, such as water-skiing, swimming, boating, and fishing. The park also provides facilities for softball and tennis and has a recreation center.

Propst Park, operated by the city and county, has nine baseball and softball fields and a tennis complex.

The Luxapalila Creek Recreation Area, located on the Tennessee-Tombigbee Waterway, has excellent picnic facilities and several boat-launching ramps for access to the waterway lakes.

Fishermen will find bass and other game fish in the well-stocked rivers and lakes. Hunters have access to the 5000-acre Wildlife Refuge located in neighboring Noxubee County, which offers deer, squirrels, turkeys, and waterfowls. The Tombigbee National Forest is only an hour's drive from town.

Columbus has two well-kept golf courses, and there is a 9-hole course at the Air Force base. Other activities available around town include horseback riding, bowling, river canoeing, and roller skating. The local YMCA serves residents as well as members.

Government

Columbus operates under a Mayor-Council form of government.

Water

Water is provided by the city of Columbus and comes from deep wells and the Luxapalila River. The water is neutral, very soft, and fluoridated. With 920 million gallons of precipitation per square mile per year, there is more than enough water available in the area. The water-plant capacity is 8 million gallons per day, nearly twice the average daily consumption and appreciably higher than peak consumption demands.

Energy

Electricity is provided by the Tennessee Valley Authority from the huge power complex that serves the entire Tennessee Valley. Distribution is by the city of Columbus.

Natural gas is distributed by the Mississippi Valley Gas Company, and fuel oil and LP gas are available locally.

Utility costs for an average two-bedroom home run about $75 per month.

Television

There is one local television station, a CBS affiliate, and the NBC station in Tupelo can be received locally. A cable system provides 11-channel coverage.

Newspaper

The local daily newspaper is:

The Commercial Dispatch
Columbus, MS 39701

The *Jackson Clarion-Ledger-News,* the *Atlanta Journal,* and the *Atlanta Constitution* are usually available locally.

For Further Information

Columbus-Lowndes Chamber of Commerce
P.O. Box 1016
Columbus, MS 39701

Department of Tourism Development
Mississippi Agricultural & Industrial Board
P.O. Box 849
Jackson, MS 39205

Mississippi Park Commission
717 Robert E. Lee Building
Jackson, MS 39201

Mississippi Game & Fish Commission
P.O. Box 451
Jackson, MS 39205

Corvallis, Oregon

POPULATION: 40,843 within the city limits
53,776 in the Benton County area

ELEVATION: 227 feet above sea level

Corvallis is situated on the west bank at the head of navigation on the Willamette River in northwestern Oregon. To the west, green hills rise gently into the lower slopes of the Coast Range. Across the river to the east, beyond the broad valley of the Willamette, rise the sharper crests of the Cascade Mountains.

The valley is rich and fertile, with fruit trees and dairy cattle on each side of the highways leading into town. The agriculture is diversified, with extensive commercial production of hay, grain, apples, pears, cherries, prunes, walnuts, filbert nuts, berries, onions, potatoes, and various vegetable crops. Other farming operations include dairying, poultry raising, and extensive plant cultivation in nurseries.

Climate

Corvallis is in the northern section of the Pacific Coastal climatic zone and has cool, dry summers and cool, wet winters. The most important single factor in the local climate is the Pacific Ocean, because the air masses over Oregon generally move from west to east. The Pacific air tends to moderate the summer heat and the winter cold. Also, the unlimited supply of moisture from the ocean provides abundant rainfall over the region.

Because of this proximity to the ocean, the climate is moderate, with normal daily temperatures in July in the high 80s. There are only about 20 days per year when the temperature reaches 90°F and above, and there are no more than 100 cooling degree days per year.

Winters are mild, with about 60 days with temperatures of 32°F and below. The first frost comes in late October and the last frost in mid-April, with about 200 days in the freeze-free growing season between. There are about 4800 heating degree days each year.

Annual precipitation averages about 50 inches and falls mainly during the winter months. Snowfall totals between 6 and 12 inches per year, though snow seldom stays on the ground very long. There are usually no more than 10 days each year in which snowfall exceeds one inch. Hail falls two or three times each year, normally in the winter months, and there may be two or three days a year with freezing rain. Thunderstorms occur infrequently in the Willamette Valley, on the average no more than five or six times per year.

Winds are moderate, generally from the northwest in winter and from all directions in the summer.

Humidity is high in the early morning hours throughout the year, but drops to a moderate 58% average in the afternoons. Corvallis receives about 70% of possible sunshine.

History

The Calapooya Indians camped on the west bank of the Willamette River, just below its confluence with Mary's River, long before the white man came to the area. The first white settlers purchased land at this choice site from the Indians in 1845. One of these settlers, Joseph Avery, established a free canoe ferry across the Willamette in order to encourage settlement — and to sell lots to those who stayed.

Corvallis, whose name is taken from the Latin phrase meaning "heart of the valley," started life as Marysville in 1851. Two years later it was renamed Corvallis.

Somehow the town escaped the rough, raw beginnings of most frontier settlements, and by 1858 a school was started, churches were being built, and steamboats were heaping freight on the new city docks. By 1878 the railroad reached Corvallis, bringing the first wave of the expansion that has continued to the present day.

Economy and Employment

Corvallis is a comfortably prospering community in which the largest single employer is Oregon State University. In recent years, business has begun to move here from California's "Silicon Valley" near San Jose, led by Hewlett-Packard's new plant. The economy is based on a solid mixture of agriculture, forestry, industry, and education.

The university employs over 5200 people, and other major employers include: Hewlett-Packard (calculators and computers, 1840); Evans Products (hardboard paneling, fiber products, 400); city of Corvallis (350); CH_2M Hill (consultants in engineering, 740); Brand-S Corp. (plywood, 290); Neptune Microfloc (water- and waste-treatment equipment, 147); and Applied Theory Associates (computer processing, 80).

Employment can also be found in retail and wholesale businesses and in smaller manufacturing companies that provide wood products, food packing, pumps, controls, dairy products, plating, poultry, sand, gravel, and concrete products.

Taxes

The state income tax varies from 4% on the first $500 of taxable income to 10% on incomes over $5000. There is no sales tax in Oregon.

Property taxes are about average for the nation, running about $1400 per year on a home selling for $65,000.

Shopping

In addition to the downtown business and shopping area, there are six suburban shopping centers. All of the everyday needs of residents can be met by the local shops and stores.

For wider variety in shopping, Portland is 85 miles to the north.

Residential Properties

Property prices are climbing, but moderately priced homes can still be found. A few typical listings are:

GOOD STARTER HOME with 1 bedroom, 1 bath, on corner lot. $39,950.

COMFORTABLE HOME with 2 bedrooms, 1 bath, wood stove. $49,900.

CLOSE-IN on ⅓ acre, with 2 bedrooms, 1 bath. $39,900.

MAGNIFICENT HOME with 3100 square feet of floor space, 5 bedrooms, 2 baths, $165,000.

Rentals are available, though it is sometimes necessary to wait for precisely what is wanted. One-bedroom apartments rent for $125 to $325 per month and two-bedroom apartments or condos rent for $175 to $415.

Safety

The FBI Crime Index rating is 72 crimes per thousand of population per year. There are no nearby hazards of any kind. In the event of a nuclear war, the Corvallis area would probably be the safest area in the entire continental United States. The Fire Insurance Rating is Class 2. On all counts, Corvallis rates unusually high in safety.

Education

The public school system includes 12 elementary, 3 intermediate, and 2 high schools.

Linn-Benton Community College is a trade and technical school serving some 3200 students from the area.

Higher education is available locally at Oregon State University, which offers undergraduate courses and graduate studies up to the doctoral level in many diverse fields. About 17,000 students attend the university.

Medical Facilities

Good Samaritan Hospital serves the area with 172 beds and general medical services. Corvallis has 110 physicians and surgeons who specialize in over 25 fields of medicine. The town also has 45 dentists.

Cultural Activities

The community is served by two libraries — the public library, which has over 108,000 volumes, and the large library of Oregon State University, which has almost 850,000 volumes.

Several excellent facilities are available for concerts, performances, lectures, and meetings, including the university's Cultural and Conference Center and the Corvallis Arts Center.

The Horner Museum offers displays and information on the history of Oregon and the artifacts of its early years.

Theater arts center on Milan Auditorium, on the university campus, where many dance, music, and theater performances are given each year.

Recreation

Locally, there are 9.7 miles of bike and jogging paths, a country club with a private 18-hole golf course, a public 9-hole course, more than 45 tennis courts, 3 racquet sports clubs, 3 public swimming pools, and several public boat landings on the river.

Oregon's rivers offer magnificent fishing for trout and steelheads. Nearby mountains and forests provide beautiful campgrounds and hiking trails. To the east, the Cascade range offers skiing and other winter sports. To the west is the Pacific coast, with deep-sea fishing and many delightful picnic areas along the coastal highway.

Government

Corvallis operates under the Council-Manager system, with an elected mayor and city council who employ a full-time city manager.

Water

With the Willamette River at its doorstep, Corvallis has an assured and ample water supply. Local water is drawn from Mary's Peak Watershed and from the river. The water system is operated by the city and has a capacity well above peak demand. The local tap water is hard and fluoridated.

Energy

Hydroelectric power is abundant in Oregon, much of it coming from a series of great dams on the Columbia River. The local electric power is supplied by Pacific Power and Light, and natural gas is delivered by Northwest Natural Gas Company.

At the present time, utility costs run about $100 per month for an average two-bedroom home.

Television

The local cable television system offers eight channels plus Showtime. Satellite packages are also available.

Newspaper
The local daily newspaper is:

The Gazette-Times
P.O. Box 368
Corvallis, OR 97339

The *Portland Oregonian* is also available locally.

For Further Information

Corvallis Chamber of Commerce
350 SW Jefferson
Corvallis, OR 97330

Travel Information Section
Department of Transportation
Capitol Mall
Salem, OR 97310

State Parks Division
300 State Highway Building
Salem, OR 97310

Employment Division
State of Oregon
850 SW 35th
Corvallis, OR 97330

This last office offers placement, counseling, and testing services to the public. They can advise on current job openings.

Fayetteville, Arkansas

POPULATION: 36,165 within the city limits
166,500 in the Fayetteville area

ELEVATION: 1400 feet above sea level

Scenic beauty, tranquillity, and comfort are all adjectives that come to mind when one visits Fayetteville. Located in rolling, wooded country in northwest Arkansas, at the western edge of the Ozarks, Fayetteville enjoys some of the best scenery, the cleanest air, the purest water, and the loveliest land in the nation. Just minutes to the south is the Ozark National Forest. To the north is huge and beautiful Beaver Lake. And surrounding Fayetteville are the rolling hills and mountains, dense woods, and open pasturelands of northwest Arkansas.

Climate

There are two major geographical regions in Arkansas, which can be more or less divided by a diagonal line cutting across the state from the northeast to the southwest. The northwestern portion, in which Fayetteville is located, comprises the interior highlands. The southeastern portion makes up the Arkansas lowlands, where there is diversified farming in the rich alluvial soils of the areas around the Mississippi, Arkansas, and White rivers.

The northwestern corner of Arkansas is hilly to mountainous, with little soil suitable for the lowland type of farming. Livestock and poultry, along with some fruit and vegetable production, are the principal enterprises of these upland farming areas.

Winters are short, but cold periods of brief duration do occur. Zero temperatures are not uncommon in January and February. Summers are long and warm, with maximum temperatures sometimes exceeding 100°F in July and August, and 2000 cooling degree days.

Precipitation is mostly in the form of showers, except for the rainy periods in late fall, winter, and early spring. The average number of days with measurable precipitation is around 100 per year. Average precipitation is 45.1 inches per year. Noontime humidity averages 53% for the year.

Rainfall is normally abundant and well distributed throughout the year, assuring well-sustained agricultural production, but sometimes storms cause local flooding. Winter and spring are the wettest times of the year, and fall is usually the driest. The Fayetteville area does have occasional snow during the winter, but it seldom stays on the ground more than a few days.

Winds are moderate, averaging 6 to 9 miles per hour, generally from the east to northeast. The amount of sunshine is 62% of possible sunshine during the year. Because of the fairly mild winters, the heating degree days amount to only 3292 per year. The area has a 180-day growing season.

History

Originally, the Ozark land was owned by the Osage Indians, who later gave way to the Shawnees, Delawares, and Cherokees. With the Cherokee Treaty of 1828, the land was opened for settlers, and many families moved in from Kentucky, Tennessee, and South Carolina.

The old Butterfield stage line ran through the area on the "Old

Wire," or government road, providing transportation west from St. Louis to San Francisco between the years of 1858 and 1861.

The Civil War reached Fayetteville with the battles of Pea Ridge and Prairie Grove. The latter, in which there were 2500 casualties, took place 12 miles west of Fayetteville in December of 1862.

"Old Main," the first building on the University of Arkansas campus, was completed in 1874 when there was no railroad closer than 150 miles away. Bricks were made on the campus, and lumber and stone were brought by wagon from the surrounding areas. Iron and glass were hauled over the mountains by ox teams. When built, it was the highest and largest building in Arkansas, and it still graces the university campus today.

Economy and Employment

The local economy is based on a solid mix of agriculture and industry. The cash value of the farm product in Washington County is the highest in the state. The largest single industry is poultry processing, and the county ranks first in the nation in the sale of broiler chickens.

Other local industries manufacture clothing, hosiery, electrical equipment, woodworking, printing, electronics, light metal, and sports equipment. With the development of recreational facilities in the area, tourism is also becoming an important part of the economy.

The University of Arkansas is the largest single employer, with 3429 full-time and 1233 part-time employees. Other major employers include: Tyson's Food (processors of eggs and chickens, 2500 employees); Levi Strauss (pants, shirts, and jackets, 500); Baldwin Piano Co. (electronic musical instruments, 500); Kearney Co. (lightning arrestors, breakers, and electrical components, 300); Hackney Brothers Truck Body Co. (refrigerated truck bodies, 100); and Standard Register Co. (printers of business forms, 300–500).

Taxes

The combined state and local sales tax is 4%, and the state income tax is about 10% of the federal income tax. The residential property tax on a home selling for $65,000 would run about $1025 per year.

Shopping

While most of the needs of residents can be supplied locally, Tulsa, Oklahoma, is only 125 miles to the west, and Little Rock is 190 miles to the southeast.

Residential Properties

A good supply of speculative housing is available in Fayetteville. Three-bedroom homes sell for $25,000 to $150,000. A few recent real estate ads read:

HOME WITH 18 ACRES. Three-bedroom, 2-bath, cedar-siding home has 2 fireplaces, dining room, living room, family room and a knotty-pine kitchen. Double carport, storage room and several outbuildings. $130,000 with owner financing.

LOVELY 4-bedroom, 2-bath two-story home. Includes utility room, fireplace, den, separate dining room, cedar siding. Located in nice neighborhood. $74,900.

OWNER WILL FINANCE this two-bedroom starter home in quiet neighborhood close to the university campus. $38,000.

NEAT FIXER-UPPER. Three-bedroom, one-bath home near university. Won't last long at $25,000.

Rentals are plentiful in Fayetteville, with one-bedroom apartments renting for $180 to $250 per month. Two-bedroom apartments or condos are available at $200 to $275.

Safety

The FBI Crime Index rating for Fayetteville is a low 41 crimes per thousand of population per year. The police force employs 46 officers and operates 15 patrol cars. The fire department has 11 vehicles and 44 employees. The Fire Insurance Rating is Class 4. There are no natural hazards in the vicinity, and the nearest manmade potential hazards are a nuclear power plant 70 miles west and an ICBM missile complex near Little Rock. Neither of these is considered to be close enough to pose a hazard for residents of Fayetteville.

Education

The Fayetteville public school system consists of a senior high school with two campuses, two junior high schools, a vocational school, and eight elementary schools. There is also a parochial elementary school. In recent years, high school seniors have consistently ranked among the best in the state, receiving a substantial number of National Merit and other scholarships.

The University of Arkansas has contributed to higher education in the area for over a hundred years. Its programs in teaching, research, and public service are constant stimulants to the educational and cultural advancement of the region. Many new industries locate in the area because of the university, and many industries employ the newly graduated students. The university also forms one of the strongest supports of the local economy, with students spending about $18 million per year in local businesses, in addition to the input of the university payroll.

Medical Facilities

Fayetteville is the regional medical center, with three well-equipped, well-staffed hospitals and a comprehensive mental-health program. Washington Regional Medical Center now has a capacity of 314 beds and provides ultramodern facilities for the finest in-patient care. The City Hospital and Geriatric Center has 105 beds, 70 of which are for long-term care. The Veterans' Administration Hospital has 234 beds devoted to the care of general medical and surgical patients.

Cultural Activities

The University of Arkansas sponsors a variety of activities in the Fine Arts Center on campus, including plays, concerts, and exhibits. The University Museum, the Greek Theater, "Old Main," and the Planetarium are special attractions. The Ozark Regional Library contains 215,000 volumes, and the university library houses another 400,000 volumes.

Recreation

For the football fan, the Arkansas Razorbacks put forth their best efforts in the University of Arkansas's Razorback Stadium, and the university basketball team has established itself as one of the leading teams in the country. The Fayetteville High School gymnasium presents a constant series of sports activities during the school season.

For the outdoors-oriented, there are scores of lakes, rivers, and streams in northwest Arkansas, and all are excellent for fishing, boating, swimming, water-skiing, canoeing, and camping. Among the best spots are: Beaver Lake, with 500 miles of shoreline and many recreation areas; Lake Wedington, with a lodge, cabins, dock, fishing, swimming, and camping; Lake Fayetteville, a new city park area with small boats, fishing, and hiking; and Lake Sequoyah, located on the White River 7 miles east of Fayetteville, with small boats, fishing, and hiking.

When the air begins to turn chilly, northwest Arkansas becomes a paradise for hunters. Among the local game are quail, ducks, deer, rabbits, squirrels, raccoons, foxes, and wolves.

Scenic campsites are available in the beautiful Ozark National Forest and lake areas, ranging from primitive areas for backpacking to electric hookups, hot showers, and dump stations for the camper-trailer group.

Fayetteville is a golfer's mecca, offering nine courses, five of which are open to the general public, virtually no waiting time, and year-round playing. There are numerous tennis courts, and the city plans to expand facilities to meet future needs.

Thirteen parks in and around the city provide facilities for picnicking, hiking, baseball, tennis, and swimming, as well as playground equipment for smaller children. Of special interest are Prairie Grove Battlefield Park, 12 miles west of Fayetteville, which has a historical museum and picnic grounds, and Devil's Den State Park, 20 miles south of town, which has facilities for picnicking, swimming, hiking, and fishing.

Senior citizens have special recreational programs that include activities such as bowling, square dancing, art, china painting, and ballroom dancing.

Government

The Council-Manager form of government in Fayetteville includes a full-time city manager and a seven-member board elected to serve four-year overlapping terms.

Water

Fayetteville's water supply is operated by the city. The water, drawn from Beaver Lake, is pure, clean, alkaline, very soft, and not fluoridated.

Energy

Southwestern Electric Power Company provides electric power within the city limits, and the Arkansas Gas Company supplies natural gas to the area. Current utility costs for the average three-bedroom home run about $100 per month.

Television

There are four television stations in the area that can be received with simple home-antenna systems, and the local cable television system provides full 12-channel coverage to local subscribers.

Newspapers

The local daily newspaper is:

The Northwest Arkansas Times
Fayetteville, AR 72701

The *Little Rock Arkansas Gazette* and other big-city newspapers are also available locally.

For Further Information

Fayetteville Chamber of Commerce
P.O. Box 4216
Fayetteville, AR 72701

Department of Parks and Tourism
State Capitol
Little Rock, AR 72201

Flagstaff, Arizona

POPULATION: 34,821 within the city limits
73,000 in the Coconino County area

ELEVATION: 6910 feet above sea level

Flagstaff is a beautiful town located at the foot of the 12,680-foot-high San Francisco Peaks in north-central Arizona, in an area of stately pine trees and quaking aspens. In the immediate environs are the famous Grand Canyon, Walnut Canyon, Oak Creek Canyon, the Petrified Forest and Painted Desert, and the Wupatki Indian ruins. Farther away but still in the vicinity are the volcanic Sunset Crater and the huge Meteor Crater.

The clear mountain air of Flagstaff attracted Lowell Observatory, one mile west of town and one of the leading astronomical observatories in the country, as well as four other observatories, including the U.S. Naval Observatory, which has a 61-inch telescope, and the Lunar Topographic Research project, located at both Sunset Crater and Meteor Crater.

Originally a cow and lumber town, Flagstaff became an important tourist center, the railhead for Glen Canyon Dam, 135 miles to the north, and trading center for ranchers in northern Arizona.

Climate

Arizona has three main topographic areas: the northeastern high plateau, elevation 5000–7000 feet; the mountainous section that divides the state from the southeast to the northwest, elevation 9000–12,000 feet; and the southwestern low mountains and desert valleys. Because of the wide publicity given to the southwestern desert area, many people think of the entire state as dry and hot. Happily, this is not the case.

At an elevation of 6910 feet, Flagstaff is in the transition zone between the high plateau and the mountains. Precipitation is moderate, at 20 inches per year, and fairly evenly divided throughout the 12 months, falling as rain in June through September and as snow the rest of the year. From November through March, storm systems from the Pacific Ocean cross the state, often bringing heavy winter snows. Summer rains often come in the form of thundershowers generated in the Gulf of Mexico.

Flagstaff has a typical mountain climate, with most of its precipitation occurring in midwinter and midsummer. There are normally no more than two or three days per year when the temperature reaches 90°F, and summer nights are always cool, with summer nighttime temperatures around 50°F. Air conditioning is not needed.

Most of the winter precipitation is in the form of snow, with an average snowfall of over 80 inches, ideal for winter sports. Highways are seldom blocked by snow, and then only for a few hours at a time.

There are only nine days per year, on average, when the temperature falls to 0°F or below. Flagstaff has 7152 heating degree days per year. The average growing season is four months long, with the last killing frost occurring in the latter part of May, and the first killing frost in the latter part of September. Because of the protection afforded by the surrounding mountains, the daily average wind velocity rarely exceeds 14 miles per hour.

History

Flagstaff got its name on Independence Day, 1876, when a centennial flag was flown from the top of its tallest pine tree. This legendary pine stood as a guide for the wagon trains traveling to California over a trail that later became U.S. Highway 66.

Flagstaff became a town in 1894, was incorporated as a city in 1928, and has been the seat of Coconino County since 1891.

Following its brief heyday as the place of the flagstaff, it became the base of extensive logging and lumber operations and a trading center for ranchers. Then, because of its proximity to so many natural wonders, it began to grow as a tourist center.

Economy and Employment

Today, Flagstaff is a busy tourist center. From April to November is "the season," when people come to cool off and visit the nearby scenic wonders. Winter tourism is also growing, because of the nearby Arizona Snow Bowl, the largest ski area in the Southwest.

Flagstaff is the center for Arizona's lumber industry, and the bulk of local employment is in lumber mills and logging camps. In addition, the area has many large sheep and cattle ranches, but no stockyards. Each fall thousands of cattle and sheep are shipped from Flagstaff to all parts of the country.

The various sawmills employ some 1500 people, and Northern Arizona University employs 1000. Other major employers in the area include: the local army ordnance depot (110 employees); Walgreen's new distributing center (200); Ponderosa Paper Products (napkins and tissue paper, 150); Spring City Knitting Co. (children's knit undergarments, 150); Gore & Associates (custom-build electrical cables, 300); and Ralston Purina (pet foods and cereals, 300). The many retail and wholesale stores and service businesses employ the remainder of the work force of 17,000.

For current job information, write:

Manager
Department of Economic Security
Employment Service
397 Malpais
Flagstaff, AZ 86001

Taxes

The state income tax is about 15% of what one would pay in federal income tax. The state sales tax is 4% and the local tax is 1%, making a total sales tax of 5%.

Property taxes are based on 10% of market value and run about $585 per year for a home selling for $65,000.

Shopping

As the market center for a large ranching and lumbering area, Flagstaff offers virtually everything residents and visitors need or want. Major national and regional chain stores are represented, along with many local enterprises.

The nearest large city for more extensive shopping is Phoenix, 141 miles to the south.

Residential Properties

Housing prices have risen in recent years, but there are many homes available for purchase at prices ranging from $55,000 to $300,000. A few typical listings:

WONDERFUL VIEW from this cul-de-sac home with 3 bedrooms, 2 baths and big country kitchen. $62,500.

CLOSE TO EVERYTHING. Well-constructed older home with 3 bedrooms, 1 bath, double garage, big yard and garden. $58,600.

RANCH HOME with 4 bedrooms, big family room, formal dining room, on corner lot with mature landscaping. $79,900.

FRENCH PROVINCIAL with 4 bedrooms, 4 baths, pool, Jacuzzi, patio, Jenn-Air stove in island kitchen. Gorgeous! Only $159,900.

Homes and apartments for rent are hard to find. One-bedroom apartments, when available, rent for $175 to $400 per month, and two-bedroom apartments run $250 to $500.

Safety

The FBI Crime Index rating is 96 crimes per thousand of population per year. City police protection is provided by a 50-member department, and county residents are served by the sheriff's office, which has 73 deputies. Fire protection is provided by a 49-member fire department. The Fire Insurance Rating is Class 5.

There are no manmade or natural hazards nearby. The local army ordnance storage depot is far enough removed from town not to be considered a hazard for residents.

Education

The local public school system provides 14 elementary schools and 2 high schools. There are also 2 private schools.

Northern Arizona University, with an enrollment of over 12,000, provides undergraduate and graduate courses to the doctoral level in arts and sciences, business, education, forestry, engineering, humanities, and environmental studies.

Medical Facilities

The local hospital has 110 beds, and there are 49 physicians and 24 dentists serving the community. For more complete medical facilities, Phoenix is 141 miles to the south.

Cultural Activities

The Museum of Northern Arizona is dedicated to the preservation and exhibition of the natural and cultural history of the Colorado Plateau, which is a diverse and unique geographic region encompassing northern Arizona and the Four Corners area. The museum, founded in 1929, offers the public exhibits and Hopi and Navajo Indian shows. It is open throughout the year.

The Flagstaff Symphony Orchestra, and Art Barn, the Pioneer Historical Museum, the Northern Arizona University Art Gallery, the Festival of Arts, and six theaters all play an important part in the cultural activities of the community.

There are four libraries: the Coconino County Law Library, with 10,700 legal volumes; the Flagstaff City–Coconino County Public Library, with 53,000 volumes; the Northern Arizona University Library, with nearly 900,000 volumes; and the U.S. Geological Survey Library, with 11,300 volumes.

Recreation

Flagstaff offers a local golf course, 3 recreation centers, 13 parks, 2 swimming pools, 12 tennis courts, an ice-skating rink, 2 ski runs, 2 sled runs, and 2 toboggan runs.

For the shooter, there are trap and skeet ranges. For the hunter and fisherman, the opportunities are almost limitless. There is excellent stream and lake fishing nearby. The fields, mountains, and forests are alive with bears, antelope, deer, elk, wildcats, turkeys, and small game birds and animals.

For nature lovers there are mountains, valleys, rivers, streams, and lakes to explore and enjoy.

Government

Flagstaff has a Council-Manager form of government, with an elected city council and a full-time city manager.

Water

The water supply is pure, soft, and slightly alkaline. Current supplies are plentiful, coming from the heavy annual snowpack in the surrounding mountains.

Energy

Southern Union Gas Company supplies natural gas to Flagstaff residents, and the Arizona Public Service Company supplies electricity from the hydroelectric plants in northern Arizona.

The average utility cost for a two-bedroom home is about $100 per month.

Television

There is one local television station, but the local cable system provides coverage on seven channels.

Newspapers

The local paper is published daily except Sunday. The address is:

Arizona Daily Sun
P.O. Box 1849
Flagstaff, AZ 86002

The *Phoenix Republic* and the *Los Angeles Times* are also available locally.

For Further Information

Flagstaff Chamber of Commerce
101 W. Santa Fe
Flagstaff, AZ 86001

Arizona Office of Tourism
501 State Capitol
Phoenix, AZ 85007

State Parks
1688 West Adams St.
Phoenix, AZ 85007

Florence, South Carolina

POPULATION: 30,170 within the city limits
59,900 in the immediate area
102,900 within Florence County

ELEVATION: 149 feet above sea level

Florence, the county seat of Florence County, is located in northeastern South Carolina about 80 miles east of Columbia in the coastal plain section of the state, near the Pee Dee River. The coastal plain area is broad and largely level, and is permeated by many tributaries of the Pee Dee River in the area of Florence County.

Florence is a major transportation center, with many trucking terminals, railway shops, and foundry and machine shops, as well as bottling, woodworking, furniture, synthetic-fiber, clothing, electronic-component, and gas-welding plants. It is an important market area for tobacco, cotton, pecans, and soybeans.

Climate

Several factors combine to give South Carolina a pleasant, mild and humid climate: its low altitude, its long coastline warmed by the Gulf Stream, and the mountains to the west that block or delay many cold-air masses approaching from the north and west.

Summers are long and warm, with normal maximum temperatures in the 80s from May through September. There are some 70 days per year with temperatures of 90°F and above. Summer temperatures are frequently relieved by thundershowers in the afternoons. There are 1950 cooling degree days per year in this area.

Winters are short and mild, with average temperatures ranging from daytime highs in the upper 50s to nighttime lows in the upper 30s from December through February. Snowfall is seldom more than 2 inches per year, and snow stays on the ground only briefly. Winter storms can bring freezing temperatures and snow and ice, and record lows have been reported in the 5° to 8°F range. The first frost normally comes in mid-November, and the last frost is generally in early March, leaving a 240-day freeze-free growing period. There are about 2400 heating degree days per year.

Precipitation is primarily in the form of rain, which is lightest in October through January. In the spring, rains tend to increase, and the heaviest rainfall comes in June and July. The total precipitation is about 47 inches per year, and rain falls on approximately one-third of the days each month in summer and one-fourth of the days in winter.

The Atlantic coastal plain in this region is subject to occasional tropical storms and hurricanes, though the distance from the ocean reduces their effect by the time they reach Florence. Tornadoes strike the state about seven or eight times per year, though the probability of a tornado striking any particular area in any given year is close to zero.

History

Like many towns throughout the country, Florence began as a railroad center. It served as a center for the movement of men and military supplies during the Civil War. Some of Florence's first public buildings grew from this military activity. The Wayside Hospital was operated for Confederate soldiers, and the stockade was built to hold captured Union soldiers.

After the war was over, the Northeastern railroad built shops in Florence, and for a hundred years this was the largest source of employment and income for the town.

The name *Florence* was bestowed by General William Wallace Harllee, president of the Wilmington and Manchester railroad, who named the junction with the Northeastern railroad line after his daughter. Early railroad maps show a station at the site named Florence as early as 1854.

In 1888 Florence County was formed, and two years later the community of Florence was chartered as a city. Growth was slow, and Florence remained a backwater until the late 1950s when DuPont moved to Florence, followed by Electromotive Manufacturing and Union Carbide.

Economy and Employment

Within the last 15 years, 35 diversified industries have chosen Florence as the site for new plants. DuPont opened a new plant for making Mylar film, followed by General Electric with a plant for making mobile radio equipment.

Today's major employers include: E. I. DuPont de Nemours & Co. (polyester films, 975 employees); Koppers Co. (electrical transmission poles and railroad ties, 775); Hannaco Knives & Saws, Inc. (industrial knives and saws, 125); Marlowe Manufacturing Co., Inc. (girls' sportswear, 700); Nucor Steel Division of Nucor Corp. (structural steel, 360); Union Carbide Corp. (welding equipment, 890); General Electric Corp. (fleet radio equipment, 1300); Fiber Industries, Inc. (polyester fibers, 850); and Stone Container Industries, Inc. (craft liner board, 597).

Other large industries and employers include: woodworking (875 employees); textiles (1800); bakeries (360); railroads (800); bottling (300); dairies (170); utilities (780); paper mills (425); and office control systems (50).

Taxes

The state sales tax is 4% and the state income tax ranges from 2% on the first $2000 to 7% on incomes over $10,000, with a $800-per-person exemption.

Property taxes are moderate, and the tax on a home selling for $65,000 runs about $585 per year.

Shopping

Since Florence serves a nine-county shopping area, it is well equipped to meet the needs of its residents. For a wider choice, Columbia is 80 miles to the west and Atlanta is 300 miles to the west.

Residential Properties

Florence has a wide variety of homes, from stately historic mansions to new condominiums. Examples of current listings are:

> GREAT OPPORTUNITY for first home. 3-bedroom 1½-bath brick home on large lot. $41,500.
>
> LARGE HOME with 4 bedrooms and 2 baths, fireplace and large master bedroom. $62,200.
>
> MAGNIFICENT VICTORIAN with assumable loan. 4 bedrooms, 2½ baths, fireplace in master bedroom, hardwood floors, Jenn-Air range, microwave, 9-foot ceilings, deck, 2400 square feet of living area. $89,000.

For those not ready to buy a home, one-bedroom apartments are available at $125 to $250 per month and two-bedroom apartments or condos rent for $250 to $350. There are sometimes waiting lists for the more desirable apartments.

Safety

Some potential hazards are closer than we like, but Florence is such a nice place that we decided to include it in this book anyhow and let the possible resident make the decision as to whether or not the hazard outweighs the advantages. A just-completed nuclear power plant is located at Lake Robinson, 25 miles away. Aside from the nuclear reactor, there are no manmade potential hazards nearby.

Earth tremors have occurred in South Carolina over the years, and the coastal plain is in a seismic hazard area. A major earthquake, centered about 90 miles to the south, occurred in 1886 and demolished more than 100 buildings in Charleston.

The FBI Crime Index rating is 95 crimes per thousand of population per year. The city police department has 78 employees and the fire department employs 58 firemen. The Fire Insurance Rating is Class 4.

Education

The public school system provides 14 elementary schools, 4 junior high and middle schools, 3 senior high schools, a vocational school, and a special-education school. In addition to the public schools, there are St. Anthony's and All-Saints Episcopal parochial schools for grades one to six, and three nondenominational private schools.

Francis Marion College is a four-year, state-supported college with an enrollment of approximately 3000 students. Named for

South Carolina's legendary "Swamp Fox," General Francis Marion, it is situated on a deeply wooded 300-acre site just east of town.

Medical Facilities

McLeon Memorial Hospital and its annex provide full medical services and 323 beds. Florence General Hospital provides another 144 beds and complete medical facilities. Also, Bruce Hospital offers 80 beds.

There are currently 74 physicians and 27 dentists serving the area.

Cultural Activities

Few communities of the size of Florence have a 50-piece symphony orchestra, but the Florence Symphony is good enough to perform in concert with national institutions such as the Atlanta Symphony. The Choral Society is an offshoot of the symphony and performs vocal classics ranging from Verdi to Broadway.

The Little Theater Guild has its own $350,000 home, a comfortable, modern, and adaptable theater, where the group produces a variety of musical and dramatic works each year. The Regional Civic Ballet Company also presents its work at the Little Theater.

The Community Concerts Association brings in stars of the concert stage throughout the year.

Francis Marion College supplements these activities with a year-round calendar of events in the performing and visual arts, including student and faculty concerts, films, plays, and art exhibitions, all of which are open to the public.

The Florence County Library, which has a main building, four branches, and two bookmobiles, serves the county and the city. It is doubling its size and shelving capacity with a new $1 million wing that includes meeting rooms and a small auditorium, as well as increased shelf space for books and periodicals. Its collection is approximately 105,000 volumes. These facilities are augmented by an interlibrary loan arrangement with every other library in the state.

Supplementing the County Library is the collection in the James A. Rogers Library of Francis Marion College, which, while intended primarily for student use, permits on-site use of its collection by the public.

Recreation

South Carolina, with its mountains, rivers, streams, lakes, and ocean beaches, has much to offer in way of recreation. To the west, the Blue Ridge Mountains offer hiking, camping, and winter skiing. To the east, the Carolina coast offers deepwater fishing, surf fishing, boating, surfing, swimming, and some of the nation's plushest pleasure resorts.

Nearby, there is much to enjoy. The city of Florence is green with parks and playgrounds that offer picnicking facilities, baseball fields, tennis courts, and basketball courts.

Golfers enjoy a 12-month season. There are about 30 golf courses within easy driving distance, but the closest to Florence are the 18-hole Country Club of South Carolina and the 18-hole Oakdale course, both open to the public, plus the private 18-hole course at the Florence Country Club.

The deep woods and open fields in the area offer a variety of hunting, from deer, quail, and doves to rabbit and opossum. The state's managed game lands are very close to Florence, and fishermen take prize fish from the Santee-Cooper river system. The Little Pee Dee and Black rivers are alive with bream and catfish. Lake Robinson is only about a 20-minute drive away and provides facilities for swimmers, water-skiers, and fishermen.

Swimmers also have access to two municipal swimming pools, and there is salt-water swimming on the coast.

Government
Florence operates under the Council-Manager form of government.

Water
The local tap water is alkaline, soft, and fluoridated. With 750 million gallons of precipitation per square mile per year and several rivers nearby, there should be ample water for the foreseeable future.

Energy
Carolina Power and Light supplies electricity to the area from fossil-fuel generators and its new nuclear power station at Lake Robinson. Natural gas is supplied by Peoples Natural Gas Company.

Utility costs for the average two-bedroom home run about $75 per month.

Television
There are two commercial stations and one public television station. Stations from Columbus, Charleston, and Charlotte, North

Carolina, can be received by rooftop antenna systems. There is also a local cable system that provides full coverage to subscribers.

Newspapers
The local daily newspaper is:

The Florence Morning News
Florence, SC 29501

The *Columbia State* newspaper is also available locally.

For Further Information

Greater Florence Chamber of Commerce
P.O. Box 948
Florence, SC 29503

In addition to requesting the usual, you may enclose $2.00, to cover printing costs, and receive the Industrial Directory, which lists all major employers in the area.

The South Carolina Commission on Aging
915 Main St.
Columbia, SC 29201

The Commission on Aging publishes a booklet, *Retiring in South Carolina,* that gives excellent information on the state and is useful even if you are not ready for retirement. It is free and highly recommended.

South Carolina Division of Tourism
Box 71
Columbia, SC 29202

Ask for their *South Carolina Trip Kit.* It's free and very informative.

Gadsden, Alabama

POPULATION: 47,526 within the city limits
100,400 within the total community area

ELEVATION: 555 feet above sea level

The state of Alabama rises in a rolling plain from the Gulf of Mexico, in the southwest, through the foothills in the central part of the state, to the southern edge of the Cumberland Plateau, the Appalachian Mountains, and the Blue Ridge Mountains, in the northeast.

Gadsden is located in the northeastern part of Alabama, in the eastern foothills at the southern tip of the Appalachian range, on the banks of the Coosa River and a manmade lake. It is 65 miles northeast of Birmingham, and 120 miles west of Atlanta.

Climate

All of Alabama has a temperate climate, with the weather approaching subtropical on the coast. The summers are long, hot, and humid, with little change from day to day. In the Gadsden area, the mountains help to alleviate the summer heat somewhat. In the average year, Gadsden has a total of about 60 days in which the temperature climbs higher than 90°F. The long hot summers bring a surprisingly moderate number of cooling degree days — a little over 2000 each year. From late June through middle August, many evenings are cooled by local afternoon thundershowers.

December, January, and February are the coldest months, though there are frequent changes between the dry, cool continental air and the mild, moist Gulf air. Severe cold is rare. The earliest frost usually arrives in October, and the last one can be expected in April. The mild winters bring an annual total of approximately 3000 heating degree days.

Precipitation throughout the year is nearly all in the form of rain, though there may be a few inches of snow each year that never stays on the ground long. Rainfall is ample, varying between 50 and 60 inches in the normal year.

While tornadoes may occur between November and May, they are likely to hit any particular spot only once in 20,000 years, so they hardly constitute an immediate and present danger. Hurricanes sometimes hit the coast but seldom travel inland far enough to bring more than a heavy rain to Gadsden.

Winter winds are generally from the north. Summer winds are generally southerly. Winds are gentle, except during storms.

For those who like gardening, the long growing season and ample rainfall provide favorable conditions year-round. For people who like outdoor sports, Gadsden receives between 50% to 60% of possible sunshine during the year. All things considered, it is a good climate to live, work, and play in.

History

While few people have heard of this small town in Alabama, almost all of us learned in school how James Gadsden negotiated the Gadsden Purchase of a portion of today's New Mexico from the Mexican government in 1854. Though the Alabama town was founded in 1840, it was named after this same James Gadsden.

The Civil War left few marks on Gadsden, though there is a statue to Emma Sansom, who guided Confederate General Nathan Bedford Forrest ("Git there fustest with the mostest") across a ford on Black Creek after the Union troops had burned the bridge.

Economy and Employment

Business and industry are growing in Gadsden, with the influx of industries moving southward from the colder northern states. Local industries manufacture textiles, iron, steel, auto tires, and various metal products.

Natural resources in the area include iron ore, timber, coal, clay, manganese, limestone, building stone, shale, chert, and sand. Agricultural products include cotton, produce, grain, and livestock.

There are many employment opportunities in business, retail, and wholesale sales, and in service industries. Major industrial employers include: Precision Products (clock and timer movements, 500 employees); Etowah Manufacturing (hamburger cookers, toaster ovens, and military space-vehicle parts, 250); Siemens-Allis Corp. (voltage regulators, 200); Dixie Tool and Die (dies, tools, jigs, and special machines, 150); and Bush Manufacturing Co. (metal fabrication, 900). Other manufacturers produce manholes, pipe, cranes, conveyors, precision machines, fuses, ammunition, containers, detergents, fencing, chairs, and rubber stamps.

Taxes

The state sales tax is 4%, and the state income tax is low, amounting to only 1.5% on the first $1000 and climbing to a maximum of 5% on taxable income above $5000.

Property taxes in Gadsden are based on an assessed value of 10% of true market value, and the tax rate is $4.50 per $100 of assessed value. Thus the taxes on a home selling for $65,000 would run about $293 per year.

Shopping

The principal shopping center is the The Mall in downtown Gadsden. In addition, there are many neighborhood shopping centers and three large centers on the outskirts of town. There is no difficulty in satisfying all ordinary needs locally.

For more sophisticated shopping, one can go to Birmingham, 65 miles to the southwest, or Atlanta, 125 miles to the east.

Residential Properties

There is never enough housing in a growing community such as Gadsden, yet prices remain quite low, compared to properties in many other parts of the country. A few typical listings are:

> LOVELY BRICK HOME with 3 bedrooms, 2 baths, living room, dining room, den with fireplace, and double garage, only $44,900.

OWNER WILL FINANCE this 2-bedroom home with living room, dining room, kitchen, half-basement, central heat and air, extra-wide single garage, $25,900.

EASY LIVING in this spacious 4-bedroom, 2½-bath home on 7 lovely acres, with living/dining room, kitchen with built-ins, den with fireplace, laundry room, office, recreation room, double garage. $89,900.

BRAND NEW BRICK home with 3 bedrooms, 2 baths, living room, dining room, den with fireplace, kitchen with built-ins, central heat and air, double garage, on large lot. $79,900.

For those not yet ready to purchase a home, rentals are available, ranging from $135 to $200 per month for one-bedroom apartments and from $175 to $345 per month for two-bedroom apartments.

Safety

The FBI Crime Index rating is 77 crimes per thousand residents per year. The police department has 107 full-time employees and the fire department has 127 full-time firemen. The city's Fire Insurance Rating is Class 4.

There are no known chemical or nuclear-waste dumps in the area, and no reports of pollution of the local waters.

Fort McClellan, 25 miles to the southeast, near Anniston, is a possible military target, and the nearest nuclear power reactor is in Scottsboro, 45 miles to the north. Neither is likely to be a hazard to the Gadsden area.

Education

Local schools are good, with five high schools, two combination junior and high schools, and seven junior and middle schools. While there are no institutions of higher learning in town, there are several in Birmingham, 65 miles away, including the University of Alabama, which has full graduate and undergraduate programs.

Medical Facilities

Gadsden is the regional center for specialized medical care for an 11-county area. There are over 600 beds available in two general hospitals, a chronic-disease hospital, a tri-county mental-health center, and five certified nursing homes.

Gadsden and Etowah County have more than 115 doctors and 41 dentists. The Etowah County Health Department, with a staff of 47, including 20 nurses and other specialists, rounds out the medical services available in the area.

Cultural Activities
The Gadsden–Etowah County Library serves the area with a collection that exceeds 130,000 volumes. It specializes in genealogy and Alabama history.

The Civic Theater, a nonprofit, nonprofessional theater, has its own building and seats 325 people. Gadsden's Concert Association and the Music Club bring various musical events to the area throughout the year. These are supplemented by an annual Marching Band Festival, a Folk Art Festival, and a local museum of fine arts.

Recreation
Gadsden has 9 parks and 22 supervised playgrounds, plus 6 recreation centers.

The Coosa River offers many opportunities along its course, with lakes both above and below town. There is a local public boat-launching facility. The river and the area lakes provide fishing, water sports, hunting, hiking, and camping facilities.

Four state parks and two national forests are within easy driving distance. A day's drive to the south brings all of the recreational possibilities of the seashores of the Gulf of Mexico, including ocean swimming, fishing, and boating.

Golfers have a choice of four private private golf courses and two country clubs. Other opportunities for residents include two local racetracks, a variety of bowling and roller-skating centers, and tennis courts in 22 locations.

Government
Gadsden, like many towns in the Old South, still relies on the antiquated Commissioner form of government, with each member of the town council serving as the commissioner of a municipal department and the mayor serving as the elected city manager.

Water
Local tap water is slightly alkaline and soft. It is supplied through a city-owned system.

Energy
Abundant hydroelectric power is available in the area from power stations on the Coosa River. Imported gas and fuel oil are expensive. Coal is cheap.

Electric power is supplied by Alabama Power Company, and natural gas is available through the Alabama Gas Corporation. Both have offices in Gadsden, and both will supply rate information on request. Coal and fuel oil for winter heating are available from local suppliers. Utility costs average about $100 per month.

Television

Four television stations can be picked up locally with home antenna systems, and a cable system offers full coverage to local subscribers.

Newspapers

The daily paper, published seven days a week, is:

The Gadsden Times
P.O. Box 188
Gadsden, AL 35909

The *Birmingham News* is also available for home delivery.

For Further Information

Gadsden Metropolitan Chamber of Commerce
P.O. Box 185
Gadsden, AL 35901

The chamber of commerce will send you a Newcomer's Guide, which contains a coupon good for one month's free subscription to the *Gadsden Times.* Be sure to ask for it.

Alabama Bureau of Publicity and Information
403 State Highway Building
Montgomery, AL 36130

Alabama Historical Commission
305 South Lawrence St.
Montgomery, AL 36104

The commission has booklets on the histories of various areas.

U.S. Forest Service
P.O. Box 40
Montgomery, AL 36101

Ask for their recreational guides to Alabama National Forests.

Galveston, Texas

POPULATION: 61,601 within the city limits
203,200 within the Galveston–Texas City area

ELEVATION: 20 feet above sea level

Galveston is located on an island just off the Texas coast in the Gulf of Mexico, 50 miles southeast of Houston. It is connected to the mainland by causeways, and a superhighway runs between it and Houston.

Galveston is a busy seaport, a bustling tourist center, and a pleasant place to live, with residences that vary from magnificent Victorian homes to ultramodern condominiums to contemporary houses in subdivisions. It offers a delightful blending of yesterday's charm and grace and today's energetic industrial development.

Climate

Located on an island surrounded by the warm waters of the Gulf of Mexico, Galveston enjoys a climate that is cooler in summer and warmer in winter than the usual coastal climate of Texas. Typically, summers are long and warm to hot and winters are brief and mild.

Normal summer daytime temperatures range in the 80s to low 90s from May through September, with nighttime lows in the 70s. There are about 3500 cooling degree days per year and about 35 days each year with temperatures 90°F and above (compared to some 90 days per year in Houston, 50 miles inland). High summer temperatures are alleviated by the southerly winds that blow from the Gulf throughout the year.

Winters have average high temperatures in the 60s and lows in the 50s, except for the three to six, and sometimes more, northers that bring arctic air down to the Gulf Coast. In normal winters, there are only four days with temperatures of 32°F and below, with those days falling between Christmas and the end of January. This assures more than 325 frost-free days in the growing season. Snow is virtually unknown. Winters bring a low 1235 heating degree days per year, and only minimal heating is required in homes.

Precipitation is about 40 inches per year, fairly evenly spread throughout the 12 months, with slightly more precipitation in July through September, mainly from the thundershowers normal to the entire Gulf Coast region. Humidity is generally high throughout the year, with nighttime humidity around 84% and afternoon lows at 71%.

Galveston is in the hurricane belt and is subject to periodic invasions by tropical cyclones. The Great Galveston Storm of September 8–9, 1900, was the worst natural disaster in United States history, with loss of life estimated at 6000 to 8000 persons. The island was completely inundated, and not a single structure escaped damage. However, after that storm, the local citizens built a huge sea wall to deflect storm-generated waves, and subsequent storms have never reached disaster proportions. With the sea wall and the present storm-warning system, Galveston has become a reasonably safe place in which to live.

History

Galveston's history stretches back perhaps 2000 years to the proud Karankawa Indians. These Indians lived off the land and sea of the Texas coast until driven off Galveston Island by Jean Laffitte's pirates in 1820.

The island was first "discovered" by Europeans in 1528, when the Spanish explorer Álvar Núñez Cabeza de Vaca and his small band were shipwrecked and imprisoned by the Karankawas for six years. After this discovery, the island dropped back into obscurity until 1785, when the Spanish returned, surveyed it, and named it Galvez, in honor of Count Bernardo de Galvez, then viceroy of Mexico.

Mexicans used the island for privateer operations until they returned from a raid one day and discovered that their sanctuary had been taken over by the famous pirate Jean Laffitte. Laffitte named his settlement Campeche and made it a haven for criminals, deserters, prostitutes, gamblers, and slave traders. He held the island until 1821 when the U.S. government drove him away.

The island remained unoccupied during the battle for Texas independence, but soon after that pioneers founded the present-day city of Galveston. From then on, the growth and prosperity of Galveston was assured. By the mid-1800s, the "Great Port" was thriving and Galveston had become the financial and cultural center of Texas and the Southwest. Cotton from the Texas fields flowed out, and goods from Europe and the eastern seaboard flowed in.

Fortunes were made on Galveston's Strand, "the Wall Street of the Southwest," where banks, insurance companies, cotton factors, and shipping companies serviced the booming port. Some of the fine Victorian residences of that period are still standing today in the older sections of town.

In the early 1900s, after the devastating storm of 1900, Galveston began losing its commercial position to growing Houston, 50 miles to the northwest and connected to the Gulf by a long ship channel that permitted ocean-going ships to bypass the port of Galveston and unload directly to the railroads that came to Houston.

After a period of economic and social depression, a renaissance began in Galveston with the restoration and revitalization of the Strand, which today remains a superb concentration of nineteenth-century commercial buildings.

Economy and Employment

Following the restoration of the downtown area, Galveston prospered. Today the tourist industry is growing, and several new hotels have been started, including a 300-room Hilton, a 150-room Ramada Inn, and a 150-room Sheraton.

The Gulf Coast oil boom has brought oil-related prosperity to the area. Shell Oil has a supply base for servicing offshore drilling rigs, and Tenneco Production is building a new dock facility and expanding its Louisiana operations to Galveston. Todd Shipyards Corporation is constructing a 40,000-ton super dry dock and expanding its pierside facilities.

As the offshore oil business has increased, so has traffic at the local airport, where commuter flights to Houston International connect Galveston to the rest of the world. A 60-helicopter fleet services the offshore oil rigs from the Galveston airport.

The University of Texas Medical Branch has been located in Galveston since 1891, and is today the largest employer on the island, with 7314 employees. Other major employers are: American National Insurance (1450 employees); Galveston Independent School District (1450); Todd Shipyards Corp. (building and repair of ships, 850); City of Galveston (750); St. Mary's Hospital (690); County of Galveston (490); Galveston Shipbuilding (ship repair, 400); U.S. Army Corps of Engineers (400); and Port of Galveston (350).

Other large employers include the Santa Fe Railway, Bredero Price (pipe coatings), American Indemnity Insurance, Thomas J. Lipton, and Guaranty Federal Savings and Loan, each with 200 to 300 employees. Heavy industry now includes companies such as Great Western Metals, Farmer's Marine and Industrial Supply, and Sanco Fabrication.

There are many smaller firms in the areas of commercial printing, millwork, sheet-metal work, wall paneling, engraving, oil-field and offshore-oil services, boat building and repair, soft-drink bottling, barging and towing services, shrimp, oyster, crab, and fish packing, sign painting, and metal fabrication.

Current employment information can be obtained by writing:

Texas Employment Commission
1922 Sealy
Galveston, TX 77550

Galveston boomed in the 1800s. It is booming again!

Taxes

So far, Texas has no state income tax. The combined state and local sales tax is 5%. The property tax is about $1381 per year on a home selling for $65,000.

Shopping

Galveston has always had a remarkable diversity of shops. Today, there are the usual chain stores to supply the everyday needs of both citizens and tourists, plus a wide variety of specialty shops offering everything from brass and pottery to books and antiques. One of the offbeat, fascinating places to browse through is a surplus store that offers military-surplus items from all eras and all parts of the world, from Civil War uniforms to British commando berets, from World War II helmets to Vietnam jungle boots.

There are three shopping malls in the area, plus several satellite shopping centers and neighborhood shopping clusters.

For those who want more variety than Galveston offers, Houston is only 50 miles away and provides virtually every shopping facility one could ask for.

Residential Properties

Homes range from historic ones that predate the storm of 1900 to the most modern in new subdivisions. These are supplemented by townhouses and condominiums, plus a variety of new apartment buildings. A few typical current listings for homes in Galveston are:

NEWLY REMODELED 3-bedroom, 2-bath home with 2000 square feet. $68,000.

BEAUTIFULLY RESTORED Historic Home, 3 bedrooms, 2½ baths in this charming cottage with old-world charm. $98,500.

CONDO with 2 bedrooms, 1½ baths, complete kitchen, washer & dryer, assumable loan. $65,000.

OLDER HOME with 2 bedrooms and den on full lot, with owner financing, $45,000.

Rentals are plentiful. One-bedroom apartments can be rented for $200 to $330 per month, and two-bedroom apartments or condos rent for $250 to $495. The chamber of commerce will provide you with a list of realtors, but the best information on the current real estate market is in the classified section of the local newspaper.

Safety

Galveston has a moderate FBI Crime Index rating of 77 crimes per thousand of population per year. There are no nearby nuclear power plants or military targets.

Police protection is provided by the Galveston Police Department, which has 147 officers and 48 cars. In the unincorporated areas nearby, protection is provided by the sheriff's department, which has 119 deputies and 48 cars.

Fire protection is provided by a 119-man department that has 20 vehicles.

Education

Galveston's Independent School District serves the island's 10,000 school-aged children, from preschool through the twelfth grade. The district includes all of Galveston Island and part of Bolivar Peninsula, and provides seven elementary schools, two middle schools, one eighth-grade school, one senior high school, and a preschool program. These are supplemented by several parochial schools and Travis Academy, a private, nonsectarian college-preparatory school.

Advanced education is available at Galveston College, a two-year college and career-training institution. Texas A & M University, whose main facility is at College Station, offers B.S. degrees in a number of marine-related subjects at its two Galveston campuses. The University of Texas Medical Branch trains medical students, nurses, and health professionals. It is a state-affiliated institution that operates several hospitals and provides training toward an M.D. degree, medical internships, and residency programs.

Other colleges and universities within an hour's drive of Galveston include: University of Houston (both the main campus in Houston and the nearer Clear Lake campus); Rice University, in Houston; Texas Southern University; South Texas College of Law; University of St. Thomas; Houston Baptist University; Lee College; San Jacinto College; Alvin Community College; and College of the Mainland.

Medical Facilities

There are eight hospitals in Galveston, with a total of 1518 beds. The University of Texas Medical Branch brings some of the country's top physicians and surgeons to the area to provide instruction to its students, thereby providing unusual medical care for patients. In addition to the hospitals, there are 20 private clinics and 120 physicians in private practice. There are 31 dentists serving the area.

Cultural Activities

The Strand Street Theater operates throughout the year, offering everything from Shakespeare to modern musicals. Each year there are a variety of road-show productions sponsored by the Galveston County Cultural Arts Council, most of which are presented at the Moody Center or in the 1894 Opera House. In addition, theater productions are offered in the summer at the Upper Deck Theater and the Long Wharf Theater.

Galveston's County Community Orchestra offers concerts throughout the season, alternating between classical and popular programs. The Dance Center offers monthly recitals and workshops in dance. The Arts Center on the Strand offers courses in the arts and a gallery for showing the works of local artists.

The Rosenberg Library, established in 1900, is the oldest free library in continuous operation in the state. It offers approximately one million volumes in its collection, along with meeting rooms and art exhibits.

Recreation

With 32 miles of beaches, Galveston provides ample opportunity for swimming and surf fishing. On the bay side of the island, there is crabbing and freshwater fishing. Charter boats are available for deep-sea fishing, and there are many places to launch your own boat if you prefer to do so.

Galveston has a yacht club, and there are many places to moor boats. Boating, water-skiing, swimming, surfing, and scuba diving are all popular sports throughout most of the year.

The island has 1 golf course, 11 ball fields, and 28 public parks. While there is no public swimming pool, Stewart Beach, a family beach, offers a guarded swimming area, a bathhouse, snack bars, and an amusement area. As the chamber of commerce says, "Come to Galveston and have fun!"

Government

Galveston operates under the Council-Manager system, with a full-time city manager and an elected city council.

Water

Water is supplied by the Galveston County Water Authority and comes from Lake Houston, the San Jacinto River, and wells in nearby Alta Loma. The system can generate more water than the maximum peak load, assuring adequate water throughout the year.

Energy

Electricity is supplied by Houston Lighting and Power Company, whose system covers the area around Houston. Power is generated from oil- and gas-fired plants and will soon be generated at the large nuclear plant at Port Lavaca, 110 miles to the southwest. Future supplies appear to be assured.

Natural gas is supplied by Southern Union Gas Company and is drawn from the large Texas gas fields nearby. It too appears to be reliable for the foreseeable future.

Utility costs, while rising, are still low in comparison to costs in many other parts of the United States, averaging $70 per month for the typical two-bedroom home.

Television

Houston television stations are near enough to be easily received in Galveston. In addition, there is a cable system offering Showtime and programs via satellite from Atlanta and Chicago.

Newspapers

The local daily newspaper is:

The Galveston Daily News
P.O. Box 628
Galveston, TX 77553

The Houston papers are also available locally.

For Further Information

The Galveston Chamber of Commerce
315 Tremont
Galveston, TX 77550

Tourist Development Agency
P.O. Box 12008, Capitol Station
Austin, TX 78711

State Department of Highways
Box 1386
Houston, TX 77001

Ask for a copy of the department's excellent highway map.

Grand Island, Nebraska

POPULATION: 33,160 within the city limits
45,200 in Hall County

ELEVATION: 1864 feet above sea level

Grand Island is located in southeastern Nebraska on the Platte River, 100 miles west of Lincoln. Despite its modest size, Grand Island is the third largest city in the state, with only Omaha and Lincoln larger. It is the trade and shopping center for a large irrigated agricultural area, dotted with dairy farms, horses, mules, and cattle. It is an important rail and manufacturing center as well. And with a growing technology in the area, Grand Island is rapidly becoming more than a prosperous agricultural community.

Underground water is plentiful and the soil is rich. The countryside is flat to slightly rolling, with scattered woods and open prairies.

Climate

Nebraska is one of the northern Great Plains states and has the climate to match: typically continental, with light rainfall, low humidity, hot summers, cold winters, great variations in temperature and rainfall from year to year, and frequent changes in weather from day to day. These changes are caused by large air masses moving in from different directions: warm, moist air from the Gulf of Mexico; hot, dry air from the Southwest; cool, dry air from the northern Pacific Ocean; and cold, dry air from northwestern Canada.

Winters are long and cold, with normal low temperatures from November through March averaging below freezing, and with occasional drops to as low as −35°F in January and February. Snow seldom exceeds 28 inches per year and occurs only about nine days per year. Winters bring about 6530 heating degree days, and there are about 152 days per year with temperatures of 32°F and below, with about 17 days during which the temperature drops to 0°F and below. The last frost in spring comes at the end of April, and the first frost in fall at the beginning of October, leaving about 160 days of frost-free growing season. Winter winds are often strong and are generally northerly, sometimes variable, shifting to westerly and even southerly, depending upon the movement of the major air masses.

Summers are short and hot, with highs around 90°F from June through August. There are 38 days per year with temperatures of 90°F and above, and about 1000 cooling degree days per year.

Precipitation is a moderate 22 inches per year, mostly falling in the summer months and often coming in the form of thunderstorms, which average about 51 per year. Tornadoes can occur, with an average of about 10 per year for the entire state.

History

Early fur traders first mapped Le Grand Ile, as it was called then, an island some 40 miles long in the Platte River. During the early days when pioneers were moving westward across the prairies, it was one of the most prominent geographical features of the Great Plains.

The first permanent settlers arrived and established a community on the island in 1857, a time when there were only some 20,000 people in the entire Nebraska Territory, most of them in Omaha. This early community took the name of the island on which it was located.

The early years of the first settlers were difficult. Rations were scarce and starvation was a constant threat. Then, in 1866, the

Union Pacific railroad reached the small community and the town's real growth began. Grand Island was incorporated as a town in 1872, after the petition for incorporation had been signed by all 105 of the taxable male inhabitants. The community grew, and by 1880 the census recorded a population of 2963. By 1900 Grand Island was a railhead for three railroads and a thriving trade and farm center.

Like most of the Great Plains states, Nebraska suffered severe hardship during the drought of the 1930s, but by the end of World War II it had recovered and was beginning to prosper again.

Economy and Employment

Because of modern agricultural methods and plentiful underground water, the region around Grand Island is one of the nation's leading agricultural areas. Grand Island is the fastest-growing industrial area in the state, with over 80 manufacturing plants producing farm machinery, auto parts, food products, and other items. As the leading retail center in central Nebraska, it offers many job opportunities in retail and wholesale trade and distribution as well.

Local manufacturing and industrial operations now total 84 diversified manufacturing plants, including: Sperry New Holland (harvesting equipment, 1150 employees); Monfort (beef packing, 1135); and Chief Industries (grain bins, steel buildings, factory-built homes, sewage-treatment systems, and signs, 530). Other local employers manufacture turbines, pumps, wall coverings, bread, ammunition, doors, mobile homes, tools, and millwork.

Taxes

Nebraska's state income tax is set at 15% of the federal income-tax obligation. The combined state and local sales tax is 4%.

Property taxes are based on full market value and the rate of taxation is $2.12 per hundred dollars of assessed value. Thus a home selling for $65,000 would be taxed about $1378 per year.

Shopping

After several modern shopping centers opened in the suburban areas, downtown retailers extensively remodeled and modernized their own area, with the result that Grand Island is now the largest shopping area between Omaha and Denver.

While shopping facilities are excellent in Grand Island, Omaha is 150 miles to the east and Denver is 402 miles to the west, for those who want greater variety.

Residential Properties

Homes are available for rent or purchase. Furnished apartments rent for $225 to $250 per month, and unfurnished homes with two bedrooms and appliances rent for $195 per month upward.

Properties for sale are offered from $20,000 upward. A few typical listings are:

OWNER MOVING and must sell this 2-bedroom 1-bath home for $18,500.

RANCH HOME with 3 bedrooms and 1½ baths on 4 acres surrounded by shade trees, about 15 miles from town. $55,000.

BRAND NEW 4-bedroom home with 2½ baths, family room, solid wood panel doors throughout, on half-acre professionally landscaped lot. $98,500.

LOVELY HOME with 1100 square feet of living space, 3 bedrooms, formal dining room, remodeled kitchen, central air and heat, large double garage with automatic openers, $39,500.

Rentals are plentiful, with one-bedroom apartments renting for $125 to $250 per month and two-bedroom apartments or condos renting for $200 to $350. The best source of information is the classified section of the local newspaper.

Safety

The FBI Crime Index rating is 64 crimes per thousand of population per year. Police protection is provided by the city police department, which has 42 full-time officers. Fire protection is provided by 40 full-time personnel, and Grand Island's Fire Insurance Rating is Class 5. Outside the city limits, the rating is Class 8 or 9, depending on the area.

There are no nearby manmade potential hazards, the nearest being 150 miles to the east at Omaha, which is the home of the Strategic Air Command headquarters and would be a primary military target in time of war.

While the Platte River has flooded in the past, the Army Corps of Engineers has constructed flood controls that should prevent further damage. Tornadoes are an ever-present possibility throughout the Great Plains, but the hazard to any individual is considerably less than that of driving or riding in an automobile.

Education

The public school system has 12 elementary schools, 3 junior high schools, and 2 high schools, with a pupil/teacher ratio of 23:1. In addition, there is a trade-technical school that provides job-oriented training for some 350 students.

The nearest institution of higher education is the University of Nebraska, located in Lincoln, 100 miles to the east, where a full program of undergraduate courses and graduate studies to the doctorate level are available.

Medical Facilities

The Lutheran Memorial Hospital and the St. Francis Medical Center provide a total of 227 beds, and there are 55 physicians and 32 dentists serving the area.

For more extensive medical care, Lincoln is 100 miles to the east, and Omaha is 50 miles farther.

Cultural Activities

The Grand Island Little Theater is an amateur community theater that presents three plays each year, one of which is usually a musical, while the Piccadilly Dinner Theater has been successful in presenting a variety of plays at its playhouse. The new auditorium at Northwest High School provides additional facilities for community entertainment.

The Community Concert Association, a 50-year-old organization, brings a variety of musical performers and performances to the community throughout the year. Nearby Hastings, Nebraska, has a symphony orchestra, and many residents of Grand Island drive the 28 miles to attend performances.

Recreation

There are 19 city parks, 2 county parks, and 1 state park in and around Grand Island. Six parks offer lighted tennis courts, and the city maintains two swimming pools.

The new YMCA-YWCA offers swimming, handball, racquetball, a fitness center, an indoor running track, and a variety of programs for all ages.

There are four large reservoirs within 100 miles of Grand Island that offer ample water-skiing and fishing opportunities. Excellent goose and duck hunting are available along the Platte River basin, a few miles from town. Pheasant hunting is superb in the area, as are quail, squirrel, rabbit, prairie chicken, grouse, and deer hunting.

There is horse racing at Grand Island's Fonner Park each spring. The park is also the location of the county fair, and livestock shows are held there throughout the remainder of the year.

Golfers have one municipal course with 18 holes and another with 9 holes. Riverside Golf Club has a private 18-hole course as well.

Government

After trying the Council-Manager form of government, the city has elected to return to the earlier Mayor-Council system, with an elected mayor and a full-time assistant who functions as the city administrator.

Water

The city supplies the water locally from 25 wells. The local tap water is acid, very hard, and not fluoridated.

Energy

Electricity is supplied by the city from its own power plant, and another plant is under construction. Natural gas is supplied by the Northwestern Public Service Company.

Utility costs average about $100 per month at the present time for a two-bedroom home.

Television

There is one local television station, and two others can be received locally. A cable service provides full coverage for subscribers.

Newspapers

The local newspaper is:

The Grand Island Daily Independent
422 West First St.
Grand Island, NE 68802

The *Omaha World-Herald* is also available locally.

For Further Information

Grand Island Area Chamber of Commerce
P.O. Box 1486
Grand Island, NE 68802

Division of Travel and Tourism
State Office Building
P.O. Box 94666
Lincoln, NE 68509

Greenville, Mississippi

POPULATION: 40,505 within the city limits
53,200 within the Greenville area
71,600 in Washington County

ELEVATION: 125 feet above sea level

Located at the western border of Mississippi, on the Mississippi River, Greenville is a deep-water harbor on Lake Ferguson, an arm of the river. A former bend of the Mississippi River forms the slack-water harbor, now protected by an earthen dike, which is over 11 miles long and is one of the best such harbors on the inland waterway system today.

Greenville is a trade, processing, and shipping center for the Mississippi-Yazoo delta region, which produces cotton, soybeans, oats, and corn. It is a region of flat, rich land, with alluvial soils that sustain a prosperous agricultural industry. Greenville is an important distribution point and retail center for a three-state area.

Climate

From the Yazoo River westward to the Mississippi lies the Delta region, with level, extremely fertile land that is devoted to extensive cotton cultivation. The hot, dry summers are well suited to cotton growing.

The climate of Mississippi is primarily determined by the huge land mass to the north and the Gulf of Mexico to the south. The prevailing southerly winds provide a moist, subtropical climate that is subject to frequent afternoon thundershowers in the summers.

In the colder season, the area is alternately subjected to warm tropical air and cold continental air, in periods of varying length. However, cold spells seldom last over 3 to 4 days. The southerly winds shift frequently to northerly during the winter. There are only about 30 days per year with temperatures of 32°F and below, and snow seldom exceeds 2 to 3 inches per year or stays on the ground long. Winters bring about 2600 heating degree days each year.

Summers are long and warm to hot, with temperatures in the 80s or higher from May through September, and temperatures of 90°F or higher about 70 days per year. Summers average 2300 cooling degree days.

The first frost in fall comes in early November and the last frost in spring is over by mid-March, giving more than 250 frost-free days each year. Precipitation averages around 52 inches per year, most of it falling in October through March, though there are frequent thundershowers in June through August. Humidity is high, averaging 73% throughout the year, but Greenville gets about 63% of possible sunshine during the year.

Tornadoes occur throughout the year, though the largest number occur in March through May. Today's tornado-warning systems are reducing the casualties and damage caused by these storms, and the chance of any particular place being struck is small. Tropical hurricanes do blow up from the Gulf of Mexico, but they lose much of their energy before reaching as far from the coast as Greenville.

History

Greenville got its start in 1829 when a group of young pioneers docked their boat at Bachelor's Bend on the eastern shore of the Mississippi River some 150 miles south of Memphis. They liked the area, stayed, and others followed.

Greenville was incorporated as a town on March 21, 1886, and since then the rich alluvial soil of the flat, fertile Mississippi Delta has provided the basis for a good living for its people.

Economy and Employment

Industry, mechanization, and automation have changed Greenville. Cotton is no longer king. The Delta now sends to market small grains, livestock, dairy products, poultry, produce, and rice. New industrial processes have led to the production of chemicals, metal products, concrete products, soybean oil, meal, fabricated metal products, fertilizers, and hardwood lumber.

The world leader in wool-carpet manufacturing has opened a large, modern plant in Greenville. A major manufacturer of hand and automatic saws is in operation here, and there are plants making metal fittings, auto parts, trailers, boilers, cable closures, and commercial and industrial stoppers.

One of the principal economic advantages enjoyed by Greenville is its unique harbor and port. A public terminal, in operation since 1958, provides handling of all types of cargo by barge, ship, rail, and truck, with facilities for warehouse and open-yard storage. Direct import-export facilities are now available, making Greenville a port with access to the entire world. And because it is located on a protected harbor, Greenville is the home of 27 privately owned towing and marine repair companies.

The Greenville Bridge, a modern steel and concrete structure spanning the 2 miles across the Mississippi River 5 miles southwest of Greenville, has made the town a key point in the movement of east-west cargo shipments as well.

Employment has remained high. The principal employers in the area are: Chicago Mill & Lumber Co. (wooden shipping containers, 335 employees); Cooper Steel (saws and rolled steel, 550); Fine Fines, Inc. (jeans, 190); Friedman Steel (scrap iron, 110); Greenville Mill (carpets, 800); Greenville Shipbuilding (towboat and barge manufacturing, 112); Hager Hinge Manufacturing, Inc. (hinges, 100); Mississippi Marine (barges and offshore supply vessels, 100); Pacific International Rice Mill (rice processing, 200); Uncle Ben's Foods (rice processing, 175); U.S. Gypsum (insulating tile and ceiling panels, 350); Utility Products (metal cable closures, 185); and 39 towing and barge companies employing nearly 1000 people.

Taxes

There is a state sales tax of 5% in Mississippi, and the state income tax is 3% on incomes below $5000 and 4% on incomes above that figure.

The property-tax rate is $1.42 per $100 of assessed value inside the city limits. Appraised values are often less than current market value, but for a newly purchased home selling for $65,000 the annual tax would run about $925.

Shopping

Greenville offers a downtown business and shopping district and three major suburban shopping centers, supplemented by several neighborhood centers. Major national chains are represented, as well as a variety of local stores and regional chains.

For shopping beyond the limits of Greenville's excellent stores, Memphis is 141 miles to the north.

Residential Properties

The average residence in Greenville is priced at about $40,000, though homes can be found on both sides of that figure. A few listings provided by the chamber of commerce are:

NEW HOME with 3 bedrooms and 1½ baths, central heat and air, 1230 square feet of living space, and a great room with fireplace. $46,000.

ON CANAL STREET. 3 bedrooms and 2 baths on a large lot, with separate den, patio. $54,900.

LARGE HOME with 3 bedrooms and 1 bath, stove, dishwasher, disposal, patio. $59,900.

OVER 3000 FEET OF LIVING SPACE in this 4-bedroom 3-bath home with living room, dining room, den, 2 fireplaces, two heating/cooling units, stove, dishwasher, disposal, and swimming pool. Separate guest house and covered patio included for $178,000.

Rentals are available, with one-bedroom apartments renting for $125 to $300 per month, and two-bedroom apartments or condos renting for $200 to $350. A note to the chamber of commerce will bring you a list of local realtors, any of whom will be happy to provide listings in the price range desired. Also, the local newspaper ads are a good place to study the local real estate market.

Safety

The FBI Crime Index rating is 98 crimes per thousand of population per year. The police department has 102 full-time and 38 part-time members, and 25 patrol cars. The fire department consists of 88 full-time members and has 8 pumper trucks, 1 snorkel, and 1 rescue vehicle. The Fire Insurance Rating for Greenville is Class 5.

There are no known natural or manmade hazards in the immediate vicinity. The nearest is a nuclear power plant 75 miles to the south, near Port Gibson.

Education

The Greenville public school system provides 12 elementary and 5 secondary schools. These are supplemented by 4 private schools.

Mississippi Delta Junior College, located 35 miles east, is a vocational-technical school providing a two-year curriculum in a variety of subjects.

Delta State University, located 35 miles to the northeast in Cleveland, is a small four-year university with about 2700 students and 160 teachers. It offers a variety of programs to the master's level.

Medical Facilities

There are two local hospitals providing a total of 389 beds and full medical care. These are supplemented by 59 doctors and 25 dentists in private practice in the community.

Cultural Activities

When people think of the blues, they usually think of New Orleans and Chicago and Kansas City, but it was in the Delta region around Greenville that the blues were born. Today, Greenville hosts an annual Delta Blues Festival in September, with many local artists participating, such as B. B. King, Bobbie Gentry, Charley Pride, Bo Diddley, and Conway Twitty. Other well-known performers come from all over the country.

Greenville can claim more published authors than any other community of its size in America, including Walker Percy, the late Hodding Carter, Ellen Douglas, Shelby Foote, Bern Keating, David L. Cohn, and the late William Alexander Percy, for whom the local library is named.

The local library's Mississippi collection includes virtually every published work by local authors, plus many of their manuscripts and first editions. The library serves both Greenville and Washington County with some 50,000 volumes.

Many sculptors, potters, photographers, and other artists make their homes in and around Greenville. Leon Koury's studio is also a classroom for student sculptors. The Greenville Art Gallery makes works of art available for public viewing.

Classical music and theater are also important in Greenville. There is a Greenville Symphony Orchestra, and the Delta Music Association brings in guest performers during the concert season.

Delta Center Stage is a local, nonprofessional theater group that gives a number of performances each year.

Recreation

Outdoors in the Greenville area is a sportsman's heaven, with the long, warm summers and short winters, the broad Mississippi River and the many lakes and streams, and the thick woods and open fields. There is excellent hunting for wild boars, turkeys, geese, quail, ducks, doves, and deer. Fishermen can take bass, white perch, pike, bream, and delicious channel catfish (some weighing up to 120 pounds) from the local waters.

Water-related sports available include sailing, motorboating, water-skiing, swimming, and canoeing — all made easily accessible by the five large lakes within 20 miles of town. The marina and the yacht club on Lake Ferguson provide ample boat mooring and storage and serve as meeting places for sailors and yachtsmen.

Golf, tennis, trapshooting, bicycling, and hiking are other favorite local outdoor sports. Three state parks in the county provide camping, picnic facilities, and wildlife trails. Other outdoor entertainment includes watching or participating in hot-air ballooning, kiting, glider flying, sail planing, and hang gliding. Baseball and softball leagues, a drag strip, art classes, ceramics classes, a bowling alley, bridge clubs, and a roller-skating club are all available locally.

The levee is both a protection from high waters on the river and a social center. Teen-agers gather there to show off their cars and pass the time of day. Youngsters use the paved slopes for skateboarding in the summer and for tobogganing on those rare days when it snows. Almost any time of year kites can be seen flying from the levee, and it is also a place for people to sit and watch the river traffic or wait for the *Delta Queen* as she slowly chugs into Greenville.

Government

Greenville operates under the Mayor-Council form of government. There are local zoning regulations and a local planning commission. The community also owns and operates the sewer system for the area.

Water

The water system is city-operated, with the water supply drawn from deep wells. The tap water is slightly alkaline, very soft, and not fluoridated. The water-system capacity is over twice the water required by the community at periods of peak consumption, so there should be ample water for many years to come.

Energy

Electricity is provided by Mississippi Power & Light. The new 750,000-kilowatt generating plant nearby assures ample power at reasonable cost for the foreseeable future.

Natural gas is supplied by the Mississippi Valley Gas Company. Fuel oil for heating is available locally for those homes that do not have natural gas piped in.

The cost of utilities averages about $100 per month for an average two-to-three-bedroom home with central heat and air conditioning.

Television

There is no local television station, but two nearby stations can be received with rooftop antenna systems, and there is a cable system that provides full 12-channel coverage.

Newspaper

The local daily newspaper is:

The Delta Democrat-Times
Greenville, MS 38701

For Further Information

Greenville Area Chamber of Commerce
P.O. Drawer 933
Greenville, MS 38701

Mississippi Park Commission
717 Robert E. Lee Building
Jackson, MS 39201

Mississippi Game and Fish Commission
P.O. Box 451
Jacksonville, MS 39205

Mississippi Department of Tourism Development
P.O. Box 849
Jackson, MS 39205

Greenville, North Carolina

POPULATION: 34,757 within the city limits
82,100 in Pitt County

ELEVATION: 55 feet above sea level

Greenville, the county seat of Pitt County, is located in eastern North Carolina on the Tar River, in the North Carolina coastal plain. It is an important market center for tobacco and forest products. Greenville is one of the largest bright-leaf tobacco markets in the world.

The countryside around Greenville is low and flat, alternating between open fields and dense woods. To the east, within a 30-minute drive, is Pamlico Sound, which offers an abundance of water-related recreation.

Climate

North Carolina is divided into three climatic areas: the Blue Ridge Mountains and the Great Smokies in the west, the Piedmont in the center, and the coastal plain in the east. Greenville is on the coastal plain, close to Pamlico Sound. Throughout the coastal plain, the soils are mostly soft sediment, with little or no underlying hard rock, and the elevation seldom exceeds 200 feet. The coastal-plain climate is modified by the proximity of the Atlantic Ocean and Pamlico Sound, which raises the average winter temperatures and reduces the summer heat. The Gulf Stream, which lies some 50 miles offshore, has little effect of this part of the coast, which is more affected by the Labrador Current that passes between the Gulf Stream and the coast.

Summer temperatures range between highs in the upper 80s and lows in the upper 60s from June into September, with only 45 days per year with temperatures of 90°F and above. Summers bring only 1450 cooling degree days per year.

Winters are mild, with temperatures ranging from the low 30s at night to daytime highs in the 50s and 60s from December into March. There are only 40 days per year with temperatures of 32°F and below, and only 3400 heating degree days per year. The last frost in spring comes in early March, and the first one in fall is not until early December, giving a 260-day frost-free period. Snowfall is seldom more than 4 to 6 inches per year, generally in December through March, and snow seldom stays on the ground for long. Snow and ice occur on an average of only once or twice each year.

Precipitation averages around 48 inches per year, more or less evenly distributed except for the peak period of July through September, with July the wettest month. The driest month is October, which averages under 3 inches of rain. Winter precipitation usually occurs in conjunction with southerly to southeasterly winds and seldom falls during cold weather.

Winds are gentle and from the south in the summers, and westerly to northerly in the winters. While summer winds average about 12 miles per hour, and winter winds even less, tropical storms have brought high winds to the area, with the highest wind ever measured in the area — 110 miles per hour — recorded at Cape Hatteras in September of 1944. Tropical hurricanes come close enough to influence North Carolina's coast about twice in an average year, but only about once in 10 years does one strike with enough force to do much damage.

History

Tobacco has been an important crop in this area since 1725, when tobacco warehouses and an inspection station for the British government were established. As the area grew and settlers moved in, cotton became the second-leading crop, until low prices made it no longer practical. Tar, another valuable export, was extracted from the longleaf-pine forests of the area.

Pitt Academy was chartered in 1787, but it was not until 1890, when the railroad arrived, that Greenville began to blossom as the hub of county life. Citizens passed a bond issue in 1903 to finance public schools, public utilities, and better streets.

In 1907, Greenville was selected by the state as the site for the proposed East Carolina Teachers' Training School, which is today's East Carolina University.

The influenza epidemic of World War I spurred the community to raise funds for a major hospital and was a major factor in the state's later decision to establish a medical school in Greenville.

Economy and Employment

Long a distribution point for farm and forest products, Greenville is now an increasingly important location for industry.

East Carolina University is the largest local employer, and East Carolina University's School of Medicine has attracted several medically related businesses. Pitt Community College has been working in cooperation with industry to train workers in needed specialties.

Between 1950 and 1969 the number of industries in Greenville tripled, and by 1979 fifteen more new manufacturers had started operations. Burroughs Wellcome, the area's largest manufacturer, moved its pharmaceutical plant here from New York, and its animal-health facility from Chicago.

Unlike many North Carolina communities, Greenville has real diversity in its economy. The tobacco industry employs 2400, mostly unskilled labor. Food and food processing employs 400; textiles, 350; lumber and forestry, 175; chemicals, 125; electrical products, 100; and pharmaceuticals, 1200.

Major employers in the area include: Burroughs Wellcome (pharmaceuticals, chemicals, and pet supplies, 1500 employees); Procter and Gamble (Pampers diapers and other paper products, 350); Carolina Leaf Tobacco (tobacco processing, 750); Eaton Corp. (electrical and gasoline fork-lift vehicles, 500); Empire Brushes (brushes, 350); Fieldcrest Mills (carpet yarns, 350); Union Carbide (batteries, 350);

Grady White Boat Works (fiber glass pleasure boats, 200); TRW Co. (rack-and-pinion steering components, 175); and Vermont American Corp. (high-speed drill bits, 175).

For current employment information, write:

Employment Security Commission
3101 Bismark St.
Greenville, NC 27834

Taxes

There is a 4% state sales tax, and the state income tax ranges from 3% on the first $2000 to 7% on taxable incomes over $10,000.

Local property taxes are modest, with rates of $1.03 per $100 of assessed value within the city limits and $.54 per $100 in the county. Assessed value is usually below actual market value, so the tax on a home selling for $65,000 would normally run about $570 inside the city limits and only $300 in the county.

Shopping

Greenville has the usual downtown business center that offers a variety of retail stores. In addition, there are five well-diversified shopping centers in outlying sections of town. Major retail chains are well represented at all locations.

For demands that can't be met by the local stores, Raleigh is only 80 miles to the west.

Residential Properties

A wide choice of housing is available, in both price and location. There are places in town and homes in the wooded countryside. Prices vary. Typical examples are:

THIS ELEGANT HOME has five bedrooms, 3 full ceramic baths, a glassed sun room, double staircase, breezeway to a double garage, huge living room with marble fireplace. All of the beauty of yesterday with today's amenities. $145,000.

OLDER HOME with 2 bedrooms, pine paneling, on a corner lot, for only $29,900.

RANCH HOME in town on corner wooded lot, with 3 bedrooms, 1½ baths, and payments under $200 for a qualified buyer. $45,900.

COUNTRY HOME with stables and kennel on 2 acres. 3 bedrooms, 2 baths, double carport, patio, many built-ins. $83,000.

TOWNHOUSES. Walk to work or school. Carpeted living room, all-appliance kitchen, 2 large bedrooms, 1½ baths, heat pump, parking. $45,000.

Apartments are available, with rentals on one-bedroom units ranging from $175 to $225 per month. Two-bedroom condos or apartments are available at $265 to $345 per month. A note to the chamber of commerce will bring you a flood of information from local real estate agents, and the local newspaper carries many ads for current offerings.

Safety

The FBI Crime Index rating is a moderate 77 crimes per thousand of population per year. The police department has 90 full-time and 7 part-time employees, and there are 78 full-time firemen. The Fire Insurance Rating is Class 4.

Seymour Johnson Air Force Base, a TAC base, is 45 miles to the southwest but should prove to be no hazard to Greenville residents. There is no other manmade potential hazard nearby, and there are no major natural hazards in the area.

Education

Greenville is better endowed with educational facilities than most communities of its size. The city provides six elementary schools, a junior high school, and a high school. There are also four parochial elementary schools and one private elementary school. Altogether, these schools have an enrollment of 5775 students.

Higher education is well served by Pitt Community College and East Carolina University. Pitt, founded in 1961, offers a comprehensive two-year program in 24 fields leading to associate degrees and in 24 technical programs, plus 14 vocational programs. There are 2500 full-time students, and another 2500 are enrolled in the continuing-education program.

East Carolina University now has over 13,000 students from 48 states, 15 countries, and all over North Carolina. It offers 105 bachelor's degree programs, 72 master's degree programs, and 5 doctoral programs. Its largest professional school is the School of Business. In addition, more than 23,000 adults take part in East Carolina's continuing-education evening classes and noncredit workshops and courses. Today, ECU is North Carolina's third-largest institution of higher learning.

Medical Facilities

East Carolina University's School of Medicine is located at Pitt Memorial Hospital in Greenville. This new hospital, completed in

1977, has 420 beds (with another 244 being added), 40 private rooms in the pediatrics area, and broad coverage in diagnostic services, surgery, cardiac care, mental health, and clinical services. There are 206 physicians and 21 dentists on the staff. The staff includes specialists in all major medical fields.

Pitt County Mental Health Center is near the hospital and provides mental-health services for the area. The Rehabilitation Center, connected to the hospital, has 55 beds and provides specialized medical services for a 27-county area. The Alcoholic Rehabilitation Center, located near town, serves a 38-county area of eastern North Carolina and is staffed with a full-time physician and a psychiatrist.

Cultural Activities

While devoting time and energy toward developing business, industry, education, and health care, Greenville has also remembered the arts and culture. The focus of culture in the region is East Carolina University. ECU has the largest art school in the Southeast. Its art gallery brings many exhibitions and shows to the area each year. Its symphony orchestra has been recognized for its quality, and the School of Music attracts many superior students. The result is more than 200 free, high-quality concerts each year for the public and the students.

The university also brings to local audiences a wide variety of performing artists, lectures, concerts, and theatrical performances. The ECU Summer Theater presents live theater in the form of musical comedies, operas, and operettas, as well as Broadway shows and special movies.

On Sunday evenings from June through August, people gather on the slopes of a grassy natural amphitheater by the river for "Sunday in the Park" performances of all types of music and dance — a joint venture of the city and the university.

In February, a Black Arts Festival features original music, poetry, and art, and the Greenville Woman's Club sponsors an annual author luncheon and writing contest. And perhaps the most fun of all is the Jaycee-sponsored Fourth of July celebration, which ends with a huge display of fireworks.

Library facilities are provided by both the Sheppard Memorial Library, with 113,412 volumes, and the ECU Library with 376,500 volumes.

Recreation

There is plenty to do in the Greenville area. There are 16 parks distributed across town, offering picnic areas, trails, play areas, paved walkways by the river, jogging paths, and a landscaped promenade. The Greenville recreation department operates four recreation centers, two baseball fields, three gymnasiums, nine playgrounds, four Little League fields, and five softball fields. Both ECU and the recreation department provide tennis courts that are open to the public.

With the Tar and Pamlico rivers at hand and Pamlico Sound and the Atlantic Coast nearby, there are many water-related recreational opportunities for residents. River Park, with one mile of river frontage, provides five fishing ponds, and the Tar River offers fishing and boating. Pamlico Sound, which offers access to the ocean, is a thirty-minute drive to the east, and the Outer Banks are only two hours away. Boating, surfcasting, and deep-sea fishing are all available along the Atlantic shore.

Swimmers can choose between the municipal pools, which open in June at Guy Smith Stadium, and the Atlantic Coast, where one can swim in the surf or in the protected sound. Water-skiing is popular both on the Pamlico River and in the sound.

Hunting is excellent along the broad coastal plain. Squirrels, rabbit, deer, quail, bears, wild boars, ducks, and doves are plentiful. Local sporting-goods and hardware stores are happy to provide information, or you can write:

North Carolina Wildlife Resources Commission
Raleigh, NC 27611

They will be happy to send full information on hunting and fishing in the area.

Golfers have two 18-hole public courses and several country clubs to choose from. Many golfers also visit the nationally rated courses at nearby Pinehurst and Southern Pines, home of the World Golf Hall of Fame.

Government

Greenville has the Council-Manager form of city government, with a seven-member city council and a full-time city manager.

Water

The city-owned water supply, drawn from the Tar River, is neutral, medium soft, and fluoridated.

Energy

Electricity and natural gas are supplied by the city. For current utilities rates, write:

Greenville Utility Commission
200 West Fifth Street
Greenville, NC 27834

Utilities average about $100 per month for a two-bedroom home.

Television
There is a local CBS station, an NBC station in Washington (North Carolina), and an ABC station in New Bern. All are readily accessible by means of a home antenna system. Local cable television is also available to subscribers.

Newspapers
The local newspaper is published daily except Saturday. It is:

The Daily Reflector
209 Cotanche St.
Greenville, NC 27834

The *Charlotte Observer,* the *Raleigh News and Observer,* and the *Richmond* (Virginia) *Times-Dispatch* are also available locally.

For Further Information

Pitt-Greenville Chamber of Commerce
P.O. Box 894
Greenville, NC 27834

The North Carolina Travel & Tourism Division
P.O. Box 25249
Raleigh, NC 27611

Greenwood, South Carolina

POPULATION: 21,568 within the city limits
54,700 in Greenwood County

ELEVATION: 665 feet above sea level

Greenwood, the county seat of Greenwood County, is located in western South Carolina, 74 miles west of Columbia and 55 miles south of Greenville, near Lake Greenwood on the Saluda River. It is a trading and processing center for a rich agricultural area in the Piedmont Plateau, with cotton, corn, and peaches its principal crops.

Buzzard Roost hydroelectric development is 16 miles to the east, at the lower end of Lake Greenwood. The lake itself is a center for water sports, hunting, and fishing.

The countryside around Greenwood is gently rolling, much of it covered with woods interspersed with open fields.

Climate

Greenwood's climate is temperate, with a strong continental influence. Summers are warm to hot, with an average of 4 days with temperatures over 100°F and about 70 days with temperatures of 90°F and above. There are usually about 2000 cooling degree days each summer.

Fall in Greenwood is the sunniest and most pleasant of the four seasons, with summer weather ending in early September. This is followed by an Indian-summer period, and prewinter cold spells begin in late November.

Winters are usually mild, though cold air does move this far south at times, broken by longer spells of above-freezing weather. There are an average of 53 days per year with temperatures dropping to 32°F and below, and about 6 days per year with temperatures of 20°F or lower. There are approximately 2500 heating degree days each winter. The growing season is about 235 days long, with the first frost arriving in mid-November and the last frost in spring occurring around the third week in March. Snow seldom exceeds 2 inches per year and does not remain on the ground more than a day or two.

Spring is marked by rapid changes, with the weather varying from occasional outbreaks of cold air in March to warm and pleasant most of the time by May.

Precipitation is about 46 inches per year, fairly evenly divided among the twelve months. Summer rainfall often comes in the form of thunderstorms.

Winds are generally northerly to westerly in the winters and southerly to westerly in the summers. Greenwood receives about 65% of possible sunshine each year.

History

The Cherokee Path, an old Indian trail, followed a route past the present-day site of Greenwood, connecting the hill towns to the lowland towns near Columbia. The first land grant in the region was made in 1744 at "a place called Ninety Six," to one Thomas Brown, and was defined as "a place 96 miles from the Cherokee nation." The name "Ninety Six" is still applied to a small town 10 miles east of Greenwood.

Scattered pioneers began locating in the area in the 1740s, and in 1747 the provisional governor of the region bought all of the land in the area from the Cherokees. Early settlers were largely English, Scottish, and Scotch-Irish, with some Germans and Huguenots as well.

In 1750 a trading post and stockade were built at Ninety Six, which eventually grew into a permanent settlement. About 1753 a London firm of land promoters and speculators were granted four great tracts of land totaling some 200,000 acres and including most of what is now Greenwood County north and west of Ninety Six. The village of Ninety Six, then little more than a barroom and a blacksmith shop, became the local seat of government when a courthouse and jail were built there in 1772, followed shortly thereafter by a church.

By the time of the American Revolution, settlers were well established in the vicinity of Greenwood, though few facts are known about them today. During the Revolution, Ninety Six was captured by the British and held as an important transportation center. It was recovered by General Nathanael Greene, but not until the British had burned everything and taken all of the residents away as prisoners.

In 1823, a young lawyer built a summer home on the road between Cambridge and Abbeville and named it Green Wood. This was the first house on the site of today's Greenwood and gave the town its name. After the railroad bypassed Ninety Six in 1852, Greenwood began to take over in importance, and it was chartered as a town in 1857. By then it had schools, a post office, a railroad, and stores and businesses to provide services for all of its 300 inhabitants.

From the opening of the first textile plant in 1891, the county has developed into a prosperous industrial area.

Economy and Employment

Today there are 45 different types of industry in Greenwood, providing a total payroll of over $250 million for the area. Because of the stable and diversified economy, unemployment has remained low.

Major employers in the area are: Greenwood Mills (with 12 plants producing fabrics, filaments, and their own castings, over 5000 employees); Grendel Corp. (spun rayon fabrics, 490); Monsanto Textiles (nylon, 1900); Oxford (ladies' blouses, 125); PMC Corp. (draperies, 175); and Riegel Textile Corp. (towels, blankets, diapers, and sportswear, 1750).

Other industrial employers include: McGraw-Edison (capacitors, 170); Moore Business Machines (business forms, 265); Neptune

Measurement Co. (meters for industry, 340); George W. Park Seed Co. (packaged seeds and garden supplies, 400); Parke Davis & Co. (medical and surgical products, 1100); Reliance Electric (electric-motor controls, 250); Robert Foundry Co. (high-volume castings, 160); Union Carbide (capacitors, 300); and Westinghouse Electric (switchgears, 250).

Agriculture is still important in the area, with crops including corn, cotton, hay and seed stock, poultry and eggs, livestock, dairy products, timber, and pulpwood. Approximately 50% of the surrounding countryside is in farmland.

Taxes

There is a 4% state sales tax, and the state income tax ranges from 2% on the first $2000 of taxable income to a maximum of 7% on incomes over $10,000.

Property taxes are moderate, and the tax on a home selling for $65,000 would run about $650 per year.

Shopping

Greenwood's shopping facilities are excellent, with most major national chain stores represented.

For wider variety, Columbia, the state capital, is 74 miles to the east. Charlotte, North Carolina, is 121 miles to the northeast, and Atlanta is 155 miles to the west.

Residential Properties

Homes are available in all price ranges, as are lots for building. The Greenwood Board of Realtors operates a Multiple Listing Service, which gives every realtor access to the full market for each client. Apartment and house rentals are available, plentiful, and inexpensive. One-bedroom apartments can be rented for $85 to $220 per month, and two-bedroom apartments for $165 to $350. Several new apartment complexes have been built in recent years.

Homes for sale are always available, and a few typical listings are:

SMALL FARM with 5½ acres and a comfortable 4-room home with electric heat, wood heater, cozy kitchen and small barn. $32,000.

ATTRACTIVE 3-bedroom home near Lander College and downtown shopping. $39,900.

GOOD LOCATION near schools, with 3 bedrooms, 2 baths, formal living and dining areas plus a den, with 1800 square feet plus fenced back yard and separate storage building on large, wooded lot. $63,000.

ON THE LAKEFRONT with 3 bedrooms, 2 baths, large recreation room, with large waterfront lot with good beach and 3 piers. $88,000.

Safety

Local law enforcement is provided within the city limits by a 52-man police force with 21 vehicles. The unincorporated areas around the city are policed by the sheriff's department, which has 22 officers on patrol in four shifts. The FBI Crime Index rating is a low 28 crimes per thousand of population per year.

Fire protection is provided by the Greenwood Fire Department, which has 50 full-time personnel and 11 firefighting vehicles. Inside the city limits, the Fire Insurance Rating is Class 4.

The county operates a countywide emergency medical service, with qualified medical technicians on 24-hour duty.

There are no known nearby manmade hazards, and the nearest nuclear plant is 60 miles to the northwest at Seneca.

Education

The Greenwood School District has 10 elementary and 4 secondary schools, with a total enrollment of 9100 students. There is also a college-preparatory independent school, Cambridge Academy, which has some 300 students enrolled in a five-year program through the twelfth grade.

Piedmont Technical College, a technical-vocational college serving seven counties, is located on the outskirts of Greenwood and provides a two-year program leading to associate degrees in business, secretarial skills, data processing, fashion merchandising, and criminal justice.

Lander College is a fully accredited, four-year state college located in the center of Greenwood. It offers B.A. and B.S. degrees in 22 major areas to about 1800 students.

For graduate studies or a wider choice of undergraduate programs, South Carolina State University is located in Columbia, 74 miles to the east.

Medical Facilities

Self Memorial Hospital is a local general hospital with 419 beds that has more than 100 physicians, representing over 30 specialties, on its staff.

There is a center for the evaluation of, and research on, genetic disorders. A local nursing home has 108 beds for long-term care, and there is also a Methodist home for the aging that is operated under the auspices of the church.

A variety of public-health services are available locally, and Beckman Center for Mental Health serves a seven-county area. Other medical facilities include a speech and hearing center, a crippled-children's clinic, a vocational-rehabilitation workshop, and special classes for the mentally handicapped.

Cultural Activities

The county library is also the headquarters for the Abbeville-Greenwood Regional Library system and has a collection of over 114,000 volumes. The system includes the library in central Greenwood, branch libraries in outlying areas, and a bookmobile service. Lander College Library has 85,000 volumes.

The Civic Center opened in 1977 and offers facilities for seating up to 4100 people for activities that include sports events, concerts, theater, banquets, conventions, trade shows, rodeos, circuses, and indoor tennis.

The Community Theater offers at least four plays and two musicals annually. The Children's Theater puts on two shows each year, and the Lander College drama department presents periodic dramatic performances.

The Community Concert Association sponsors three to four classical-music performances each year.

Recreation

Directly behind the Civic Center is a complex consisting of five softball fields, one baseball diamond, and eight lighted tennis courts. Inside the Civic Center, the city's recreation department offers daily activities that include courses in quilting, ceramics, artificial flower making, and painting.

Golfing is available at the Greenwood Country Club, the Ware Shoals Country Club, the Star Fort Country Club in Ninety Six, Cedar Lake Golf Course (public), Parkland, and Cokesbury Hills Country Club.

Swimming pools are located at the YMCA in Ware Shoals, at Greenwood Country Club, and at the Seaboard Recreation Center.

Located on the shores of Lake Greenwood is a state park that offers facilities for swimming, boating, camping, fishing, and picnicking. A number of fishing camps and boat landings are located around the lake's 200-mile shoreline.

Government

Greenwood is governed under the Council-Manager plan.

Water

The municipal water supply comes from nearby Lake Greenwood, and maximum supply is 40% higher than maximum demand. The local tap water is slightly alkaline, very soft, and not fluoridated. The supply of water appears to be more than adequate for the foreseeable future.

Energy

Electricity is supplied by Duke Power Company, through the city's public works department, and comes from fossil-fuel, hydroelectric, and nuclear power plants. Natural gas is also delivered through the city-owned system. Propane gas and fuel oil are available locally.

At the present time, utility costs average about $100 per month for the typical two-to-three-bedroom home.

Television

Excellent television reception is available from three stations representing the three major networks — one in Greenwood, one in Spartanburg, and one in Asheville, North Carolina. Full coverage is also available through the local cable system.

Newspapers

The local paper is published daily except Sunday. It is:

The Index Journal
Greenwood, SC 29648

The State, published in Columbia, is also available locally.

For Further Information

Greenwood Chamber of Commerce
Box 980
Greenwood, SC 29648

South Carolina Division of Tourism
Box 78
Columbia, SC 29202

South Carolina Department of Parks
Suite 113, Edgar Brown Building
1205 Pendleton St.
Columbia, SC 29201

Hannibal, Missouri

POPULATION: 18,811 within the city limits
37,300 in Ralls and Marion counties

ELEVATION: 491 feet above sea level

Mark Twain's name is the first thing that comes to mind when Hannibal, Missouri, is mentioned. He grew up here and later wrote Hannibal into his books about Huck Finn, Tom Sawyer, and Becky Thatcher.

Located on the west bank of the Mississippi River some 110 miles northwest of St. Louis and 20 river miles downstream from Quincy, Illinois, Hannibal is a river port, rail center, and growing industrial community located on the line between Ralls and Marion counties.

Hannibal is an attractive town with a variety of nineteenth-century homes and business buildings. From the river up both sides of

Broadway stand simple pre–Civil War Federal-style buildings as well as Italianate Victorian, Gothic Revival, and Queen Anne style houses and mansions.

Climate

Missouri is an inland state with a climate that is primarily continental. There are frequent changes in weather, both from day to day and from season to season. It is in the path of cold air moving down from Canada and warm, moist air coming up from the Gulf of Mexico, and is also influenced by dry air from the west.

Normal winter temperatures range from the 40s in the daytime to the 20s at night from December through February, though extremes have been recorded as high as 84°F and as low as −22°F in these months. Snow has been known to fall as early as October and as late as May, though most of the annual 18 inches of snow falls between November and March. It is unusual for snow to stay on the ground for more than a week or two before it melts. Winds in winter are westerly to northwesterly and gentle, except during storms that blow down from Canada. Winter brings about 4900 heating degree days per year.

Summers bring normal daytime highs of 75°F in May, in the 80s from June through September, and 70°F in October. However, extremes as high as 115°F have been recorded in July and August. Summer winds are usually southerly or southwesterly and gentle, and there are approximately 1500 cooling degree days per year.

Summers average 46 days of temperatures 90°F and above, and winters bring an average of 83 days of temperatures 32°F and below. The last frost in spring usually comes before mid-April, and the first frost in fall does not usually arrive until late October. There are a total of 210 frost-free days per year, on the average. Sunshine averages 65% of possible sunshine throughout the year.

Precipitation comes in the form of rain in the summers and usually snow in the winters, with total precipitation fairly evenly spread throughout the year. Thunderstorms bring rains that are sometimes very heavy and are most frequent from April to July. Total annual precipitation is about 36 inches.

The state of Missouri averages about 10 tornadoes per year. These have been observed during every month of the year, with about 70% occurring during March through June, mostly between 4 and 6 P.M.

Missouri is subject to frequent changes in temperature. While winters are cold and summers are hot, prolonged periods of either very cold or very hot weather are unusual. Every winter normally has periods of mild, above-freezing weather, and summers normally have occasional periods of dry, cool weather to break up the hot, humid periods.

History

The 1811 earthquake that centered in New Madrid, Missouri, some 250 miles south of Hannibal, was responsible for the founding of Hannibal. One man who had lost his property in the New Madrid quake was granted new land upriver by the state to replace what he had lost. This 640-acre parcel was on the west bank of the Mississippi River, some 125 river miles north of St. Louis. The Hannibal Company was formed to promote this site near Bear Creek, and the company name was given to the budding community.

The first settler in Hannibal was Moses D. Bates, who opened a trading post. With the Mississippi River at his door, his business flourished and the community began to grow.

While the two most important factors in the launching of Hannibal into the world were the earthquake and the Mississippi River, it was Mark Twain and his writings that immortalized Hannibal. Twain came to Hannibal with his family in 1839 as a four-year-old child with an active imagination. The Clemens family lived in Hannibal for fourteen years – years during which Samuel Clemens learned the things that brought his stories to life.

The Clemens family home has been preserved in Hannibal. There is a Mark Twain museum, and the drugstore, the doctor's office, Rockliffe Mansion, the Garth House, and the Mark Twain Cave are all open to the public as part of the Mark Twain heritage.

Hannibal was incorporated as a city in 1839.

Economy and Employment

As the home of Mark Twain, Hannibal has a steady tourist trade, with some 250,000 visitors each year. Originally a trade center on the Mississippi River, it has remained so over the years. Today there are 2 railroads, 16 trucking companies, 2 bus lines, a municipal airport, and a very active port on the Mississippi River, with 9 barge companies working out of the city.

In addition, there is increasing industrial development in the area, with major employers including: Watlow Hannibal (electric heating elements, 115 employees); Universal Atlas Cement (170); Atlantic Building Systems (fabricated steel buildings, 140); American Cyanamid (agricultural chemicals, 375); and companies manufacturing coin-handling supplies, deviled ham, and boots and shoes, and doing commercial printing. Altogether, 30 diversified industries provide approximately 1800 industrial jobs.

For current employment information, write:

Job Service
Missouri Division of Employment Security
203 North Sixth St.
Hannibal, MO 63401

For assistance and information on starting a new business, write:

Director
Hannibal Industrial Council
Box 230
Hannibal, MO 63401

Taxes

Sales taxes, including state, county, and city taxes, total 4⅝%. The state income tax ranges from 1.5% on taxable incomes of $1000 to 6% on taxable incomes above $9000 per year.

The property tax on a home selling for $65,000 runs about $1425 per year.

Shopping

Hannibal has downtown and suburban shopping centers, with many regional and national chains represented. For greater variety, Quincy is 30 miles by road to the north and St. Louis is 110 miles to the south.

Residential Properties

Housing in Hannibal is 67% owner-occupied. Most of the homes are detached, though there are some duplexes and apartments. Homes are available for purchase, but rentals are hard to find. One-bedroom apartments rent for $150 to $260 per month, and two-bedroom apartments for $175 to $325.

The average cost of preowned homes is currently about $35,000. A few typical examples are:

4 BEDROOMS, 1½ baths, brick ranch-style home on 120′ × 90′ lot, in very good condition with full basement, carpeted floors, and 2-car garage. $61,900.

LIKE NEW. 4-year-old frame bungalow with 3 bedrooms and 1 bath. $33,500.

SPLIT-LEVEL 3-bedroom home with 1½ baths and single-car garage, full carpeting. $39,500.

Safety

There are no nearby manmade hazards. The city is on a bluff above the river, so flooding has never been a danger.

The FBI Crime Index rating is a moderate 68 crimes per thousand of population per year. The police department has 38 full-time members, and the fire department also has 38. The Fire Insurance Rating is Class 6.

Education

Hannibal has six elementary schools, one junior high school, and one high school, plus a trade and technical school that offers 16 vocational training programs.

For a broad undergraduate curriculum and graduate education, the University of Missouri at Columbia is located 100 miles to the southwest of Hannibal.

Medical Facilities

There are two hospitals in Hannibal. Levering Hospital has 117 beds, 2 obstetrical rooms, 4 operating rooms, and 3 emergency rooms, and St. Elizabeth Hospital, established in 1915 by the Sisters of St. Francis, now has 150 beds, 38 physicians on staff, and an effective hospital auxiliary.

In addition, the area offers assorted health-care facilities and clinics, two nursing homes, an ambulance district, the Mark Twain Emergency Squad, 26 physicians, and 13 dentists.

Cultural Activities

Hannibal has the Community Concert Series, the Community Chorus, the Men's Chorale, the Art Club, the Ice House Theater, the Theater Guild, the Arts Council, the Fine Arts Museum, and the public library, which has over 48,000 volumes.

Recreation

The countryside around Hannibal is beautiful, with rolling bluffs along the Mississippi River and flat, rich farmland interspersed with woods filled with wildlife, especially white-tailed deer, ducks, quail, and doves.

The 60 miles of waterway contain many species of fish. Most sought after is the channel catfish — and if you haven't tasted channel cat fresh from a river or lake, you haven't tasted fish!

Two golf courses, an 18-lane bowling alley, a roller-skating rink, a swimming pool, the YMCA, 20 tennis courts, and rivers and lakes for boating and water-skiing round out Hannibal's recreational opportunities.

Government

Hannibal operates under the Mayor-Council system of government. City-owned facilities include the water-supply and electricity utilities, both operated by a board of public works.

Water

Tap water is neutral, hard, and fluoridated. It is drawn from the Mississippi River and treated in the city-owned water plant, which has a capacity larger than the highest peak demand. With the river at the doorstep, there is no likelihood of a water shortage, but there is a constant possibility of upstream pollution.

Energy

Natural gas is supplied by the Great River Gas Company. Electricity is supplied by the Hannibal Board of Public Works, which offers a *Customer Handbook* giving full information on water, electricity, and sewer services. Their address is:

Hannibal Board of Public Works
4th & Broadway
Hannibal, MO 63401

Television

There is one local television station, a CBS affiliate, and the NBC station in Quincy is easy to receive. For complete coverage, there is a local cable system.

Newspapers

The daily newspaper is:

The Hannibal Courier-Post
200 North Third St.
Hannibal, MO 63401

The *St. Louis Post-Dispatch*, the *St. Louis Globe-Democrat*, the

Kansas City Star and *Times,* the *Chicago Tribune,* and the *Chicago Sun-Times* are all available locally.

For Further Information

Hannibal Chamber of Commerce
P.O. Box 230
Hannibal, MO 63401

Division of Tourism
308 E. High St.
Jefferson City, MO 65101

Hattiesburg, Mississippi

POPULATION: 40,882 within the city limits
64,888 in Forrest County
139,961 within the Hattiesburg trading area

ELEVATION: 144 feet above sea level

Hattiesburg is located in southeastern Mississippi, at the confluence of the Bouie and Leaf rivers, 70 miles north of Gulfport and the Gulf of Mexico. It is a rail, trade, shopping, and industrial center for a prosperous farming and lumbering area.

The countryside is flat, wooded, and broken with many waterways and a few rolling hills. The soil in the area is lacking in natural fertility, except along the streams, and is generally better for forestry than for crops.

Climate

The prevailing southerly winds provide a moist, subtropical climate in Hattiesburg. Afternoon thundershowers are common in the summer, bringing relief from the heat. Summers are long and warm to hot, with high temperatures in the upper 80s to 90s from May through September. There are about 75 days per year with temperatures of 90°F and above. The area has about 2700 cooling degree days per year.

Winters are brief and mild, with seldom more than 20 days per year in which temperatures drop to 32°F and below. Normal winter temperatures range from highs in the 60s to lows in the 40s, broken by occasional northers that drop temperatures to freezing and below for a few days. Snow is virtually unknown, and the first frost does not arrive until the end of November. The last frost occurs by the last week of February, giving 270 frost-free days in the growing season.

The humidity in Hattiesburg is high, averaging around 75% throughout the year, but the area enjoys about 63% of possible sunshine. Precipitation is about 56 inches per year, fairly well distributed throughout the year, though slightly less in October and slightly more in the thunderstorm season of midsummer.

Tropical cyclones, or hurricanes, can occur between August and October, though the inland location of Hattiesburg is considerable protection from the full force of the storms.

History

During the early days of American colonization, the Hattiesburg area was covered in forest, inhabited occasionally by bands of Choctaw Indians. The white man came and the Indians died or moved westward, but nothing much happened in this portion of Mississippi until Civil War days, when Captain William Harris Hardy, a Confederate soldier, statesman, and engineer, found the lovely spot where the Leaf and Bouie rivers joined. He picked it for settlement, and in 1881 named it for his wife, Hattie. The town was incorporated in 1884.

Early settlers were attracted by the large stands of virgin pine timber. These forests were the major source of wealth in the area for many years.

With plentiful rain, fast-growing timber, and good rail and water transportation, the area became a busy trade center for an area that included the 10 surrounding counties. In recent years, Hattiesburg has been called the Hub of South Mississippi.

Economy and Employment

For many years, timber was the principal source of income in the area, and it is still important today, with local plants producing building materials and other products.

Industry began diversifying after World War II and now includes plants producing wearing apparel, chemicals, paper products, handbags, machinery, and boxes. Poultry and meat processing have grown in importance, and the most recent growth has been in tourism and conventions. Scott Paper Company has completed a 135,000-square-foot plant in Hattiesburg, employing 400, and another paper plant is under construction. Downtown Hattiesburg is working on a $1 million improvement project, and the area's economy is healthy and prospering.

Unemployment has remained low as the economy continues to expand and new plants continue to move in from northern states. Major employers include: Big Yank (men's work clothes, 521 employees); Hercules, Inc. (chemicals, 935); Marshall Durbin Poultry Co. (425); Price Brothers (concrete pipe, 153); Mississippi Tank Co. (steel tanks, 200); Neco Electrical Products (650); Masonite Corp. (lumber products, 177); and a number of smaller companies that make handbags, boxes, pipe, and machinery.

For local job information, write:

Mississippi State Employment Service
Hattiesburg, MS 39401

Taxes

Mississippi has a 5% retail sales tax, and the state income tax is 3% on the first $5000 above deductions and 4% for earnings above that figure.

The property tax depends on location. Inside the city limits, the tax rate is $1.582 per $100 of actual value, while it is $.981 per $100 in the unincorporated areas outside the city limits. Thus, a house selling for $65,000 inside the city limits would be taxed approximately $1028 per year, while a residence in the county would be taxed about $638 per year.

Shopping

Hattiesburg has a downtown business area supplemented by six suburban shopping centers. Many major national and regional chains are represented. As the trade and shopping center for an area with a population of 139,000, Hattiesburg is better equipped than most towns to serve the local residents.

For shopping beyond the capacities of local stores, there are Mobile, Alabama, 97 miles to the southeast, and Jackson, Mississippi, 83 miles to the northwest. And New Orleans, 115 miles to the southwest, is a shopper's paradise.

Residential Properties

The local newspaper carries ads for available housing, both for rental and for purchase. A few typical listings are:

> IN PETAL [a suburb of Hattiesburg], a 3-bedroom, 2-bath home on large 100 × 150 lot, with den and 5.25% assumable loan. $43,500.
>
> BRICK RANCH HOME on large wooded lot with 3 bedrooms and 2 baths plus fenced back yard. $48,000.
>
> CLOSE IN with 3 bedrooms, 2 baths, family room, fireplace, double garage, plus workshop and screened back porch. $50,000.
>
> BEAUTIFUL brick home with 4 bedrooms, 2 baths, family room, den, central heat and air, on 110 × 200 wooded lot, $61,500.

Rentals are available, with one-bedroom apartments renting for $150 to $225 per month and two-bedroom apartments or condos for $165 to $375.

Safety

Hattiesburg's FBI Crime Index rating is 54 crimes per thousand of population per year. The local police department serves the community with 92 full-time and 28 part-time employees. The fire department has 93 full-time personnel, and the city has a Fire Insurance Rating of Class 5.

There is no nearby manmade hazard at present, but there is a possibility that a site near Richton, Mississippi, 22 miles to the east, will be designated as a storage area for nuclear waste. Since this site would not be in the same river drainage system as Hattiesburg, it is not considered an appreciable hazard. However, persons working in Hattiesburg and looking for rural property might be well advised to avoid the Richton area until the question has been resolved.

Education

The Hattiesburg public school system has a 16.44:1 pupil/teacher ratio, which is better than many comparable communities today.

Higher education is well served locally by a vocational branch of Pearl River Junior College, by William Carey College, and by the University of Southern Mississippi. William Carey College is a coeducational, fully accredited institution with over 2500 students, operated under the direction of the Baptist Church and offering a four-year college program. The University of Southern Mississippi is a four-year state-supported institution with over 10,000 students enrolled in a broad variety of studies.

For graduate studies leading to masters' and doctoral degrees, Mississippi State University, near Columbus, is 172 miles north, and the University of Mississippi, near Oxford, is 231 miles north.

Medical Facilities

Forrest General Hospital, which has 420 beds, and Methodist Hospital, which has 205 beds, provide excellent and complete facilities for the area. There are 118 physicians in private practice serving the area as well.

Cultural Activities

The Concert Association, organized in 1939, brings in performers of national and international fame for concerts at Thomas Hall Auditorium on the campus of William Carey College. The Little Theater, first organized in 1930, presents plays in the American Building, a local landmark, while the Civic Light Opera gives performances in Saenger Theater.

A local art association sponsors an annual art show and provides classes in cooperation with the city's recreation department. The Department of Theater Arts at the University of Southern Mississippi offers both theater and dance programs.

The public library serves the local residents with 75,000 volumes, and the 400,000-volume collection of the university is also available to local residents during the school year.

Recreation

The city's recreation department conducts an active recreational program, operating seven playgrounds, three swimming pools, baseball fields, and basketball courts, plus senior-citizen activities, kite-flying contests, gun shows, boxing tournaments, and talent shows.

Hattiesburg has two 18-hole public golf courses plus a par-3 course, two country clubs, a community center, and two bowling alleys. The city maintains 24 parks with camping and picnicking facilities, and 9 tennis courts. The university maintains another 10 tennis courts on campus.

The numberless lakes, ponds, streams, and rivers in the area offer endless opportunities for the fisherman. For the saltwater fisherman, the Gulf Coast is only 70 miles to the south. Boating enthusiasts have Ross Barnett Reservoir, with launching ramps and rental boats, 90 miles to the north, and the Gulf Coast, 70 miles to the south, offers much to choose from in boat rentals, launching areas, and charter trips for deep-sea fishing.

Government

Hattiesburg is operated under the Mayor-Council system, with elected council members serving as commissioners of city departments.

Water

Water is supplied locally by the city of Hattiesburg. The water is drawn from deep wells and is neutral and very soft. The water system can generate approximately one-third more water than maximum peak demand, assuring adequate supplies in the foreseeable future.

Energy

Electricity is provided by the Mississippi Power Company, and comes mostly from gas-fired steam power plants. Gas is supplied by the Wilmut Gas & Oil Company.

Utility costs are low, with the cost of utilities for an 1800-square-foot home averaging about $53 per month.

Television

There is one local UHF television station, and the local cable system provides 10-channel service to subscribers.

Newspapers

The local daily newspaper is:

The Hattiesburg American
Hattiesburg, MS 39401

The *New Orleans Times-Picayune* is also available locally.

For Further Information

Hattiesburg Area Chamber of Commerce
204 W. Front St.
Hattiesburg, MS 39401

Mississippi Department of Economic Development
P.O. Box 849
Jackson, MS 39205

Mississippi Game and Fish Commission
P.O. Box 451
Jackson, MS 39205

Department of Tourism Development
P.O. Box 849
Jackson, MS 39205

Houma, Louisiana

POPULATION: 32,607 within the city limits
50,466 in the Houma area
94,393 in Terrebonne Parish

ELEVATION: 15 feet above sea level

Terre bonne means "good earth," and a visitor can quickly see why the area was given this name. Terrebonne Parish (county) is the perfect example of southern Louisiana bayou country. The parish has a total area of 1893 square miles — 1336 square miles of land and 557 square miles of water. Like most of southern Louisiana, it is composed of low, flat land varying from prairies and wooded areas about 12 feet above sea level to bayous, lakes, and salt marshes in the southern areas.

The area is dotted with stately, historic, antebellum homes beside oak-lined bayous (a bayou is an arm of a lake or river). The semitropical climate permits exotic blooming plants such as bougainvillea and hibiscus to thrive. In the mild climate, local residents (Cajuns) grow their own vegetables in bayouside gardens also laden with citrus fruits, figs, pomegranates, and other fruits.

Off the beaten tourist track, Houma is only one hour from New Orleans and two hours from Baton Rouge. It is now one of the top areas in the nation in production of oil and gas, and its fisheries are among the busiest.

Climate

Houma is in southernmost Louisiana, in an area that is low and often marshy, with numerous sluggish streams or bayous that flow through lakes and marshes to the Gulf of Mexico. The present industrialization of the area is due, in large part, to the mild climate and the unfailing water supply.

Summers are moist and semitropical, with frequent afternoon thundershowers. From May through October, the daily maximum temperature averages in the 80s or above, with 69 days per year with temperatures 90°F and above, usually in June through August. Summers bring 3000 cooling degree days per year.

Winters are mild, with minimum temperatures generally in the 40s and 50s from November through April, though northers have brought below-freezing temperatures to the area. Normally, however, freezing temperatures occur only about once every seven years.

With 62 inches of rain per year, the humidity averages 75% to 80%. Rainfall occurs throughout the year, with a bit more falling in June through August, in the form of thundershowers. October and November are the driest months, averaging only around 3 inches of rain per month. Total rainfall in the region measures 1078 million gallons per square mile per year.

Winds are normally gentle and southerly throughout the year, except when northers bring cold air down from the north, or when a tropical storm moves up from the Gulf of Mexico. Houma is outside the normal range of tornadoes, but tropical storms and hurricanes do hit the Louisiana coast on occasion. Houma is far enough from the Gulf to avoid the brunt of most storms, however.

History

The Houma Indians were living in the Terrebonne area when Henry de Tonti and Sieur d'Iberville visited in the late seventeenth century. In 1765, the influx of Acadians began. Exiled from their homes in Canada, they followed the Mississippi River southward and finally found refuge in Louisiana. Terrebonne Parish was created in April 1822, and Houma was incorporated in 1843.

In the early days of the parish, numerous waterways provided the principal means of communication and travel. Settlements and plantations sprang up along these bayou roads. The present highway system grew from the early towpaths along the banks of the bayous that were used when there was not enough wind to push the sail-powered boats upstream. Travel in and out of the area was provided by steamboats on Bayou Lafourche, 10 miles to the east, which connected with the several steamboat lines plying the long, broad Mississippi River.

The early economy of the parish was primarily rural and agricultural, and at one time the chief industry was growing sugar cane and making sugar and molasses.

The shrimp industry in the area began 75 years ago with a Cantonese named Lee Yim, who introduced a shrimp-drying process to local fishermen. With the introduction of the shrimp trawl in 1917, it became possible for fishermen to take in larger catches, boosting shrimp production and giving an impetus to the Houma fishing industry that lasts to this day.

Economy and Employment

The Lirette Oil Field, 18 miles south of town, is the site of the first oil to be discovered in the area. Ever since that first oil field, the area has flourished. More oil and gas fields have been discovered. Texaco is one of the largest firms in the local oil industry, and Getty Oil Company has a plant for removing propane and butane and selling the dry gas. Seven gas companies are presently taking gas from the local fields. Houma is booming, and all indications are that it will continue to boom for a long time. Both on- and off-shore oil drilling is continuing steadily, oil-related businesses are swamped with orders, and the traditional industries are holding their own.

Shrimp fishermen now bring in more than 50 million pounds of shrimp per year. There are 52 producers of oysters in Houma, and 185 trappers, who take in half a million pelts each year with a value of over $2 million. In the fresh water of the bayous, four companies harvest over 8000 pounds of crawfish each year.

Agriculture today includes sugar cane, meat packing, food processing, soybeans, truck crops, citrus fruits, and livestock.

Among the major employers are: Avondale Shipyards (900 employees); Delta Services (steel structures, 1650); Offshore Caterers, and Offshore Food Services (both are catering services, with a combined employment of 1175); and steel-fabricating plants employing over 2000. The petroleum industry employs around 8000 people in the area, and service businesses employ another 8000. Retail trade employs 8500, shipbuilding a total of 2600, water transportation employs 2340, and the seafood fishing and processing industry another 665.

Taxes
The combined state and local sales tax is 5%. There is no city or parish income tax, and the state tax is low, with a rate of 2% on the first $10,000 of taxable income, going up to a high of 6% on incomes over $50,000.

The local property tax is also low, averaging about $895 per year on a home selling for $65,000.

Shopping
Needs not met locally can easily be filled by a one-day shopping trip to New Orleans, 57 miles to the northeast via an excellent highway.

Residential Properties
Rentals are plentiful, ranging from one-bedroom apartments for $165 to $350 per month to two-bedroom apartments for $190 to $465 per month. Homes for sale are represented by these typical ads:

> THREE bedroom 2½ baths, living room, den with wet bar, brick, central air and heat, workshop, fenced yard, $60,000.
>
> EASTSIDE. 2-bedroom brick home, central air and heat, large lot, $50,000.
>
> CUTE 4-bedroom brick home, 1½-bath, central heat and air, priced in the low 40s.
>
> BEAUTIFUL 3-bedroom, 2-bath home with 1620 feet of living area on ½-acre lot, $70,000.

In addition to these, there are numerous mobile-home parks where mobile homes can be purchased for considerably less than conventional homes.

For some unexplained reason, most of the real estate ads in the local newspaper do not indicate price, so it takes a few letters to local realtors to obtain full information on current real estate listings and prices.

Safety
There are no manmade hazards close to Houma, and, despite the low elevation, flooding is not a danger. The hazard of tropical storms

is overrated by the national news media, and the chance of any one location being hit by a tropical storm or hurricane is really quite small.

The FBI Crime Index rating is a moderate 59 crimes per thousand of population per year. The police department has 84 employees and 25 cars, and the parish sheriff's department has another 105 employees and 77 vehicles. The local fire department has 69 full-time employees and 40 volunteers and operates six trucks and two snorkel trucks. The area has a Class 4 Fire Insurance Rating.

Education

There are 34 elementary schools, 4 middle high and high schools, 2 private schools, and 2 vocational-technical schools.

Nicholls State University in nearby Thibodaux is only 30 minutes away by bus or car. The Louisiana Marine and Petroleum Institute was established in 1977 and specializes in maritime courses, including offshore oil- and gas-related skills, offshore fishing, and various other skills such as marine diving and underwater exploration. Its site is on the Houma Navigation Canal.

For the best that Louisiana has to offer, Louisiana State University and Louisiana A & M are both located in Baton Rouge, the state capital, which is 90 miles to the north.

Medical Facilities

Terrebonne General Hospital, which has 200 beds, serves all of the parish with an intensive-care unit, a nursing home, and full hospital facilities.

The parish has 111 physicians, including some nonresident physicians at the South Louisiana Medical Center. There are 34 dentists. The Houma Medical and Surgical Clinic and the Terrebonne Regional Mental Health Clinic also serve the area.

Cultural Activities

The parish library has 121,959 volumes available to the public.

Le Petit Théâtre de Terrebonne is a nonprofessional little-theater group with 900 subscribers that uses local talent to produce an average of five plays per year.

In New Orleans, only an hour away, an endless variety of shows, exhibits, concerts, and performances are available.

Recreation

Houma has two private golf courses, one an 18-hole course at Ellendale Country Club, the other a 9-hole course at Houma Golf Club.

Locally, there are 3 bowling alleys, 4 roller-skating rinks, 2 swimming pools, 12 lighted baseball and softball parks, 13 tennis courts, and a variety of other facilities.

For those who prefer to create their own recreation, there are unlimited opportunities for fishing and hunting in the area around Houma. Boating opportunities range from rowboating in the shade of cypress trees on quiet bayous to offshore fishing in the Gulf of Mexico, which is only a few miles away.

And for those whose favorite recreation is sampling new dishes, there is a diet-breaking variety to choose from: crab, shrimp or crawfish boil, crawfish étouffée, seafood gumbo, jambalaya, and oysters in many forms. These are all Cajun dishes developed from a combination of French and local cooking.

Government

Houma is governed by a Mayor-Council system. In Louisiana, council members are called aldermen.

Water

The water is alkaline and hard, and comes from an endless source — the Intracoastal Waterway and Bayou Black. The local system is municipally owned and operated, and plant capacity is well above the maximum demand.

Energy

The city of Houma has its own municipally operated power plant, which provides electric power for about four-fifths of the city area. The outside areas and the remainder of the city are served by Louisiana Power and Light and by South Louisiana Electric Cooperative. A municipally owned gas-distribution system brings a plentiful supply of low-cost natural gas to local homes. Utility costs run about $90 per month for the average two-bedroom home.

Information on current rates for electricity and gas can be obtained by writing City Clerk, City of Houma, Houma, LA 70360.

Television

Houma is within easy reach of the many stations in New Orleans, and there is a local cable system as well.

Newspapers

The local newspaper is:

The Houma Daily Courier
312 School St.
Houma, LA 70361

The *New Orleans Times-Picayune* is also available locally.

For Further Information

Houma-Terrebonne Chamber of Commerce
P.O. Box 328
Houma, LA 70361

South-Central Planning and Development Commission
P.O. Box 846
Thibodaux, LA 70301

Louisiana Department of Transportation & Development
Office of Highways
Baton Rouge, LA 70804

Ask for their excellent highway map, which is free.

Texaco Waterways Service
135 East 42nd St.
New York, NY 10017

Ask about the coastal Louisiana waterways and receive a free brochure.

Office of Tourism
P.O. Box 44291
Baton Rouge, LA 70804

Jackson, Tennessee

POPULATION: 49,131 within the city limits
74,546 in Madison County

ELEVATION: 425 feet above sea level

Jackson is in the center of western Tennessee, about 85 miles northeast of Memphis and 131 miles southwest of Nashville, on the south fork of Forked Deer River. This is an area of gently rolling hills and delta farmlands, where agriculture is still an important part of the economy.

Jackson is also an industrial city, with a variety of manufacturing. It is a trade and shipping center for a large agricultural area and is also a medical center for western Tennessee.

Climate

Western Tennessee has warm, mild, humid summers and mild winters. Humidity averages about 80% at night throughout the year and drops to about 60% in the afternoons. The area receives about 60% of possible sunshine throughout the year.

During the winter, temperatures range from highs in the 50s to lows in the 30s from December through February. The last frost is over by the end of March, and the first frost in fall comes in the first week of November, leaving about 230 days in the frost-free growing season. Snow seldom totals more than 6 to 8 inches per year, falling mostly in December to early March and never staying on the ground for long. There are about 3400 heating degree days per year.

Summers are warm, with average daily highs in the 80s and 90s from May through September, and there are about 64 days per year with temperatures of 90°F and above. There are about 2000 cooling degree days per year.

Spring and fall bring pleasant weather, with daytime highs in the 60s and 70s and cool nights.

Precipitation averages about 48 inches per year, fairly evenly spread throughout the 12 months, though August through October are somewhat drier than the rest of the year. Winds are normally gentle and southerly except when they shift to westerly or northerly during winter cold spells.

Severe storms are relatively infrequent in the area, since it is east of the major tornado area and south of the main area of blizzards. Damage from tropical storms is rare, and blizzard conditions occur about once in 40 years. Thunderstorms are frequent but seldom damaging.

History

The Jackson area was the home of the Mound Builders before A.D. 850 and was part of the hunting grounds of the Chickasaw Indians when the white man first arrived. When the first settlement on the banks of the Forked Deer River began in 1806, it was called Alexandria, in honor of the surveyor who moved there from Virginia. It was a small river port and an early shipping center because it was navigable by the flatboats of that era. Madison County was established in 1821, and friends of "The General" Andrew Jackson prevailed on the legislature to name the county seat Jackson in his honor.

The settlers quickly learned that the rich alluvial soil was perfect for cotton. By 1840, more than 5000 bales were shipped each year, and by the time of the Civil War 21,000 bales were produced annually. The Civil War raged around and through Jackson, and there are many markers today to commemorate battle and camp sites.

Jackson was an early center for various churches. The Christian Methodist Episcopal denomination established Mother Liberty Christian Methodist Episcopal Church in 1849, and St. Luke's Sanctuary was built in 1844. The First Baptist Church was built in 1837, Methodists began Andrew Chapel in 1820, Cumberland Presbyterians organized in the area in 1872, and Catholics began a mission shortly after the Civil War. United Pentecostals established a congregation in the early 1900s.

Jackson students met in rented buildings until 1883, when the site for the College Street School was purchased. This began the development of the area's public school system.

Economy and Employment

Agriculture dominated the lives of the local residents until an influx of industries in the 1960s. Conalco's construction in 1955 anticipated the boom that really began when the American Olean Tile Company opened in the Madison County Industrial Park in 1962.

Today's economy is based on industry, trade, services, retailing, and agriculture. Agriculture is no longer dominated by cotton but includes soybeans, beef cattle, and hogs. With some 480,000 people living in the 17-county trade area, Jackson is an important retail and trade center.

The largest employers in the area are the combined medical facilities of the four hospitals, and the associated medical services. Other major employers include: American Olean Tile Co. (ceramic wall and floor tiles, 219 employees); Bemis Co. (industrial sheeting, twine, and fabrics, 950); Bendix Corp. (auto parts, 455); Bruce Hardwood Floors (378); Coca-Cola (204); Consolidated Aluminum (aluminum foil and sheet, 608); International Paper Co. (specialty, grocery, and plastic bags, 291); Oakley Fashions (women's apparel, 325); Owens-Corning (fiber glass, 900); Procter & Gamble (food products, 760); Quaker Oats (food products, 531); and Rockwell International (tools, 1025).

Jackson also has employers in the fields of asphalt production, electronic components, lithographic plates, printing, dairy products, adhesives, wood products, bread, concrete products, cans, metal processing, brick and clay products, saws, and optical products.

Taxes

The combined state and local sales tax is 6%, and the state income tax is limited to 6% on income from interest and dividends.

Residential property taxes are based on an assessment of 25% of market value, and the tax on a home selling for $65,000 would run about $585 per year inside the city limits.

Shopping
In addition to the central shopping district, there are several regional and neighborhood centers attracting shoppers from a large 17-county area. Major chains have joined with the hundreds of locally owned stores to attract over $340 million in annual retail sales.

For greater variety, Memphis is 85 miles to the southwest and Nashville is 131 miles to the northeast.

Residential Properties
Homes can be found in all price ranges, from small starter homes for under $30,000 to spacious luxury homes for over $100,000. Typical listings are:

MOVE IN today to newly decorated 2-bedroom home on a large lot with trees, eat-in kitchen. Only $25,900.

OWNER WILL FINANCE this 4-bedroom 3½-bath home in prime location. 2400 square feet, large private clubroom overlooking a private German beer garden. $69,900.

ASSUME LOAN on this almost-new 3-bedroom 1½-bath home on a quiet street. $44,800.

TWENTY ACRES of woods and pasture, only 9 miles from town. 3-bedroom, 2-bath log home. $80,000.

BEAUTIFUL 4-bedroom, 3-bath home on 1¼-acre wooded lot in choice residential area. $99,900.

Apartments are plentiful, with one-bedroom apartments renting for $155 to $310 per month and two-bedroom apartments or condos renting for $195 to $425. The chamber of commerce will send a list of apartments that are available in town. In addition, the chamber will provide a list of realtors and send you a copy of *Homeparade*, which gives a monthly listing of homes for sale. All of this is free.

Safety
The FBI Crime Index rating is 81 crimes per thousand of population per year. There are 130 uniformed police officers, and the fire department has 150 members. The Fire Insurance Rating is Class 3A.

There are no natural hazards and no manmade hazards or military target areas nearby.

Education

The Jackson Public School System has eight elementary schools, three junior high schools, and one senior high school. Private schools include Old Hickory Academy, a Montessori school, a Catholic school, and Jackson Christian School.

There are five institutions of higher learning in Jackson. Jackson State Community College is a state-supported two-year college offering associate degrees in 29 areas of study.

Lambuth College, founded in 1843, is a four-year liberal-arts Methodist-supported college that offers B.A. degrees in arts, science, music, and business administration.

Lane College, founded in 1882 by the Christian Methodist Episcopal Church, has 673 students enrolled in B.A. programs in 14 areas of study, including preprofessional training in medicine, dentistry, nursing, and law.

Union University is the city's oldest educational institution, dating back to 1825. Sponsored by the Baptist Church, it offers four-year degree courses in the fields of arts, science, music, and nursing to 1345 students.

West Tennessee Business College, founded in 1929, is a privately owned business college with 300 students.

Vocational training is offered at the State Area Vocational-Technical School, and cosmetology courses are offered by Jackson Beauty Academy and the McCollum and Ross University of Beauty Culture.

For graduate studies, the University of Mississippi, in University, Mississippi (near Oxford), is about 100 miles south.

Medical Facilities

Jackson is the medical and health-care center for the 480,000 persons in the surrounding 17-county area. The major facilities are Jackson–Madison County General Hospital, Parkway General Hospital, Jackson Specialty Hospital, and Jackson Mental Health Psychiatric Hospital, together providing 853 hospital beds. Their combined facilities offer virtually every medical care that could be asked for. Jackson also has five nursing homes, with a total of 459 beds.

In addition, there are 133 doctors in private practice and 43 dentists, plus 18 dental hygienists.

Cultural Activities

The Jackson–Madison County Library serves the community with 79,654 volumes. In addition, the various college libraries contain another 270,000 books, many of which are available for the use of the local residents.

The coliseum, which has a seating capacity of 6000, and the Jackson Civic Center, seating 2200, provide facilities for athletic events, concerts, conventions, trade shows, and the Miss Tennessee Pageant.

Many of the cultural needs of the community are met by the Arts Council, the local colleges, and the parks and recreation department. Under the auspices of the Arts Council are the Jackson Symphony Orchestra, the Art Association, and the Writers' Group.

The Community Concert Association is responsible for many dramatic and musical presentations featuring world-renowned artists. The Theater Guild presents stage productions of plays and musicals, using semiprofessional talent from a large area.

Lambuth College has the only planetarium in western Tennessee. It is open to the public for a nominal fee.

Recreation

Because of the moderate climate, Jackson residents can enjoy outdoor activities much of the year. Parks are scattered throughout the city. Muse Park features 100 acres of nature trails, picnic areas, playgrounds, lighted ball parks, and tennis courts. Five state parks are within easy driving distance and provide many facilities for outings.

The city maintains 10 playgrounds, as well as lighted fields for the Little League and softball leagues. Two city parks have lighted tennis courts. Other city facilities include gymnasiums, game rooms, senior-citizen centers, an indoor tennis court, and a swimming pool.

Golfers have a choice of three public golf courses and a driving range plus three private golf and country clubs. Three colleges and the Jackson Golf and Country Club maintain tennis courts.

For the outdoorsman, there are many opportunities within easy driving distance. This area of Tennessee is noted for its hunting and fishing. For information on places to hunt, fish, and camp, write:

Tennessee Department of Conservation
Division of Tourism Information
2611 West End Avenue
Nashville, TN 37203

Government
Jackson is governed by the Commission system, as is Madison County, though the commissioners no longer have direct control over city departments as they once did.

Water
Tap water is neutral, very soft, and fluoridated. Water is provided by the city's utility division.

Energy
The city's utility division provides electricity and natural gas, as well as water, sewer, and trash-collection services. A $30 deposit is required to establish all these services, after which the consumer is billed for current use.

The present cost of utilities for the average two-to-three-bedroom home is about $85 per month — somewhat lower than the national average, because electricity is drawn from the huge Tennessee Valley Authority at special low rates.

Television
There is one local network television station, and a local cable company provides full-channel coverage.

Newspapers
The daily newspaper is:

The Jackson Sun
Jackson, TN 38301

The *Memphis Commercial Appeal* and the *Nashville Tennessean* are also available locally.

For Further Information

Jackson Area Chamber of Commerce
P.O. Box 1904
Jackson, TN 38301

Tennessee Tourist Development
505 Fesslers Lane
Nashville, TN 37210

Jefferson City, Missouri

POPULATION: 33,794 within the city limits
54,200 in Cole County

ELEVATION: 628 feet above sea level

Jefferson City, the state capital, is located in the center of Missouri on the Missouri River, some 127 miles west of St. Louis and 145 miles east of Kansas City. It is a commercial and processing center for an agricultural area. Jefferson City has railroad shops and increasing light industry, coupled with a busy rail and river transportation center.

The countryside is slightly rolling and wooded between the open farmlands. The broad Missouri River flows along the northeast side of town, and the airport is located across the river.

Climate

Missouri has four definite seasons, though temperatures can vary considerably from the norm in any of them. Winters are short and sometimes quite sharp, with normal temperatures dropping below freezing at night from December through March. Arctic storms can drop temperatures to well below zero on occasion. Spring and fall bring mild weather, with cool nights and warm days. There are about 102 days per year with temperatures of 32°F and below, and the frost-free growing period averages 220 days a year, with the last frost in spring coming about the first of April and the first frost arriving in the first part of November. There are about 4900 heating degree days each year.

Summers are warm to hot, with normal highs in the upper 80s from June through August, but record highs have reached 115°F in July and there are about 46 days per year with temperatures 90°F and higher. There are some 1500 cooling degree days per year.

Annual precipitation is a comfortable 36 inches, well spread out throughout the year. Winters bring about 15 inches of snow, which normally falls during November to March. There is about 65% of possible sunshine each year. Humidity is moderate, ranging from 75% at night to 57% in the afternoons. Winds are westerly to northerly in winter, shifting to southerly in the summer, and are generally moderate all year. There are an average of about 10 tornadoes per year throughout the entire state.

History

The federal government donated land for the express purpose of establishing a state capital in Missouri, and on the last day of 1821 the legislature established Jefferson City at its present site on the Missouri River. The new capital was named for Thomas Jefferson, and many of the first settlers in the town were from Charlottesville, Virginia, near Jefferson's home.

When the site was picked, three families were already living there. Daniel M. Boone, son of the famous pioneer, and Major Elias Bancroft were commissioned to plan and lay out the town. Records show that Boone was paid $4.00 for 120 days of work, and the first lots sold at an average price of $32.75 each.

The first capitol building, completed in 1826, faced the river and was located on the site of the present governor's mansion. When a fire destroyed it in 1837, it was replaced with a new building on the present site. This building has been expanded over the years and is still the state capitol today.

Jefferson City was slow to recover from the Civil War, but by the turn of the century new industries began to appear and electric lights were installed. Since then, growth has been slow and steady, much of it based on government in the early years, and only recently on industry and commerce.

Economy and Employment

Today, more and more industries are opening offices and plants in Jefferson City, expanding the economic base. In addition to industry, the growing governmental agencies and the expanding retail and wholesale businesses help maintain a sound and broadly based economy.

Government is one of the largest employers in the area. For information on openings in state government, write:

Director, Personnel Division
State of Missouri
123 East Dunklin
Jefferson City, MO 65101

The current major industrial employers include: Benchmark Tool Co. (makers of tools, 257 employees); Chesebrough-Pond (cosmetics, 975); DeLong (steel fabrication, 180); Footwear Distribution Center, 138); *News Tribune* (106); Scholastic, Inc. (distributors of school materials, 235); Von Loffman Press (textbooks, 500); and Westinghouse Electric (underground transformers, 1120).

There are many openings from time to time in the retail and wholesale businesses. For current job information, write:

Missouri State Employment Service
407 Jefferson
Jefferson City, MO 65101

Taxes

The Missouri state income tax ranges from 1.5% to 6% of taxable income. There is a combined state-city sales tax of 4%.

Property taxes are based on one-third of market value and total $5.10 per $100 of assessed value, so that the tax on a home selling for $65,000 would run about $1110 per year.

Shopping

Because Jefferson City is an important regional center, a wide selection of merchandise can be found locally. Principal shopping areas include the downtown business district and five major shopping centers. In addition, there are many neighborhood stores located throughout the city.

For those persons desiring wider shopping opportunities than are offered locally, St. Louis is 127 miles to the east and Kansas City is 145 miles to the west. Both cities have cosmopolitan shopping facilities.

Residential Properties

Many rentals are available in the $300–$400 price range for two- and three-bedroom apartments. One-bedroom apartments rent for $115 to $210 per month, and the rent for two-bedroom apartments ranges from $160 to $405. Homes for sale can be found in almost any price range desired. A few typical listings are:

> COMFORTABLE, QUIET LIVING at an affordable price with 100% owner financing. Charming older 2-story home with 3 bedrooms, deck, big kitchen, new carpet and paint, beautiful acre lot. $39,900.
>
> IN QUIET NEIGHBORHOOD. 3-bedroom, 3-bath home with family room with fireplace, large deck, with lots of privacy. $53,500.
>
> NEAT AND CLEAN 3-bedroom split foyer home with new decoration, family room opening onto concrete patio, sundeck off of dining area. $42,900.
>
> STARTER HOME with 2 bedrooms and new carpeting. Remodeled in 1974. $19,900.

The *Capital News* and the *Post-Tribune,* the local morning and evening newspapers, carry ads in every issue, though the Sunday *News and Tribune* carries more. Write and ask about sample copies.

Safety

The crime rate in Jefferson City is a low 44 crimes per thousand of population per year, according to the FBI Crime Index. The police department has 73 employees, 22 cars, 5 motorcycles, and 3 K-9 dogs. Fire protection is provided by 64 employees in the local fire department, which is equipped with two ladder trucks, six pumpers, one chemical truck, one rescue truck, one rescue boat, and an arson-investigation truck. There are four fire stations throughout the city. The Fire Insurance Rating for Jefferson City is Class 5.

There are no nearby nuclear or military installations that might prove hazardous to local residents. Tornadoes, as already mentioned, are always a possibility, though not nearly as much of a danger as driving to the local supermarket.

Education

The Jefferson City public school system provides classes for students from kindergarten through the twelfth grade, plus special facilities for handicapped children and adults. Educational television is available through the local cable system. There is also a vocational-technical high school to train young people for entry into industry. Other educational facilities include private nursery schools and kindergartens, plus parochial schools operated by the Catholic and Lutheran churches.

Higher education is available locally at Lincoln University, founded originally for education of black Civil War veterans. Today it provides higher education for some 2300 students in seven undergraduate programs and five graduate-degree programs.

Within just a few miles of Jefferson City are a number of excellent universities. The University of Missouri–Columbia, which has 24,000 students and offers both undergraduate and graduate courses, is only 30 miles to the north.

The University of Missouri–Rolla, with 4400 students, is 65 miles southeast of Jefferson City. It specializes in mining and engineering, and nearly 80% of its faculty members hold Ph.D. degrees.

Linn Technical College, located 20 miles east of Jefferson City, is Missouri's oldest residential, degree-granting, two-year, industrially related technical institute.

Medical Facilities

Hospital care is available at Memorial Community Hospital, St. Mary's Hospital, and Charles E. Still Osteopathic Hospital, which have a combined total of 491 beds. There are 43 physicians and surgeons, 22 dentists, and 27 osteopaths practicing in Jefferson City.

For special medical problems, both St. Louis and Kansas City offer superior medical facilities.

Cultural Activities

The City Symphony Orchestra and the Community Concert Association provide musical programs throughout the year and present many world-famous guest artists. Numerous art exhibits are sponsored by the Capitol City Council on the Arts. There is an active Writers Guild for local authors and students of writing.

The Little Theater and the Children's Theater provide several performances locally each year. Lincoln University and the branches of the University of Missouri all offer many programs throughout the year that are open to the public.

The Thomas Jefferson Regional Library, completed in 1975, serves four counties with a collection of some 200,000 volumes. The state library, with its fine law collection and 181,000 volumes, is also available to the public. Lincoln University's library contains another 120,000 volumes.

Recreation

The city's six main parks, totaling 1100 acres, offer a wide variety of year-round activities and facilities, including picnic tables, barbecue pits, playground areas, rest rooms, ball fields, three outdoor swimming pools, an indoor pool, a refrigerated ice rink, two lakes for all-year fishing, a 1000-seat amphitheater, an 18-hole golf course, racquetball courts, and lighted tennis courts. Craft and hobby classes are available for all age groups, and there are special recreational activities for the handicapped.

There are two private country clubs with facilities for golf, swimming, and social activities. An ultramodern YMCA was completed in 1978 and provides numerous facilities including a swimming pool, gymnasiums, handball courts, a health club, and 12 acres of park land for outdoor sports.

A short drive to the south is the huge Lake of the Ozarks, with nearly 1400 miles of shoreline, posh resort hotels, nightclubs, and unlimited opportunities for fishing and water sports.

Government

Local government is under the Mayor-Council system.

Water

The local water supplier is the Capital City Water Company. Tap water is neutral, hard, and not fluoridated. With the Missouri River flowing by town, the water supply is assured.

Energy

Electricity and gas are supplied by the Missouri Power & Light Company. Utility costs run about $100 per month for the average two-to-three-bedroom home.

Television

There is one local network television station, and the cable television system provides full-channel coverage to subscribers.

Newspapers
There are two daily newspapers, the *Capital News* (mornings) and the *Post-Tribune* (evenings), and also the *News and Tribune* (the combined Sunday edition). All are published by:

The News Tribune Company
210 Monroe
Jefferson City, MO 65101

The *Kansas City Star* and *Times,* the *St. Louis Globe-Democrat,* and the *St. Louis Post-Dispatch* are available locally as well.

For Further Information

Jefferson City Area Chamber of Commerce
P.O. Box 776
Jefferson City, MO 65102

Missouri Division of Tourism
Box 1055
Jefferson City, MO 65101

Jonesboro, Arkansas

POPULATION: 31,118 within the city limits
64,569 in Craighead County

ELEVATION: 320 feet above sea level

Jonesboro is located in northeastern Arkansas, 69 miles northwest of Memphis, 133 miles northeast of Little Rock, and 239 miles south of St. Louis, in the broad Mississippi River alluvial-plains area. The land is generally level, with forested hills and open pasturelands. The town itself is located on a plateau known as Crowley's Ridge, in an area of farms, forests, streams, and lakes.

The rich soils in this region provide fertile ground for a variety of crops, including rice, cotton, and soybeans. The local forests include pine and hardwoods, mostly oak.

Climate

The climate of Jonesboro is typical of the broad cotton belt that extends from eastern Texas eastward and northward to the Atlantic Ocean. Precipitation averages 50 inches per year, spread fairly evenly throughout the year but somewhat heavier in November through May. Humidity averages about 80% in summer and drops to 60% in winter.

Summers are long and warm to hot, with 72 days per year with temperatures of 90°F or above and approximately 2000 cooling degree days. On the other hand, winters are brief and mild, with only 3232 heating degree days and only 57 days with temperatures of 32°F or below. The last spring frost comes around March 30 and the first winter frost comes around the end of October or in early November. The growing season averages from 225 to 260 days per year. There is usually some light snow in December through March, but as a rule it stays on the ground only briefly.

Winds are moderate, averaging between 7 and 12 miles per hour throughout the year, generally blowing from the northeast to the northwest in winter and southerly in the summer.

History

As the chamber of commerce in Jonesboro puts it, "There is a commonness in our name and really nothing in our history or development which suggests uniqueness." Jonesboro is a small, growing agricultural town and railroad crossing. Like countless other little towns, it went virtually unnoticed as our nation grew to maturity. There were no great rivers to make Jonesboro a port and no great abundance of natural resources to attract heavy industry.

With the world passing by as Jonesboro slowly grew and developed, the town has retained many more of the things that make a small town a good place in which to live than other towns that were more progressive.

Economy and Employment

While the foundation of the local economy is agriculture, industry is becoming increasingly important. Unemployment is low, and the future in Jonesboro looks good for local residents.

Rice and soybeans are the staple crops, and Jonesboro has the world's largest rice mill. Cotton is still important, and wheat and other grains are increasing in importance. Row-crop farming, cattle, pigs, watermelons, vegetables, and even flowers add to the local agricultural production. There are almost 1300 farms in Craighead County.

Major employers include: Arkansas State University (460 employees); W. A. Krueger Co. (one of the largest printers of magazines and commercial publications in the nation, 375); Penn Athletic Products (tennis balls, 185); ACA Division of DuPont (automatic clinical analyzers, 360); Colson Caster Division (casters and wheels, 300); Flintrol, Inc. (insect-control devices, 100); Frolic Footware (Hush Puppies, 650); General Electric (small-horsepower motors, 550); FMC Corp. (machinery, 321); Riceland Foods (the largest rice mill in the world, 300); and the two hospital-medical centers (870).

For current employment information, write:

Employment Security Division
528 West Monroe
Jonesboro, AR 72401

Taxes

Arkansas has a 3% state sales tax, and the state income tax averages about 10% of the federal income tax.

Residential property taxes are based on an assessment of 20% of true market value and average about $990 per year on a home selling for $65,000.

Shopping

As a trade and shopping center for a large agricultural area, Jonesboro can meet most normal needs. For wider variety, Memphis is only a little over an hour's drive to the south and is the usual choice of local residents.

Residential Properties

Prices for homes range from $20,000 to over $100,000. A few typical offerings are:

4-BEDROOM BEAUTY. Kitchen just remodeled with new appliances. One bedroom has outside entrance. Good value at $47,500.

BUNGALOW with real charm. 3 bedrooms, 2 baths, separate garage. $31,250.

ELEGANT COLONIAL for the discriminating buyer. 5 bedrooms, recreation room, 3½ baths, beautifully landscaped. Won't last long at $93,000.

CUTE 2-BEDROOM starter home. Needs a little sprucing up. $21,400 for quick sale.

One-bedroom apartments are available from about $160 to $275 per month, and two-bedroom units rent for $180 to $310 per month. For current real estate listings, write:

Jonesboro Board of Realtors
P.O. Box 1013
Jonesboro, AR 72401

Safety

Jonesboro's crime rate is low, with an FBI Crime Index rating of 44 crimes per thousand of population per year. The police department employs 43, including 39 uniformed policemen. Fire protection is provided by a department with 56 firemen. The Fire Insurance Rating is Class 5. There are no potential hazards closer than Blytheville Air Force Base, a SAC base at which nuclear weapons are stored, 40 miles to the east.

Education

The city has five elementary schools, two middle schools, and Jonesboro High School. In addition, there is the Area Vocational Technical School on the high school campus. Jonesboro also offers a parochial school, a business college, a beauty school, and a practical-nursing school.

Arkansas State University's main campus, in Jonesboro, has over 7600 students and offers majors in 74 undergraduate and 51 graduate areas. It has a beautiful 483-acre campus in town, which is supplemented by several rural farms.

Medical Facilities

St. Bernard's Regional Medical Center, founded in 1900, now serves a 15-county area with 275 beds and a modern diagnostic center. It has a staff of over 100 physicians and 650 employees. Craighead County Memorial Hospital primarily serves the local community and has 98 beds, a growing staff of 24 physicians, and over 220 employees. Both hospitals have 24-hour emergency services.

Two ambulance services have registered and highly trained technicians. There are several nursing homes for senior citizens, as well as an Area Health Education Center that is staffed in part by medical students on clinical rotation of a year's duration.

Cultural Activities

Jonesboro has an active Fine Arts Council that has involved the community in the arts. One example of this involvement is the construction of the Forum, a municipally owned auditorium that has attracted at least one event every two days since it first opened. There are also the Northeast Arkansas Symphony, the Jazz Society, a community chorus, and many touring artists and performers who come to Jonesboro.

Arkansas State University's outstanding College of Fine Arts annually provides audiences with award-winning art shows and drama and music performances.

Local library facilities include the public library, which has over 60,000 volumes, and the university library, which has more than 476,000 volumes, all of which are available for use by the public.

Recreation

The city owns a golf course, tennis courts, swimming pools, parks, playgrounds, and a family camping area, all open to the public. The recreation department sponsors football, baseball, softball, and many arts and crafts programs. Facilities are available for bowling, roller skating, archery, boating, and fishing.

For hunters, the golden fields skirting the borders of town are full of quail and doves. The nearby ricelands offer some of the best duck hunting in the world. The rivers, streams, and lakes that dot the landscape in all directions are a paradise for fishermen and provide areas for swimming, boating, hiking, camping, and picnicking.

Government

The city operates under the Mayor-Council system, with an elected mayor and a 12-member council.

Water

The local tap water is soft, neutral, fluoridated, and free from pollution, and with 17 million gallons of water per capita for the area, there is ample water for all needs.

Energy

Jonesboro was the first city in Arkansas to develop an agreement with a major power company. The result is assured electrical power for the future, at reasonable rates. Power is generated from the low-cost coal available locally. Utility costs average around $80 per month for a two-bedroom home.

Television

There is a local ABC station, and stations from nearby cities, including Little Rock and Memphis, can be received easily.

Newspapers
The local daily newspaper is:

The Jonesboro Sun
Jonesboro, AR 72401

Newspapers from Little Rock, Memphis, and several other big cities are available locally.

For Further Information

Greater Jonesboro Chamber of Commerce
P.O. Box 789
Jonesboro, AR 72401

Department of Parks and Tourism
State Capitol
Little Rock, AR 72201

1st Bank and Trust (WELCOME)
P.O. Box 1209
Jonesboro, AR 72401

This bank has offered to send prospective residents a free one-month subscription to the *Jonesboro Sun,* a map of Jonesboro, and a "1st Welcome Kit" containing information about utilities, schools, license registration, and many other things a new resident would want to know. Just write and ask.

Joplin, Missouri

POPULATION: 38,893 within the city limits
86,958 in Jasper County

ELEVATION: 1039 feet above sea level

The gateway to the Ozarks, Joplin is located in southwestern Missouri, 70 miles west of Springfield and 150 miles south of Kansas City. It is a rail, shipping, and processing center for a region producing grain and livestock. There are dairying, fruit growing, and lead and zinc mining in the area.

In recent years, Joplin has expanded its industrial base to more than 150 manufacturing firms. This is an area of superb scenery, clean air and water, and a relatively mild climate.

Climate

Missouri is an inland state and its climate is primarily continental. There are frequent changes in the weather, both daily and seasonal. The state is in the path of cold air moving down from Canada, warm, moist air coming up from the Gulf of Mexico, and dry air moving in from the west.

The months of December through February are cold, with highs in the 40s and lows in the 20s. There are about 100 days per year with temperatures 32°F and below, and winters bring about 4000 heating degree days per year. The last frost in spring is about April 10 and the first frost in fall comes at the end of October, giving about 203 frost-free days in the growing period each year. Snowfall is light at 13 inches per year and falls in November through March.

Spring and fall are pleasant, with temperatures climbing into the high 60s to mid-80s in the days and dropping to the 50s and 60s at night. Summer is short and hot, with about 41 days per year with temperatures of 90°F and above. There are about 1900 cooling degree days per year.

Precipitation is about 41 inches per year, ranging from about 2 inches per month in December through February to 5 inches per month in May and June. Thunderstorms occur about 60 days per year, mostly in the summer months, and tend to cool off the hot afternoons. Winds are moderate and normally from the southeast except during winter storm periods. Humidity is moderate, and there is about 63% of possible sunshine each year.

History

Originally Missouri was Indian country. The first white men began to move into the Joplin area in the early 1800s, mostly from Tennessee and Kentucky. In the mid-1800s, galena was discovered near Joplin and lead mining began, only to be halted by the Kansas-Missouri feuds and the Civil War. By 1870, mining was again active and some 20 prospectors were working in the Joplin Creek area.

By 1871 the valley was filling with small box houses and tents. John C. Cox laid out a town east of Joplin Creek and named it in honor of his friend, the Reverend Harris G. Joplin. By March of 1872 the town had grown enough to be merged with the town of Murphysburg, and the two were incorporated as Union City. A year later it was learned that the incorporation was illegal, and the two towns separated and began feuding, but by 1873 they patched up their quarrels and merged again under the name of Joplin.

With the coming of the first railroad in 1875, the future of the town was assured and it began to grow and settle down. As the mining began to play out, Joplin turned to manufacturing, retail, wholesale, medical, cultural, and entertainment activities and became a center for the four-state area of southwest Missouri, northwest Arkansas, northeast Oklahoma, and southeast Kansas.

Economy and Employment

In addition to being the wholesale and retail trade center for a large area, Joplin is a prospering center for industry, finance, education, medicine, and America's surface transportation network. All of this leads to a varied and stable economy with above-average employment security. Today there are more than 150 manufacturing firms in Joplin, producing over 100 different products. These range from small metal-working shops to large plants employing hundreds of people. Fully developed industrial sites are awaiting the arrival of further industry.

Among Joplin's major employers, with over 500 employees, are: Eagle-Picher Industries (agricultural chemicals, insulating materials, and precision sheet-metal products); Motorola (transformers and video-display devices); and Sperry-Vickers (hydraulic units). Manufacturers with more than 200 employees are: American Fixture Co. (store fixtures); Atlas Powder Co. (commercial explosives and fertilizers); Cardinal Scale and Manufacturing Co. (industrial weighing equipment); FAG Bearing Corp. (ball and roller bearings); Fox DeLuxe Pizza Co. (frozen pizza); Junge Baking Co. (bread); La Barge, Inc. (cables and cable harnesses for missile, aircraft, and computer industries); Miller Manufacturing Co. (industrial work clothing); Missouri Steel Casting Co. (special steel castings); and Tamko Asphalt Products, Inc. (asphalt roofing products).

There are many companies employing fewer than 200 that manufacture a wide variety of items including explosives, chemicals, machinery, lawn mowers, caskets, pallets, fertilizers, clothing, instruments, furniture, dog food, shoes, ball bearings, and dairy products.

Taxes

The state income tax ranges from 1.5% to 6% on taxable income. There is a combined city-state sales tax of 5%. Property taxes are based on an assessed value of one-third of market value. Taxes on a home selling for $65,000 would run about $1430 per year.

Shopping

As the trade and shopping center for a large area, Joplin has over 500 retail outlets in the downtown area and also has the new, enclosed

Northpark Mall, Eastmoreland Plaza, and other areas. For all normal needs, the local resident need go no further.

For those who want a wider selection, Kansas City is 150 miles to the north and Tulsa, Oklahoma, is 100 miles to the southwest.

Residential Properties

Homes available in Joplin are considerably less expensive than in many other parts of the nation. A few typical listings are:

> COUNTRY LIVING without the work. Nearly new 3-bedroom in restricted subdivision with formal and informal living areas. 2 full baths and over one-acre lot. $69,900.
>
> NEAT AND CLEAN 2-bedroom home with dining room, utility room, carpeting, garage, new siding, storm shutters, private owner financing, $16,900.
>
> CLOSE-IN STARTER HOME. 2 bedrooms, stone walls, large living and dining area with fireplace, small basement, detached stone garage. $32,500.
>
> CONTEMPORARY 2-story with 3 bedrooms, 2 baths, huge great room, massive fireplace, on 1½ acres. $79,900.

Rentals are plentiful and inexpensive, with one-bedroom apartments available from $75 to $195 per month and two bedroom apartments or condos for $125 to $350. Furnished mobile homes can be rented for $125 to $250 per month, depending on size and location.

Safety

The FBI Crime Index rating is a moderate 78 crimes per thousand of population per year. Police protection is provided by the Joplin police department, which has 67 sworn personnel supplemented by a trained reserve force. The department operates a 24-hour ambulance service, and a dispatching service for all emergency services can be reached by dialing the 911 emergency number. Fire protection is provided by a department with 68 firefighting personnel. There are four fire stations and a total of 15 pieces of equipment. The city of Joplin has a Class 5 Fire Insurance Rating. There are no nearby manmade potential hazards.

Education

Joplin's school district includes an area extending into Jasper and Newton counties and covers some 70 square miles. It provides 14 elementary schools, 2 junior high schools, 2 senior high schools, and a technical school for over 7850 local students. In addition, there are several private and parochial schools.

Missouri Southern State College, located on 350 acres at the northeast edge of Joplin, is the educational and cultural center of a nine-county area in southwestern Missouri. It offers courses leading to bachelors' degrees in a number of areas in liberal arts, business administration, and teacher education. It also offers masters' degrees in education and business administration in cooperation with Southwest Missouri State College in Springfield.

Ozark Bible College, which has 800 students, is also located in Joplin.

For broader educational opportunities, several universities are within a 200-mile radius. Among these are: University of Missouri at Rolla, 169 miles to the northeast; University of Missouri at Kansas City, 130 miles to the north; Southwest Missouri State University, at Springfield, 57 miles to the east; and the University of Kansas, at Lawrence, 176 miles to the north.

Medical Facilities

A health-care center for the four-state region of southwestern Missouri, northwestern Arkansas, northeastern Oklahoma, and southeastern Kansas, Joplin has three modern hospitals that offer a broad range of services. St. John's Medical Center, with 367 beds, specializes as a rehabilitation center for Parkinson patients in addition to providing normal hospital services. Freeman Hospital, with 144 beds, specializes in caring for critical patients and provides prenatal and child care as well as a continuing-education program for physicians and surgeons. Oak Hill Osteopathic Hospital, with 98 beds, provides gastroenterological services and a cardiology department. These hospitals are supplemented by several nursing homes with a total of 370 beds, plus two mental-health and retardation diagnostic centers.

Currently, there is one physician for each 1161 persons in the area served by Joplin.

Cultural Activities

Many local events take place at Memorial Hall, which has a seating capacity of 3000. It hosts banquets, sports events, concerts, and community meetings. Spiva Art Center, on the campus of Missouri Southern State College, presents art and educational exhibits and serves Joplin and the surrounding area.

The Joplin Little Theater produces several shows each year for local residents and visitors. The Community Concert Association brings ballet companies, symphony orchestras, and individual musicians to Joplin.

Library services are provided by the public library, which has two branches and a 71,250-volume collection. In addition, Missouri Southern State College has a library with 95,000 volumes. Of special interest is the beautiful Post Memorial Art Reference Library, a noncirculating library open to the public that provides reference services on all aspects of art history, painting, sculpture, architecture, furniture design, and archaeology.

Recreation

There are four 18-hole golf courses — one public and three private — for golfers in the Joplin area. There are also 20 public tennis courts, 13 of which are lighted, and there are numerous private and school-owned courts as well.

Joplin provides 932 acres of public parklands distributed among 20 parks that have a variety of facilities. Eight major lakes and dozens of clear-water streams offer residents a wide variety of water-related recreation. There are four city swimming pools open to the public, and one can also swim at the local lakes.

Government

Joplin operates under the Council-Manager form of government, with a full-time city manager and an elected city council. The city budget is about $12 million, and there are more than 365 city employees.

Water

Joplin's water is soft, neutral, and not fluoridated. It is supplied by the Joplin Water Works Company from Shoal Creek, a clear Ozark stream just south of the city. The plant has access to enough water to generate more than twice the present daily demand, and supply greatly exceeds even peak demand. The water is pure, tasty, and plentiful.

Energy

Electricity is supplied by the Empire District Electric Company. Electricity rates are in the lowest 25% of rates in the United States. Natural-gas service is provided by the Gas Service Company, which supplies natural gas throughout Missouri, Kansas, Oklahoma, and Nebraska. Local coal mines offer low-cost coal for heating.

Utility costs for the average two-bedroom home run about $75 per month.

Television
There are three local television stations and a cable system that provides 27 different program services to local subscribers.

Newspapers
The local daily newspaper is:

The Joplin Globe
Joplin, MO 64801

The *Kansas City Star* and *Times,* the *St. Louis Post-Dispatch,* the *St. Louis Globe-Democrat,* and the *Oklahoma City Oklahoman* are also available locally.

For Further Information

Joplin Chamber of Commerce
112 W. 4th
Joplin, MO 64801

Missouri Division of Tourism
308 E. High St., Box 1055
Jefferson City, MO 65101

Kinston, North Carolina

POPULATION: 25,110 within the city limits
59,819 in Lenoir County

ELEVATION: 44 feet above sea level

Kinston is located on the Neuse River on the coastal plain of North Carolina, between New Bern and Goldsboro, about 60 miles inland from Pamlico Sound on the Atlantic Coast. The countryside is flat, with woods along the banks of the river and between the open fields.

Tobacco is still the chief industry and source of income in Kinston, one of the leading leaf-tobacco markets of the world, though other industries are moving into the area.

Climate

The climate of the coastal plain is modified by the proximity of the Atlantic Ocean, which raises winter temperatures and reduces the average day-to-night temperature range.

Summers are generally warm to hot, with about 45 days with temperatures of 90°F and above and temperatures in the 70s and 80s from April through October. There are about 1450 cooling degree days per year.

Winters are generally mild, with daily ranges from highs in the 50s to lows in the 30s and only about 40 days per year with temperatures of 32°F and below. There are about 3400 heating degree days per year. The first frost comes in early December and the last frost is in early March, resulting in approximately 260 frost-free days in the growing season. Snowfall is seldom more than 4 to 6 inches per year, falling in December through March and seldom remaining on the ground more than a short time.

Precipitation is about 48 inches per year, fairly evenly divided throughout the 12 months, though it is somewhat lighter in April and May and September through December. About 865 million gallons of precipitation per square mile fall in this area each year. Humidity averages about 75%, and there is about 65% of possible sunshine each year.

Winds are generally gentle, southerly in summer and veering to westerly and even northerly in winter.

History

Kinston was established in 1740 by William Heritage, a prominent planter and jurist, as a trading post for planters in the area. Originally it was called Kingston. In 1762 it was authorized as a town by the Royal Governor. The first trustees of the town laid out the streets, which today still bear the names given them by those trustees, in honor of themselves — Caswell, McLewean, Bright, Shine, and Gordon. While bitterness still remained after the American Revolution, the *g* was dropped from the town's name and it became Kinston.

Early industry included a buggy factory and a shoe-manufacturing company. Later Kinston acquired a shipyard and was the site for the building of the Confederate ironclad ship *Neuse*, which was used briefly before the war ended. Today its unrestored hull lies on the bank of the Neuse River a few hundred feet from the site of its launching.

Kinston has long been a transportation center, a meeting place at the convergence of old Indian trails and later, when the first settlers began carving settlements and plantations out of the wilderness, a gateway to the fertile lands and forests of the interior. The river, which once handled considerable traffic, is now so silted up that it is no longer usable for transportation, but it is still a favorite fishing and canoeing waterway for local residents.

For many years Kinston was a one-crop town, dependent entirely on tobacco, but after World War II industry began finding its way to this pleasant and peaceful area.

Economy and Employment

Today, Kinston is still one of the world's leading tobacco centers, but tobacco is no longer the only source of employment. Kinston also produces chemicals, Dacron, textiles, foods, boxes, fertilizers, meats, lumber and wood products, concrete products, and furniture. Agriculture, no less than other industries, has progressed, with a resulting diversification into soybeans, beef, swine, and poultry production.

The active Lenoir County Industrial Development Commission works with firms interested in locating in the area and has been instrumental in bringing in much of the town's new industry.

As a result of the postwar shift toward industry, employers now include: Albain Shirt Co. (men's shirts, 450–500 employees); Austin Carolina (tobacco, 800–1000 seasonal employees); Barrus Construction Co. (paving and grading, 400); Buehler Products, Inc. (electric motors, 225); E. I. DuPont de Nemours (Dacron fiber, 3000); Glen Raven Mills (synthetic yarns, 250); Hampton Industries (shirts, 1200); Joy Manufacturing Co. (cable rubber products, 175); Smithfield Packing Co. (meats, 400); Texfi Knit I (polyester fabrics, 550); and West Co. (stoppers for the pharmaceutical industry, 300).

In addition, there are many smaller businesses, including foundries, feed and seed outlets, lumber companies, concrete-products companies, jewelry manufacturers, and box makers.

Information on the local employment situation can be obtained by writing:

Employment Security Commission
2100 Presbyterian Lane
Kinston, NC 28501

Taxes

North Carolina has a 3% state sales tax, to which Kinston adds a local sales tax of 1%. The state income tax ranges from 2% on the first $2000 earned to 7% on incomes over $10,000, with a $2200 exemption for heads of households and a $700 exemption for each dependent.

Property taxes are currently $1.12 per $100 of assessed value. The tax on a home with a market value of $65,000 would run from $406 to $730 per year, depending on assessed value.

Shopping

Kinston has a good central business and shopping district, plus three excellent suburban shopping centers. Many major chains are represented, and the local stores more than adequately meet the day-to-day needs of local residents.

For wider choices in shopping, Raleigh, the state capital, is about 80 miles to the northwest via an excellent four-lane highway.

Residential Properties

There are two sources of current information on available housing in Kinston — the local newspaper and the local realtors. The chamber of commerce will provide a list of realtors. The *Kinston Free Press* is published daily and carries ads for both rentals and properties for sale. A few typical listings are:

> GOOD STARTER HOME with 3 bedrooms and 1 bath, aluminum siding, oil heat, assumable loan, freshly painted interior. Annual property taxes run $254.33. A bargain at $29,900.
>
> BUILT IN 1948, this 3-bedroom 1-bath brick veneer home has 2 screened porches, well, oil heat, 2-car carport, on 94 × 98 wooded lot. Taxes of $209.94 per year. $30,000.
>
> BEAUTIFUL BRICK HOME with 3 bedrooms, 2 baths, 1537 square feet of living area, on 100 × 200 heavily wooded lot. Taxes are $239.50 per year. Assumable loan of 8½%. New heat pump, fenced back yard. $49,900.
>
> ROOMY 2285-square-foot home with 3 bedrooms, 2 baths, sun room, separate living and dining rooms, garage, oil heat and central air conditioning. Taxes are $400.52 per year and there is an 11% 30-year loan that is assumable. Beautiful trees on 120 × 140 corner lot. $49,900.

Rentals are plentiful and inexpensive. One-bedroom apartments are available for $75 to $150 per month, and two-bedroom apartments or condos are available for $100 to $200.

Safety

The nearest potential manmade hazard is Seymour Johnson Air Force Base, 24 miles to the west, near Goldsboro. As a Tactical Air Command Base, it is a potential military target.

The FBI Crime Index rating is 77 crimes per thousand of population per year. Police service is provided by a 64-employee department with 18 vehicles. Kinston has a Class 4 Fire Insurance Rating, and the local fire department has an extensive fire-prevention and safety program, an ample water supply, and good equipment.

Education

Kinston has a public school system with 9 schools to serve the area, supplemented by 1 private school and 3 parochial schools. There are also 12 day-care centers for younger children.

Higher-education needs in Kinston are served by a school of nursing and a two-year community college. Lenoir Community College has eight modern buildings on its campus, with a Learning Resources Center that houses 40,000 books, 330 periodicals, and 17 newspapers. Its curriculum is shaped to fit the needs of local youth being trained to serve in local business and industry.

East Carolina University, another possibility, is only 28 miles away, in Greenville. It is a state-supported university offering a full four-year program plus graduate programs leading to a variety of doctoral degrees. ECU is only a 30-minute commute from Kinston.

Medical Facilities

Lenoir Memorial Hospital is a nonprofit general hospital serving a wide area with 281 beds and 61 physicians on the staff, most of whom are also in private practice.

Cultural Activities

Kinston is deeply involved in the arts. The Community Council for the Arts, founded in 1965, is dedicated to promoting, stimulating, and coordinating artistic activity in Kinston and Lenoir County. The Arts Center is open to the public daily as a learning center, offering classes in music, dance, sculpture, painting, theater, voice, and weaving. It also has a gallery that exhibits the works of local artists and craftsmen.

Three theater groups serve the community. The Kinston-Lenoir Community Theater presents plays for local residents. The Moppet Theater and the high school theater involve the youth of the community in theatrical productions.

The Community Chorus presents regular concerts, and the annual street fair involves most of the community, either as participants or as viewers. The North Carolina Opera Company and the East Carolina Symphony bring regular concerts to Kinston each year.

Further cultural activities, including drama, concerts, and lectures, are provided at East Carolina University, only 28 miles away.

Recreation

Kinston's recreation department provides a year-round program offering chess, bridge, drama, golf, physical-fitness, day camps, gymnastics, swimming, sewing, basket weaving, yoga, soccer, baseball, football, tennis, karate, badminton, table tennis, volleyball, and more. The city provides 21 lighted tennis courts, 12 lighted athletic fields, one 9-hole golf course, 3 swimming pools, 7 recreation centers, 3 gyms, a ceramic shop, many picnic areas, and a physical-fitness trail.

Private enterprise in Kinston offers two modern bowling alleys, excellent roller-skating facilities, and even flying lessons. Two private country clubs provide golf, tennis, swimming, and other activities for their members. Several stables in the area offer boarding, breeding, and training for horses, and the area specializes in hunting horsemanship. The area has four different show circuits each year.

Hunters will find that Lenoir County is full of game. During certain seasons, hunting for deer, quail, rabbit, doves, squirrels, and raccoons is permitted on nearby public wildlife gamelands for those with special licenses. Fishermen have a broad range of choices, from saltwater fishing along the Atlantic coastline to freshwater fishing on three of the best fishing rivers of the state — the Neuse, the Tar, and the Chowan. Fish in these rivers include striped bass, largemouth bass, crappie, bream, shad, and trout.

Government

Kinston operates under the Council-Manager system, with a full-time city manager supervising the day-to-day operations of the city.

Water

Local tap water, provided by the city of Kinston, is slightly alkaline and very soft. The 865 million gallons of rainfall per square mile per year and the proximity of the Neuse River ensure that the water supply is more than sufficient.

Energy

Electrical energy is supplied by Carolina Power and Light to the city's distribution system. The hydroelectric, nuclear, and fossil-fuel generating plants in the state appear to be adequate for meeting present and immediate future needs. Natural gas is available from the city, but many houses use oil for winter heating.

Utility costs for the average well-insulated 1500-square-foot home run about $100 per month at current utility prices.

Television
Three major network television stations can be received on home antenna systems, and there is a cable system offering subscribers full-channel coverage.

Newspapers
The local daily newspaper is:

The Kinston Free Press
2103 North Queen St.
Kinston, NC 28501

Other newspapers available locally include the *Raleigh News and Observer* and the *Wilmington Star.*

For Further Information

Kinston/Lenoir County Chamber of Commerce
P.O. Box 157
Kinston, NC 18501

North Carolina Division of Travel & Tourism
P.O. Box 15249
Raleigh, NC 17611

Lafayette, Louisiana

POPULATION: 79,511 within the city limits
150,000 within the greater Lafayette area

ELEVATION: 40 feet above sea level

Lafayette is a town of contrasts, a mix of Cajun culture and modern university life, bayou fishing and thriving industry. It is located in the heart of "Acadia country," in south-central Louisiana on Vermilion Bayou, 45 miles north of the Gulf of Mexico and 145 miles west of New Orleans.

Lafayette was originally important as the trading center for an agricultural area growing sugar cane, rice, cattle, cotton, and sweet potatoes. Those items are still produced, but today Lafayette is caught up in the Louisiana oil boom and is considered one of the major oil cities in the nation.

Despite the current boom, the old culture is still very much alive. French is still heard on the streets and in the restaurants, and the Cajun food is still among the best in the world.

Climate

Southern Louisiana is mostly low and level, with elevations generally less than 60 feet above the Gulf of Mexico. Water runoff is by means of numerous sluggish streams, or bayous, that flow through lakes and marshlands into the Gulf.

The rapid industrialization of southern Louisiana is partly due to the mild climate and the unfailing water supply. Precipitation is in the form of rain and is fairly evenly distributed throughout the year, except from July through mid-September when cooling thunderstorms are frequent. Total annual precipitation is about 57 inches. The area receives 1061 million gallons of rain per square mile per year, which is equal to 16.6 million gallons per capita per year.

Summers are long and warm to hot, with normal maximum temperatures above 70°F from March through October. There are some 80 days per year with temperatures of 90°F and above, and temperatures sometimes exceed 100°F for brief periods during June through September. There are about 2900 cooling degree days per year in the area.

Winters are short and mild, with only 1450 heating degree days, and there are seldom more than five days per year with temperatures below 32°F. Even in the coolest months of November through February, the normal daily maximum temperatures are in the middle to high 60s and the minimum temperatures are between the mid-40s and 50s.

Winds are generally gentle, except during occasional tropical storms, and usually blow from the south throughout the year. Tropical storms, sometimes developing into hurricanes, are one of the potential hazards of living in the coastal areas near the Gulf of Mexico. During an 84-year period, 92 tropical cyclones have moved into Louisiana or have come close enough to affect the coastal area. Of these, 29 were of hurricane intensity, with winds of 74 miles per hour or more at some point within the storm area. The tropical-storm period is generally from July through October, peaking in September.

It is reassuring to remember that the chances of any particular storm hitting any particular area are small, and the inland location of Lafayette tends to protect it from the main force of coastal storms. Any hurricane affects only a relatively small area for a brief time, and hurricane frequency is really quite low. Hurricanes do occur, but they are not a good reason to avoid living in southern Louisiana.

History

The colonization of Lafayette began when the Acadians settled in Louisiana after being expelled from Nova Scotia. The story of that exile can be read in Longfellow's famous poem "Evangeline." The Acadians brought with them French culture and the French language. They lived by trapping, fishing, and minor truck farming. From these Acadians, today called Cajuns, came the superb cuisine, the love of independence, and the joy of life that characterize the area.

Originally an Acadian village called Vermilionville, Lafayette began growing when the Southern Pacific railroad built a railhead and division point there in the latter part of the nineteenth century. Growth spurted again when oil was found in the area in the early years of the present century, and when the state began to develop the University of Southwestern Louisiana there. These three influences of transportation, education, and petroleum were the major forces that shaped Lafayette's development from the tiny fur-trading and farming community of a hundred years ago into the busy, modern town of today. A fourth influence on local development came with the addition of light industry.

Economy and Employment

The Heymann Oil Center in Lafayette is sometimes called the Million Dollar Mile and is one of the major oil-industry centers in the Gulf Coast area. There are over 1000 oil-related companies in the Lafayette area, and over half of them are located in this center. Almost every major oil company in the world is represented here. Today Lafayette's largest areas of employment are the petroleum industry, wholesale and retail trade, service industries, and government.

Originally the economy of Lafayette Parish depended on lumbering, and later it was based on sugar cane and cotton. Today agriculture, while still important, has fallen behind oil production and increasing industrialization as an economic force. Crops today include soybeans, rice, cotton, sugar cane, and corn. The beef-cattle industry is developing, and there is a small dairy industry as well.

With its network of good highways and its strategic location, Lafayette serves as a trading area for over 500,000 people. It is a distribution center for building materials, electric appliances, oil, gasoline, coffee, auto parts, canned foods, and many other items.

Industry in the area includes canneries and dehydration facilities for sweet potatoes and other vegetables, and the manufacture of building materials, electrical appliances, auto parts, furniture, door frames, moldings, metal parts and fabrication, millwork, brick and concrete, bakery and creamery products, cordage, and various products for oil fields and marine, industrial, and home use.

Major manufacturers in the area include: American Manufacturing, Inc. (cordage and twine, 160 employees); L. A. Frey & Sons, Inc. (meat packers, 252); Dowwell Fluid Services (chemicals, 250); Reamco, Inc. (oil-field equipment, 280); Union Camp Corp. (lumber and particleboard, 95); and Southern Structures, Inc. (prefabricated modular buildings, 160).

Since 1975, an average of 26,000 new workers a year have found jobs in Lafayette. Even unskilled workers can earn around $15,000 a year, and millionaires are so plentiful that the *New York Times* has featured an article about them.

For current information on the local employment situation, write:

Lafayette Area Office of Employment Security
Lafayette, LA 70503

Taxes

Despite the local wealth, property taxes in Lafayette are moderate. Residential property is assessed at 10% of market value, and a tax exemption is available on homes valued at $50,000 or less. The property tax on a $65,000 home would run about $853 per year.

The combined state and local sales tax is 5%. The state income tax is low, with a maximum of 6% tax on taxable incomes over $50,000 and a $12,000 income exemption for a married head of family. There is no city or parish income tax.

Shopping

Serving a trading area of 500,000 people, and with a large number of millionaires living in the area, Lafayette offers more varied shopping facilities than many cities of several times the population. The principal shopping area is not surprisingly called Oil Center, and there are at least 15 other shopping centers in the community. All of the major retail department-store chains, variety stores, and chain food markets are represented, as well as a wide variety of specialty shops.

Shopping for food is one of the more enjoyable occupations in Lafayette, with many types of seafood, crawfish, peppers, and spices available here that cannot be found elsewhere. For an introduction to the superb Cajun cuisine, there are restaurants in every price range that cater to every taste.

Residential Properties

Because of the current boom in the area, the demand for housing has been exceeding the supply, and higher prices than elsewhere have resulted. Typical ads in the local real estate columns read:

> EXCELLENT CONDITION. Three-bedroom, 2-bath home featuring new carpet, vinyl and wallpaper. Freshly painted inside and out. $76,000.
>
> IN PRESTIGIOUS NEIGHBORHOOD. Large four-bedroom 2-bath with den, large living and dining combination and spacious country kitchen. Fenced back yard. Monthly notes of only $581 to qualified buyer. Price is $180,000.
>
> MOM WILL LOVE this spacious kitchen and then enjoy the large family room. Four bedrooms, 2 baths. $85,000.
>
> NEAT AND CLEAN. Two bedrooms, 1 bath, garage. Ideal starter home. $39,900.

Apartments are plentiful but expensive, with one-bedroom apartments renting for $200 to $400 per month and two-bedroom apartments or condos renting for $350 to $700 per month.

Safety

There are no manmade hazards nearby, not even air pollution, and the only possible natural hazard is the unlikely possibility that one will be in the direct path of a hurricane. The crime rate in the area is moderate, with an FBI Crime Index rating of 90 crimes per thousand of population per year. The Lafayette police department has 186 full-time officers and the fire department has 205 employees. The Fire Insurance Rating is a low Class 2.

Education

Schools in Lafayette range from nursery schools and day-care centers to 23 elementary schools, 8 junior high schools, and 5 high schools in the public school system. In addition, there are 14 parochial elementary schools and 6 parochial high schools. Lafayette also has a special program designed to locate, and provide services for, the gifted as well as for those who are mentally impaired or retarded.

Higher education in Lafayette is provided by the University of

Southwestern Louisiana, which has an enrollment of some 15,000 and a curriculum covering liberal arts, engineering, commerce, and science. Graduate degrees are available in 36 areas, including the state's only Ph.D. program in computer science.

Lafayette Parish Vocational School offers cooperative education in child care, food service, office education, trade, and industry. Training is provided in everything from air conditioning to welding.

Louisiana State University, in Baton Rouge, is only an hour's drive to the north and offers excellent graduate and undergraduate programs.

Medical Facilities

Lafayette has four hospitals with a combined capacity of 793 beds. There are a number of specialized treatment centers, including centers for mental health and for handicapped children.

Cultural Activities

The Lafayette public library system consists of a central library, seven branches, and one bookmobile, with a total of over 150,000 volumes. During the school year, the large and varied collection in the library of the University of Southwestern Louisiana is open free of charge to residents of Louisiana.

The Natural History Museum and Planetarium has a year-round series of programs in the fields of astronomy, antiques, energy, archaeology, music, and local geography. It sponsors over 70 workshops and field trips.

There are also the Lafayette Museum and the Wildlife Museum, both open to the public. The Art Center for Southwestern Louisiana has both permanent and rotating exhibits. Musical and theatrical groups regularly schedule performances in Lafayette.

The area is known for its many festivals, including the Festival Acadiens, the International Rice Festival (in nearby Crowley), the Breaux Bridge Crawfish Festival, the Mardi Gras, the Cajun Music Festival, the Rayne Frog Festival, the Louisiana Sugar Cane Festival, and the Dairy Festival and Fair in Abbeville.

Recreation

The warm climate permits residents and visitors to enjoy a wide variety of recreational activities throughout the year. The Lafayette Parks and Recreation Department has a well-organized sports program that includes baseball, soccer, tennis, martial arts, boxing, and swimming.

There are two public 18-hole golf courses — City Park and Les

Vieux Chenes de Lafayette. In addition, there are several private clubs that have golf courses. There are also many private health clubs and spas in the area that offer tennis, racquetball, swimming, saunas, whirlpool baths, and various health and physical-fitness services.

The area has an abundance of places suitable and available for boating, camping, and fishing, many within minutes of Lafayette. For the hunter, the state has set aside 35 wildlife-management areas. A list of these is available from the Louisiana Department of Wildlife and Fisheries. Fishing is available on the many bayous, lakes, and bays within a forty-mile radius, and deep-sea fishing in the Gulf of Mexico can be arranged in Morgan City, 65 miles to the southeast.

Spectator sports are provided by the local university's football, basketball, track, and other teams, which compete in the Southland Conference. Louisiana State University (LSU), an hour to the north in Baton Rouge, competes in the Southeastern Conference and against national opponents.

Government

Like most towns and cities in Louisiana, Lafayette has a Mayor-Council form of government, with an elected council constituting the legislative branch of local government and an elected mayor serving as the chief executive and head of the executive branch.

Water

Tap water is neutral, soft, and plentiful, with 16.6 million gallons of precipitation per capita per year in the area.

Energy

Located in the heart of an oil and gas area, Lafayette has plentiful energy. Within the city limits electricity is supplied by the city of Lafayette. Natural gas is supplied by Trans-Louisiana Gas Company. Current rate information can be obtained by writing the City of Lafayette, 733 Jefferson St., Lafayette, LA 70503.

Utility costs for an average two-to-three-bedroom home average about $100 per month at current rates.

Television

There are four local television stations, plus a cable system that provides coverage of all major networks and programs.

Newspapers
The local daily newspaper is:

The Daily Advertiser
221 Jefferson St.
Lafayette, LA 70501

There are several weekly newspapers in the area, and many major newspapers, such as the *New Orleans Times-Picayune*, are available for home delivery.

For Further Information

Greater Lafayette Chamber of Commerce
P.O. Drawer 51307
Lafayette, LA 70505

Office of Tourism
P.O. Box 44291
Baton Rouge, LA 70804

Van Eaton & Romero
Homes for Better Living
3703 Johnston St.
Lafayette, LA 70503

Van Eaton & Romero will send any prospective resident an excellent little book entitled *A Newcomer's Guide to Lafayette.* It's free and well worth asking for.

Lake Charles, Louisiana

POPULATION: 75,621 within the city limits
160,000 in Calcasieu Parish

ELEVATION: 20 feet above sea level

Lake Charles is located in southwestern Louisiana on the Calcasieu River 37 miles from the Gulf of Mexico. Houston is 141 miles to the west and New Orleans 205 miles to the east. It is a seaport with a 35-foot-deep channel connecting it to the Gulf and is the trading center for a timber and rice-growing area surrounded by large deposits of sulfur, natural gas, and petroleum.

Lake Charles is only about 120 years old — not very old as towns go in Louisiana. It is not as busy and prosperous as some other places in the state, where the offshore oil boom has changed life so drastically in the past few years. It does not have the climate of Southern California. But it is a town in which everything seems to fit together and work well. The economy is thriving, a mix of light and heavy industry, shipping, railroad transportation, and agriculture. It has good communications systems, medical facilities, educational institutions, and recreational opportunities.

Climate

Lake Charles is located on the low coastal plain adjacent to the Gulf of Mexico. The Gulf is the primary influence on the climate of the area, bringing southerly winds most of the year and an average humidity of 75% or higher, as well as annual precipitation of some 56 inches. Precipitation is fairly evenly spread out throughout the year, with frequent thunderstorms in the summer months. There is about 63% of possible sunshine each year.

The climate is warm to hot and humid, with seldom more than 7 days per year with temperatures of 32°F or below and a 309-day frost-free growing period. Summers, which last from May into October, are long and hot, with daytime temperatures in the 80s and 90s and nighttime temperatures in the 70s. There are 90 days per year with temperatures of 90°F and above and some 3000 cooling degree days each year.

Winters are short and mild, with normal temperatures ranging from daytime highs in the 60s to nighttime lows in the 40s from December through February. During this period, residents can expect five or six northers, during which arctic air blows down on strong north winds and drops temperatures sharply for a few days. Snow is almost unknown. There are only 1200 heating degree days per year.

Tornadoes are very rare in this Gulf Coast area, but tropical cyclones (hurricanes) can bring high winds and heavy rains. Lake Charles's inland location provides considerable protection from the worst effects of hurricanes striking the coast.

History

Originally, Indians lived and traded in the Lake Charles area. The first white settlers were a married couple named LeBleu from Boudreaux, France, who arrived in 1771 and lived peacefully among the Indians for many years until other white settlers began to move in. One of the early settlers who joined the LeBleu family was Charles Sallier, also from France. He settled near the shores of Lake Charles and gave his name to the lake and the community, which were both originally called Charley's Lake and later formalized into Lake Charles.

The Spaniards called the river flowing through Lake Charles the

Rio Hondo, but the French settlers preferred the Indian name *Quelqueshue*, which meant "Crying Eagle." From this the name Calcasieu evolved.

Growth was slow until a lumber mill and schooner dock were established in 1855. This began a profitable trade with Texas and Mexican ports. When the railroad arrived, a new era really began. By 1866 the community had a newspaper, a bank, and a chamber of commerce. A few years later, a new industry, a rice mill, gave impetus to rice growing in the area.

Years passed and little more happened until the 1920s, when the people of the town raised the money for dredging a channel to the Gulf of Mexico and built docks on Lake Charles, establishing the town as a deepwater port.

With the development of oil and gas fields in Louisiana, the petrochemical industry began to develop in Lake Charles, and today it is one of the most important parts of the economy.

Economy and Employment

Industry in southwest Louisiana has provided a solid base for a healthy economy. The petrochemical industry is the major source of employment, and many manufacturers use the abundant mineral resources in the area.

Heavy industry provides the primary base for economic stability. This is supplemented by agriculture, including the raising of cattle and horses and the growing of grains, soybeans, and timber, as well as by marine industries and fisheries. For many years the nation's number-one rice port, Lake Charles is now a major importing center for the southern United States, handling more than 3.5 million tons of freight annually.

Some of the major employers in the area include: Cities Service Corp. (petroleum refining, 2100 employees); Pittsburgh Plate Glass Co. (glass, 2100); Firestone Corp. (synthetic rubber, 500); American Press (newspaper, 170); Coca-Cola (125); Borden's (milk products, 100); Olin Corp. (chemicals, 1100); Hercules Corp. (chemicals, 500); United Gas Pipe Line Co. (90); and Continental Oil (petroleum distribution, 100).

There are six local employment agencies, and the chamber of commerce will provide their addresses. For current job information, write:

Louisiana Department of Employment Security
1028 Enterprise Blvd.
Lake Charles, LA 70601

Taxes

Louisiana's state income tax ranges from 2% on the first $2000 of taxable income to a top rate of 6% on taxable income over $50,000 per year. The combined city and state sales tax is 5%. Property taxes are low and work out to about $203 per year for a home selling for $65,000.

Shopping

As a result of today's prosperity, residents can find almost anything they need or want locally, but for wider choices Houston is a three-hour drive to the west and New Orleans is four hours to the east.

Residential Properties

With the current economic growth in Lake Charles, housing is not as plentiful or easy to find as in some less-prosperous places. However, it can be located, and the newspaper real estate ads are the best source of current information. A few typical current listings are:

> FIRST HOME in Sulphur [10 miles west of Lake Charles]. Assume mortgage balance of $12,500, with payments of $175 on this small frame house. Total $18,500.
>
> CHARMING 3-bedroom 1-bath home in choice subdivision away from traffic and industry. $35,000.
>
> HANDSOME CEDAR HOME near high school. 3 bedrooms, 2 baths, fireplace, huge covered patio, lovely trees on large lot. $65,000.
>
> NEW BRICK HOME with 3 bedrooms, 2 baths and professionally landscaped yard. $81,900.

Rentals are plentiful, with one-bedroom apartments renting for $185 to $325 per month, and two-bedroom units for $200 to $550.

Safety

Lake Charles has a low FBI Crime Index rating of 55 crimes per thousand of population per year. Police service is provided by a department with 143 employees, 25 patrol vehicles, 13 detective units, 2 motorcycles, and 2 parking-regulation vehicles. Certified officers have to complete a six-week training course at Louisiana State University and one year of in-service training.

Fire protection is provided by the Lake Charles fire department, which has 134 employees, five fire stations, six fire-engine companies, two ladder companies, and several reserve units. The Fire Insurance Rating is Class 2.

There are no known nearby manmade hazards.

Education

The Lake Charles public school system is part of the Calcasieu Parish school system and provides public education from kindergarten through the twelfth grade. The public schools are supplemented by the Episcopal Day School (grades one through eight) and several Catholic schools, including St. Louis High School.

Sowela Technical Institute and Delta School of Business provide specialized vocational and technical training.

McNeese State University, in Lake Charles, is a fully accredited university providing undergraduate and graduate education in the fields of business, education, engineering, humanities, sciences, and the arts.

For a broader choice of fields or for graduate studies to the doctoral level, Louisiana State University, in Baton Rouge, is 125 miles to the east.

Medical Facilities

There are three full-service hospitals in Lake Charles and another in Sulphur, 10 miles to the west, providing a total of 838 beds and 84 bassinets. There are also seven nursing homes with a total of 1076 beds. Lake Charles has 161 physicians representing virtually every field of medicine. There are also 93 dentists in local practice.

For the rare case that cannot be handled locally, both Houston and New Orleans have some of the finest medical facilities in the world.

Cultural Activities

Art, theater, music, and dance are all important contributors to the cultural atmosphere of the city. The Lake Charles Art Associates, the Artists Club of the Gulf Coast, and the Arts Club of West Calcasieu provide art activities and exhibitions throughout the year.

The Civic Symphony Orchestra presents three annual concerts, and the Community Concert Series brings in touring groups and soloists for local performances. Each year the Messiah Chorus of over 230 voices stages its famous Handel oratorio, which is broadcast nationwide.

Two theater groups are active, providing adult and children's theater and classes in theater arts. The Lake Charles Civic Ballet and several other dance and ballet organizations bring modern and classical dance to the area.

Library facilities include several public-library branches and mobile units. McNeese State University has a rare-book collection. Combined, the Calcasieu Parish Library and the McNeese State University library offer over 350,000 volumes for public use.

Recreation

Because of the mild climate, most of the recreational opportunities in the Lake Charles area are out-of-doors. After work, there is always time for fishing, golfing, or strolling on the beach.

A little farther away, sports fishing on the Gulf of Mexico offers tarpon, marlin, barracuda, snapper, bluefish, and many more. Good freshwater fishing is found in nearby bayous, rivers, and lakes. Crabbing and shrimping are as close as Lake Charles and the Gulf of Mexico, and speckled trout run strong in big Calcasieu Lake. Area waterways offer boatmen more than 50 miles on which to travel. Charter boats are available for group fishing trips in the Gulf. Water-skiing, powerboating, sailing, swimming, and skin diving are all popular and readily available.

Camping and picnicking are always popular at the nearby parks and along the Calcasieu River. Duck hunting is very popular in the area, and at two large game preserves nearby, hunters can find quail, doves, and deer.

The city maintains 30 parks and playgrounds covering more than 561 acres and offering year-round programs in a wide variety of sports and hobbies.

Golfers have five 18-hole courses to choose from, four of them public and one, at Lake Charles Golf & Country Club, private. These are supplemented by a putting course and several driving ranges. Other available activities include bowling, baseball, softball, tennis (26 courts), and swimming in 4 local pools. There are also several sports clubs for hunters, shooters, boaters, yachtsmen, water-skiing enthusiasts, and fishermen.

Government

Lake Charles operates under a Mayor-Council system, with a full-time mayor as the chief executive and a seven-man council as the part-time legislative body.

Water

Water is supplied by the Greater Lake Charles Water Company and comes from numerous local wells. The tap water is alkaline, soft, and not fluoridated.

Energy

Electricity is supplied locally by the Gulf States Utility Company from fossil-fueled generating plants, mainly powered by the plentiful natural gas in the area. Natural gas is supplied by Entex, Inc.

Utility costs, while rising, are still low in comparison to the rest of the nation and run about $90 per month for the average two-to-three-bedroom home.

Television

There is one local television station, an NBC affiliate. A cable system provides full-channel coverage to subscribers. Because of the flat terrain, stations from Beaumont, Port Arthur, Lafayette, and even Houston can usually be picked up by home antenna systems.

Newspapers

The local daily newspaper is:

The Lake Charles American Press
P.O. Box 2893
Lake Charles, LA 70602

The *Beaumont Enterprise* is also delivered locally.

For Further Information

Greater Lake Charles Chamber of Commerce
P.O. Box 3109
Lake Charles, LA 70602

Louisiana Office of Tourism
P.O. Box 44291
Baton Rouge, LA 70804

The Newcomers Club
℅ Michelle Hale
1531 Janet Drive
Lake Charles, LA 70605

For information you can't get through the chamber of commerce, ask Michelle to help.

Las Cruces, New Mexico

POPULATION: 44,916 within the city limits
69,500 in the area

ELEVATION: 3896 feet above sea level

Las Cruces is located in south-central New Mexico at the junction of two major interstate highways, 45 miles north of El Paso and 225 miles south of Albuquerque, in the heart of the fertile Mesilla Valley. It is surrounded by mountain ranges on three sides: the Organ Mountains, the San Andres Mountains, and the Franklin Mountains on the east; the Caballo Mountains on the north; and the foothills of the Goodsight Mountains on the west. The closest are the Organ Mountains, which rise to a majestic 9119 feet at the eastern edge of the city.

To the west, the Rio Grande (the Rio Bravo del Norte, to the

Mexicans) flows southward through the Mesilla Valley toward El Paso, where it turns eastward and forms the boundary between Texas and Mexico.

Climate

The key to the prosperity of Las Cruces is the moderate climate, which provides four well-defined seasons and few extremes. With low rainfall and 85% of possible sunshine annually, agriculture would be difficult without the water from the Rio Grande for irrigation.

Maximum temperatures range from the 70s in March and April to the high 80s and 90s from May through September, followed by cooler weather in October. There are over 100 days per year with temperatures of 90°F or above, though the heat is not unpleasant since the summertime daytime humidity is only 25% to 30%. Annual humidity averages only a low 40%. There are about 2000 cooling degree days per year.

Precipitation is seldom more than about 8 inches per year, and most of that falls from June through October, frequently in the form of thundershowers, of which there are some 40 per year. Snowfall is less than 2 inches per year and disappears quickly.

Winters are mild to cold, depending on the arctic air masses that pass over the continent. There are usually only 52 days per year with temperatures of 32°F or below, though below-zero temperatures have been recorded. The last frost usually comes around the end of March and the first one around the end of October, with 200 days between them. The area has about 3000 heating degree days per year.

Tornadoes are rare. Winter winds from the north and west can be stiff and uncomfortable, but summer winds are generally from the southeast and gentle.

History

Indian villages were in the Las Cruces area long before 1535 when Álvar Núñez Cabeza de Vaca led a group of Spanish explorers through the pass at El Paso and up the Rio Grande. Later, Coronado and the conquistadors marched through the Mesilla Valley, but it was not until 1598 that the first colonists, led by Don Juan de Oñate, moved into the area. The Indians found the new settlement on the Rio Grande a fine source of loot, and their constant raids caused the Spanish to build cavalry forts and stockades to protect the settlers.

The name Las Cruces dates back to 1830 when a group of 40

travelers from Taos camped in the area and were massacred by Apache Indians. A field of crosses marked the burial ground of these travelers, and those who later traveled El Camino Real (the Royal Highway) westward came to know the spot as Las Cruces — The Place of the Crosses.

The area was initially a Spanish possession, then became a part of Mexico. In 1848 the United States acquired it by the Treaty of Guadalupe Hidalgo. The townsite of Las Cruces was surveyed the following year. Las Cruces officially became a town in October of 1907.

Economy and Employment

Agriculture was the first industry in Las Cruces, and today it is still an important part of the local economy. Irrigated from the Rio Grande, local crops include onions, lettuce, tomatoes, alfalfa, cotton, and pecans. One of the most valued crops is chili peppers, grown in many varieties and processed by four local companies.

Las Cruces is the marketing center of southwestern New Mexico, second only to Albuquerque as the leading business community in the state. Employment opportunities include many jobs in both wholesale and retail trade and many service industries.

The major employer in the area is the government. Many Las Cruces residents work at White Sands Missile Range or Holloman Air Force Base. Some 8000 residents of Las Cruces are employed at the missile range, and another 2000 military personnel live in the city. New Mexico State University is the next largest employer, with 6000 employees, including the teaching staff.

Memorial General Hospital employs 735. Other employers include: L'EGGS Products (hosiery, 870 employees); Stahmann Farms Pecan Products (450); City of Las Cruces (650); Wells Lamont Corp. (work gloves, 135); Sandyland Nursery (100); SEMCO Manufacturing, Inc. (sound control products, 100); and Furtex West, Inc. (highpile synthetic fabrics, 100). In addition, various contractors at White Sands employ another 600.

Taxes

New Mexico has a 3.5% sales tax. The state income tax ranges from 0.6% on the first $2000 of taxable income to 6.7% on taxable income above $100,000.

The real property tax rate is $3.271 per $100 of assessed value within the city and $2.319 per $100 in the unincorporated areas. Assessment is based on one-third of true market value. Thus the taxes on a $65,000 home within the city limits would run about $710 per year.

Shopping

There is a large and busy downtown shopping area with many excellent stores. In addition, there are seven suburban shopping centers, the largest being Town North with 28 stores. Retail outlets include many chain stores such as Safeway, J. C. Penney, White House, Skagg's, Albertson's, TG&Y, Piggly Wiggly, Sears, Montgomery Ward, K-Mart, Thrifty Drug, and Gibson's.

As a trade and shopping center for a large area, Las Cruces offers shopping choices that are normally quite adequate, but for more variety, El Paso is only 45 miles to the south via an excellent freeway.

Residential Properties

Housing in Las Cruces ranges from old but solid homes built in the 1920s and 1930s to brand-new modern homes. Prices range accordingly. Examples of current listings are:

> TOP OF THE LINE custom brick home for the discriminating buyer, only 2 miles north on 2 irrigated acres. 3 bedrooms, 2 with private baths. 3 fireplaces, study, owner financing. $98,000.
>
> OLD ADOBE on a large grassy lot with 3 bedrooms, country kitchen, dining room, fireplace in living room. Recently remodeled. $43,000.
>
> STARTER HOME with 3 bedrooms and 1 bath on fenced lot. $29,500.
>
> FOR FAMILY AND ENTERTAINING. Lovely 4-bedroom, 3-bath home with magnificent view of the mountains. Large living room, formal dining room, screened porch, good assumable loan. $87,500.

Apartments and house rentals are scarce at the present time. One-bedroom apartments cost from $180 to $250 per month, and two-bedroom apartments are $225 to $300. The chamber of commerce will send for the asking a free copy of *Southern New Mexico Homes Illustrated,* a biweekly publication full of real estate ads.

Safety

The FBI Crime Index rating for Las Cruces is 89 crimes per thousand of population per year. There are about 200 employees in the combined police and fire department.

Holloman Air Force Base, at Alamogordo, 66 miles to the northeast, Fort Bliss, 45 miles southeast at El Paso, and White Sands

Missile Range, over 60 miles to the northeast, are potential military targets, but fortunately there are mountain ranges between Las Cruces and all three locations, so the town should be relatively safe in the event of an attack. There are no other known manmade or natural hazards in the area.

Education

Las Cruces is served by 15 kindergartens, 15 elementary schools, 5 junior high schools, 2 high schools, 3 private and parochial schools, and the Doña Ana County vocational and technical school.

Higher education is represented by New Mexico State University, which has 12,500 students and a broad curriculum. Located on a 6250-acre campus, it offers five undergraduate colleges, a graduate school, and a division of continuing education. There are over 100 undergraduate degree programs in 11 major areas. Graduate programs offer 34 degrees at the master's level and 17 at the doctoral level. Because of its proximity to White Sands Missile Range, the university has one of the world's most extensive collections of photographs of planetary objects.

Medical Facilities

Las Cruces has a modern hospital with 183 beds that is currently being expanded to accommodate another 103 beds. There are 77 doctors and 28 dentists in the community.

For further medical service, El Paso, only 45 miles away, has 14 hospitals with over 2000 beds and provides every type of medical care.

Cultural Activities

The Thomas Branigan Memorial Library serves the community with 77,240 volumes, and the New Mexico State University library, which is open to the public, has an additional 680,000 volumes.

The university offers and sponsors concerts, symphonic groups, lectures, plays, art exhibits, readings, choral groups, and chamber-music groups.

Las Cruces has a community theater group that performs about five productions per year. There are several community concert groups, as well as associations of writers, artists, and musicians.

Recreation

Organized recreational facilities in Las Cruces include an auto race-track, 2 bowling alleys, 14 parks, 17 racquetball courts, 40 tennis courts, 2 skating rinks, 15 ball fields, 5 swimming pools, and 6 golf courses. For those who prefer to make their own recreation, the Rio Grande provides many opportunities, with picnic spots, swimming, and occasional canoe races and downstream rafting.

White Sands, a national monument as well as a missile range, includes 244 square miles of pure white gypsum sand in dunes that rise as high as 45 feet. It offers many recreational opportunities, from photography to sand surfing and painting.

To the east, in the high, cool pine country, is Lincoln National Forest, which offers camping, picnicking, hunting, fishing, hiking, boating, and even winter skiing.

Elephant Butte Reservoir, 53 miles to the north on Interstate 25, is the largest and most popular water-recreation area in the state. It offers boating, fishing, water-skiing, and swimming, as well as camping along the shores.

For a taste of another culture, Juarez, Mexico, is just across the river from El Paso and offers dog and horse racing in addition to shopping and a wide choice of Mexican restaurants. And speaking of food, the real connoisseurs of Mexican-American food agree that the Mexican food in southeastern New Mexico is the best.

Government

The city is governed by the Council-Manager system.

Water

The local tap water is alkaline, hard, and not fluoridated, and is supplied by the city of Las Cruces from 23 deep wells with a daily capacity of 22 million gallons — a bit above the maximum daily peak load.

Energy

El Paso Electric Company supplies electricity to the area, and El Paso Natural Gas Company provides natural gas to the city's distribution system. Rates for both can be obtained from the Las Cruces chamber of commerce. For heating other than natural gas, many homes use fuel oil, which is available locally from several sources, and coal, which comes from northern New Mexico. Utility costs for an average two-to-three-bedroom home run about $100 per month.

Television

There is one local television station, and most of the El Paso stations can be received with adequate antennas. A cable system offers 12 channels to local subscribers.

Newspapers
The local daily newspaper is:

The Las Cruces Sun News
Las Cruces, NM 88001

In addition there is a weekly, the *Las Cruces Bulletin,* and the *El Paso Times* is available for home delivery.

For Further Information

The Las Cruces Chamber of Commerce
Drawer 519
Las Cruces, NM 88004

Tourist Division
Bataan Memorial Building
Commerce & Industry
Santa Fe, NM 87503

State Park Commission
P.O. Box 1147
Santa Fe, NM 87501

Lewiston, Idaho

POPULATION: 27,972 within the city limits
31,600 in Nez Perce County
6900 in Clarkston, Washington (across the river)

ELEVATION: 738 to 1600 feet above sea level

Lewiston is located on the western border of north-central Idaho at the confluence of the Snake and Clearwater rivers, approximately 110 miles south of Coeur d'Alene and Spokane. Mountains rise sharply to the east, high prairie areas are to the north and south, and the Snake River valley trails off to the west. The Clearwater River valley cuts eastward into the mountains at the north edge of town.

An older section of town, an area of tree-lined streets, pleasant parks, and a mix of old and new housing, is situated on the bluff overlooking the two rivers. Lewis-Clark State College is located here. Lewiston is a business, trade, and shopping center for a large area with a population of some 133,000.

Climate

The rugged Bitterroot Mountain chain rises in the northeastern part of Idaho, forming the boundary between Idaho and Montana and providing a barrier to the free flow of air from the north. The lowest part of the state is Lewiston, at the confluence of the Snake and Clearwater rivers, and the highest point is 12,655 feet at Mt. Borah in Custer County. Although the Lewiston area is 300 miles from the Pacific Ocean, it is nevertheless influenced by the maritime air borne eastward on the prevailing westerly winds. Winters, particularly, have greater cloudiness and greater precipitation because of this Pacific air.

Since elevation has much to do with annual average temperatures, Lewiston has the highest average in the state, but this does not mean that the winters are warm. Winters in the Lewiston area are generally cold, though sometimes broken by mild spells. From November through March, nighttime temperatures average below freezing and daytime temperatures range from the low 30s to the high 40s. During winter blizzards, temperatures can drop to as low as −22°F. Normal winters have 5550 heating degree days and 101 days with temperatures 32°F and below. The first frost arrives in mid-October and the last frost seldom comes before the end of April, allowing for about 171 days of growing season.

Summers are warm to hot, with cool nights. Highs as high as 109°F have been recorded, but normal highs range from 70°F in May to 88°F in July. Summer nights are usually cool, with temperatures in the 40s and 50s, though they sometimes drop to near-freezing as late as June. There are usually no more than 500 cooling degree days per year and only around 36 days with temperatures of 90°F and above.

Precipitation is light, averaging 16 to 20 inches per year, fairly well divided among the months, except for July through September, which are drier. Winter snowfall averages around 24 inches, falling mostly in November through March. Humidity ranges from 71% in the early mornings to a low of 46% in the afternoons. There is normally about 66% of possible sunshine each year.

Winds in winter are variable, generally from the south through southeast. Summer winds are westerly, as a rule.

History

The area around Lewiston is the home of the Nez Perce Indians. The first white men known to pass through this area were Lewis and Clark, in the course of their westward explorations. They camped at the junction of the Clearwater and Snake rivers on October 10, 1805, and again a year later on their return.

For the next 30 years, the legendary mountain men were the only white men to visit the area. Then, in 1835, the first permanent settlement was started about 12 miles south of today's Lewiston. Here a pioneering couple founded a mission, farmed, and taught school for the Indians.

More traders and trappers visited the area, and by the time Elias Davidson Pierce came through in search of gold in 1860, a large reservation had been set aside for the Nez Perce. Pierce illegally entered their reservation and found gold on the north fork of the Clearwater River. The resulting flood of gold miners from California and the East resulted in the founding of Lewiston in 1861. Lewiston, which is located at the head of navigation on the Snake River, began as a seaport and distribution point for the miners. It is the farthest inland of all ports in the Pacific Northwest, but it is nonetheless classified as a seaport.

In 1863 Congress created the Idaho Territory, an area including what is now Idaho, Montana, and most of Wyoming, and the new territorial governor named Lewiston as the state capital. By 1865, southern Idaho had grown so much that it had enough voting power to move the state capital from Lewiston to Boise. For some time thereafter there was a legal battle over possession of the state seal and the state archives. Boise eventually won.

The Nez Perce Indians resented the reduction of their reservation and the white man's refusal to stay out. This finally led to violence, and in 1877 the Nez Perce won a fleeting victory at White Bird Canyon, just south of Lewiston. Federal troops pursued the Indians, driving them into northern Montana, then to Oklahoma and Kansas. Eventually they were permitted to return to their Idaho reservation.

Meanwhile the battle between northern and southern Idaho continued, with northern Idaho proposing to annex itself to the state of Washington. Washington rejected this idea and Congress began to fight to retain Idaho intact. In 1890 Idaho became the forty-third state. Lewiston continued its growth as a seaport serving a largely agricultural area, even though mining continued.

Economy and Employment

Lewiston's port handles barges with capacities of up to 12,000 tons carrying cargo to and from ports all over the world. The major downstream cargoes are grain and wood products, with grain shipments exceeding one million tons per year. A number of grain terminals, bulk loaders, and container-handling facilities have been built on a site facing the Clearwater River near its junction with the Snake River.

Today's economy is diversified and soundly based. Major areas of employment include wholesale and retail trade, service industries, government, education, lumber and timber products, and paper and allied products.

The largest single employer in Lewiston is Potlach Corporation (lumber, plywood, paperboard, and tissue products, 2700 employees). Other major employers include: Omark Industries (primers and bullets for ammunition, 555); St. Joseph's Hospital (347); City of Lewiston (250); Camas Prairie Railroad (223); and Twin City Food, Inc. (food processing, 350). Other area employers are engaged in the manufacture of electronic components, milk products, bread, signs, and building supplies.

Taxes

Idaho has a 3% state sales tax. The state income tax is higher than in many states, starting at 2% on the first $1000 of taxable income and climbing to 7.5% on incomes over $5000.

Property taxes in Idaho are limited by law to 1% of full market value, so the maximum allowable tax on a $65,000 home would be $650.

Shopping

Since Lewiston serves as the shopping and trading center for a market area containing 133,000 people, it has better shopping facilities than most towns of its size. Supplementing the downtown shopping district are several shopping centers: Southgate, with 10 stores; Sunset, with 11; and Town & Country, with 3. Just across the Washington border, Clarkston's downtown center has 5 stores. Most stores remain open Monday and Friday evenings. Retail outlets include Sears, Montgomery Ward, Radio Shack, Albertson's, Payless, IGA, Firestone, and several western chains such as Great Western and Lewis & Clark.

Spokane, 114 miles to the north with a population of 341,000, offers a wider choice for shoppers needing more than local stores can provide.

Residential Properties

Housing is relatively inexpensive in Lewiston, with homes ranging in price from $24,000 upward.

CLOSE-IN COTTAGE with 2 bedrooms, spacious living room and dining area, full basement. Owner financing. $35,000.

SWEEPING VIEWS of valley from 3-bedroom 2-bath home with recreation room and another bath in lower level. Fireplaces up and down. Nearly 1500 square feet with a full basement. $78,500.

SMALL BUT COZY one-bedroom cottage with fireplace on large tree-shaded lot. Only $28,700.

FORTY ACRES with 3000-square-foot solar home with copper plumbing, double-pane windows. Two springs on land, easy drive to town. $100,000, with owner financing.

LESS THAN RENTING to live in this mobile home with double insulation, electric heat, fireplace. Utilities seldom exceed $50 per month. $13,500.

The Multiple Listing Service of Lewiston and Asotin County, Washington, publishes a monthly *Seaport Homefinder* that lists homes currently available in the area. Ask the Lewiston chamber of commerce for a copy.

Rentals are available in Lewiston, with one-bedroom apartments renting for $200 to $295 per month. Two-bedroom apartments or condos cost about $225 to $425 per month.

Safety

The FBI Crime Index rating for Lewiston is a low 56 crimes per thousand of population per year. The police department has 53 employees and eight patrol cars, and the fire department has four stations with 46 full-time personnel and 25 active and 20 standby volunteers. The Fire Insurance Rating is Class 4.

There are no nearby manmade hazards closer than the nuclear power plant and storage facilities located at Richland, Washington, 110 miles to the west.

Education

The Lewiston public school system operates seven elementary schools, two junior high schools, and one high school, providing education from kindergarten through the twelfth grade. Five parochial schools also provide schooling for all grades.

Lewis-Clark State College, in Lewiston, is a small state-supported four-year college with about 2400 students. It was founded in 1893 as a teachers' college and has since expanded to include nursing, business administration, criminal justice, and vocational training in its curriculum. Students may work toward a one-year vocational diploma, a two-year associate degree, or a four-year baccalaureate degree.

The University of Idaho, located in Moscow, Idaho, only 30 miles to the north, offers undergraduate and graduate degrees to the doctoral level.

Eight miles west of Moscow, in Pullman, Washington, Washington State University offers a complete curriculum for undergraduate degrees and graduate degrees to the doctoral level, to a student body of some 17,500.

Medical Facilities

St. Joseph's Hospital serves the area with a staff of 60 physicians and dentists, 347 employees, and 125 beds. There are about 100 physicians and dentists in private practice in the area, many of whom are also on the hospital staff. Other health facilities include three nursing homes and a city health department that provides a variety of services.

Cultural Activities

Lewiston has two libraries open to the general public: Lewiston City Library, which houses 55,000 volumes, and the Nez Perce County Free Library, which has 56,363 volumes.

The Community Concert Association brings concerts and performers to the area each year, and the Symphony Orchestra provides regular concerts. The Civic Theater presents live theater, and the community is also served by the Lewis-Clark Art Association, the Valley Art Center, and Civic Arts, Inc.

Recreation

The recreational opportunities in the area are perhaps Lewiston's chief attraction, particularly for people who love the out-of-doors. The city offers two public and two private 18-hole golf courses, several football, baseball, and softball fields, three bowling alleys, numerous tennis courts, and three swimming pools.

All four seasons permit outdoor recreation. Fishermen can take steelhead, salmon, rainbow trout, smallmouth bass, and sturgeon from nearby waters. Hunters can find moose, goats, bighorn sheep, black bears, grouse, ducks, ring-necked pheasants, and valley and mountain quail.

Skiing and snowmobiling are available nearby during the winter. The Clearwater and Snake rivers provide boating almost all year round, including sailboating. Those who wish may simply pack a picnic lunch or dinner and head for one of the many parks on either the Clearwater or the Snake; a favorite stream; or a nearby campground. Those who want more excitement can find it in a whitewater canoe trip on the Snake River from Lewiston through Hell's Canyon.

Dworshak Dam, on the North Fork of the Clearwater, has created a 55-mile-long reservoir that offers recreation for boaters, swimmers, water-skiers, and fishermen. This lake is surrounded by numerous parks with facilities for camping, picnicking, boating, and group activities. For information on Dworshak Reservoir, write:

U.S. Army Corps of Engineers
Walla Walla District
Walla Walla, WA 99362

Ask for their pamphlets entitled *Dworshak Reservoir Recreation Guide* and *Lower Snake River Recreation Guide.* They're free.

Government

Lewiston has a Council-Manager form of government.

Water

Lewiston operates its own water district, drawing the water supply from rivers, wells, and gravity-fed reservoirs. The system has a pumping capacity of 11 million gallons per day. The local tap water is slightly alkaline and very soft.

Energy

Electricity is provided by Washington Water Power Company from hydroelectric plants on the Snake River. An ample supply of power is assured for the foreseeable future. The same company also supplies natural gas to the area. Rate information can be obtained by writing their Lewiston office. Utilities for the average home run about $65 per month at the present time.

Television

There are two television stations in Lewiston plus a 10-channel local cable system.

Newspapers

The daily newspaper is:

The Lewiston Morning Tribune
Tribune Publishing Co.
Lewiston, ID 83501

A weekly, the *Clarkston Herald,* is published across the river in Clarkston, Washington.

For Further Information

Greater Lewiston Chamber of Commerce
Hotel Lewis Clark
Lewiston, ID 83501

Idaho Division of Tourism
State Capitol Building
Boise, ID 83720

Medford, Oregon

POPULATION: 42,800 within the city limits
136,900 in Jackson County

ELEVATION: 1380 feet above sea level

Medford, the county seat of Jackson County, is located in southwestern Oregon on Bear Creek, 10 miles from its confluence with the Rogue River. From its beginnings a hundred years ago as a depot on the Oregon and California railroad, Medford has become the center of a growing agricultural and industrial area with a sound and expanding economy.

Because of its pleasant climate, Medford has become the home of many retired persons. Tourists are drawn to the numerous nearby attractions, such as Crater Lake and the Oregon Shakespeare Festival in nearby Ashland.

Climate

Medford is located in a valley formed by Bear Creek and the Rogue River. On the east the Cascade Mountains form a barrier, and to the west and north lies the Coast Range, while to the south are the Siskiyou Mountains.

The climate is moderate but characterized by marked seasonal changes. Late fall, winter, and early spring are damp, cloudy, and cool. Late spring, summer, and early fall are warm, dry, and sunny because of the prevailing dry continental high-altitude winds during this period. Winds are normally very light in the valley, generally from the south in winter and from the northwest the rest of the year.

The Siskiyous and the Coast Range form a "rain shadow" that results in a relatively light annual rainfall, usually no more than 19 inches, most of which falls during the winter. The scant summer rains are usually in the form of thundershowers. Snowfall is heavy in the surrounding mountains, providing good winter skiing, but light in the valley floor, where it seldom remains on the ground more than 24 hours. Fog is frequent in the valley floor during winter and early spring, but it seldom remains longer than three days, usually only one or two days. Smoke from the numerous sawmill refuse burners reduces visibility to 1 to 3 miles in the morning hours.

Temperatures are seldom extreme. In winter, the daily average minimum dips slightly below freezing during December and January. High temperatures in the summer average slightly below 90°F, though there are about 67 days per year with temperatures 90°F and above. Winters usually have about 92 days of temperatures of 32°F and below, but no more than 4 days per year when the temperature fails to rise above that figure. There are about 4800 heating degree days and 800 cooling degree days per year. The average growing season is 170 days, from April 30 to October 17.

History

Founded in 1886 as a depot on the Oregon and California railroad, Medford was named after the city in Massachusetts. The next year it was incorporated as a town, and it grew rapidly as a freight center.

Always a prosperous agricultural area, it became the center of the Rogue River pear boom of 1900–1910. After World War II, increasing industrialization broadened the economic base. Tourist trade began to increase with the improvement of Interstate 5, which now runs from Mexico to Canada, passing through Medford.

Economy and Employment

Today's economic base in Medford is broader than ever before. Agriculture is still one of the most important industries, and pears are still the chief crop. Forest products, taken from 1.5 million acres of commercial timberland, have become equally important. Industry is growing, with over 7000 people employed in manufacturing. There are more than 200 manufacturing plants in the Medford area involved in lumber, plywood, and various types of machinery and equipment manufacturing, fruit packing, and grain processing.

As the industrial, trade, and service center of southern Oregon and northernmost California, Medford offers many jobs in wholesale and retail trade and services. Government employment also accounts for a large portion of the labor market.

Some of the major manufacturers in the area are: Balteau-Standard (transformers, 102 employees); Boise Cascade (lumber, 900); Harry & David Division of Bear Creek Corp. (fresh-fruit packers, 650 to 2200, depending on the season); Medford Corp. (lumber and particleboard, 875); and 3M Co. (microfilm-related items, 320).

Major nonmanufacturing employers include: Pacific Northwest Bell Telephone (381); Pacific Power & Light (350); Providence Hospital (528); Rogue Valley Memorial Hospital (935); and Sears, Roebuck & Co. (160).

Current job information can be obtained from:

Oregon Employment Division
P.O. Box 910
Medford, OR 97501

Taxes

Oregon has no state sales tax, but the state income tax is higher than many, starting at 4% on the first $500 and climbing to 10% on incomes over $50,000, with a $2000 exemption for family heads and an exemption of $1000 per dependent.

Property taxes are based on an assessment of 81.6% of true market value. The current tax rate is $1.54 per $100 of assessed value, so the tax on a home selling for $65,000 would amount to approximately $817 per year.

Shopping

As a trade and shopping center for a large area, Medford has stores that are larger and have a wider variety of offerings than do many towns of its size. There is a good central downtown business and shopping district, supplemented by seven malls and shopping centers in the area. Most major retail chains are represented, plus several excellent local and regional stores.

Because of Medford's isolated location, there is no big city nearby for convenient shopping for things that cannot be obtained locally. Portland is 276 miles to the north via Interstate 5, and San Francisco is 364 miles to the south. The result is that local merchants are extremely helpful in filling special needs of local residents.

Residential Properties

Rent for apartments or duplexes ranges from $280 to $395 per month for one-bedroom apartments and from $350 to $475 for two-bedroom apartments. Houses for rent range from $375 to $700 per month. Homes sell for $50,000 to $250,000 and up. Mobile-home space rentals range from $100 to $200 per month.

A few typical listings for homes for sale are:

3-BEDROOM, 2-bath home with 1152 square feet, gas and forced-air heating. Price $56,900.

3-BEDROOM, 2-bath home, with 1144 square feet, electric heat pump. Price $57,350.

5-BEDROOM, 3-bath home with over 2000 square feet of living space, electric ceiling cable heating, for $77,500.

4-BEDROOM, 2-bath home with 2014 square feet of living space, electric heat pump/air conditioning, built in 1980, for $99,500.

The chamber of commerce can provide a list of local real estate agents, and the local newspaper offers listings of current rentals and homes for sale.

Safety

Medford is one of the safest possible areas in the event of almost any manmade disaster. This part of Oregon is in the least danger from radioactive fallout of any place in North America below the Arctic Circle.

The FBI Crime Index rating is 99 crimes per thousand of population per year. Police service is provided by the city's 75-member force, and the city fire department has 70 members. The Fire Insurance Rating is Class 3. There are no nearby manmade hazards. Natural disasters are also unlikely. Earthquake hazard is minimal since Medford is not on a fault line.

Education

Medford's school district serves a population of about 54,000, with 10,000 students and a student/teacher ratio of 24:1 in the 14 elementary schools and 20.3:1 at the secondary level.

Southern Oregon State College, in Ashland, 16 miles southeast on Interstate 5, is a four-year institution with 8 divisions, 23 academic departments, and 6000 students. Continuing-education programs are available there to meet the needs of business and industry in the area.

Rogue Community College is a two-year facility in Grants Pass, 28 miles to the northeast on Interstate 5. It has an open-door admission policy and offers low tuition to local residents.

Oregon Institute of Technology is the state system's polytechnic college in nearby Klamath Falls, offering degrees in engineering, health, and industrial and business fields.

Medical Facilities

Medford is the regional medical center for southern Oregon. Rogue Valley Memorial Hospital has 264 beds and offers a complete range of treatment specialties, including open-heart surgery, a burn center, and cancer treatment. Providence Hospital, which has 168 beds, is a general medical and surgical hospital offering a pain clinic, a physical-rehabilitation program, a poison-control and drug center, and a family-planning center.

Cultural Activities

The area offers many cultural choices, from concerts and theater to exploring historic Jacksonville, a 120-year-old gold-mining town 5 miles from Medford that has a museum, shops, old homes, antiques, and an annual music festival each August.

The annual Oregon Shakespeare Festival, in nearby Ashland, attracts visitors from all over the world from June through September. Performances are offered in three theaters — the Angus Bowmer Theater, the Outdoor Elizabethan Stage, and the Black Swan.

The Rogue Valley Symphony, located in Ashland, provides concerts for the area throughout the year.

The Jackson County library system has a main library in Medford and 12 branches, serving the entire county area with 262,266 volumes.

Recreation

There is a wide selection of recreational opportunities for residents of Medford. Three public golf courses and the Rogue Valley Country

Club course serve the area's golfers. In summer there is swimming in two outdoor pools, and year-round swimming is offered at the indoor pool at the YMCA, which also offers handball and racquetball facilities to residents.

Nearby Howard Prairie Lake offers fishing and camping, and there is salmon and steelhead fishing on the Rogue River. All of southern Oregon is a hunter's paradise, with an abundance of bears, deer, quail, doves, and rabbit. The nearby parks and wilderness areas offer a wide range of opportunities for hiking and camping.

Skiing is available at nearby Mt. Ashland from Thanksgiving through April on 22 ski runs, including challenging downhill and cross-country runs. The area also offers snowmobiling, ice fishing, and sled-dog racing each winter.

Boating and water-skiing are available at several nearby lakes, and raft trips extending from one to four days are offered on the Rogue River.

The Rogue Valley is home for hot-air-balloon flights out of Ashland from May through September, and glider flying and soaring are based at Montague. Spectators and qualified participants can enjoy or take part in the NASCAR, auto-cross, kart, and motorcycle races that take place regularly at Jackson County Sports Park.

Government

Medford has a Council-Manager form of government, and Jackson County has the equivalent with a three-member board of commissioners and a county administrator.

Water

Water is supplied by the city of Medford from Big Butte Springs, supplemented by the Rogue River as required. The total demand is about one-third of available system supply. The local tap water is neutral, very soft, and not fluoridated.

Energy

Electricity is supplied locally by Pacific Power and Light. Because of the abundance of water, most of Oregon's power is supplied by hydroelectric plants.

Natural gas is supplied by C P National from pipelines that bring gas up from California's gas fields.

At present utility rates, the average home pays about $100 per month for all utilities combined.

Television
Because of Medford's isolated position in southern Oregon, residents are dependent on the local cable television system for reception.

Newspaper
The local newspaper, published daily except Saturday, is:

The Medford Mail Tribune
P.O. Box 1108
Medford, OR 97501

Single copies cost $2.00 by mail.

For Further Information

Greater Medford Chamber of Commerce
304 S. Central Ave.
Medford, OR 97501

Oregon Travel Information
101 Transportation Building
Salem, OR 97310

Monroe, Louisiana

POPULATION: 56,338 within the city limits
132,400 in the Monroe SMSA

ELEVATION: 82 feet above sea level

Monroe, the parish seat of Ouachita Parish, is located in northeastern Louisiana, about 100 miles east of Shreveport, in a prosperous agricultural area producing forestry products, beef, cottonseed, and paper products. The nearby gas fields support chemical and carbon-black production, and local industry includes the manufacture of furniture and clothing.

The countryside around Monroe is flat to slightly rolling, well wooded between the open fields. The Ouachita River twists and turns its leisurely way between the communities of Monroe and West Monroe.

Climate

The climate of northeastern Louisiana is ideal for the cotton that grows in the fields around Monroe. The principal influences that determine the climate of Louisiana are its subtropical latitude and its proximity to the Gulf of Mexico.

In summer the prevailing southerly winds provide moist, semitropical weather with frequent thundershowers. Summers are long and warm, with temperatures in the 80s to low 90s from May through September. There are some 2500 cooling degree days per year in the area, and about 85 days per year with temperatures of 90°F and above.

Winters are generally mild, with daytime highs around 60°F and lows in the 40s, except when arctic air brings northers that can drop temperatures to below zero in January and February. Normal winters have only 31 days with temperatures 32°F and below. The last spring frost comes by the first of March and the first frost in fall seldom arrives much before the first of December, providing a growing season of some 240 days. There are about 2000 heating degree days per year.

Precipitation in the Monroe area is plentiful throughout the year, slightly heavier in November through January and slightly less in June through October, except for thunderstorms in July. Annual precipitation averages about 50 inches per year. Snow is rarely as much as 2 inches per year and never stays on the ground for long. Humidity averages about 84% at night and 58% in the afternoons throughout the year. There is about 70% of possible sunshine for the year, with more in summer and slightly less in winter.

History

In 1542, Hernando de Soto's band of weary Spanish explorers traveled up the Ouachita River toward the Mississippi. Commissioned by Spain to find and establish a new route to India and discover new sources of gold and jewels, they failed in their attempts. Shortly after passing this way, de Soto, weary, disillusioned, and sick, died of a fever.

After this, no white men showed up for nearly 200 years. In 1719, the French established a trading post called Prairie de Canots on the banks of the Ouachita, but it was not until after the French and Indian War in 1763 that a permanent settlement was started at this location.

When Louisiana was ceded to Spain, Don Juan Filhiol was sent to take command of the small post, which later became Fort Miro, and he tried to develop productive farms around the military post. The region grew and developed as a purely agricultural area until 1819, when the *James Monroe,* the first steamboat to come up the Ouachita, arrived. The boat docked at Fort Miro on May 1, 1819, and made such an impression on the local settlers that they named their village Monroe, in honor of the steamer.

Life prospered on the Ouachita, sedately in Monroe, on the east bank, and less so in Trenton, on the west bank. Monroe was a quiet trading town, while Trenton was a brawling cotton port filled with gambling and drinking boat crews and dockworkers. Trenton thrived briefly, then the port moved downstream to Cottonport, and in 1882 a permanent steel bridge was built across the Ouachita to Cottonport, which later became West Monroe.

In 1916, the first gas field was discovered, and it played an important part in the growth of Ouachita Parish.

Economy and Employment

With the discovery of gas in the vicinity, carbon-black plants, paper mills, and other industries began moving into the area to use the low-cost fuel. By 1950 the hardwood forest had been depleted and had been replaced by extensive pine forests that provided materials for both the paper mills and the growing lumber industry.

As Monroe grew, so did its trade. Today Monroe is an extensive trading center as well as a financial, medical, professional, recreational, and cultural center for some 400,000 people in 13 parishes in Louisiana and 2 counties in Arkansas. As a trading and shopping center, Monroe provides employment to more people in retail and wholesale businesses than in any other field. The second-leading employer is the government, with 19% of the work force, followed by manufacturing with 17%, services with 15%, and construction with 9%.

To supplement present facilities, the Monroe Port Commission is working with the U.S. Corps of Engineers to develop a site for a public port terminal and a water-oriented industrial park on the Ouachita River. Present facilities now handle over 1.3 million tons of cargo annually.

Some of the major employers in the area are: Manville Forest Products Corp. (kraft paper, cartons, and shipping containers, 2800 employees); Guide Division of General Motors (auto headlamps, 825); I. M. C. Chemical Group, Inc. (chemicals, 530); Selig Manufacturing Co. (upholstered furniture, 260); International Minerals & Chemical Corp. (anhydrous ammonia for agriculture and industry, 500); Bancroft Bag, Inc. (paper bags, 175); Plymouth Tube (drawn tubular products, 100); and the city of Monroe (1264).

Monroe has three publicly owned industrial parks totaling 500 acres that provide space and facilities for an increasing number of new industries, including Sunbelt Manufacturing, Malone and Hyde, Sol's Pipe Yard, and Louisiana Industries.

Taxes

The combined state and city sales tax is 6%. The state income tax does not reach 6% until taxable income exceeds $50,000.

Property tax rates vary according to location, with rates slightly higher in Monroe than in West Monroe. Within Monroe's city limits, the tax on a $65,000 home runs about $244 per year.

Shopping

Since they serve a trading area of some 400,000 people, Monroe and West Monroe are so well supplied with excellent stores that there is seldom any need to travel beyond the community for shopping. However, greater variety can be found in Shreveport, 100 miles to the west, and New Orleans, 270 miles to the south.

Residential Properties

The average home sells for about $56,000, though homes can be found in a wide range of prices. A few typical listings are:

> LOVELY 3-bedroom 2-bath home with den and many built-ins. Big lot with lots of trees. $48,500.
>
> NORTHSIDE HOME with swimming pool, 2 bedrooms, over 1900 square feet of living space, separate living room and den, fireplace, fenced yard, plenty of trees. $77,000.
>
> JUST REDUCED. 3 bedrooms, 2 baths, hall, with added wing that could be an efficiency apartment. 2 kitchens. $36,000.
>
> GORGEOUS 2-story home on a full acre just outside West Monroe, with 5 bedrooms, 4 baths, living room, dining room, den, family room, office, large gazebo, carport, double garage, lawns, trees, and more. $100,000.

Rentals are plentiful and moderate in cost, with one-bedroom apartments renting for $175 to $200 per month and two-bedroom apartments or condos renting for $225 to $350.

Safety

The FBI Crime Index rating for Monroe is 89 crimes per thousand of population per year. Police protection is provided in Monroe by a department with 106 full-time policemen and 29 squad cars, while West Monroe has another 38 full-time policemen and 13 squad cars.

The unincorporated areas are protected by the Ouachita Parish sheriff's department, which has 115 deputies and 16 patrol cars.

Fire protection in Monroe is provided by seven stations manned by 120 full-time firemen. Monroe enjoys a low Class 3 Fire Insurance Rating. West Monroe has 32 full-time firemen and a Class 5 Fire Insurance Rating.

There are no serious natural hazards in the area. While areas of Monroe flooded after the winter storms of 1982–83, the flooding took place in low-lying areas that should never have been developed in the first place. Anyone buying a home in Monroe should avoid these low areas situated in the flood plain of the river.

Education

The Monroe City school system operates 12 elementary, 3 junior high, and 3 high schools. The Ouachita Parish system includes 15 elementary, 10 junior high, and 5 high schools. Over 30,000 students attend the two systems. In addition, parochial and private schools serve a combined enrollment of 2100 and the local state vocational-trade school has an enrollment of 550.

For higher education, Monroe has Northeast Louisiana University, a public-supported institution with an enrollment of 11,000 students and a faculty and staff of 900. Louisiana State University, located 200 miles to the south in Baton Rouge, has an enrollment of nearly 50,000 and offers courses through the doctoral level in a very wide choice of subjects.

Medical Facilities

St. Francis Medical Center Hospital has 417 beds, E. A. Conway Memorial Hospital has 138, and Glenwood Hospital has 176. Together they offer complete medical coverage for the community and surrounding area.

Over 130 doctors and 49 dentists are in private practice in the area, supplemented by the Ouachita Parish unit of the Public Health Service.

Cultural Activities

The Ouachita Parish Public Library has over 223,000 volumes and an annual circulation of over 550,000. In addition, the Northeast Louisiana University reference library is open for use by the public.

Monroe has something for everyone. The civic center, located in the heart of town, is a 31-acre complex that includes an arena, a theater, a conference hall, and parking for more than 2000 automobiles. The conference hall seats 1000 for banquets and 1200 for concerts. The convention center has a full stage (adjustable for size), dressing rooms, and complete theater equipment.

The Monroe Symphony Orchestra offers concerts throughout the year, and the Twin City Ballet Company gives two major performances each year. The Little Theater provides the community with live theater performances during the season, and Northeast Louisiana University regularly presents lectures, concerts, theatrical performances, and individual artists for both students and local residents.

In addition, Monroe offers a number of programs such as the Artist-in-Residence program, senior-citizen art classes, a children's arts day camp, and an annual festival of the arts.

Recreation

Six recreation centers in Monroe offer league competition for children and adults in basketball, volleyball, and badminton. There are four municipal swimming pools. Golfers have access to one 18-hole public golf course, three 9-hole public courses, and the 18-hole private courses at Bayou DeSiard Country Club and Pine Hills Country Club.

Owing to the mild climate, residents can participate year-round in such sports as golf, tennis, swimming, fishing, and jogging. The parish-owned recreation area at Cheniere Lake, a 3600-acre lake, offers facilities for camping and picnicking, as well as playgrounds. The lake offers outstanding fishing for bream, white perch, bass, catfish, and buffalo fish.

Water sports opportunities are plentiful in the area. The Ouachita River is one of the most beautiful rivers in the world and offers boating, water-skiing, and swimming. There is a municipal dock at Forsythe Park and a private dock, both located on the Ouachita River. Other bodies of water, such as Lake D'Arbonne, Moon Lake, Black Bayou, Bussey Lake, and Bayou DeSiard offer boating, picnicking, fishing, water-skiing, and swimming.

Other outdoor activities available include a rifle range, archery, camping, canoeing, rowing, woodlife survival training, and hunting. Hunters will find five major areas available to them, with over 77,000 acres of varied woodland, fields, and streams. There is an abundance of deer, squirrels, turkeys, doves, ducks, and rabbit.

Government

Monroe is governed by the Mayor-Council system, with an elected mayor and five councilmen. The new government center includes a city hall, a municipal court, a police department, and a jail.

Water

Water supplies are ample in Monroe, with 902 million gallons of precipitation per square mile per year in the area. Water is supplied locally by the city of Monroe. Local tap water is alkaline, very soft, and not fluoridated.

Energy

Electricity is supplied by Louisiana Power and Light Company from generating systems run primarily by plentiful natural gas. Natural gas comes from the huge nearby gas fields and is supplied locally by Louisiana Gas Service Company.

As in the rest of the nation, utility costs are rising in Monroe, but rates remain lower here than in many communities. At current rates, the occupant of an average two-to-three-bedroom home can expect to pay about $50 to $60 per month for utilities.

Television

There are four local television stations and three local cable systems, providing full coverage to all residents.

Newspapers

There are two daily newspapers, the *Monroe News-Star* (evenings) and the *Monroe Morning World* (mornings), both printed by the same publisher and combined in the weekend editions. For information on both, write:

Monroe News-Star & World
Monroe, LA 72101

The *New Orleans Times-Picayune* and the *Shreveport Times* are also available locally.

For Further Information

Monroe Chamber of Commerce
141 DeSiard St., Suite 120
Monroe, LA 72101

Louisiana Office of Tourism
P.O. Box 44291
Baton Rouge, LA 70804

Muskogee, Oklahoma

POPULATION: 40,011 within the city limits
66,939 in Muskogee County

ELEVATION: 602 feet above sea level

Muskogee is located in northeastern Oklahoma, 115 miles east of Oklahoma City and 45 miles east-southeast of Tulsa, near the confluence of the Verdigris, Grand, and Arkansas rivers. Surprisingly, despite its great distance from the Gulf of Mexico, Muskogee is a seaport, since it is situated on the Arkansas River, which flows into the Mississippi River in southeastern Arkansas and thence into the Gulf of Mexico.

Located in the heart of Oklahoma's "Green Country," Muskogee is surrounded by low, gently sloping hills that blend into a rich, flat to rolling farming area containing the world's largest concentration of manmade lakes. Drive in almost any direction from Muskogee and you will reach water within 5 to 30 minutes. Because of all the lakes, recreational possibilities abound. The area offers excellent camping, boating, restaurants, motels, cabins, and lodges.

Climate

Muskogee's climate is continental, with hot summers and mild winters. Summers bring some 70 days with temperatures of 90°F and above and about 2000 cooling degree days per year. Annual precipitation is close to 42 inches and is well distributed throughout the year. Spring is the wettest season, with about one-third of the year's total precipitation. Winter is the driest season, with only 16% of the yearly total. Thunderstorms account for much of the rainfall, especially in the spring. During an average year, Muskogee has about 53 thunderstorms. The average daily relative humidity is about 55% in the summer and 60% during the winter. About one-third of the days are clear during an average year, and the area receives 65% of total possible sunshine.

Winters are comparatively mild with an occasional norther that lasts only a few days. There are normally only 5 days per year with temperatures that fail to climb above 32°F, and there have only been 12 days in the past 30 years in which the temperatures dropped to zero or below. Snowfall averages about 7 inches per year, with most of it falling in January and February. Usually, snows are light and remain on the ground only a short time. The frost-free growing season averages 215 days a year, with the last spring freeze coming at the end of March and the first fall frost occurring in early November. There are about 3500 heating degree days per year.

Prevailing winds are southerly, except during January and February when they tend to be northerly. The average annual wind speed is 10 miles per hour, though strong, gusty winds of 30 to 40 miles per hour accompany outbreaks of cold weather, when Canadian air blows in on a norther.

Tornadoes can occur in the area, as they can throughout the rest of the Great Plains region. One of the most damaging storms to hit the area occurred on April 12, 1945, when a tornado killed 13 persons and injured 113.

History

During the building of the Missouri, Kansas & Texas railroad (the Katy line), the crews worked a section at a time, and the end of the completed section was called a terminus. This was the place beyond which loaded trains could not go. In the summer of 1871, such a terminus brought about the founding of Muskogee, named after the Muscogee or Creek tribe of local Indians.

When the activities of the terminus ended with the opening of the next section of completed line, the railroad left behind a collection of tents and shacks. The U.S. government had made a treaty with the Indians that required the construction of an Indian Agency building in the area, and one was begun in 1875 on a hill just northwest of the abandoned tents and shacks. From its beginnings in this agency building, Muskogee became the most important city in the Indian Territory, and it was on this spot that the government negotiated with the several Indian tribes of Oklahoma.

Muskogee was incorporated as a city on March 19, 1898, and has grown ever since, from what was once a bald, open prairie into the present busy town.

Economy and Employment

Muskogee's economy is diversified, with local industries involved in the processing or production of rare metals, glass, clothing, steel and iron, boxes, precision optical equipment, and meat and dairy products. In addition, the operations of the port of Muskogee are an increasingly important part of the local economy.

Over 25,000 people are employed in the area, with 792 involved in agriculture, 5021 in manufacturing, 6267 in government, and 5042 in wholesale and retail trade.

Major manufacturers and processors in the area include: Acme Engineering and Manufacturing Corp. (makers of ventilating and cooling equipment, 465 employees); Brockway Glass Co. (glass containers, 625); Coburn Optical Industries (machines for optical laboratories, 400); Container Corporation of America (corrugated shipping containers, 137); Corning Glass (Pyrex glass products, 625); Fort Howard Paper Co. (tissue paper, 600); and Muskogee Iron Works (structural steel and iron, 250).

Taxes

Property taxes in Muskogee are based on an assessment of 15% of market value. The tax rate within the city limits is $9.244 per $100 of assessed value. A home selling for $65,000 would be taxed approximately $902 per year. There is a homestead exemption for owner-occupied residential housing.

There is a combined state and city sales tax of 8%, and the state income tax ranges from 0.5% on the first $2000 of income to 6% on income over $15,000.

Shopping
Muskogee has a nine-block central shopping and business center supplemented by several neighborhood centers. Many major national and regional chains are represented, including J. C. Penney, Sears, K-Mart, TG&Y, Thrifty Drug, and Safeway.

For a greater selection than can be found locally, Tulsa is only 45 miles away via the Muskogee Turnpike, and Oklahoma City is 115 miles to the west.

Residential Properties
So far, housing demands in Muskogee have not exceeded the available supply. Typical listings include:

10% VA ASSUMPTION on this home. Pay only $6100 down and make payments of $261. Detached garage, storm windows, near school. $32,500.

SOUTH OF TOWN on 6¼ acres of good pastureland. $59,500.

10¼% ASSUMABLE LOAN on 1501-square-foot 3-bedroom 2-bath home with fireplace, central heat/air and built-in kitchen. $50s.

SUPER OLDER HOME in good area with 2/3 bedrooms, formal dining room, fenced yard. $36,500.

Rentals are available, with one-bedroom apartments renting for $125 to $190 per month and two-bedroom apartments or condos for $150 to $325.

Safety
Muskogee's FBI Crime Index rating is 81 crimes per thousand of population per year. The community is patrolled 24 hours per day by a 94-man police department. The fire department has five fire stations and 81 employees, and the city has a Class 4 Fire Insurance Rating.

The nearest manmade hazard is a nuclear power plant about 40 miles to the north. Tornadoes can be a hazard for people living in lightly built or mobile homes, though the tornado warning system has reduced the hazard in recent years.

Education
The public school system in Muskogee provides 11 elementary schools, 3 junior high schools, and 1 high school. There are also 2 parochial schools, a Montessori school, a school for the blind, and a vocational-technical school.

Bacone College is a two-year liberal-arts college that was begun in

1880 under the auspices of the American Baptist Home Mission Society to bring higher education to the Indians. Today its students represent 55 Indian tribes and come from all 50 states.

Other colleges and universities within a 50-mile radius of Muskogee include: Connors State College, 18 miles away in Warner; Northeastern Oklahoma State University, 24 miles away in Tahlequah; Tulsa University, 45 miles away in Tulsa; and Oral Roberts University, also in Tulsa.

Medical Facilities

Muskogee has two hospitals: Muskogee General Hospital, which has 362 beds, and the Veterans' Administration Hospital, which has 247 beds and serves only veterans. The General Hospital has a staff of 125 doctors and 19 dentists, and more are in private practice in the community. Nine nursing homes in the area have a total capacity of 575 beds, and a city-county health unit, opened in 1968, provides full public-health services.

Cultural Activities

The public library, which was founded in 1908, now has a collection of some 90,000 volumes and serves about 30,000 patrons. Recent additions offer rooms for meetings of groups of up to 300 people and are used by various civic, cultural, and educational groups throughout the year.

A complete, modern, and flexible Civic Assembly Center can seat more than 3700 persons in its auditorium, 450 in a combination banquet–meeting room, and 850 for dinner. Exhibit space totals 10,000 square feet.

School plays and civic productions are performed in the 1000-seat Fine Arts Auditorium, and the Community Concert Association brings ballet, piano concerts, vocal groups, and instrumental groups to town throughout the year.

Recreation

Muskogee maintains 32 public parks totaling over 2200 acres. Scattered throughout the park system are picnic facilities, barbecue grills, water, rest rooms, playground equipment, tennis courts, baseball diamonds, swimming pools, and benches. The city's recreation department arranges and sponsors a wide variety of community recreation programs for all ages. Team sports thrive in Muskogee, with bowling leagues, baseball, softball, basketball, and tennis.

Muskogee has one of the most modern and active YM-YWCAs in Oklahoma. In addition to working with young people, the "Y" provides many special classes for adults, makes meeting rooms available, and has a Businessman's Health Club, complete with equipment, pool, steam room, and masseur.

The Muskogee Country Club has an outstanding 18-hole golf course, and a 9-hole course is located at the Meadowbrook Country Club. In addition, two public courses are provided by the city.

Three public swimming pools are operated during the late spring and summer in the largest city parks. Both country clubs, the Elk's Club, and the YM-YWCA also operate pools.

Eastern Oklahoma offers excellent hunting and fishing for a wide variety of game and fish. Three great rivers converge at Muskogee — the Arkansas, the Verdigris, and the Grand. The Arkansas is navigable from Muskogee to the Mississippi and thence to the Gulf of Mexico. Webber's Falls Lake provides the harbor for the port of Muskogee, and around Muskogee, within a 30-minute drive, are four more beautiful lakes that offer many opportunities for water sports and fishing.

Government

Muskogee is governed by a Council-Manager arrangement. There is an area planning commission to develop future plans for Muskogee and to coordinate all planning of federal, state, and local governments within the area.

Water

The local tap water is alkaline, soft, and not fluoridated. With the three rivers at the town's doorstep, there is no likelihood of the city ever suffering from a water shortage. Water is supplied by the city's water department.

Energy

Electricity is provided by the Oklahoma Gas & Electric Company. Natural gas is supplied by Oklahoma Natural Gas Company. Given the vast number of oil and gas fields in Oklahoma, plus the operating nuclear power plant 40 miles north of Muskogee, it appears that there will be adequate power for the foreseeable future.

Current electrical and gas rates may be obtained by writing the local chamber of commerce. Utility costs currently average about $100 per month for a two-to-three-bedroom home.

Television

There is currently no television station in Muskogee, but stations in Tulsa and Fort Smith, Arkansas, can be received on home antenna systems. In addition, a local cable system provides full coverage with stations from Tulsa, Fort Smith, Oklahoma City, Atlanta, Dallas, and Chicago. Also available are Home Box Office, Showtime, and news and religious channels.

Newspaper

The local daily newspaper is:

The Muskogee Daily Phoenix and Times Democrat
P.O. Box 1968
Muskogee, OK 74401

For Further Information

Muskogee Chamber of Commerce
P.O. Box 797
Muskogee, OK 74401

Oklahoma Industrial Development and Park Department
Information Division
Will Rogers Memorial Building
Oklahoma City, OK 73105

Tourism Promotion Division
Tourism and Recreation Department
500 Will Rogers Memorial Building
Oklahoma City, OK 73105

Nacogdoches, Texas

POPULATION: 27,103 within the city limits
45,300 in Nacogdoches County

ELEVATION: 277 feet above sea level

Nacogdoches (pronounced nack-ah-doe'chiz) is situated in the heart of the Piney Woods of East Texas, 130 miles northeast of Houston and 140 miles southeast of Dallas. The county seat of Nocogdoches County, it is a retail and wholesale trading center for a wide lumbering and agricultural area.

Not only the oldest town in Texas, Nacogdoches is also one of the most successful. One key to its success and growth is Stephen F. Austin State University, which has kept the economy steady, even during some difficult times.

Nacogdoches is a town of red-brick buildings and brick-red land.

The downtown central square, a relic of an earlier century, is now the center of a prosperous and energetic business community.

Climate

Because of its location between the Gulf of Mexico and the high plateaus and mountain ranges of the North American continent, Texas has widely diverse climatological regions, from the semiarid western plains to the tropical Rio Grande Valley, from the cool-temperate mountain regions of the Big Bend to thickly wooded eastern Texas.

Nacogdoches, located in the Piney Woods of East Texas, has a humid subtropical climate with hot summers and mild winters. Rainfall averages between 45 and 50 inches a year, distributed more or less evenly throughout the year. Winter storms bring hail two or three times a year, and sometimes a light snowfall will cover the ground for a day or two, though normal winters seldom bring even a trace of snow.

Humidity varies throughout the day, from 70 to 80% around sunrise to 50 to 60% in the early afternoons. It remains fairly constant throughout the year, with an annual average humidity of 75% — which makes for luxurious gardens but also increases the effect of hot summer afternoons or cold winter mornings.

In winter, the normal daily minimum temperature is about 40°F, and there are only about 20 days a year with temperatures dropping to 32°F or below. In summer, daily temperatures vary between 70–80°F minimum and 90–100°F maximum, with about 100 days per year when the temperature exceeds 90°F. This climate pattern gives Nacogdoches a low 1750 heating degree days each winter, but the long, hot summers bring a total of some 2500 cooling degree days. Air conditioning is more important than heating, though both are necessary for comfort.

Winds in the Piney Woods are normally gentle and generally from the south to southeast off the Gulf of Mexico, though winters always bring several chill northers. Tropical cyclones (hurricanes) sometimes threaten the Texas coast but seldom carry much energy as far inland as Nacogdoches. Tornadoes are infrequent in East Texas, usually striking in the areas west of Dallas and Houston.

History

Nacogdoches is an old community, claiming to be the oldest town in Texas. Cabeza de Vaca, the Spanish explorer, got lost while marching along the Texas coast and was captured by a group of

Indians. He escaped, and in 1528 carried back to Mexico City a description of the rich, wooded land occupied by the Caddo Indians. It was these Indians of the Hasinai confederacy who named the land *tejas*, which, in their tongue, meant "friend."

According to Indian legend, the communities of Nacogdoches, in present-day Texas, and Natchitoches, in western Louisiana, were founded by the twin sons of a long-ago chief of the Caddo tribe. It was the commerce between these two communities that beat out the pathway that later became part of the Spaniards' Camino Real — the Old San Antonio Road.

About 1700, the early Spanish mission builders began to colonize the Nacogdoches area, but they gave up about 1720 because of constant raids by the French, who had a firm hold on the Louisiana Territory to the east. In 1779, Nacogdoches became a permanent settlement, retaining the old Indian name.

Economy and Employment

Modern Nacogdoches is a progressive, growing community offering exceptional opportunities to new residents. The economy is broad-based and stable. Once primarily a cotton market town, Nacogdoches is now involved in truck farming, poultry raising, forestry, light industry, and education.

While much of the local industry is based on forestry and agriculture, new industries are moving in. The principal employer is Stephen F. Austin State University, and other major employers include: Bright Coop Co. (makers of poultry coops and pallets, 145 employees); International Paper Company (plywood, 335); Moore Business Forms (printers, 242); Nibco of Texas (brass valves, 430); Plus Tex Growers (feed and chicks, 230); Sun Terrace (outdoor furniture, 270); Texas Farm Products (poultry feeds, pet foods, animal feeds, fertilizers, and chicks, 554); and Valmac Industries (poultry, 245).

There are many other employers in the area, including manufacturers of transformers, furniture, boat trailers, candy, flanges, and motor homes.

Taxes

Texas does not have a state income tax, but there is a 5% state and city sales tax. Property taxes are moderate. On a home selling for $65,000 the annual tax would be $1235 inside the city limits and somewhat lower outside.

Shopping

In addition to the downtown area, which has five department stores, discount stores, and supermarkets, there are two suburban shopping centers.

For wider variety in shopping, both Houston and Dallas are within a three-hour drive.

Residential Properties

Financing the purchase of a home is always a problem, but many property owners in Nacogdoches will provide financing for buyers at lower interest rates. A few typical listings are:

> GREAT LOCATION only 3 blocks to college. 3 bedroom, 2 bath with double garage, nice trees and large backyard. $69,500.
>
> EXCELLENT EXECUTIVE HOME with 4 bedrooms, dining room, large family room, and 2½ baths. Don't miss this at $73,900.
>
> PLENTY OF TREES on this 4-acre property with 2 bedrooms and one bath. $34,000.
>
> OLDER 2-bedroom home on 10 acres with 2 barns and 2 large storage buildings, close to town, for $32,500 with owner financing at 10%.

Rentals are scarce at present, but the situation is improving. One-bedroom apartments currently cost from $175 to $350 per month, and two-bedroom apartments or condos rent for $200 to $700.

Safety

The FBI Crime Index rating for Nacogdoches is a very low 33 crimes per thousand of population per year, one of the lowest in the nation. Police protection is provided by a 55-officer police department, and the fire department has 52 full-time employees.

There are no nearby manmade hazards, and the area is too far inland to be seriously threatened by hurricanes.

Education

The local public school system includes five elementary schools, one middle school, one junior high school, and one senior high school. The outlying areas are served by two additional school districts, each with its own middle schools and high schools.

Nacogdoches has been a center of higher education for a long time. Nacogdoches University (no longer in existence) was founded in 1845 under a charter from the Republic of Texas. Today, Nacogdoches and the area are served by Stephen F. Austin State University, established in 1921, which has a current enrollment of 9500 students who come from 43 states and 20 foreign countries. It offers a four-year program leading to various bachelors' degrees.

For a wider choice in undergraduate studies or for a complete selection of graduate studies, there are the University of Houston, 130 miles to the southwest in Houston, and Southern Methodist University (SMU) in Dallas, 140 miles to the northwest.

Medical Facilities

Nacogdoches Medical Center Hospital, which has 150 beds, and Memorial Hospital, which has 184 beds, provide modern and complete medical care. A 24-hour emergency medical service is available. Over 60 doctors and 30 dentists practice in the area.

Cultural Activities

The public library, with 40,000 volumes, and the Stephen F. Austin State University library, with 375,000 volumes, are both open to local residents. The Hoya Memorial Library, with its 10,000-volume collection, is also open to the public.

Much of the cultural life of the community centers on the university. Its Fine Arts Auditorium hosts many performing artists and groups throughout the year. In addition, the Lamp-Lite Players, a local nonprofit, nonprofessional theater group, offer dinner, musicals, and drama to the area.

Recreation

Nacogdoches has seven city parks with picnic facilities, playgrounds, jogging areas, swimming pools, softball fields, and 38 tennis courts. The town also has a skating rink and a bowling alley.

Golfers have a choice of the public Woodland Hills Golf Course, which offers 18 holes, golf carts, and a driving range, and the private course of the Piney Woods Country Club.

Sam Rayburn Reservoir is a 114,000-acre lake where there are facilities for swimming, boating, fishing, and camping. Toledo Bend Reservoir, to the east of Nacogdoches, is a 186,000-acre lake for fishing, boating, and camping. Lake Nacogdoches, a recently completed 2200-acre lake, offers fishing, boating, sailing, and waterskiing. Located 12 miles west of town, it also offers a good swimming area, picnic and rest-room facilities, and public boat ramps.

Government

Nacogdoches has an unusual blend of the old and the modern, with a city manager working under the Commissioner form of government. It seems to work here.

Water

Because of the plentiful rainfall in East Texas, water has never been a problem. The municipal water supply is very soft, coming from deep wells. The water is neutral and not fluoridated. Most important of all, it tastes good!

Energy

Since Nacogdoches is located near the East Texas gas and oil fields, natural gas is plentiful. Though no longer as cheap as it once was, energy is still cheaper here than in many areas. Entex, Inc., supplies natural gas locally, and electricity is supplied by Texas Power & Light Company. Utility costs for the average two-bedroom home run about $85 per month at present.

Television

Nacogdoches has one television station and a cable system that offers eight additional channels plus home movies.

Newspapers

The local daily newspaper is:

The Daily Sentinel
P.O. Drawer 68
Nacogdoches, TX 75961

Both the *Houston Chronicle* and the *Dallas News* are available locally.

For Further Information

Nacogdoches Chamber of Commerce
P.O. Box 974
Nacogdoches, TX 75961

Tourist Development Agency
P.O. Box 12008, Capitol Station
Austin, TX 78711

Texas Employment Commission
2103 South Street
Nacogdoches, TX 75961

The Texas Employment Commission can provide current information on job openings.

Natchez, Mississippi

POPULATION: 21,732 within the city limits
38,171 in Adams County

ELEVATION: 215 feet above sea level

Natchez, in southwestern Mississippi, is the oldest settlement on the Mississippi River and is, from a historical standpoint, one of the most interesting cities in America. Before the white man arrived, Natchez was the site of the Grand Village of the Natchez Indians, whose culture reached its peak in the mid-1500s.

Life in Natchez has always centered on the river, which made it one of the most important ports of the 1800s. At one time, more than half of the millionaires in the United States lived in the plantations and townhouses of Natchez.

Today, Natchez is a trade and shipping center for a region producing livestock, timber, and cotton. Industry is moving in, and there are 400 oil wells in the county. Modern Natchez is a blend of history and progress, of today, yesterday, and tomorrow.

Climate

Several factors influence the climate of this portion of Mississippi: the Gulf of Mexico to the south, the large continental land mass to the north, the subtropical latitude, the prevailing southerly winds, and the Mississippi River itself. Generally, the area has long, hot summers and brief, cool winters.

The prevailing southerly winds provide a moist, semitropical climate with conditions often favorable to afternoon thundershowers. When the air-pressure masses shift to bring westerly or northerly winds, periods of hotter and drier weather interrupt the prevailing summer humidity. The high humidity and hot days and nights from May to September can be uncomfortable without air conditioning. Relief comes in the form of thundershowers during many afternoons. There are about 60 thunderstorms per year.

Summer maximum temperatures average in the 80s and 90s from May through October, with some 80 days per year with temperatures of 90°F and above. The area has 2750 cooling degree days per year.

The winter season is alternately subjected to warm, tropical air and cold continental air. Cold spells seldom last more than three to four days and the ground rarely freezes. However, the cold northers of winter can bring sudden, sharp drops of temperature. Winter temperatures seldom fall below 32°F, with only about 20 days per year dropping that low or lower. Normal daily minimums in the winter are generally in the low to mid-40s. Frosts are not frequent, and the first frost seldom arrives before the end of November. The last frost comes by early March. There are 1800 heating degree days per year.

Rainfall averages around 57 inches per year, with rain occurring about 10 days per month except in the drier months of September through November, when rain falls only 7 or 8 days per month. Snowfall is rare and snow stays on the ground for no more than an hour or two at the most, with an average snowfall of well below one inch per year. Total precipitation in the area amounts to over 1000 million gallons per square mile per year and provides an ample 20 million gallons per capita per year.

Natchez is south of the normal range of tornadoes and far enough inland to escape the force of the occasional hurricanes.

History

Natchez takes its name from the Natchez Indians who lived in the area long before the white man. They were an agricultural nation whose culture reached its peak in the mid-1500s and then began to decline, though their Grand Village, where Natchez stands today, remained an active Indian center until 1729.

In 1682, Robert Cavelier, Sieur de La Salle (better known in our schoolbooks as simply La Salle), floated down the Mississippi from French Canada with a group of soldiers and a priest, looking for the mouth of the river. They picked the present site of Natchez as the most desirable location on the long river. From this first contact made by La Salle's party until 1716, the relations between the Indians and the French were cordial. After the French established nearby Fort Rosalie in 1716, relations deteriorated, until in 1729 the Indians massacred the French garrison there. The French retaliated in force and the Natchez Indians vanished as a nation.

In 1763 the British acquired the Natchez territory, but in 1779 the Spanish captured the town. Much of today's city was laid out by a Spanish engineer of that period. But the Spanish did not hold Natchez long, either. In 1797, Andrew Ellicott arrived in Natchez as the representative of George Washington to fix the boundary between the United States and Spanish territories. In 1798 the Spanish evacuated their fort and surrendered the town to the United States. Natchez was made the capital of the new territory and was incorporated as a city in 1803.

Because of the booming trade that began between the new United States and the Spanish-dominated West Indies and Mexico, Natchez suddenly became a point of focus for the adventurers seeking easy fortunes. Flatboats moved up and down the Mississippi and were sometimes dismantled and converted into houses in the growing town. The river waterfront was lined with warehouses, wharves, and shops built on pilings over the water. On an upper street, named Silver Street, were buildings of a better and more permanent type. Buildings on the edge of the bluff overlooking the river had one floor facing onto Middle Street or Royal Street and the higher floor facing onto the more prestigious Silver Street.

The wealth of early Natchez came from the busy commerce on the Mississippi River, but as the town's wealth grew, its foundation on the riverbank crumbled away as the result of frequent landslides and erosion, so that today more than 160 acres of the original city have disappeared into the broad river below. In the winter of 1811–1812 the New Madrid earthquake, centered 300 miles north of

Natchez, shook the town and sent huge swells churning down the river, creating mudslides and tearing boats loose from their moorings. Landslides ripped away much of the already weakened waterfront. Today all that remains of "Natchez Under-the-Hill," the old portion of town below the bluff that supports today's town, is Silver Street and a few old buildings that were missed by the river and the landslides.

Above the bluff, Natchez continued to prosper, and today it is a pleasant mixture of the old and the new, with many old mansions and with new industries springing up around the outskirts of town.

Economy and Employment

Today Natchez is a trade and shipping center for an agricultural region producing livestock, timber, and cotton. Industry includes meat packing, pecan processing, and the manufacture of auto tires and tubes, furniture, boxes, wallboard, rayon pulp, and wood products. With 400 oil wells in Adams County, industrial port facilities on the Mississippi River, and a grain elevator, Natchez has a broadly based economy.

There are two railroads and two airlines serving Natchez, and U.S. highways 84 and 61 intersect here. There is a toll-free bridge across the Mississippi, connecting Natchez to east-central Louisiana and providing ready access to the major market and business centers of the South.

The major employers in the area are: International Paper Co. (processors of wood pulp, over 1100 employees); Armstrong Rubber Co. (tires and tubes, 1100); Diamond International (egg cartons, 380); and Johns-Manville Sales (insulation board, 200).

Current job information can be obtained from:

Mississippi State Employment Agency
807 Main Street
Natchez, MS 39120

Taxes

Mississippi has a state sales tax of 5%. The state income tax ranges from 3% on the first $5000 of taxable income to 4% on incomes above that figure. The residential property tax on a home selling for $65,000 would run about $609 per year.

Shopping

In addition to the downtown center, Natchez has nine shopping centers with some 65 stores, including many major national and regional retail chains. Local facilities are fully adequate for normal needs.

For more extensive shopping, Baton Rouge, Louisiana, is 90 miles to the south, and New Orleans is 54 miles beyond that.

Residential Properties

While there are many modern homes available, Natchez has some of the most beautiful and remarkable antebellum homes in the country. From time to time these become available on the market, offering buyers a wonderful opportunity to restore and live in a national landmark.

Typical listings for contemporary homes include:

GREAT NEIGHBORHOOD. Next-to-new 3-bedroom, 2-bath home with detached carport and screened breezeway. Central air/heat. $64,500.

STARTER HOME. 2 bedrooms, 1 bath. Cute and clean with single garage, rambling roses, and 2 pecan trees. Won't last at $33,900.

EXECUTIVE 4-bedroom, 3-bath home with all the amenities and then some. Beautifully forested lot in excellent area. $87,000.

BEST BUY IN TOWN. 4 bedrooms, 2½ baths, huge backyard, 2-car garage with workshop. $75,000 firm.

Rentals are available, with one-bedroom apartments renting for $125 to $350 per month and two-bedroom condos or apartments renting for $175 to $550.

Safety

Crime in Natchez is moderate, with an FBI Crime Index rating of 92 crimes per thousand of population per year. Police service is provided by 54 full-time policemen. The local fire department has 46 full-time members, and the town has a Class 5 Fire Insurance Rating.

There are no nearby manmade hazards. Since Natchez is situated on a bluff above the Mississippi, floods are not a hazard.

Education

The Natchez-Adams school district has eight elementary schools and six high schools to serve the town and the surrounding area. There are also five local parochial schools.

Copiah-Lincoln Junior College, in Natchez, is a vocational-technical training center that also offers college-level courses. Natchez Junior College also offers two-year college courses.

For more extensive higher education, there are: Louisiana State

University in Baton Rouge, 93 miles to the south; another campus of Louisiana State University in Alexandria, 56 miles to the west; and Alcorn State University at Lorman, Mississippi, 26 miles to the north.

Medical Facilities

Jefferson Davis Memorial Hospital, Natchez Community Hospital, and Charity Hospital serve the needs of the community with a total of 366 beds. Supplementing the hospitals are three nursing homes. There are fifty physicians in private practive in the community, many of whom are also on the staffs of one or more of the hospitals, and there are fifteen dentists practicing locally.

Cultural Activities

The Judge George W. Armstrong Public Library serves the community with 71,168 volumes. The local Little Theater offers productions in February, May, and November. Each March there is the famous Spring Pilgrimage, a month-long tour of 36 antebellum homes. Coupled with the pilgrimage is a show entitled "Southern Exposure," an irreverent satire of the South.

Other activities during the year include: the Antique Show and Sale, sponsored by the Natchez Garden Club each May; the Junior Tennis Open Invitational in June; a high school rodeo in June; the Old Natchez Territorial Fair in September; the Mississippi Medicine Show, a riverboat review presented in connection with the Spring Pilgrimage; and a large number of antique and crafts fairs throughout the year. Natchez also has a museum, a gallery of old photographs, and an art association.

Recreation

Natchez offers a variety of recreational opportunities. There are 8 local parks with swimming pools, 10 tennis courts, and picnic facilities. Duncan Park, in town, has a 9-hole golf course and lighted tennis courts. In addition to the Duncan Park course, there is a country club with an 18-hole course. Seventeen ball fields provide summer recreation for all ages, as do the city's youth centers and the senior citizens' center.

Hunting in the Homochitto Forest and fishing in the Mississippi River backwaters are permitted under a combined hunting and fishing license for $13.50 per year, which permits hunters to bag one deer and one turkey per day during the season. Residents under the age of 16 or above the age of 65 do not require either hunting or fishing licenses.

Government

Natchez operates under the Mayor-Council system, with an elected mayor and a board of aldermen. The mayor is the chief executive and manager of the city.

Water

The local water is alkaline, very soft, and plentiful. There is a city-operated water system with a plant capacity that exceeds peak demand. Water supply and quality appear to be sufficient for all needs for the foreseeable future.

Energy

Electricity is provided by Mississippi Power & Light through three local distributors. With several nuclear power plants along the Mississippi, both above and below Natchez, the electrical needs of the area appear to be assured. Gas is supplied from a number of gas fields in Mississippi and Louisiana by Mississippi Valley Gas Company.

Utility costs for an average two-to-three-bedroom home run about $75 per month.

Television

Three television stations can be received with home antenna systems, and a local cable system provides coverage on 12 channels.

Newspapers

The local daily newspaper is:

The Natchez Democrat
Natchez, MS 39120

The *Jackson* (Mississippi) *Clarion-Ledger* and *News* and the *New Orleans Times-Picayune* are also available locally.

For Further Information

The Natchez–Adams County Chamber of Commerce
P.O. Box 725
Natchez, MS 39120

State of Mississippi
Department of Economic Development
Jackson, MS 39205

Department of Tourism Development
P.O. Box 849
Jackson, MS 39205

Ottumwa, Iowa

POPULATION: 27,354 within the city limits
40,306 in Wapello County

ELEVATION: 651 feet above sea level

Ottumwa is in southeastern Iowa on the Des Moines River, 90 miles southwest of Des Moines. The river divides the city, with the business section and the older residential parts all located on the north bank. North Ottumwa is hilly and still contains many fine old homes and public buildings. South Ottumwa is flatter and contains the newer residential sections, schools, and newer industries.

Southeastern Iowa is a rich, gently rolling agricultural area and has long been an important commercial, rail, and industrial region with rich coal resources. Ottumwa is the trade, shopping, and transportation center for a large, fertile part of the state.

Climate

Because of its latitude and its interior continental location, Iowa's climate is characterized by marked seasonal variations. During the six warm months of the year, the prevailing moist, southerly flow of air from the Gulf of Mexico provides plentiful rainfall. In winter, the prevailing northwesterly flow of dry Canadian air makes the weather cold and relatively dry.

At intervals throughout the year, air masses from the Pacific Ocean move across the Rockies and reach Iowa, bringing comparatively mild and dry weather. The Indian summers of autumn are a result of these Pacific air masses. Sometimes, hot dry winds blow up from the southwest desert areas, bringing temperatures that soar into the 100s and air so dry it desiccates the crops.

Temperatures vary widely. Winters, from December through February, bring temperatures from around freezing to well below that figure, with some 128 days per year with temperatures 32°F and below. The last frost in spring usually comes in the last week of April, and the first frost arrives about the middle of October. Because of the long, sometimes very cold winters, the area has some 6100 heating degree days per year.

Summers are generally mild, with highs normally in the 80s from June through August. Only some 30 days per year have temperatures of 90°F and above, and there are approximately 1000 cooling degree days per year. Spring and fall provide mild days and cool nights.

Snowfall is about 30 inches per year, falling mostly in November through March. Rainfall is a moderate 32 inches per year, and humidity averages about 82% at night, falling to a low 61% in the daytime. There is about 62% of possible sunshine per year in the area.

History

Ottumwa's recorded history started with an Indian chief named Appanoose, who along with his small band of followers established a village on the north bank of the Des Moines River. He called his village Ottumwa, which meant "strong-willed and persevering."

Unlike most American communities, Ottumwa cannot trace its history back to a single settler, other than the Indian chief Appanoose. The first white settlers arrived all at once — 2000 of them on May 1, 1843. The previous autumn, the United States government had purchased all of the land along the Des Moines River from the Fox and Sac tribes for a few cents an acre, but settlement of the land was forbidden until the following May. On the last day of April, throngs of anxious families waited at the starting line for the signal that would start the land rush. At the stroke of midnight, federal troops sent the pioneers racing toward their new claims.

With the coming of the railroad, Ottumwa became an important shipping point for a large agricultural region, but over the years the community has had to fight a continuing battle with the river. For years, Ottumwa bore the well-earned title of Flood City and battled rising waters almost every year.

The city won. The floods have been tamed and the last serious flood was in 1947. With the conquering of the river, more industries began to follow John Deere, which opened a factory in Ottumwa in 1900. The city won another battle when John Morrell, Ottumwa's largest employer, closed its meat-packing plant in 1973. Instead of crying for help, the citizens and businessmen of Ottumwa went out and found new industries to replace Morrell, including another meat packer, George A. Hormel & Company.

Economy and Employment

Today, Ottumwa's economy is broadly based and healthy. It has been named an All-American City and was the location chosen by Dr. Milton Friedman, Nobel Prize winner, for the filming of the conclusion of his award-winning television series, *Free to Choose.*

With three railroads and Amtrak serving the town, Ottumwa is a shipping, trading, shopping, and business center for an 11-county area of southeastern Iowa and northeastern Missouri. It is a growing community with more than 50 manufacturing firms and allied companied producing or processing such diverse products as hay and forage, harvest implements, meat products, automotive supplies, factory-built homes, fiber-glass bathtubs and shower units, agricultural knives, kitchen cabinets, and metal awnings.

Among Ottumwa's major employers are: John Deere's Ottumwa Works (harvesting implements, 2250 employees), George A. Hormel & Company (meat products, 800); Everco Industries (auto parts, 315); and Al-Jon (auto crushing and recycling, 70). A total of 3900 people work in the town's 47 largest plants. In the past five years, there have been no work stoppages in any of these plants for any reason.

Other employment opportunities exist in Ottumwa's many retail, wholesale, and service businesses, with about 12,000 people employed in nonmanufacturing and nonagricultural jobs.

Taxes

Iowa has a 3% state sales tax, and the state income tax ranges from 0.5% on the first $1000 of income to 6% on taxable incomes over $7000. Net incomes under $5000 are not taxable.

Property taxes are higher than in some other best towns, averaging about $1430 per year on a $65,000 home.

Shopping

As the shopping and trading center for an 11-county area, Ottumwa is better able to provide for the shopper than many communities of its size.

For more extensive shopping, Des Moines is only 90 miles to the northwest and Kansas City is 216 miles to the southwest.

Residential Properties

Rentals are never plentiful but can usually be located in the price range desired. Unfurnished one-bedroom apartments rent for about $150 to $325 a month, and two-bedroom apartments rent for $180 to $375, though the newer and more desirable ones may run to $450.

Homes for sale are always available, often with owner financing at interest rates below the current lending rate. A few typical examples are:

WELL-KEPT 3-bedroom ranch home with 1½-car garage and new room. Good location with bus, banking and shopping nearby. Under $40,000.

ATTRACTIVE 3-bedroom ranch with lots of landscaping, fenced back yard, new furnace and water heater. Owner financing. $34,500.

EXTRA-NICE 3-bedroom ranch home with 1½ baths near school, with family room in finished basement and attached garage with workshop. $45,000.

OLDER 3-bedroom home with large yard, trees and shrubs, garage and much more. Contract terms. $20,000.

Safety

The crime rate is low in Ottumwa and always has been. The FBI Crime Index rating is 46 crimes per thousand of population per year. Law enforcement is provided by a 34-man police department, and fire protection is furnished by the city's fire department, which has 42 full-time employees. Ottumwa's Fire Insurance Rating is Class 5 and 6 within the city limits, and Class 7 and 8 in the surrounding county areas. The lower ratings are in the older areas, so check with an insurance agent before selecting a home.

There are no nearby manmade hazards, the closest being the nuclear power plant about 70 miles to the southeast at Burlington.

Education

Ottumwa's public school system provides 12 elementary schools, 3 junior high schools, and 1 high school. Indian Hills Community College merged with Ottumwa Heights College in 1979 to form a single, unified trade, technical, and junior-college program for local students.

The nearest four-year college is William Penn College in Oskaloosa, Iowa, an independent church-supported school with about 600 students.

The University of Iowa is 76 miles northeast in Iowa City and offers a wide variety of programs leading to bachelors', masters', and doctoral degrees.

Medical Facilities

St. Joseph's Hospital, operated by the Sisters of the Humility of Mary, is a fully accredited general hospital with 160 beds, 40 of them designated for long-term health care. Ottumwa Hospital is publicly owned and offers 208 beds. Together, the two hospitals represent an investment of over $6 million for the provision of health care to the community. They offer a unique 24-hour-a-day telephone hotline for parents who need pediatric help or advice, as well as special facilities and services for orthopedic surgery, alcohol and drug abuse counseling, physical and respiratory therapy, and pediatrics.

The new Ottumwa Clinic adjoins the Ottumwa Hospital, and over half of the area's 42 doctors are located there.

Cultural Activities

As in former eras, the citizens of Ottumwa believe in producing their own culture and entertainment. Local events include the Amateur Iowa Art Show in May, a buffalo-burger feed in June, the Summer Music Festival and the Fourth of July celebration in July, and the antique airplane reunion, the four-day Oktoberfest, and the Ozark Opry in fall.

Many area residents support Southeast Iowa Symphony, which gives six concerts a year.

The Community Players offer three stage productions each year, one of which is usually a musical. Ottumwa Heights College also has a theater group and presents four musical and dramatic shows each school year.

Recreation

Ottumwa has something for everyone. There are 5 swimming pools, 16 tennis courts, and two 18-hole golf courses — one a municipal course, the other belonging to the private Ottumwa Country Club. The country club also offers swimming and tennis for its members. The local YMCA, which has a new family center, offers activities including boys' clubs, teen nights, swimming, gymnastics, yoga, guitar lessons, indoor soccer, and racquetball. It has many other programs for men, women, and children.

Boating enthusiasts have the Des Moines River, and some trailer their sailboats or powerboats to Rathbun or Red Rock reservoirs. Fishermen use the river, nearby state parks, and the two federal reservoirs. Both federal reservoirs are within 40 miles of Ottumwa and both offer extensive facilities for boating, swimming, camping, water-skiing, and picnicking. Only a few hours farther away are the Minnesota and Wisconsin lakes to the north and the beautiful Missouri Ozarks to the south.

The area also offers excellent hunting for small game, quail, pheasants, wild turkeys, and ducks.

Government

Ottumwa is governed by a Mayor-Council system, with an elected mayor and four commissioners.

Water

The Ottumwa Water Works provides tap water that is slightly alkaline and soft. With the Des Moines River at its doorstep, Ottumwa's water supply seems assured forever.

Energy

Electricity is supplied by Iowa Southern Utilities Company, which has a new local $300 million coal-fired generating plant. Since some of the nation's largest coal fields are in the general area, power should be available for the foreseeable future. Natural gas is piped in from the Texas and Louisiana fields and distributed by Iowa-Illinois Gas and Electric Company. There are adequate supplies for the present.

At present, local utility costs average about $85 per month for the average home.

Television

There is a local ABC-affiliated television station, and the local cable system brings all major networks to local subscribers.

Newspapers
The local daily newspaper is:

The Ottumwa Courier
Ottumwa, IA 52501

The *Des Moines Register* is also available locally.

For Further Information

Ottumwa Area Chamber of Commerce
P.O. Box 308
Ottumwa, IA 52501

Travel Development
250 Jewett Building
Des Moines, IA 50309

Ponca City, Oklahoma

POPULATION: 26,248 within the city limits
49,750 in Kay County

ELEVATION: 1003 feet above sea level

Ponca City is located in the broad, flat, open prairie country of northern Oklahoma near the Kansas line, 105 miles north of Oklahoma City and 95 miles south of Wichita, Kansas. The Arkansas River is a couple of miles to the southeast and huge Kaw Lake is only 10 miles to the northeast.

Ponca City is a trade, processing, and shipping center in a large grain, livestock, and oil region in the Oklahoma plains country. The local economy has a growing industrial base.

The town was originally named Ponca after the Ponca Indians who lived and hunted in the area, but popular usage of the name

Ponca City caused the post office to change the name to the present one in 1913.

Climate

Oklahoma is located in the southern Great Plains, where the terrain is mostly rolling plains that slope downward from west to east, broken here and there by scattered hilly areas. The climate is mostly continental. Summers are long and sometimes very hot. Winters are shorter and less rigorous than in the northern Great Plains states, and periods of extreme cold are infrequent.

High temperatures in November through March average in the 40s and 50s, and low temperatures are in the 30s and high 20s, though during this period extreme highs have reached the 80s and extreme lows have reached −20°F. Snowfall is usually 8 to 10 inches each year, falling mostly from December through early March. There are 3800 heating degree days each winter and 90 days with temperatures of 32°F and below. The first frost in fall comes in the last week of October, and the last spring frost occurs in the first week of April, leaving some 200 days in the frost-free growing period.

Summer temperatures range from daily lows in the 50s and 60s to daily highs in the 80s and 90s from mid-April to mid-September or later. There are about 70 days per year with temperatures of 90°F and above, and highs in the hundreds occur from June through September. There are about 1800 cooling degree days each year.

Precipitation averages around 30 inches per year, lighter in November through March and somewhat heavier in May and June. The area can sometimes be subject to extremely heavy rains as well as summer droughts. Thunderstorms occur about 50 days per year, generally in the spring and summer months, and are sometimes accompanied by hail. Tornadoes occur throughout the Great Plains, including the Ponca City area, though the chances of any single spot being struck are quite low. Skies are mostly clear, with about 68% of possible sunshine each year. Winds are generally southerly except for the occasional northers that drop temperatures sharply.

History

Ponca city began all at once, in 1893, with the opening of the Cherokee Strip. The U.S. government gave a private developer the right to sell certificates for a drawing for acquiring lots in the newly opened area. More than 2000 people gathered at the proposed site and drew lots. They organized a government by popular assembly.

Economy and Employment

Originally a farming community, Ponca City became an increasingly important petroleum center with the discovery of oil and natural gas in the area. Today it has two large refineries with a combined daily capacity of more than 100,000 barrels. The town also produces more than 75 million pounds of carbon black each year.

Wholesale and retail trade are increasing with the growth in population and income in the area. The greatest expansion in the past year has been in manufacturing. The largest single employer in the area is CONOCO, which employs 845 in its refinery and 3380 in financial, research, engineering, and service positions. The second largest is Huffy, the world's leading bicycle manufacturer. With almost 10 acres of manufacturing and warehouse space and a work force of 600, Huffy offers many opportunities for employment in factory, clerical, supervisory, and technical positions.

Other employers include: Merz, Inc. (makers of special truck bodies for oil fields, 415 employees); Smith-Gruner (rotary oil-field drill bits, 290); Nickles Machine Corp. (diesel-engine parts, 100); and Continental Carbon (carbon black, 80). Other fields of production include pipe fabrication, concrete products, chrome plating, dairy products, clothing, oil-field equipment, cans, electronics controls, transfomers, vacuum systems, and custom welding.

For current job information, write:

Oklahoma Employment Security Commission
1201 West Grand
Ponca City, OK 74601

Taxes

There is a combined state and local sales tax of 4%. The state income tax ranges from 0.5% on the first $2000 of income to 6% on taxable income over $15,000.

The property tax rate is $7.989 per $100 of assessed value, based on 14% of true market value, so a home selling for $65,000 would be taxed approximately $728 per year.

Shopping

Ponca City has an excellent but small business and shopping district, plus several neighborhood shopping centers. The local stores and branches of national chains are quite adequate for the daily needs of local residents.

For more extensive shopping, Oklahoma City is less than two hours to the south via an excellent interstate highway.

Residential Properties

New housing has generally kept pace with the increasing population, so adequate choices are available for the newcomer. Typical listings are:

EASY LIVING in this 4-bedroom home on 1½ acres with a beautiful view. Two living areas and a double fireplace, double garage. $88,500.

FIXER-UPPER. An older 2-bedroom frame home, clean and FHA approved. $19,900.

COUNTRY SETTING for this 3-bedroom mobile home on 2 landscaped acres with new steel storm cellar and 2-car garage. $32,000.

NEW CONDO with 2 bedrooms and 1 bath, patio, energy efficient. $42,000.

OLDER two-story home with 3 bedrooms, central heat and air, living room, dining room, large lot, comfortable family living. $44,900.

Rentals are available but not plentiful. One-bedroom apartments rent for $200 to $400 per month, and two-bedroom condos or apartments rent for $250 to $500.

Safety

The FBI Crime Index rating for Ponca City is a low 56 crimes per thousand of population per year. The police department has 60 full-time officers. The fire department has 66 employees, and the city has a Fire Insurance Rating of Class 5.

There are no nearby nuclear installations or other manmade hazards. Tornadoes are always a hazard in the Great Plains, but the modern tornado warning program provides Ponca City with adequate advance notice.

Education

The public school system serves the area with eight elementary schools, two junior high schools, and one high school. In addition, there are two parochial schools serving students from kindergarten through the sixth grade.

Vocational training is offered at the Pioneer Area Vocational Technical School, located on a 40-acre site in the Airport Industrial Park complex. It provides courses in a large variety of technical, vocational, health, and business subjects.

While there is no institution of higher learning inside the city limits, Ponca City is relatively close to a number of colleges and universities. The nearest is Northern Oklahoma College, a two-year state-supported community college offering courses leading to various associate degrees. It is only 14 miles west at Tonkawa.

Oklahoma State University, at Stillwater, 40 miles to the south, offers a broad curriculum to undergraduates and graduates alike.

Farther away is the University of Oklahoma, at Norman, just south of Oklahoma City, which offers a full curriculum to the doctoral level.

Medical Facilities

St. Joseph Medical Center Hospital has 203 beds and is supplemented by three nursing homes. There are 51 physicians and 10 dentists serving the area.

The Bi-State Mental Health Foundation is also located in Ponca City and serves seven counties in Oklahoma and one in Kansas, providing in-patient and out-patient service and 24-hour emergency service for psychiatric patients. This facility also provides programs for the treatment of alcoholism, hearing and speech defects, and drug abuse.

Oklahoma City, less than two hours away, offers more extensive medical facilities and services if required.

Cultural Activities

The City Cultural Center contains an Indian museum, a studio, and a D.A.R. museum, plus meeting-room facilities. Ponca City also offers a Community Concert Series, the Art Center, local theater performances at the Ponca Playhouse, and a seminar and conference center. The Ponca City library has some 60,000 volumes.

For a greater variety of concerts, theater, and music, Oklahoma City is 105 miles south.

Recreation

There are many recreational opportunities in the area. The city provides an 18-hole public golf course, lighted tennis courts, indoor and outdoor swimming pools, 14 public parks, and a supervised sports program. Golfers also have access to the local country club course.

Lake Ponca is only 2 miles from town and offers fishing, waterskiing, boating, sailing, a playground for children, and camping and picnicking areas.

Kaw Lake, 10 miles northwest of town, was created by impounding the waters of the Arkansas River. It now provides 17,000 acres of recreational water in Oklahoma's rolling hill country. Unlike many such lakes, Kaw Lake is uncluttered with commercial enterprises. There are opportunities for boating, swimming, camping, and picnicking on and around the lake.

In the nearby brush- and tree-covered countryside, hunters can find rabbit and quail. Duck and goose hunting are popular in season, and fishing is excellent on the lakes and in the river.

Government

City government is by the Council-Manager system, with a city commission and a full-time city manager.

Water

The city-supplied water comes from Lake Ponca and 67 wells nearby. Tap water is neutral, hard, and not fluoridated.

Energy

Electricity is supplied by the city from hydroelectric plants on the Arkansas River that are operated by private industry. Natural gas is provided by the Oklahoma Natural Gas Company from a number of gas wells in northern Oklahoma.

The cost of utilities averages around $75 per month for the typical two-bedroom home.

Television

There is no local television station, but good home antenna systems will bring in stations from Oklahoma City, Tulsa, and Wichita, Kansas. The local cable television system provides 12 channels of coverage for subscribers.

Newspapers

The local newspaper, published daily except Saturdays, is:

The Ponca City News
Ponca City, OK 74601

Also, the *Oklahoma City Oklahoman* is available locally.

For Further Information

Ponca City Area Chamber of Commerce
Box 1109
Ponca City, OK 74602

Oklahoma Industrial Development
4024 North Lincoln
Oklahoma City, OK 73152

Oklahoma Tourism & Recreation Dept.
504 Will Rogers Memorial Building
Oklahoma City, OK 73105

Prescott, Arizona

POPULATION: 20,081 within the city limits
56,400 in Yavapai County

ELEVATION: 5364 feet above sea level

Newcomers driving into Prescott have a feeling they have seen it all before. They have. More Western movies have been filmed in the Prescott-Sedona area than perhaps anywhere else except in the desert areas east of Hollywood. Prescott is located in a mountainous, pine-clad section of west-central Arizona, surrounded by some of the most beautiful and picturesque country in the nation.

Scenery is not Prescott's only asset. Located in a mile-high basin among pine-dotted mountains that are rich in minerals, Prescott is a growing manufacturing center as well as the trading center for a large agricultural and livestock-producing area.

While smaller than many of the towns listed in this book, Prescott has much to offer the person or family looking for the small-town way of life.

Climate

Located in a mile-high valley on the western edge of the central mountainous section that divides Arizona, Prescott has a climate that is cooler than that of Phoenix, 100 miles to the south, and warmer than that of Flagstaff, 91 miles to the north. All four seasons are mild and dry, with cool summers and cold winters.

Summers have about 50 days during which temperatures climb to 90°F and above, and there is a total of about 1000 cooling degree days per year. Winters bring an average of 131 days with temperatures of 32°F and below, with 4362 heating degree days. The growing season is approximately 215 days.

Precipitation is low, totaling only 18 inches per year, with most of it coming in the form of rain in July and August and as snow from November through March. Often the summer rains come as thundershowers that move north from the Gulf of Mexico to the mountains.

Many people feel that Prescott has the best climate in Arizona. Summer daytime temperatures are normally in the high 80s, but the nights always cool off to the 50s, with a humidity of seldom more than 45%. Winter daytime temperatures are usually in the 40s, with lows in the teens to the twenties at night.

History

Archaeologists estimate that the earliest settlers in the Prescott area were there at least 25,000 years ago. Large Indian settlements there declined about A.D.1300, leaving behind some of the tourist attractions of today.

Spanish explorers passed through the area in the sixteenth century, looking for, but not finding, the gold that had lured them westward and northward from settlements in Mexico and on the Gulf of Mexico.

In 1863 placer claims were established along Lynx Creek, 5 miles from today's Prescott. More discoveries were made along Kasayampa, Turkey, Big Bug, Granite, and Antelope creeks. This new wealth had such an impact that President Lincoln established the Arizona Territory that same year, naming Prescott the territorial capital.

Prescott was named after historian William H. Prescott, whose

research also resulted in the naming of many of the town's present-day streets, such as Montezuma, Cortez, and Alarcon. It was a roaring mining camp in its earliest days. The first saloon was opened on the bank of Granite Creek, but "Whiskey Row" developed along Montezuma Street, where 20 saloons served miners and cowboys 24 hours a day.

As people moved into Prescott to exploit the needs of the miners and cowboys, mercantile enterprises, livery stables, and two newspapers opened up to supplement the three breweries and proliferating saloons and bawdy houses. The first school opened in 1864, the same year Prescott officially became a town.

Prescott remained the territorial capital for only three years, after which the government was transferred to Tucson. In 1877, Prescott became the capital once again, but in 1899 it lost the honor permanently to Phoenix.

On the night of July 14, 1900, the worst possible disaster for a frontier town — fire — hit Prescott. Despite the efforts of a capable volunteer fire department that pumped the town's reservoir dry, 5 of Prescott's largest hotels, 25 saloons, and more than 50 other business establishments were lost. The financial loss was $1.5 million — in today's dollars, perhaps twenty times that.

Prescott has had its share of unusual people. George Ruffner, frontier sheriff and cowboy, was a one-man police force who made history on the Arizona frontier. When he died in 1933, at the age of 71, he was Arizona's oldest active peace officer.

Bucky O'Neill was another colorful resident — a sheriff, mayor, and sometime newspaperman who helped organize the famous Rough Riders of Spanish-American War fame. He rode beside Teddy Roosevelt and died on a Cuban hillside.

Economy and Employment

Prescott is the administrative headquarters for the Prescott National Forest, which has an annual payroll of nearly $2 million. Other major government employers in the area include the Arizona Department of Transportation; the Veterans' Administration Center at Fort Whipple; Yavapai County; the City of Prescott; and the Prescott public schools.

The fastest-growing sector of the economy is manufacturing. The Morris-Maler Manufacturing Company makes women's blouses and employs approximately 230 people. Other major employers include: U.S. Electrical Motors, a division of Emerson Electric Corporation, with over 500 employees and an annual payroll of over $4 million;

Airborne Navigation Corp. (navigation equipment, 90); the Veterans' Administration Hospital (434); and Aquarium Pump Supply (pumps, 80). Cyprus-Bagdad Corp. maintains a large open-pit copper mine and refinery 66 miles west of Prescott.

Cattle and sheep raising are the main agricultural activities, and mining is still important. Tourism is increasing, and the area is beginning to be discovered as a desirable place for retirement.

For current employment information, write:

Manager
Department of Economic Security
234 Grove Ave.
Prescott, AZ 86301

Include a stamped, self-addressed envelope to ensure a quick reply.

Taxes

The combined state and local sales tax is 5%. Arizona's state income tax amounts to approximately 15% of the federal income tax.

Property taxes are based on an assessment of 15% of market value, and the tax rate is $12.05 per $100. Thus the tax on a home selling for $65,000 would be approximately $1175 per year.

Shopping

As the trading center for a large mining and livestock-raising area, Prescott offers good shopping facilities. As in many frontier towns, downtown commerce centers on the county courthouse square. In this central area, and in outlying shopping centers, are many national and regional chains and local specialty shops.

For more extensive shopping, Phoenix is about 100 miles to the south.

Residential Properties

At present, there are many homes and apartments available for purchase or rental. A few typical listings of homes for sale are:

NEAT, WELL-KEPT 3-bedroom, 2-bath home in good neighborhood with owner financing. A bargain at $58,600.

PERT AND PRETTY with picket fence and close enough to walk to town. Two bedrooms, one bath, and single garage. $39,900.

LARGE, SPACIOUS AND GRACIOUS. This one is immaculate and ready for occupancy. Three bedrooms, 3 baths, outsize double garage high enough for boat storage. $79,900.

BEST VIEW FOR MILES. High on a hill with wide decks and cozy fireplaces in living and family rooms. Four bedrooms and two baths. Great financing at $88,500.

One-bedroom apartments currently rent for $200 to $350 per month, and two-bedroom units for $250 to $500.

Safety

Prescott's FBI Crime Index rating is 56 crimes per thousand of population per year, making it one of the safest of the best towns. The police department has 22 officers and 7 other employees. The fire department operates from four stations and has 54 employees. The Fire Insurance Rating is Class 4.

There are no natural or manmade hazards in the area.

Education

Prescott's public school system provides five elementary schools, two junior high schools, and one senior high school. There are also a privately operated nursery school, parochial schools, and other schools, including a private college preparatory school.

Yavapai Community College is a two-year state college with a technical-vocational program and an academic-transfer program.

Prescott Center College is a four-year experimental liberal-arts college.

Embry-Riddle-Arizona, also in Prescott, is a small university offering a degree in aeronautical science.

For broader choices in higher education, Arizona State University is located 100 miles to the south in Tempe, a suburb of Phoenix, and offers undergraduate and graduate studies to over 36,000 students.

Medical Facilities

Yavapai Community Hospital, with 138 beds, offers a full range of medical services to the area. There is also a Veterans' Administration Hospital for veterans.

There are 32 doctors and surgeons, 22 dentists, 9 chiropractors, 2 podiatrists, 3 osteopaths, 2 orthodontists, 2 orthopedists, 5 optometrists, 2 opticians, and 2 ophthalmologists serving the community.

Cultural Activities

The public library has a new modern building and serves as headquarters for a countywide system that houses over 72,000 volumes.

Prescott is a center of western art and is the home of many painters and sculptors working in this field. The annual George Phippen

Memorial Western Art Show brings many western artists and visitors to the courthouse square.

The Phoenix Symphony Orchestra presents four concerts each season in Prescott's Hendrix Auditorium. The local concert association brings music, dance, and other performances to the auditorium during the year, and Yavapai Community College brings various artists and performers to the college for students and the general public.

The old Territorial Governor's Mansion has been restored and is now a museum. It is the site of the annual Folk Arts Fair.

Recreation

Prescott is located in an area that encourages outdoor activities. Its most famous event is the spectacular Frontier Days Celebration, which centers on the world's oldest continuous rodeo. This celebration, held each Fourth of July weekend, has its roots in the traditional cowboy contests of territorial days.

Each August, during the dark of the moon, the Smoki People, a "tribe" of non-Indians living in Prescott, stage their now-famous Ceremonials and Snake Dance. Organized in 1921, the Smoki have developed their entertainment into a huge pageant dedicated to the reproduction of old Indian ceremonials.

For the golfer, Antelope Hills Golf Course, rated as one of Arizona's best, is open throughout the year and is one of the few courses in the nation whose pro shop is connected to an airport by a taxi strip. The 18-hole, 6827-yard course has served as the site for the U.S. Open and the U.S. Amateur regional qualifying rounds. Prescott Country Club, about 15 miles from town, is privately owned, but its 18-hole course is open to the public. It offers members a swimming pool, tennis courts, shuffleboard, a dining room, and clubhouse activities.

In the nearby Prescott National Forest, hiking, backpacking, camping, picnicking, and other outdoor activities are popular with residents and visitors. The forest service maintains public campgrounds in five locations within 10 miles of town, all with rest rooms, picnic tables, and fireplaces.

The city provides 15 softball fields, some of which also double as soccer and football fields in season, and maintains an Adult Center that offers programs in crafts, languages, sewing, round and ballroom dancing, quilting, shuffleboard, bridge, pool, and group travel. Two local gun clubs provide pistol and rifle ranges, as well as trapshooting and skeet shooting.

Fishermen in the Prescott area are fortunate in that there is no closed season on any species of fish, and no limitation on day or night fishing. A fishing license is required. Near Prescott are Lynx Lake, Watson and Willow lakes, Goldwater Lake, and Granite Basin Lake, all open for fishing.

Hunters can find seven species of game: deer, javelinas, elk, turkeys, antelope, bighorn sheep, and buffaloes. In addition, bears and mountain lions are also classed as game animals. Predators and non-game animals such as foxes, skunks, coyotes, jaguars, weasels, bobcats, ocelots, and porcupines may be taken at any time if one has a valid hunting license.

Government

Prescott has a Council-Manager form of government, with an elected mayor and city council employing a full-time city manager.

Water

Tap water is neutral, pure, soft, and not fluoridated. The supply appears adequate to accommodate considerable population growth.

Energy

Electricity is supplied by the Arizona Public Service Company from hydroelectric plants nearby. Natural gas is distributed by Southern Union Gas Company.

Utility bills in this area average about $100 per month for a two-bedroom home.

Television

A local cable television system provides major network coverage, and a weather/music channel and Home Box Office are also available.

Newspapers

The local newspaper, published daily except Saturday, is:

The Prescott Courier
P.O. Box 312
Prescott, AZ 86302

There is also a weekly newspaper, the *Prescott Paper,* which is published on Wednesdays and contains only local news.

The morning and evening editions of the Phoenix papers are available locally.

For Further Information

Prescott Chamber of Commerce
P.O. Box 1137
Prescott, AZ 86302

Arizona Office of Tourism
501 State Capitol
Phoenix, AZ 85007

Quincy, Illinois

POPULATION: 42,048 within the city limits
71,622 in Adams County

ELEVATION: 482 feet above sea level at the Mississippi River
600 feet above sea level in the northeast section of town

Quincy rests on the bluffs overlooking the Mississippi River in western Illinois. It has a good river harbor and is an important river port as well as a trading, industrial, and distribution center for a rich grain- and livestock-producing area.

Items manufactured in Quincy include metal wheels, air compressors, agricultural equipment, and truck and tractor bodies.

Among Quincy's claims to fame are the well-known people who were born there, including actress Mary Astor and actors John Anderson, Fred MacMurray, and John Livingstone (better known as the Lone Ranger).

Climate

The Illinois climate is typically continental, with cold winters, warm summers, and frequent brief fluctuations in temperature, humidity, cloud cover, and wind direction. The excellent soil and well-distributed 40 inches of annual precipitation are responsible for the excellent agricultural productivity of the area. The countryside is flat but well drained.

Winters are cold, with daytime high temperatures in the 40s and nighttime lows in the 20s and 30s from December through February. Extreme lows can reach −22°F, and there are normally 83 days per year with temperatures of 32°F and below. The last frost in spring is about April 10, and the first frost in fall comes about October 20, giving the area a 210-day frost-free growing season. Winters bring about 4900 heating degree days per year. Snowfall averages about 18 inches per year, falling from November through March. Winter winds are westerly to northwesterly.

Summers are warm to hot, with temperatures exceeding 90°F about 46 days per year, though the average daytime highs are in the upper 80s and the average nighttime lows are in the 60s from June into September. There are about 1500 cooling degree days per year.

Precipitation is fairly evenly distributed throughout the year, with slightly heavier rainfall in March through June. Thunderstorms are frequent in the summer months, often cooling off the hot afternoons. Humidity is moderate, and there is about 65% of possible sunshine each year.

History

Quincy's modern history began with John Wood and Willard Keys, who sailed into Quincy Bay in 1820. The bay is a natural harbor, the largest on the Mississippi, and the two enterprising Yankees felt it would be a good place for a town. Two years later they returned and founded the town, naming it Quincy after the already named Quincy Bay.

Quincy grew up as a river town, a town of riverboats and rivermen, pioneers and gamblers, merchants and speculators. Together they built warehouses and the mansions on the bluffs above the bay. Early immigrants from Ireland and Germany built neighborhoods of working-class houses and fine Italianate mansions.

After the Civil War, Quincy rivaled Chicago in size and importance as a shipping and rail center. It flourished until the railroads found more direct routes to Chicago. But while Quincy was losing importance as a shipping center, it was quietly developing industry and trade.

Today Quincy is a major Middle Western repository of architecture. It is filled with Federal and Greek Revival structures, Italian villas, and the slated mansard roofs characteristic of Second Empire architecture.

Economy and Employment

Today Quincy has a sound balance of manufacturing, wholesale and retail trade, and service industries. The new Edward Schneidman Industrial Park is attracting new industry at an increasing rate. Because of the growing cost of overland transportation, the economical river transportation system is regaining some of its former importance. Five barge lines service Quincy, and the waterfront is active. Employee turnover rate and unemployment are below the national average.

Major industries in Quincy are: Gardner Denver Co. (makers of air compressors and pumps, with over 1500 employees); Electric Wheel Division of Firestone (wheels, rims, hubs, spindles, 1500); Harris Corp. (broadcast equipment, 1000); Moorman Manufacturing Co. (poultry and livestock feeds, 800 to 1200); and Colt Industries (compressors, 400 to 800). Other major employers include Huck Fixture Co., Quincy Paper Box, Quincy Soybean, and Davis Cleaver Produce.

Taxes

Illinois has a flat state income tax of 2.5% of net income. There is a state sales tax of 4% and a local sales tax of 1%, making a total of 5% for Quincy.

Property taxes are based on an assessed value of one-third of market value. The tax rate is $6.2101 per $100 of assessed value, so a home selling for $65,000 would be taxed approximately $1345 per year.

Shopping

There are three major shopping areas in Quincy, and numerous neighborhood stores. All normal needs can be met locally, but for more extensive shopping St. Louis is only 120 miles to the southeast.

Residential Properties

Rentals are available, either in apartment buildings or separate houses. One-bedroom apartments rent for $90 to $250 per month. Two-bedroom apartments rent for $165 to $325 per month, and three-bedroom townhouses can be rented for $350 to $400.

There are homes for sale in all price ranges. A few sample listings are:

WITHIN WALKING DISTANCE of Quincy Mall, this 2-bedroom home has living room, dining room, kitchen, full basement, and is close to schools. $28,750.

VERY CLEAN 3-bedroom home with 2-car garage, fully carpeted with central heat and air. Attractive financing. $46,500.

LOW-INTEREST LOAN on this 3-bedroom 1½-bath brick ranch home on 1¼ acres. Large fireplace in big living room. Spacious country kitchen with all appliances, 2-car garage, full basement, close to schools and shopping. $63,900.

LARGE HOME with over 2700 square feet, 4 bedrooms, 2 baths, family dining room, big kitchen with walnut cabinets, range, oven, dishwasher. All this on 5 acres with 2-car garage and owner financing. $88,900.

Safety

The FBI Crime Index rating for Quincy is a low 64 crimes per thousand of population per year. The local police department has 64 full-time officers, 14 civilian personnel, 10 vehicles, an emergency TAC squad, and a communications tie-in with the county sheriff. Fire protection is provided by 5 fire stations in town with 71 firemen, 6 line pumpers, 3 reserve pumpers, a reserve aerial truck, and a rescue truck. The Fire Insurance Rating is Class 4.

There are no known nearby manmade hazards. The nearest nuclear-storage area is in Burlington, Iowa, 60 miles to the north. While the Mississippi River has flooded in the past, the Army Corps of Engineers has provided flood controls that should prevent any future danger from flooding.

Education

There are 21 public and private elementary schools in Quincy, with a total enrollment of almost 7000. Adams County has another 11 schools with an enrollment of about 2400.

High schools include 4 county schools, grades nine through twelve, a parochial high school, also grades nine through twelve, a city public high school for ninth and tenth grades, and a city public high school for grades eleven and twelve.

John Wood Community College is a two-year public liberal-arts and vocational college with 4500 full-time and part-time students.

Quincy College is a four-year Catholic liberal-arts college with 1200 students.

Gem City College is a private vocational school offering courses in horology, business, fashion, merchandising, and cosmetology.

For higher education outside of Quincy, the University of Missouri at St. Louis, 120 miles to the southeast, offers a broad curriculum for undergraduate studies and graduate studies to the doctoral level.

Medical Facilities

There are two hospitals serving Quincy: Blessing Hospital, which has 278 beds, and St. Mary Hospital, operated by the Franciscan Sisters of the Poor, which has 277 beds and specializes in drug-abuse therapy, psychiatry, and inhalation therapy. The Illinois Veterans' Home Hospital has 50 beds and a nursing home with 513 beds for veterans.

There are over 85 doctors, 26 dentists, 2 orthodontists, 9 chiropractors, 2 osteopaths, and 3 podiatrists in the community. Two large clinics and a family-practice center supplement the other medical services.

For more specialized medical services than are available locally, St. Louis is only a couple of hours away and has some of the best medical facilities in the nation.

Cultural Activities

The Quincy public library has over 128,000 volumes, and the Great River Library System provides interlibrary loans, making available the services and collections of virtually every other library in the state of Illinois. Also, the Quincy College Library has a collection of 182,000 volumes.

The Symphony Orchestra gives several concerts each year, and the Civic Music Association brings in artists for an annual series of programs. The Little Theater is active in bringing live stage performances to the community.

Other local organizations include the Society of Fine Arts, the Sunday Music Series, the Progressive Playhouse, the Junior Theater, the Photographic Society, and the music and theater departments of Quincy College, all of which bring cultural and artistic activities to the community throughout the year.

Recreation

The Quincy Park District operates 19 parks containing some 1400 acres of parkland, on which are provided a 27-hole golf course, 26 tennis courts, 29 horseshoe courts, 8 softball/baseball fields, and 5 boat launches. The district also operates Quinsippi Island, an island in the Mississippi that has a marina, a reconstructed pioneer village, an Indian museum, and a miniature railway.

Siloam Springs State Park, 25 miles east of Quincy, offers fishing, boating, camping, hunting, horseback riding, and picnicking. Wakonda State Park, 14 miles northwest of Quincy, offers similar facilities.

Private country clubs offer two 18-hole golf courses, swimming pools, tennis courts, and clubhouses. There are also six private boat clubs, a racquet and tennis club, and a swim club.

Government
Quincy operates under the Mayor-Council system, with a mayor and a board of aldermen.

Water
Local water is drawn from the Mississippi River and treated at the local water plant. Thc tap watcr is alkaline, soft, and fluoridated. Since the water comes from the river, the supply is unlimited. The only potential problem would be from upstream pollution, which means that the water supply must be constantly monitored for purity.

Energy
Electricity is supplied by the Central Illinois Public Service Company from a variety of fossil-fuel and nuclear generating plants. Natural gas is supplied by the same company and comes from gas fields in Texas, Louisiana, and Oklahoma.

Utility costs at present run about $100 per month for the average two-to-three-bedroom home.

Television
The two local television stations are affiliated with NBC and CBS. Other nearby stations can be received on home antenna systems, and there is a cable system that provides movies and full-channel coverage to subscribers.

Newspapers
The local daily newspaper is:

The Quincy Herald-Whig
Quincy, IL 62301

Several weekly newspapers are also published in the area. The *St. Louis Post-Dispatch* and the *Chicago Tribune* are available locally.

For Further Information

Quincy Area Chamber of Commerce
314 Main St.
Quincy, IL 62301

Office of Tourism
222 South College St.
Springfield, IL 62706

Redding, California

POPULATION: 42,005 within the city limits
108,700 in Shasta County

ELEVATION: 560 feet above sea level

Redding, located on Interstate 5 in north-central California, is the tourist center for California's northern mountain region because of its nearness to the Lassen and Shasta Park areas. It is on the Sacramento River at the upper end of the huge Sacramento Valley, between the Sierra Nevada on the east and the Trinity Alps portion of the Coast Range on the west.

The region is prosperous, with an economy based on a stable blending of tourism, mining, lumbering, and farming.

Climate

To the east of Redding the Sierra forms a barrier against the extremely cold air of the Great Basin in winter, though on occasion cold air moves southward between the mountain chains. To the west, the Coast Range breaks the storms moving in from the Pacific. The temperature pattern is intermediate between the maritime and continental, with hot summers and moderate winters.

Temperatures in winter range from highs in the 50s to lows in the 30s and 40s, with occasional drops into the 20s. There are 2700 heating degree days per year and about 275 days of frost-free growing season, with the last frost coming at the end of February and the first at the end of November. There are about 25 days with temperatures 32°F and below.

Summers are long and hot with temperatures in the 90s from June through September and about 100 days per year with temperatures of 90°F and above. Extreme maximum temperatures of 114°F have been reached in all four of these months. There are normally 1900 cooling degree days per year. Sunshine averages about 75% of possible sunshine per year.

Precipitation is about 22 inches per year, mostly in November through March, and snow is seldom more than 2 inches per year and only stays on the ground briefly. Prevailing winds are westerly, swinging to the northwest in winter and to the southwest in summer.

History

Two men shaped the history of Redding, men with names almost alike — Pierson B. Reading and Benjamin B. Redding. Reading was one of the first pioneers in the lumber industry in Shasta County, starting operations in 1843. He and his partner obtained a Spanish land grant for 26,000 acres along the Sacramento River. Reading built a home, stocked his ranch with cattle and horses, and planted northern California's first grapevines and the state's first cotton. In 1862 he mapped out a town near the mouth of Clear Creek, where it runs into the Sacramento River.

The railroad arrived in 1872, four years after Reading's death. With the railroad came a man named Benjamin Redding, land agent for the Central Pacific railroad. The railhead near the townsite begin to develop, and the legislature named the town Reading, after its original developer. The railroad refused to recognize the name and insisted that the town be named for their land agent, Redding. In 1880 the townspeople and the legislature gave in and accepted the railroad's name. By then, there were 9492 residents, of which 1326 were Chinese, 1037 Indian, and 53 black.

As a railway, shopping, and trading center, Redding has grown slowly and prospered.

Economy and Employment

Following World War II, the well-established lumber and wood-products industry began to be supplemented by cabinetmaking companies, foundries, dairying, cement manufacturing, boat building, and many other new enterprises. In addition, Redding became the gateway to a very large and increasingly popular recreational area known as the Golden Circle, which contains Shasta Dam, Mt. Shasta, Lassen Volcanic National Park, Lake Almanor, Whiskeytown Lake, Trinity Lake, and Burney Falls. These attractions bring a steady flow of tourists to Redding and make retail trade a very important part of the local economy.

Retail trade employs 20% of the work force, and another 20% are employed in service industries. Government employs 24%, of which two-thirds are in education. Manufacturing accounts for 11%, of which about half are involved in the production of lumber and wood products and half in various light industries. Mining and construction employ 7%, wholesale trade 4%, finance and insurance 4%, and agriculture only 3%.

Major employers in the area include: Roseburg Lumber (350 employees); Champion Building Products (plywood, lumber, and boxes, 470); Simpson Lee Paper Co. (paper products, 600); Jhirmack Enterprises (beauty-salon products, 237); and Calaveras Cement (109). Other employers include the Memorial, Mercy, and Shasta hospitals (1100 employees in all); Pacific Telephone (392); Shasta College (327); and CH_2M Hill, Inc. (consulting, 190).

With the slowdown in the building trades, unemployment has risen in the lumber and wood-products industries, but other fields of employment seem unaffected at this time.

Taxes

The state and local sales taxes total 6%, and the state income tax ranges from 1% on the first $2630 of taxable income to 11% on incomes over $20,450.

Property taxes are assessed at 1.0208% of full market value, under the limitations of Proposition 13. This means that a home selling for $65,000 would pay approximately $665 in taxes per year.

Shopping

As an important tourist center for the large surrounding area, Redding's shopping facilities are better than would be expected for its size. The new Downtown Mall, located in the center of town, is a completely enclosed, climate-controlled shopping area with ample multilevel parking.

For wider variety, San Francisco is about 220 miles to the south.

Residential Properties

The median purchase price in 1981 for an existing single-family home was $73,000. Rentals are comparably high, with two-bedroom apartments running $285 to $365 per month and single-bedroom apartments running about $210 to $300. Executive homes rent for $500 a month and up.

A few typical offerings of homes for sale are:

COUNTRY HOME with 3 bedrooms and 1200 square feet of living space, on ½ acre with trees and a small barn and single garage. $54,900.

COMFORTABLE 3-bedroom home with utilities, built-in pool, deck with barbecue, and a dining-family room. $63,500.

$12,500 DOWN will get you into this 3-bedroom, 1½-bath home with plush carpets, tile countertops, large bedrooms and tree-shaded lot on quiet cul-de-sac. $95,000 with assumable loan.

LARGE FAMILY HOME with 4 bedrooms, 2½ baths, view of mountains, family room with wet-bar, inside utility room, landscaped and fenced. $115,000 with assumable first and owner will carry second.

Safety

Redding's FBI Crime Index rating is 85 crimes per thousand of population per year. The police department has 70 officers and patrolmen, 20 technicians, 30 enclosed vehicles, and 4 motorcycles. Fire protection is provided by a fire department with 19 officers, 34 firemen, 5 dispatchers, 17 fire vehicles, and 6 other vehicles. The Fire Insurance Rating is Class 4.

There are no natural hazards except for California's ever-present earthquake potential. There are no manmade hazards closer than Sacramento's nuclear power plant and Tactical Air Command Base (TAC) 163 miles to the south and Eureka's nuclear power plant 158 miles to the west, on the other side of the Coast Range.

Education

There are fourteen elementary schools and five high schools serving Redding and the surrounding area. In addition, there are five private schools for students in kindergarten through the twelfth grade.

Shasta College, in Redding, is a two-year junior college with 8000 students in various fields including liberal arts, preprofessional studies, and career programs in accounting, administration of justice, agriculture, auto technology, banking, clerical skills, computer studies, electronics, engineering, journalism, and other areas leading to A.A. and A.S. degrees.

The nearest four-year university is California State University at Chico, 72 miles to the south.

Medical Facilities

There are three excellent hospitals in Redding. Memorial Hospital has 132 beds and specializes in cardiology, orthopedics, and respiratory and cardiac rehabilitation. Mercy Hospital, with 260 beds, specializes in surgery, obstetrics, pediatric/neonatal care, cancer treatment, and trauma therapy. Shasta General Hospital, with 75 beds, specializes in mental health.

Cultural Activities

Much of the local culture is centered on Shasta College, which has a 2300-seat amphitheater and a College Theater with 477 seats. The latter is the home of the Community Theater and the Summer Festival of the Arts.

The Shasta Symphony Orchestra performs several times a year for local audiences, and the Community Concert Series brings top-quality musical and dance performances to town.

For larger events and conventions, the Redding Civic Auditorium seats over 2000 and the outdoor College Sports Stadium seats 3000.

The county library serves the community with 154,967 volumes, and the Shasta College library supplements that with some 65,000 volumes.

Recreation

Redding is in the center of a huge outdoor recreational area. Locally, there are 20 developed parks and playgrounds and 6 golf courses, and nearby there are 4 major lakes: Shasta, Whiskeytown, Lake Britton, and Trinity.

Within a 75-mile radius of Redding are many rivers, lakes, mountains, state and national parks, and huge wilderness areas. Lake

Shasta is the most impressive body of water in the area, with 370 miles of shoreline. It is a haven for houseboaters, and fishermen take bass, crappie, trout, catfish, and giant sturgeon from the lake. The nearby Trinity Alps Wilderness Area and Trinity Lake are popular attractions. Trinity Lake holds the state record for smallmouth bass at 9.14 pounds and has a great kokanee salmon fishery. Lake Siskiyou is probably the most beautiful of all northern California lakes. It has a fine campground and offers outstanding fishing.

The McCloud River, east of Mt. Shasta, offers great fly fishing for trout. The Pit River, home of the Pacific Gas and Electric power stations, is another fine trout-fishing area. White-water canoe and raft trips are available on the Sacramento River.

In wintertime the ski slopes of Mt. Shasta and Mt. Lassen are excellent. Both areas have dining and lodging facilities nearby.

Government

Redding has the Council-Manager form of local government.

Water

Water is supplied by the municipal water department, which draws its supply from local rivers and lakes. There is more than enough good water for the foreseeable future. The local tap water is slightly acid, very soft, and not fluoridated.

Energy

Electricity is supplied by Redding Municipal Utilities and is drawn from Pacific Gas and Electric Company's vast northern California system. Much of the power is generated in the many huge hydroelectric plants on the nearby rivers.

Natural gas is supplied by Pacific Gas and Electric Company and is piped to the area from the central and southern California gas fields.

At present rates, utilities cost about $200 per month for the average two-to-three-bedroom home.

Television

There are two local television stations, and the local cable television system provides full coverage for subscribers.

Newspapers

The local daily newspaper is:

The Redding Record Searchlight
P.O. Box 2397
Redding, CA 96099

The San Francisco and Sacramento papers are also available locally.

For Further Information

Greater Redding Chamber of Commerce
P.O. Box 1180
Redding, CA 96099

Department of Parks & Recreation
State of California
P.O. Box 2390
Sacramento, CA 95811

Rocky Mount, North Carolina

POPULATION: 41,573 within the city limits
64,700 in the immediate area

ELEVATION: 121 feet above sea level

Rocky Mount is located in the coastal plains area of northeastern North Carolina, some 50 miles east-northeast of Raleigh, on the Tar River. Located on the border of Edgecombe and Nash counties, and serving both counties, it is a shipping and trading center for tobacco and cotton growers.

One of the largest leaf-tobacco markets in the world, Rocky Mount has several drying plants, warehouses, and auction centers. Other local crops include cotton, corn, peanuts, and pine timber.

Area manufacturers produce textiles, clothing, concrete, metal products, chemicals, electrical equipment and supplies, and stone, glass, and clay products.

Climate

Situated in the broad coastal plain of North Carolina, Rocky Mount is about 60 miles from any large body of water and twice that distance from the Atlantic Ocean. While weather in this area is moderated by the ocean, Rocky Mount is far enough inland to miss the force of the sometimes violent Atlantic storms.

There are four distinct seasons in this region. Summers are warm and sometimes hot, with highs in the 80s and 90s from June through August and into September. Summers bring about 48 days with temperatures 90°F and above, and there are about 1500 cooling degree days per year. Fall and spring bring highs in the 60s and 70s and lows in the 40s and 50s.

Winters are generally short and mild, with lows in the mid-30s from December into March and about 41 days with temperatures of 32°F and below. There are about 3500 heating degree days per year. The last frost of winter comes around March 18 and the first fall frost arrives around the end of November, leaving 254 days between frosts. Snowfall totals about 6 inches per year and occurs generally in December through March.

Precipitation is about 50 inches per year, fairly evenly divided throughout the 12 months, except for the thunderstorm season of July through September when there is somewhat higher rainfall. Winds are generally moderate, blowing from the north to northwest in winter and from the south to southwest in summer.

History

There isn't much history of note in Rocky Mount's past. It was a small tobacco and cotton town and stayed that way for many years. It first belonged to the Tuscarora Indians, who settled beside the rocky mounds at the Great Falls on the Tar River.

In 1744 the first gristmills and sawmills were built beside the falls. By 1818 the first cotton mill began operation. The Civil War and the Reconstruction era slowed the modest growth of the community, but in 1867 Rocky Mount was incorporated as a town with a population of 300.

By 1900 the population had increased to 3000 as a result of the growth of the tobacco and cotton markets and the development of the railroad line through town.

From 1900 until after World War II, not much happened to Rocky Mount. It grew slowly and quietly.

Economy and Employment

North Carolina is the largest tobacco manufacturing state in the nation, and Rocky Mount is one of the largest tobacco markets. But tobacco is no longer its only source of income. The city maintains a varied and vigorous economy bolstered by rapid industrial expansion. During the past decade, more than a dozen blue-chip companies have located plants in the Rocky Mount area. The city's economic profile includes textiles, timber products, pharmaceuticals, electronics, insurance, banking, transportation, steel fabrication, furniture manufacturing, locksets and security systems, plastics, power systems, and food services.

The area's cost of living has remained below the national average, as have construction costs, and the temperate climate contributes to a lower-than-average cost for fuel, clothing, and housing.

There are employment opportunities in a wide variety of fields in Rocky Mount. Some of the major employers are: Abbott Laboratories (one of the world's largest pharmaceutical companies, 1500 employees); China American Tobacco Co. (processors and exporters of tobacco, 1000); Burlington Industries (drapery fabrics, 2100 employees in four local plants); Schlage Lock Co. (producers of 5 million to 6 million locksets each year, 700); Ilco-Unican Security Systems (key machines, keys, security systems, and cabinet hardware, 400); Barcalounger Co. (reclining chairs, 500); Polylok Corp. (drapery materials, 1000); Texfi-K, Inc. (yarns, 1000); London Mills (velour and velvet-pile fabrics, 500); and Masonite Corp. (particleboard, 500).

There are many smaller companies involved in the area of food production, tobacco, textiles, apparel, lumber and wood products, furniture, metals, machinery, construction, utilities, finance, insurance, real estate, and many services.

Taxes

The state and local sales taxes total 4%, and the state income tax ranges from 3% on the first $2000 of taxable income to 7% on incomes over $10,000 per year.

Property taxes arc $1.64 per $100 of assessed value in the Edgecombe County half of town and $1.42 per $100 of valuation in the Nash County part. A $65,000 home would be taxed $1066 per year in Edgecombe County and $923 in Nash County.

Shopping

Rocky Mount has a downtown shopping area plus neighborhood shopping centers. All day-to-day shopping needs can be met locally. For more extensive shopping, Raleigh is 50 miles to the west.

Residential Properties

Houses and apartments are available for rent or purchase. One-bedroom apartments rent for $100 to $200 per month. Two-bedroom apartments can be rented for $175 to $275 per month, and three-bedroom houses rent for $275 to $450 per month.

Many homes are available for purchase. A few typical listings are:

OWNER WILL FINANCE this 3-bedroom 2-bath brick home in excellent condition, with fenced yard, patio, 20 × 30 workshop, insulated, paneled, and many other features. $46,500.

20-YEAR-OLD 4-bedroom, 2-bath home paneled with knotty pine and a fireplace in the living room. Only $35,000.

OLDER HOME with 3 bedrooms, 1½ baths, den, living room, and kitchen. $23,500.

EXECUTIVE HOME with 3 large bedrooms, 2 baths, living room, dining room, and den with fireplace, for a family who likes outdoor activities, with privacy fencing and 18′ × 36′ pool. Home is 2053 square feet and priced at $96,500 with a 9% assumable loan.

Safety

Rocky Mount's FBI Crime Index rating is 88 crimes per thousand of population per year. Police protection is provided by the Rocky Mount Police Department, which has 100 uniformed officers. The fire department has 87 employees operating five engine companies. The Fire Insurance Rating is Class 4.

There are no nearby manmade hazards.

Education

Fourteen public schools, two private schools, and one parochial school provide education for the youth of the community.

Higher education is available at two technical colleges, Nash Technical Institute and Edgecombe Technical Institute, and at North Carolina Wesleyan College. Founded in 1956, North Carolina Wesleyan has a 200-acre campus just north of town. It offers programs leading to Bachelor of Arts, Bachelor of Science in Technology, and Bachelor of Science in Nursing degrees.

Nash Technical Institute offers two-year Associate of Applied Science degrees in 17 areas, and Edgecombe Technical Institute awards Associate of Applied Science degrees in 11 areas.

Several internationally known institutes of higher learning are within a hundred-mile radius of Rocky Mount: North Carolina State University in Raleigh, 42 miles to the west; University of North Carolina in Chapel Hill, 65 miles west; Duke University in

Durham, 59 miles west; and East Carolina University in Greenville, 42 miles to the southeast.

Medical Facilities

Rocky Mount offers some of the finest health care available in North Carolina. Nash General Hospital is a 300-bed facility opened in 1971, and Rocky Mount Sanitarium opened a new 50-bed facility in 1980. Edgecombe General Hospital, 16 miles to the east in Tarboro, supplements local health care. The area is served by a large number of physicians with a wide range of specialties, and over 20 dentists.

For more specialized medical care, there are the facilities of North Carolina Memorial Hospital, located on the campus of the University of North Carolina in Chapel Hill; the world-famous Duke Medical Center, in Durham; and Pitt Memorial Hospital, in Greenville. All are within one and a half hours of Rocky Mount.

Cultural Activities

When the local citizens talk about "The Tank" they are not talking about water or jail but about the Rocky Mount Arts and Crafts Center, which is housed in a converted railroad water tank. On the first floor of the Tank is an art gallery. On the second floor is the Tank Theater, which offers major productions each year. The third floor houses classrooms for arts and crafts classes.

North Carolina Wesleyan College forms the center of much of the community's cultural life. The Wesleyan Players present a varied program throughout the year, ranging from Shakespeare to modern musicals. The Performing Arts series brings distinguished artists to the area. In the past they have featured Duke Ellington, the Atlanta Contemporary Dance Company, and others.

The Braswell Memorial Library, in Rocky Mount, is supplemented by the collection of the Wesleyan College library. Both libraries are open to the public.

Recreation

Rocky Mount has 40 city parks, a children's museum, lighted tennis courts, a YMCA, a YWCA, and numerous swimming pools. The city also offers one public 18-hole golf course and one 9-hole course. These are supplemented by two 18-hole private courses and two 9-hole private courses.

The nearby reservoir offers fishing, sailing, swimming, water-skiing, or just sunbathing for the less energetic. Canoeing is available on the Tar River or on the nearby Pamlico and Albemarle sounds.

Hunters will find deer and other game nearby. Fishermen can fish in the Tar River or in the sounds. Within easy driving range is the Atlantic Ocean for deep-sea fishing.

Government
Rocky Mount operates under the Council-Manager system, with a full-time city manager and an elected city council.

Water
The water system is city-owned and supplies water that is alkaline, very soft, and fluoridated. Given the ample rainfall and the proximity of the Tar River, the water supply should never be a problem for the community.

Energy
The city also operates the gas, electrical power, and sewer systems. Heating is primarily by oil, with some homes depending more and more on wood. Utility costs, including oil for heating, run about $100 per month for the average two-bedroom home.

Television
While some stations can be received on home antenna systems, most residents subscribe to the local cable television system, which provides full-channel coverage.

Newspapers
The local daily newspaper is:

The Rocky Mount Telegram
150 Howard St.
Rocky Mount, NC 27801

The *Nashville Graphic* (Nashville, North Carolina) and the *Rocky Mount News & Observer* are weekly papers available locally.

For Further Information

Rocky Mount Area Chamber of Commerce
P.O. Box 392
Rocky Mount, NC 27801

North Carolina Division of Travel & Tourism
430 North Salisbury St.
Raleigh, NC 27611

Roswell, New Mexico

POPULATION: 39,698 within the city limits
51,900 in Chaves County

ELEVATION: 3577 feet above sea level

Located in southeastern New Mexico near the Pecos River, Roswell began as a frontier trading post and is now the largest trade and shopping center in a huge area bounded by Albuquerque, 200 miles northwest, Amarillo, 215 miles northeast, Lubbock, 174 miles east, and El Paso, 206 miles southwest.

To the west of Roswell are the high ranges and eastern slopes of the Rocky Mountains. To the east, across the Pecos River, are the broad high plains of eastern New Mexico and western Texas.

Around Roswell the land is flat to gently rolling, with wide fields of cotton, alfalfa, sorghum, and other commercial crops, as well as miles of rich rangeland dotted with beef cattle and sheep. It is big, wide-open country.

Climate

The climate in Roswell is generally mild in winter and warm to hot in summer, with four distinct seasons. Winter temperatures normally range from highs in the 50s to lows in the 20s, with occasional cold spells that bring north winds and drop the temperatures below zero. There is little precipitation in winter. Snowfall totals perhaps 8 inches a year and never stays on the ground for long. There are about 3800 heating degree days each winter. The first frost arrives in the first week of November, and the last frost comes during the first part of April, leaving about 208 days in the frost-free growing period. There are about 100 days per year when the temperature drops to 32°F or below, generally at night only.

Summers are hot from June through August, with daily maximum temperatures in the 90s but with generally cool nights. There are about 90 days per year with temperatures of 90°F and above and about 1500 cooling degree days per year. The heat is relieved by the low humidity, which averages 54% at night and drops to 38% in the afternoons.

Winds are generally from the southeast through most of the year, shifting to westerly in the winter, with occasional northers bringing sharp drops in temperature.

Rainfall is only about 14 to 16 inches per year, and agriculture depends heavily on irrigation from the vast underground aquifers of the region. Precipitation occurs about three to four days per month except in the summer, when it is a bit more frequent, increasing to five or six days per month. Roswell receives some 75% to 80% of possible sunshine each year.

History

Roswell began in 1869 when a professional gambler named Van C. Smith built two adobe buildings to house a general store, post office, and hotel. When he filed the first claim to the land, he named it for his father, Roswell Smith.

In 1877 Captain Joseph C. Lea bought out Smith's claims and thereby earned the title of "Father of Roswell." Mrs. Lea's efforts on behalf of education and civic improvement attracted settlers to the area, and by 1880 Roswell had become an important trading center. In 1891 it was incorporated as a town.

The discovery of plentiful artesian water in 1890 was the greatest single factor in the rapid growth of the town.

Economy and Employment

Farming, made possible by utilization of the still-plentiful underground water, covers 100,000 acres in Chaves County, a county ranking high in the production of feeder beef, feeder sheep, and sheep wool. This area is also ideal for the raising of quarter horses. Roswell is within a short drive of five major racetracks, including the famous Ruidoso Downs, and the First National Bank in Roswell is known as "the horseman's bank."

Because of its location, Roswell has become the center of retail and wholesale trade and distribution for a huge area. Its climate, low taxes, and low utility costs have attracted many new industries. The former Walker Air Force Base has been converted into the new Roswell Industrial Air Center, with sites and facilities for industrial, commercial, educational, and recreational use.

The greatest number of jobs are in the retail, wholesale, and service businesses that serve the huge surrounding area. Because of the steady influx of industry, jobs in that field are also increasing. At present the major industrial employers in the area are: Transportation Manufacturing Corp. (makers of Greyhound buses, 700 employees); Levi Strauss (jeans, 545); Holsum Baking Co. (breads, 210); and Glovers, Inc. (meat packing, 595). In addition, there are a number of firms that employ from 10 to 75 people in the manufacture of such diverse items as sheet-metal products, concrete brick, glass Christmas ornaments, cardboard tubing, aircraft parts, jewelry, pyrotechnics, plastic pipe, maps, fiber-glass products, and feed troughs.

For local job information, write:

New Mexico State Employment Service
601 North Main
Roswell, NM 88201

Taxes

New Mexico is one of the few states operating without a budget deficit. There is a 4% sales tax in Roswell — 3% for the state and 1% for Roswell. The state income tax amounts to about 8% of the federal income tax.

Property taxes are based on an assessed value of one-third of the current appraised value, at a rate of $3.25 per $100. A home selling for $65,000 would be taxed approximately $702 per year.

Shopping

As the trading and shopping center for an area larger than New Hampshire and Vermont put together, Roswell is well equipped to fill virtually all the needs of local shoppers. There is a downtown shopping area, and there are eight suburban centers where many national and regional chains are represented.

For greater choice, Albuquerque is 200 miles to the northwest and El Paso is 206 miles to the southwest.

Residential Properties

New construction has kept pace with Roswell's growth, and homes are always available for rent or purchase. Rentals are available at the Roswell Industrial Air Center as well as in town.

A few typical listings of homes for sale are:

CLOSE TO HIGH SCHOOL. 3 bedrooms, 2 baths, brick ranch home with formal living and dining rooms, double fireplace, lots of storage, $61,500.

ON CUL-DE-SAC. 3-bedroom, 1-bath home with fenced yard and mature landscaping. $28,900.

ALL BRICK 3-bedroom 1½-bath home with fenced yard and mature trees. $38,500.

SPACIOUS 4-bedroom, 1½-bath home with lawn and shrubs, central air and heat. $69,000.

Apartment rentals range from $150 to $450 per month for one-bedroom apartments and from $200 to $600 per month for two-bedroom apartments or condos.

Safety

Roswell's FBI Crime Index rating is 66 crimes per thousand of population per year. The police department has 94 full-time personnel, and the Chaves County sheriff's department and the New Mexico state police provide police services outside the city limits.

Fire protection is provided by five fire stations and 64 full-time firemen. The fire department has nine pumpers, a snorkel truck, two crash trucks, and one emergency and rescue vehicle. Roswell has a Fire Insurance Rating of Class 5.

There are no manmade or natural hazards in the area. The nearest possible hazard is a proposed nuclear waste dump near Carlsbad, New Mexico, 77 miles to the south.

Education

The Roswell public school system operates 16 elementary schools, 4 middle schools, and 2 high schools. In addition, the area has 4 private kindergartens, 3 nursery schools, and the New Mexico Military Institute (NMMI).

NMMI (called "Nimmie" by local residents and students) has been a landmark in Roswell since 1891, when it was established as the Goss Military Institute. It became a territorial school in 1893 and was renamed New Mexico Military Institute. Mandated by state law to be a "military institute for education and training of the youth of this country," NMMI has been named a Distinguished Military School by the Department of the Army (or War Department) every year since 1909. Today, NMMI is a high school and a two-year college offering both junior and senior ROTC. It is one of the few schools where a college student can obtain an army officer's commission in just two years, after which he may then be deferred from active duty while completing his baccalaureate degree elsewhere.

Eastern New Mexico University–Roswell Campus is a two-year junior college providing academic, vocational, and technical courses.

Southwestern Business College is a privately operated business college offering secretarial and business courses.

In addition, there are a number of dance, cosmetology, and other private trade schools in the area.

The nearest four-year university offering undergraduate and graduate studies is New Mexico State University at Las Cruces, 186 miles to the southwest, which offers a broad curriculum through the doctoral level.

Medical Facilities

Roswell is the medical center for southeastern New Mexico, with over 50 physicians, 15 dentists, 3 osteopaths, 1 podiatrist, 8 chiropractors, and 6 optometrists. There are two well-equipped hospitals in the city. Eastern New Mexico Medical Center has 94 beds and St. Mary's Hospital has 118 general beds and 120 nursing-home beds. In addition, there is a geriatrics department at St. Mary's, plus four nursing homes in town.

Cultural Activities

The Roswell public library serves the community with 57,000 volumes, and New Mexico Military Institute has 55,835 volumes in its library.

The Museum and Art Center features a planetarium and classroom plus the Goddard Rocket and Space Wing.

Various programs are scheduled annually by the Community Concerts Association, the Symphony Orchestra Society, and the Community Little Theater.

New Mexico Military Institute and Eastern New Mexico University also provide many programs throughout the year.

Recreation
Roswell's eight city parks offer a variety of facilities, including swimming pools, tennis courts, a carousel, and a zoo. Four recreation centers offer activities for all age groups. Roswell has two football stadiums, one baseball field, and many softball facilities. Lighted tennis courts are open to the public at both high schools and in Cahoon Park.

Three golf courses, open all year, provides some of the best golfing in the southwest. The municipal course and the NMMI course both offer 18 holes, while the Roswell Country Club offers a 9-hole course.

The YMCA offers many programs for the entire family and has an Olympic swimming pool and courses in swimming and water safety.

Bottomless Lakes State Park, just east of town, offers swimming, water sports, picnic grounds, camping, playgrounds, fishing, and horseback riding.

Bitter Lakes National Wildlife Refuge, just north of town, offers designated fishing and hunting areas.

Two of the finest ski areas in the nation are within easy driving distance — at Sierra Blanca and Cloudcroft. Both have snow-making machines that assure skiing even when the snow is insufficient.

Another recreational area within easy driving distance is the Lincoln National Forest, with plenty of fishing, hunting, skiing, and hiking. Driving time is about 45 minutes. And the Carlsbad Caverns are less than three hours' drive south of Roswell.

Government
Roswell operates under the Council-Manager system, with a mayor, 10 city-council members, and a full-time city manager.

Water
Municipal water is provided by the city of Roswell from 21 deep artesian wells. The water is pure, free of bacteria or pollutants, alkaline, very hard, and not fluoridated. The supply appears to be adequate for the immediate future, though all of the water tables in the Great Plains area are being diminished by continuous irrigation.

Energy
Southwestern Public Service Company serves a 45,000-square-mile area, including Roswell and southeastern New Mexico. Its electrical generating capacity appears to be well above present needs.

Natural-gas service is provided by the Gas Company of New Mexico, and gas is piped in from several southwestern gas fields. The supply appears to be adequate for many years to come unless diverted elsewhere by government order.

Present utility costs run about $75 per month for the average two-bedroom home.

Television
There are two local television stations, affiliated with CBS and NBC. The local cable system covers the remaining channels.

Newspapers
The local paper, published daily except Saturday, is:

The Roswell Daily Record
P.O. Box 1897
Roswell, NM 88201

The *Albuquerque Journal* and the *El Paso Times* are also available locally.

For Further Information

Roswell Chamber of Commerce
P.O. Drawer 70
Roswell, NM 88201

New Mexico Tourist Division
Bataan Memorial Building
Santa Fe, NM 87503

San Angelo, Texas

POPULATION: 73,141 within the city limits
84,784 in Tom Green County

ELEVATION: 1908 feet above sea level

San Angelo, the county seat of Tom Green County, is located in west-central Texas, about 180 air miles northwest of San Antonio, at the confluence of the North Concho and Middle Concho rivers. It is the educational, cultural, medical, trade, and shopping center for an area larger than New England.

With the development of nearby Twin Buttes Reservoir, Nasworthy Lake, and O. C. Fisher Lake, San Angelo has also become a center for tourism.

The area around San Angelo is gently rolling, broken by the rivers and lakes nearby.

Climate

San Angelo is located at the lower edge of the High Plains, where the climate is alternately influenced by the moist, warm tropical air from the Gulf of Mexico, the dry air from northern Mexico, and the arctic air from Canada.

Summers are long and warm to hot, with temperatures during May through September ranging from highs in the upper 80s and 90s to lows in the 60s and 70s. There are 113 days per year with temperatures of 90°F and above, and the area has some 2500 cooling degree days per year. Summer temperatures have reached as high as 109°F in June and July, and there are usually several days per year with temperatures over 100°F.

Winters are short and mild, except during the usually brief northers, with about 2225 heating degree days per year. Normal winter temperatures range from highs in the 50s and 60s to lows in the 30s and 40s, with only 42 days per year with temperatures of 32°F and below. The last frost is over by late March, and the first frost in fall does not arrive before mid-November, resulting in a frost-free growing season of 235 days or more.

Precipitation is a low 24 inches per year. Winters are dry and clear, while showers often occur in spring and late summer. Snow seldom exceeds an inch or two and is never on the ground for long. San Angelo enjoys about 73% of possible sunshine per year, with sunshine more than 250 days a year. The average humidity is a low 56%.

There are about 50 thunderstorms each year, as well as several northers that bring arctic air and sometimes drop winter temperatures to sub-zero levels. Tornadoes can occur, though the chance of any one place being hit is slight. High westerly winds sometimes cause blowing dust, though dust storms are rare.

History

Ben Ficklin's stage stop, on the road between San Antonio and El Paso, was established on the South Concho River about four miles from today's San Angelo, but it was wiped out by a disastrous flood in 1882.

Frequent Indian raids led to the establishment of Fort Concho where the North and Middle forks of the Concho River join. Around the fort grew a town, a typical wide-open two-gun town with saloons and gambling houses. Texas longhorn cattle were herded down Chadbourne Street, a main thoroughfare of today's San Angelo.

Wool was brought into San Angelo by wagon even before the Santa Fe railroad extended this far in 1888. The Gulf Coast railroad also had its terminus here, and San Angelo became the primary wool market in the United States, with 1 million pounds of wool handled the first year.

Since 1903, San Angelo has been the shipping point and trade center for the immense territory of western Texas, as far west as the Pecos River.

From 1903 to 1923, the area to the south and west of San Angelo developed into the most prosperous sheep- and cattle-raising section in the country. To the north and east, innumerable farms produced bumper crops of cotton, oats, and grain sorghum.

Then, in 1923, oil was discovered nearby and started the boom that still continues in San Angelo.

Economy and Employment

San Angelo's economy is well diversified, with a good balance of employment that ranges from farm products to jet aircraft, from oil to tourism, from education to the military.

Industry is steadily growing as northern manufacturers find that energy costs are lower and living is more pleasant for their employees in San Angelo. In addition, San Angelo is still an important cattle market and remains the world's largest wool market.

Job opportunities are widely varied. Major fields of employment are: education, 4400 jobs; Goodfellow Air Force Base, 3300; transportation, communications, and utilities, 2210; services, including motels and resorts, 1250; medical and professional services, including hospitals, 2790; construction, 1090; food processing, 940; oil production, 490; mining, 840; and retail and wholesale trade, 7420.

Among the major employers are: Ethicon, a subsidiary of Johnson & Johnson (over 1600 employees); Mitsubishi Aircraft (500); Barry's of San Angelo (footwear, 300); Pool Company (oil-field machinery, 400); and General Telephone (2000 in the San Angelo area).

Taxes

Texas has no state income tax. The state sales tax is 4% and the San Angelo sales tax is 1%, making a total of 5%.

Local property taxes are based on an assessment of 45% of true market value, and the tax on a $65,000 home would be approximately $1190 per year.

Shopping

Since San Angelo serves as the trade and shopping center for an area larger than New England, it is unusual to find shopping needs that cannot be met by the local facilities. The excellent downtown business and shopping area is supplemented by 10 suburban shopping centers.

For those who feel the need to shop in a larger city, San Antonio is 217 miles to the southeast and Dallas is 253 miles to the northeast.

Residential Properties

There is a wide variety of housing to choose from in San Angelo, from majestic classic southern homes with 12-foot ceilings to modern townhouse condominiums. A few typical current listings are:

FRESHLY PAINTED 3-bedroom, 1½-bath home with large family room. $49,000.

COUNTRY LIVING on 6 lots with a 3-bedroom 1½-bath home with large kitchen. Low $30's.

WARMTH AND BEAUTY in this 3-bedroom home with big lawn in a desirable neighborhood close to shopping. $83,500.

ATTRACTIVE brick home with 3 bedrooms and 2 baths, roomy closets, on quiet corner. $40's.

Apartments are available, with one-bedroom apartments renting for $200 to $290 per month and two-bedroom apartments or condos renting for $250 to $500 per month.

Safety

San Angelo's FBI Crime Index rating is a moderate 59 crimes per thousand of population per year. The local police department has 115 uniformed officers and the fire department has 134 employees.

There are no nearby manmade hazards. The local Goodfellow Air Force Base is a school for military police and is not considered a military target. Tornadoes can strike in the area, but the present-day warning system reduces the danger.

Education

San Angelo has 36 public schools, including 3 high schools, and provides education to 16,000 students from kindergarten through the twelfth grade.

Higher education is available locally at Angelo State University, which has a 287-acre campus and serves 5600 students. It provides a complete range of courses through the masters' level. A new business administration and computer school was completed in 1982.

Medical Facilities
There are four hospitals in the city, providing a total of more than 700 beds. Hospital services includes a renal-care unit and private psychiatric care. A geriatrics center serves the needs of the elderly, including the many retirees who have moved here from other areas. There are over 100 physicians in private practice and on the hospital staffs.

Cultural Activities
San Angelo's three public libraries contain more than 288,274 volumes, and the Angelo State University library, which houses over 142,000 volumes, is available for use by local residents during the school year.

Most of the city's cultural life revolves around the university, which sponsors a community theater, a symphony orchestra, and frequent concerts throughout the year.

The new Convention Center has a variety of facilities and attracts top entertainers in many fields.

Recreation
Because of the mild, dry, sunny climate, outdoor activities are possible on almost any day of the year. The city park system includes some 275 acres of developed and undeveloped parkland and includes public swimming pools, a golf course, tennis courts, basketball courts, baseball diamonds, and soccer fields. The Concho River flows through downtown San Angelo.

Within minutes of San Angelo are Twin Buttes Reservoir, O. C. Fisher Lake, and Lake Nasworthy, all of which offer excellent fishing, water-skiing, and other water sports.

Hunters come to the area from all over Texas to hunt for deer, turkeys, quail, doves, rabbit, ducks, and javelinas.

Government
The city is governed by the Council-Manager system.

Water
San Angelo operates its own water department. The tap water is alkaline, very hard, and not fluoridated.

Energy

San Angelo gets its electricity from West Texas Utilities Company, which obtains its power from eight steam-generating plants and one gas-turbine plant, providing a total of 863 megawatts of power for a system that supplies 167 communities and 18 rural cooperatives in west-central Texas. Current rates can be obtained by writing:

West Texas Utilities
P.O. Box 5021
San Angelo, TX 76902

Natural gas is supplied by the Lone Star Gas Company, which draws its supply from nearby gas wells. Current rates can be obtained by writing:

Lone Star Gas Co.
111 West Twohig
San Angelo, TX 76903

The cost of utilities for a typical two-to-three-bedroom home averages about $85 per month.

Television

There is only one local network television station, but the local cable service provides full-channel coverage to subscribers.

Newspapers

The daily newspaper is:

The San Angelo Standard Times
P.O. Box 5111
San Angelo, TX 76902

The *Dallas News* and the *Dallas Times-Herald* are also available locally.

For Further Information

San Angelo Chamber of Commerce
500 Rio Concho Drive
San Angelo, TX 76903

Travel & Information Division
State Dept. of Highways & Public Transportation
Austin, TX 78763

Tallahassee, Florida

POPULATION: 80,759 within the city limits
159,542 in the Tallahassee area

ELEVATION: 190 feet above sea level

Tallahassee is the state capital of Florida and the county seat of Leon County. It is located in the northern part of the state where the panhandle joins the peninsula, 166 miles west of Jacksonville, 194 miles east of Pensacola, and 20 miles north of the Gulf of Mexico.

This is an area of rolling hills, lakes, streams, stately magnolias, and moss-laden oak trees. To the west lie the Ochlockonee River and Lake Talquin. To the north, the county boundary is the Georgia-Florida state line. To the southeast, the St. Marks River flows toward the Gulf.

It would be hard to find a more attractive town anywhere in the world. Tallahassee has many of the things that chambers of commerce like to brag about: natural beauty, a colorful heritage, lots of small-town charm, a mild and generally pleasant climate, and many friendly, hospitable people.

Climate

Tallahassee has the mild, moist climate common to the Gulf states. Summers are long, warm, and relatively humid. Winters, although punctuated with occasional northers, are generally mild because of the nearby Gulf of Mexico.

Temperatures vary from average lows and highs in January of 43°F and 65°F, respectively, to average lows and highs in July of 72°F and 91°F, respectively. There are normally some 80 days per year, mainly in June through August, when temperatures are 90°F and above. In winter, there are seldom more than 20 days, in December through February, when the temperature drops below 32°F. There are only some 1485 heating degree days per year in the area, but the long summers bring 2750 cooling degree days.

The annual rainfall of more than 50 inches provides 950 million gallons of water per square mile and 20 million gallons per capita per year. Humidity ranges from about 50% to 65% during the afternoon hours to about 85% to 95% during the night and early morning hours. Rainfall occurs throughout the year, but is heaviest in the months of June through September.

Prevailing winds are southerly except during September through December when they are often northerly. Tornadoes can occur in all seasons, but are most frequent in spring. Generally, tornadoes in Florida do not cover wide areas, and damage has not been extensive. Tropical storms and hurricanes can, of course, hit anywhere along the Gulf Coast, but Tallahassee's location 20 miles inland is good protection from the severity of such storms, and storms are generally less severe in this area than in the southern parts of the state.

History

The area around Tallahassee was known to Europeans long before the Pilgrims landed at Plymouth Rock. It is thought that Ponce de León landed in this area on his second voyage in 1521. Pánfilo de Narváez definitely passed through the area in 1528, and in 1539–40 Hernando de Soto spent the winter at or near the site of Tallahassee.

The original inhabitants of the area were the Apalachee Indians, now extinct. By 1675, there were seven Franciscan missions in the immediate vicinity of Tallahassee. The most important of these missions was San Luis de Talimali, on the western outskirts of the present city.

Early in the eighteenth century, expeditions of Englishmen and Creek Indians from South Carolina raided the missions and dispersed the local Indians, after which the area was occupied by Seminole Indians, relatives of the Creeks. The name of Tallahassee was derived from the Seminole Indians, who called the area *tal-a-hass-ee,* meaning "old town" or "old place."

The United States acquired Florida from Spain in 1821, and Andrew Jackson became the first governor. Under a later governor, a central location for a territorial capital was ordered, and in 1823 Tallahassee was chosen. The first session of the new Legislative Council met in Tallahassee on November 8, 1824.

The town was laid out symmetrically, with Capitol Square at the center. Four other public squares were established, and broad streets were built. The first lots were sold in April 1825, and on December 9, 1825, Tallahassee was incorporated as a city. At that time it had 50 houses, a church, a schoolhouse, 2 hotels, 7 stores, an apothecary's shop, a printing shop, 2 shoemakers, 2 blacksmiths, 3 carpenters, a tailor, and 3 bricklayers. Most of these establishments were clustered around Capitol Square.

The fertile lands of middle Florida quickly attracted settlers from the older southern states, who established large plantations that they worked with slave labor. The capital became the trade center for the area, and St. Marks, 20 miles to the south, was its shipping point.

Tallahassee began as a rough-and-ready frontier community, but as it grew, its citizens built fine and stately homes. Several notable examples still stand, including The Grove, The Columns, and Goodwood.

The first capitol building was the wooden one built in 1826. In 1839 the present brick capitol was begun. It was completed in 1845, the year Florida was admitted to the Union. The new capitol was remodeled from 1902 to 1920 and enlarged in 1921–22 and again in 1938 and 1947. In 1970 an extensive expansion was approved for the capitol complex and is now underway. In spite of all of these changes, the central portion of the building is still the old brick capitol of 1845.

Economy and Employment

Tallahassee's economy is based on Florida's three major employment sectors — agriculture, industry, and tourism. In addition, local, state, and federal government are crucial to the city's economy.

Two outstanding universities greatly broaden the economic base.

Looking ahead, the outlook for Tallahassee is far better than for many communities of its size. Its trade area encompasses 12 counties, 3 of which are in Georgia, that have a combined population of over 350,000. The effective buying income for this area is estimated at close to $2 billion per year.

Unemployment is below the state average because of the stability of the local economy. Light industry is encouraged and is moving in. The average household income is one of the highest in the state. During recent years, Florida's economy has grown faster than that of the nation as a whole, and this growth is expected to continue.

The largest public employers are: the State of Florida (26,200 employees in Tallahassee); local government (6600); the federal government (1300); Florida State University (3650); Florida A & M University (1200); and Tallahassee Memorial Medical Center (1800). In the private sector, the major employers are: Olin Corp. (rocket propellants, 300 employees); Wayne H. Coloney, Inc. (machinery and ammunition handling systems, 309); Seminole Refining (petroleum products, 110); Publix Markets (food stores, 750); Central Telephone (987); Holiday Inns (200); Capitol City First National Bank (195); McDonald's (260); Borden Dairy (100); and the Municipal Code Corporation (city legal codes, 125).

For current job information, write:

State of Florida Employment Office
1307 North Monroe St.
Tallahassee, FL 32303

Taxes

Florida's taxes are lower than most, with a state sales tax of 4% and no state income tax.

Residential property taxes are moderate. The tax on a home selling for $65,000 would be about $815 per year.

Shopping

Shopping needs for most residents can be met locally, but the nearest large shopping centers are in Jacksonville, 166 miles to the east, and Atlanta, 261 miles to the north.

Residential Properties

Even in Tallahassee, it is a buyer's market in housing. While prices of homes have risen across the nation, including here, there are still bargains to be found. A few examples of recent ads are:

OLDIE BUT GOODIE. Lovely old 5-bedroom home with lots of appeal. Over 2600 square feet of spacious room, 2 fireplaces and 3½ acres of gardens with many varieties of trees and shrubbery. Only $58,000.

CLOSE IN NEAR LAKE AND PARK. This 2-bedroom townhouse with private patio is in an ideal location to walk to shopping, schools, and church. Take an evening stroll around the lake and feed the ducks. $42,000.

IN TOWN 3-bedroom home, fenced yard, large oak tree, detached two-car garage just right for a shop. $36,000.

GREAT INVESTMENT opportunity. 4-bedroom home in very good rental location, close in to downtown and university. See it today at $38,000.

Apartments are available, with one-bedroom units renting from $195 to $300 per month and two-bedroom apartments or condos renting for $245 to $525 per month.

Safety

There are no manmade hazards nearby, the nearest being the nuclear reactor and power plant at Dothan, Alabama, 100 miles to the northwest. Hurricanes are always a possibility, but none have done serious damage in the area in recent years.

Tallahassee's FBI Crime Index rating is 90 crimes per thousand of population per year. The police department has 127 uniformed members and 79 other employees. In addition, the county sheriff's department is headquartered in town. The fire department operates five fire stations and employs 119 uniformed members plus 5 nonuniformed personnel. Tallahassee was the first city in the state to achieve a Class 2 Fire Insurance Rating, which contributes real savings in insurance premiums to local residents and businesses.

Education

In addition to its public school system and a number of private schools, Tallahassee is well-endowed with institutions of higher learning, with two four-year universities, one two-year college, and the Lively Area Vocational Technical School.

Florida State University consists of a graduate school and 10 undergraduate divisions and has over 22,000 students. It offers a research and computer center, two particle accelerators, and an active research institute.

Florida A & M is the state's leading agricultural and mechanical university, with a total of approximately 6000 students in its graduate school and seven undergraduate divisions.

Tallahassee Community College offers courses to those who

wish to transfer after two years to four-year institutions and to those who are interested in completing their education in two years.

Medical Facilities

The medical needs of the area are met by the city-owned Tallahassee Memorial Regional Medical Center, with 771 beds; the privately owned Capital Medical Center, a medical and surgical facility with 180 beds; three nursing homes with a total of 240 beds; and several mental-health facilities.

There are over 160 physicians and dentists in private practice in Tallahassee.

Cultural Activities

Tallahassee offers a remarkable array of cultural activities. The University Symphony Orchestra/State Symphony of Florida presents its concert season from September through June of each year. The Florida State Opera, under the auspices of Florida State University, operates the Ruby Diamond Auditorium and presents annual grand opera and festivals, as well as various special artists.

The Tallahassee Little Theater, which has its own 142-seat facility, presents various types of drama. The FSU Leisure Program Office is responsible for programs throughout the year in dance, theater, and instrumental and vocal music.

Facilities for additional programs and presentations include the Conradi Studio Theater at FSU, which has 500 seats and was built in 1971; the Lee Hall Auditorium of Florida A & M University, which has 1500 seats; Moore Auditorium at FSU, which has 403 seats; Opperman Music Hall at FSU, a concert hall seating 500; and Charles Winter Wood Theater at Florida A & M, which has 650 seats and was built in 1956.

Libraries are well represented in Tallahassee. The Leon County public library has 178,732 volumes; Florida A & M University library has 318,098 volumes; Florida State University library has 1,050,000 volumes; the State Library of Florida has 348,919 volumes; the Tallahassee Community College library has 56,545 volumes; and there are many governmental library facilities with collections specializing in law, government, agriculture, history, education, and industry.

Recreation

Like the rest of Florida, the Tallahassee area offers much in the way of outdoor recreational opportunities.

Golf is played throughout the year in Tallahassee on four public 18-hole courses and one 9-hole course, all within fifteen minutes of downtown. Capital City Country Club is noted throughout the Southeast for its annual George Washington Golf Tournament, held in February, and its Shamrock Golf Tournament in March. This is a private club that welcomes visitors who are guests of members. Killearn Golf and Country Club, another private club, is the home of the PGA Invitational Tallahassee Open. Its course is over 7000 yards long. Florida State University's 18-hole course is open to the public during the summer. Winewood Golf Club is a private club that has an 18-hole, par 72, 6685-yard course.

The countryside around Tallahassee attracts many hikers who enjoy the abundant wildlife and wildflowers. Hunting is prime in the heavily forested areas around Tallahassee that abound with deer, turkeys, quail, doves, raccoons, opossum, ducks, and geese. The city is located in the path of a waterfowl flyway, and lakes north of town provide many ducks and geese for hunters each year. Bear hunts can be organized in the national forest nearby.

Greyhound racing buffs can enjoy nightly races during the season at the track in Monticello, 25 miles from town. And a jai alai fronton is located in Gadsden County, some 35 miles west of Tallahassee. It operates during January through June and offers pari-mutuel betting. For drag-race fans there is the Tallahassee Speedway Park, which has a strip for drag racing.

Spectator sports include a full high school athletic program and the many events at Florida State University and Florida A & M University. Both are noted for their intercollegiate athletics.

Swimmers have a choice of three city-operated pools open from mid-May through Labor Day, as well as a number of lakes and, of course, the nearby beaches at Shell Point, St. Theresa Beach, St. George Island, and St. Andrews State Recreation Area.

Boating is excellent on the rivers, lakes, and coastal bays as well as in the Gulf itself. Shell Point, only 30 miles south of Tallahassee, has a large marina on the Gulf. The fishing town of St. Marks, about 8 miles upriver from the Gulf, has good boat facilities, including a yard capable of handling large boats, a yacht club, and grocery stores for last-minute shopping before leaving for a weekend on the water.

Wakulla Springs, 15 miles south of Tallahassee, is the world's deepest natural spring. The area around it offers a lodge and restaurant, glass-bottom boat tours, jungle cruises, swimming, and nature trails.

A special attraction in the area is the FSU "Flying High" circus, an internationally known student circus group that holds its annual home show at FSU during the first two weekends of May.

The North Florida Fair each fall and the Tallahassee Festival in spring are annual highlights in Tallahassee.

Government

Tallahassee has a Council-Manager form of government, with the city manager serving as the chief executive and reporting only to the five-member city commission.

Water

The local tap water is alkaline, soft, not fluoridated, and plentiful. With 950 million gallons of rain per square mile per year in the area, and with the numerous lakes and rivers, there is ample good water for every need.

Energy

Located between the nuclear power plants at Dothan, Alabama, 100 miles to the northwest, and Crystal Springs, Florida, 150 miles to the southeast, Tallahassee has access to ample electrical power for the foreseeable future. Electricity is supplied through the Talquin Electric Co-operative. Natural gas is piped in from the large gas fields of Louisiana and Mississippi and distributed locally by the Tallahassee City Utilities Department.

Current utility costs average around $85 per month for an average two-bedroom home.

Television

There are three local television stations, and the local cable system provides full coverage for subscribers.

Newspapers

The local daily newspaper is:

The Tallahassee Democrat
227 North Magnolia
Tallahassee, FL 32302

The *Florida Flambeau* is published five days each week, and the *Capital Outlook* is a weekly local newspaper.

For Further Information

Tallahassee Area Chamber of Commerce
Box 1639
Tallahassee, FL 32302

Division of Tourism
505 Collins Building
Tallahassee, FL 32304

Tupelo, Mississippi

POPULATION: 23,896 within the city limits
53,600 in Lee County

ELEVATION: 284 feet above sea level

Tupelo is the county seat of Lee County and is located in northeastern Mississippi, 97 miles southeast of Memphis. A trade, processing, and shipping center for a rich agricultural area, Tupelo is also characterized by growing industrialization.

An old town with a history that began before the famed Natchez Trace passed through, connecting Nashville with Natchez, Tupelo is also a modern town and one of the first cities in the Deep South to be named an All-American City.

The beautiful countryside is flat to gently rolling, with thick woods, moss-covered oaks, and open fields broken by streams, ponds, and lakes.

Climate

The climate of this area is similar to that of all of Mississippi in that the controlling factors are the huge land mass to the north and the Gulf of Mexico to the south. The prevailing southerly winds create a moist, semitropical climate. The high humidity of 70% tends to produce uncomfortable summers that are fortunately cooled by the frequent afternoon thundershowers.

Summers are long and warm to hot, with daily maximum temperatures in the 80s to 90s from May through September and some 70 days per year with temperatures of 90°F and above. The area has about 2200 cooling degree days per year.

Winters are brief and mild, though temperatures can drop well below freezing during winter storms that blow down from Canada. Normal winter temperatures range from highs in the 50s to lows in the 30s and 40s from mid-November through mid-February. Winter storms can drop the temperatures as low as a record −8°F, and there are usually about 55 days per year with temperatures of 32°F and below. There are approximately 2900 heating degree days each winter. The last frost usually comes by the last week in March, and the first frost usually does not arrive before the first week in November, resulting in some 220 days of growing season.

Precipitation varies, with about 11 days of rain and 5 to 6 inches of precipitation each month from December through March. The months of August through October have the least rain, while thunderstorms are frequent in July. Total precipitation averages 52 inches per year, and rain falls about one-third of the days throughout the year, except for the brief dry period during September and October. The area enjoys about 60% of possible sunshine each year.

Winds are generally gentle and southerly except during the cold winter storms, when winds can become quite strong from the northwest through the northeast.

History

The original inhabitants of the Tupelo area were the Chickasaw Indians. During their time, the Natchez Trace was an important Indian trail, de Soto spent a winter in the area, and Bienville led the French against the Indians. The Indians remained in the area until 1832, when the United States government took the land under the Treaty of Pontotoc.

Following the Chickasaw exodus, the Natchez Trace was opened up as a military road and land was sold to settlers from the eastern seaboard, many from the Carolinas. By the end of a decade of settling the area, the new settlers had become well-to-do farmers. A store was built, other buildings were added, and the village began to grow.

When the Mobile and Ohio railroad laid its tracks 2 miles east of the existing village, the townspeople moved over to the marshy land covered with Tupelo gum trees. The present town, named for the gum trees, began with a store, two saloons, and a temporary railroad station.

In 1866, Lee County was created and named after General Robert E. Lee, and Tupelo was chosen as the county seat. Four years later Tupelo was incorporated as a town, a free school system was begun, and progress returned to the area.

Soon another railroad, electric lights, and cotton gins brought further progress. People began to tire of living in a boggy swamp beside the railroad, and in 1886 drainage was begun, bonds were issued, and 1000 acres were reclaimed. By 1891 there were 2 newspapers, 2 schools, 3 hotels, 7 churches, 5 factories, 30 businesses, an ice house, a tin shop, 6 brickyards, and an opera house. The population was 1525.

Industry began with a cotton mill, one of the first in the state, and other industries followed, including a cottonseed-oil mill, a fertilizer factory, a shirt factory, a dress factory, and the nation's first fish hatchery.

The boll weevil wiped out the cotton fields in 1916 and economic disaster struck Tupelo. Local businessmen and former cotton farmers united and began agricultural diversification that brought dairying, livestock raising, and poultry farming to the area.

Economy and Employment

A very active Community Development Council in Tupelo has brought many new businesses and industries to the area. Within the past 25 years the community has risen to a position of leadership in manufacturing in the Mid-South.

Tupelo's location at the junction of two railroads, U.S. highways 45 and 78, Mississippi Highway 6, and the famous Natchez Trace Parkway has contributed greatly toward making it the trading center of a large area. The 9 counties surrounding Lee County form a 10-county area that is primarily rural with small family farm units. This is Tupelo's trade area.

Agricultural production in the area includes dairy products, poultry, beef, soybeans, pork, vegetables, and forest products. While cotton production is declining, other agricultural areas are increasing rapidly, with poultry, eggs, and broiler production exceeding $6 million in sales per year. Meat production exceeds $8 million a year. The local prosperity is reflected in bank deposits of over $600 million.

Natural resources in the region include clay, cement rock, wool rock, limestone, and natural gas and petroleum, in addition to the forests of the area.

Some of the major employers in the area are: Air-Cap Manufacturing Co. (makers of power mowers, 735 employees); Daybrite Lighting (fluorescent lights, 625); FMC Corp. (belt conveyors, 430); Lucky Star Industries (men's and boys' jeans, 540); Mid-South Packers (meat products, 640); Purnell's Pride (poultry and eggs, 675); and Rockwell International (power tools, 700).

Other major employers include several clothing manufacturers, furniture companies, and makers of machinery and tools, dyes, ice cream, pillows, boxes, fertilizer, castings, tubs, and paint.

Taxes

The state sales tax is 5%, and the state income tax ranges from 3% to 4%. There are no city or county sales or income taxes.

Residential property taxes are quite low. The annual tax on a home selling for $65,000 would amount to only about $325.

Shopping

As the trading and shopping center for a 10-county area, Tupelo has better-than-average shopping facilities. Memphis is only two hours to the northwest via an excellent highway.

Residential Properties

A few examples of local residential listings are:

THREE BEDROOMS, 2 baths, 1500 square feet, with brick exterior, 2-car carport, central heat and air, fireplace. $53,500. Taxes $300.00 per year. Utilities $75 per month.

SEVEN ROOMS with 3 bedrooms, 2 baths, on 100 × 150 lot. 1567 feet of living space, brick exterior, 2-car carport, central heat and air, fireplace. $57,500. Taxes $300 per year. Utilities $80 per month.

EIGHT ROOMS, 4 bedrooms, 3 baths, 2075 square feet, on 155 × 180 lot, with brick exterior, central heat and air, fireplace, 2-car carport. $84,000. Taxes $285.00. Utilities, $100 per month. House is 5 years old.

TEN-ROOM HOME with 4 bedrooms, 3 baths, 2-story, 2900 square feet on 134 × 175 lot, with brick exterior, central heat and air, fireplace, 2-car carport, 1½ years old. $134,900. Taxes $250 per year. Utilities $100 per month.

Apartments are available for rent, with one-bedroom units renting for $155 to $195 per month. Two-bedroom apartments or condos rent for $255 to $295 per month.

Safety

Tupelo's FBI Crime Index rating is a low 59 crimes per thousand of population per year. The police force consists of 65 full-time officers and is equipped with 10 cars, 12 motorcycles, and 9 other vehicles. The fire department has 75 firemen, 7 pumper trucks, and 1 rescue unit equipped to handle airport emergencies. The Fire Insurance Rating is Class 5.

There are no nearby natural or manmade hazards. The nuclear power plant near Corinth, 50 miles to the north, is the nearest potential hazard. Tupelo is in a low seismic-risk area, but this is not considered a serious hazard to residents.

Education

The Tupelo and Lee County school systems provide five elementary schools for grades one through five, one sixth-grade school, a junior high school for grades seven and eight, one ninth-grade school, and Tupelo High School for grades ten through twelve. In addition, there is a vocational/technical school that offers instruction in many areas, including drafting, electricity, and auto repair.

Further vocational and technical education is available at Itawamba Junior College and at Tupelo Vocational and Educational Center. At both schools students can gain two years of college credit while studying in fields applicable to today's industries.

Tupelo is the home of one of the branch centers of the University of Mississippi, where undergraduate and graduate courses are offered to some 1700 students.

The main campus of "Ole Miss" (the University of Mississippi) is located in Oxford, 49 miles to the west, and provides a full curriculum of graduate and undergraduate studies.

Medical Facilities

The North Mississippi Medical Center in Tupelo serves a large area in northeastern Mississippi with full hospital services, including a new cardiac center. It has 588 beds, and many of the community's 72 physicians are on the hospital staff.

In addition, there is a Regional Rehabilitation Center in Tupelo that provides outpatient services to the handicapped. There are 115 physicians and 30 dentists in private practice in the area.

Cultural Activities

The Lee-Itawamba Library System library serves the surrounding community with 165,000 volumes.

The Symphony Orchestra gives concerts throughout the year in the Civic Auditorium. The Community Theater, a dramatic and dinner theater, offers various performances throughout the year featuring local talent and guest artists.

Memphis, 97 miles to the northwest, is close enough to permit local residents access to its many cultural events.

Recreation

There are 10 public parks in the Tupelo area, providing a variety of facilities and activities, including picnic areas, playgrounds, a soccer field, swimming, softball fields, tennis courts, nature trails, and fishing.

Golfers have several local choices. Tupelo Country Club has an 18-hole course, plus tennis courts, a swimming pool, and dining facilities. Bel-Aire is a 9-hole golf course, and the Natchez Trace Golf Club has an 18-hole golf course plus swimming pool, clubhouse, pro shop, and banquet room.

Tombigbee State Park, 6 miles from town, has a 120-acre spring-fed lake and a lodge for banquets, parties, and reunions. The park offers boat launches, camping, fishing, nature trails, playgrounds, tennis, vacation cabins, and water sports.

Dam Site 6 Lake offers camping, fishing, boating, and picnic areas.

Lake Lamar Bruce offers fishing, boating, swimming, and picnic areas, with 340 acres of open water.

Lake Piomingo is a private lake with cabin sites, boating, fishing, and a swimming area.

Government

Tupelo operates under the Mayor-Council plan. An elected mayor and aldermen run the local government.

Water

With 900 million gallons of precipitation per square mile per year in the area, there is a more-than-adequate water supply. Local tap water is neutral, soft, and fluoridated.

Energy
Electric power is supplied to Tupelo by the Tennessee Valley Authority and is distributed by the City of Tupelo Water and Light Department. Gas service is supplied by the Mississippi Valley Gas Company, and both bituminous coal and fuel oil are available locally.

For an average 1500-square-foot home with good insulation, utility costs average around $85 to $100 per month.

Television
There is one local television station in Tupelo, and stations in Memphis, Tennessee, and Birmingham, Alabama, can be received on good home antenna systems. A local cable television system provides full coverage of all channels for local subscribers.

Newspapers
The local daily newspaper is:

The Daily Journal
Tupelo, MS 38801

The Memphis and Birmingham papers are also available locally.

For Further Information

Community Development Foundation
P.O. Drawer A
Tupelo, MS 38801

The Community Development Foundation is Tupelo's equivalent of a chamber of commerce.

Department of Economic Development
Division of Tourism
State of Mississippi
P.O. Box 22825
Jackson, MS 39205

Mississippi Game and Fish Commission
P.O. Box 451
Jackson, MS 39205

Victoria, Texas

POPULATION: 50,703 within the city limits
65,000 in Victoria County

ELEVATION: 93 feet above sea level

In Victoria, residents call their town "The Best-Kept Secret in Texas." In many ways it is. Victoria is located on the Guadalupe River in southern Texas, 116 miles southeast of San Antonio and 40 miles inland from the Gulf of Mexico. The favorable climate and abundant water, gas, and oil have helped make it a busy trade and shipping center for a large and prosperous ranching, agricultural, and petroleum-producing area.

Since 1962, when the opening of the Victoria Barge Canal connected the town with the Intracoastal Waterway, business and industry have boomed in Victoria.

Climate

Victoria's climate is affected more by the Gulf of Mexico than any other single factor except its southern latitude. The predominant winds are from the southeast, off the Gulf, tempering the heat and bringing Victoria more rain than falls in the drier areas to the west.

Summers are long and hot. Daily temperatures range between highs in the 80s and 90s and lows in the 60s and 70s from May through October, bringing some 3200 cooling degree days per year. There are about 115 days per year with temperatures of 90°F and above.

Winters are short and mild, except for the few chill northers that blow in each year and bring about 11 days with temperatures of 32°F and below. These northers are usually sudden in their arrival, cause abrupt drops in temperature, and seldom last more than three or four days. There are only 1200 heating degree days for the area each year. Frosts are mild and only occur between mid-December and mid-February, resulting in about 300 frost-free days in the growing season.

Precipitation is about 32 inches per year, fairly evenly divided throughout the year, with slight peaks in May and September. Rain occurs on only about one-fourth to one-third of the days each month. There is no snow. Humidity varies between highs of about 82% in the early morning hours and lows of 52% in the sunny afternoons. There is about 62% of possible sunshine each year.

Hurricanes are always a threat to the Texas coast, though Victoria's inland location tends to protect it from the full force of storms that strike this part of the coast. In September 1961 the great hurricane Carla, the largest hurricane on record, moved inland over Port Lavaca with winds estimated at 175 miles per hour. While the damage to the coastal area was severe, partly due to an 18.5-foot tide, Victoria was not badly damaged.

Tornadoes, while frequent in the northern areas of Texas, are virtually unknown this far south.

History

Before the white man's arrival, the Victoria area was shared by four Indian tribes, the Lipans, the Toncahuas, the Comanches, and the Karankawas. Then in 1530, only 38 years after Columbus made his historic voyage, a Spanish expedition led by Cabeza de Vaca was shipwrecked on the Gulf Coast. The friendly Lipans and Toncahuas helped the Spanish party, who recovered and returned to Spain to tell of this lovely coastal area with a river bordered by stately pecan trees.

Robert Cavelier, Sieur de La Salle, established a tiny fort here but was driven away by disease and hostile Comanche and Karankawa Indians. The Spanish learned of this French incursion into their territory and in 1689 sent an expedition led by Captain Alonzo de León, who named the river for the patron saint of Mexico, La Señora de Guadalupe. The Spanish established a mission and a fort, but the difficulty of maintaining communication with Mexico City was too much to cope with and the mission and settlers moved away, some to today's town of Goliad, some in the direction of San Antonio.

After that, not much happened to the site until 1805, when a new settlement was established under Martin de León and named Nuestra Señora de Guadalupe de Victoria. When Texas gained independence from Mexico, the name was shortened to Victoria.

Martin de León laid out Victoria in accordance with European and Mexican tradition, with a central market square. Today, Victoria's city hall stands on the site of this square.

Victoria's Mexican heritage lives on today in the magnificent old buildings, in the street names, and in the atmosphere of the community.

Economy and Employment

Victoria County has a total agricultural income of over $32 million a year. Crops include grain sorghum, corn, rice, hay, pecans, honey, soybeans, cotton, and peaches. Farmers raise beef cattle, poultry, hogs, sheep, and horses.

The major change in the local economy came with the discovery of oil in southern Texas. This was followed, in the years after World War II, by growing industrial development, much of it based on the nearby petroleum production. Victoria's economy is healthy and growing. Unemployment has remained low and retail sales have remained high.

Employment opportunities range from clerical jobs in local businesses, to teaching positions at the local schools and colleges, to highly technical jobs in the petrochemical industry. The major employers in the area are: Union Carbide (a large petrochemical plant, 1400 employees); Victoria Independent School District (1330); E. I. DuPont de Nemours & Co. (petrochemicals, 1300); DeTar Hospital (600); City of Victoria (600); Citizens Hospital (530); Skytop Rig Co. (servicing and drilling of oil wells, 500); Victoria Bank & Trust Co. (386); Safety Steel (reinforced buildings and railroad flatcars, 275);

Central Power & Light (254); Sears, Roebuck & Co. (233); and many smaller firms in a wide range of manufacturing and service industries.

Taxes

Texas has no state income tax, and the retail sales tax is 4%.

The property tax rate for both city and county is $1.41 per $100 of assessed value. The tax on a home selling for $65,000 would run about $915 per year.

Shopping

All the everyday needs of local residents can be met in the attractive downtown center or in the seven suburban shopping centers. For wider choices, San Antonio is 116 miles to the northwest and Houston is 120 miles to the northeast.

Residential Properties

Victoria offers many choices in residential living, from small apartments to the new Tanglewood and Mayfair Terrace subdivisions. Typical listings are:

SPACIOUS 3-bedroom, 2-bath home with fully equipped kitchen, living area with fireplace, ceiling fans and wet bar. Double garage with opener, skylight, loft and landscaping. $107,500.

CLOSE TO SCHOOLS AND SHOPPING. 3-bedroom, 2-bath home with fireplace and ceiling fan in den, fenced yard, double garage, lawn. $69,900.

INVESTMENT OR STARTER HOME. Two-bedroom home on corner lot with trees and detached 2-car garage. $42,000.

IN PORT O'CONNOR, 27 miles from Victoria, a furnished 2-bedroom home on 75 × 100 lot. $25,000.

SHORT DRIVE TO PLANT. 3-bedroom, 2-bath home with fireplace, nice lawn, lots of trees. $35,000.

Apartments are plentiful, with one-bedroom units renting for $250 to $350 per month and two-bedroom apartments or condos renting for $325 to $650.

Safety

Victoria's FBI Crime Index rating is 63 crimes per thousand of population per year. Police protection is provided by a 103-man police department and fire protection by a 72-man fire department that includes 24 emergency medical personnel, 3 ambulances, and 2 rescue boats, plus fire engines, an aerial truck, a snorkel truck, and other units.

The nearest manmade potential hazard is the nuclear plant at nearby Lavaca Bay, about 30 miles to the southeast. Natural hazards are limited to the possibility of hurricanes, though Victoria's inland location is the best safeguard against the major force of such storms.

Education

The public school system has 17 elementary schools, 3 junior high schools, and 2 high schools. These are augmented by 6 private and parochial schools.

Higher education is provided by an unusual "2 + 2 = 4" program, in which Victoria Junior College offers a two-year program applicable either to an associate degree or as the first two years of a four-year bachelor's-degree program that is continued at the University of Houston, Victoria campus. The university offers the last two years of the four-year program, granting B.A. degrees as well as providing graduate work toward a master's degree.

For a broader curriculum in a larger school, there is the University of Houston's main campus in Houston, 120 miles to the northeast, as well as the very good and very large University of Texas at Austin, 123 miles to the north.

Medical Facilities

Two hospitals serve the area with a combined total of 407 beds. These are augmented by four nursing homes with a total of 498 beds. There is also a private clinic with 30 beds.

Victoria has 110 doctors and 33 dentists in private practice, and the Gulf Bend Community Mental Health center provides aid in all areas of mental health.

For some of the finest medical care available in the world, Houston is 120 miles to the northeast.

Cultural Activities

Victoria offers a broad range of cultural events and activities. It has a Civic Theater Group, a Community Center Annex, an Exhibition Hall, and a huge 48,000-square-foot Show Barn. The local symphony orchestra and the community theater offer performances throughout the year, and the University of Houston provides the community with a wide range of special events, including livestock shows, a Bach Festival, and the Oil & Gas Exposition.

The public library serves the community with 58,646 volumes.

This is supplemented by the Victoria Junior College library, with 43,500 volumes, and the library of the University of Houston, Victoria campus, which has 75,000 volumes. Both of these libraries are open to residents during the school year.

Recreation

Because of the warm climate, almost every day of the year is suitable for outdoor activities. Twenty-seven miles southeast of Victoria is Port Lavaca, which has the world's longest fishing pier. Almost every type of Texas saltwater fishing is only minutes away from Victoria. Deep-sea fishing boats are available for full-day or half-day trips into the Gulf. Surf fishing is available along Matagorda Island, and bay fishing is excellent in Matagorda and Lavaca bays. Other water-related sports in the area include water-skiing in the old gravel pits just outside of town and swimming and boating along the shores and in the nearby bays.

Riverside Golf Course is an excellent 18-hole course with a tree-bordered fairway. Victoria Country Club also maintains an 18-hole course for members and guests.

Riverside Park, which has 562 acres of woodland, faces onto 4.5 miles of the Guadalupe River. It has 200 picnic areas, many with tables, benches, and barbecue pits. In addition, the park has playground equipment and a boat ramp on the river, and there are also hiking areas, exercise trails, and a duck pond. Smaller city parks offer baseball fields and other playgrounds.

The area has numerous softball fields, a model-airplane testing and racing area, an excellent zoo, and numerous tennis courts. In nearby Goliad, La Bahia Downs offers spring and fall horse racing.

The Aransas National Wildlife Refuge, on San Antonio Bay, and the Welder Wildlife Refuge, nearby, provide opportunities to view wildlife such as deer, turkeys, geese, ducks, and whooping cranes in their natural habitats.

For history buffs, there are several magnificent old missions, the McNamara house, and the Nave Museum. There is even an old gristmill, driven by a windmill, that was brought over from Germany in 1860.

Government

Victoria is governed by the Council-Manager system.

Water

The city-supplied water is plentiful, neutral, soft, and not fluoridated. The water comes from deep wells, and the system's maximum pumping capacity is 3 million gallons per day higher than peak load, so the supply should be adequate for all local needs for some time to come.

Energy

Electricity is supplied by Central Power & Light in town, and by the Victoria County Electric Co-op in rural areas. Electricity comes from gas-fired steam-generating plants in southern Texas, and will also come from the Lavaca Bay nuclear plant when it goes into service. Electric power supplies appear to be adequate for future needs.

Natural gas, drawn from gas wells in southern Texas, is supplied by Houston Pipeline Company and is distributed in Victoria by Entex, Inc. Because of the large gas fields in southern Texas, the future needs of the area appear to be assured.

Current utility rates can be obtained through the chamber of commerce, but at present the cost of utilities can be expected to average about $100 per month, with much of the cost going into operating air conditioning during the long, hot summers. For those families who can be comfortable with attic fans and ceiling fans, the cost per month would be much lower.

Television

There is one local television station, and the local cable system provides 11-channel coverage to subscribers.

Newspapers

The local daily newspaper is:

The Victoria Advocate
Victoria, TX 77901

The *Houston Chronicle*, the *Houston Post*, and the *San Antonio Express* and *News* are available locally.

For Further Information

Victoria Chamber of Commerce
P.O. Box 2465
Victoria, TX 77901

Travel & Information Division
State Dept. of Highways & Public Transportation
Austin, TX 78701

Vincennes, Indiana

POPULATION: 20,589 within the city limits
41,561 in Knox County

ELEVATION: 421 feet above sea level

Vincennes, the county seat of Knox County, is located on the Wabash River 51 miles north of Evansville and 59 miles south of Terre Haute. Surrounded by fertile farmlands, it is the oldest town in Indiana and is today an attractive residential community as well as a busy retail and industrial center.

The countryside is gently rolling with open fields and patches of woodland, dotted here and there with orchards and small farms.

Climate

The Indiana climate is one of warm summers and cool winters, a climate of four distinct seasons. The weather during any season is subject to change, however, as surges of polar air move southeastward or tropical air moves northeastward. These changes are more frequent and more pronounced in winter, which may be unusually cold. Summer, too, may be unusually cool. On the other hand, a summer may be unusually warm and a winter mild, if tropical air predominates.

These contrasting forces of warm and cold air are responsible for the thunderstorms and cyclones generated in the area. Severe storms that damage property and may cause loss of life are most frequent in the spring.

Winters vary from mild to cold. Average winter temperatures range from highs in the 40s to lows in the high 20s and low 30s, but extremes of 77°F in January and −17°F in February have been recorded. Snowfall averages about 18 inches per year, mostly in December through March. The last frost is usually in the first week of April and the first frost comes in the first week of November, resulting in 216 days of growing season. There are approximately 4500 heating degree days per year.

Spring and fall are pleasant and mild, and summers can be quite hot. Normal summer temperatures range from highs in the upper 80s to lows in the upper 60s, though extremes as high as 112°F in July and as low as 32°F in May and September have been recorded. There are about 1500 cooling degree days per year, and 43 days with temperatures 90°F and above.

Rainfall averages around 42 inches per year, with rain fairly well distributed throughout the year except for the spring rains in March through May that are heavier than those during the rest of the year. There is about 65% of possible sunshine each year, mostly in the summer and fall. Cloudiness is greatest in the winter.

Winds in winter are generally northerly, and those in summer are for the most part southerly.

History

About 1732, a young French lieutenant was sent to the lower Wabash River by his government in Canada to establish a post and fortification. He chose a site near a friendly Piankeshaw Indian village where for centuries thousands of buffaloes had forded the Wabash.

When the French were defeated by the British in 1763, the post named Vincennes was turned over to the victors. It remained a fort until 1779, when it was captured by a band of frontiersmen led by Colonel George Rogers Clark.

Following the American Revolution, the Continental Congress organized the "Territory Northwest of the River Ohio" and appointed William Henry Harrison to govern it. In 1804, Harrison built Grouseland on the outskirts of Vincennes, and he lived there until 1812. In 1813 the territorial capital was moved to Vincennes.

Vincennes has many old, historic buildings, including the old Territorial Capitol; Vincennes University, which was founded in 1801; the first newspaper office in Indiana, which was built and opened in 1804; and the Old State Bank, constructed between 1836 and 1838.

Economy and Employment

Vincennes is a busy retail and trading center for a rich farming area that produces corn, soybeans, wheat, peaches, and apples. In addition, there are many dairy farms. Natural resources include oil, bituminous coal, natural gas, sand, and gravel.

The local Area Development Organization is making available a number of excellent industrial sites to attract new business to the area. Local industries include manufacturers of glass, batteries, shoes, structural steel, and paper products.

Major employers are: Hamilton Glass Products (glass fabrication, 350 employees); Essex International (magnet wire, 330); Prestolite (batteries, 150); Vincennes Steel (150); Packaging Corporation of America (paper and plastic containers, 125); Hoover Universal (auto-seat springs, 108); and Universal Scientific (printed circuits, 123).

Taxes

The Indiana income tax is 1.9% of adjusted gross income. The state sales tax is 4%.

Property taxes are based on an assessed value of one-third of true market value, and a home selling for $65,000 would be taxed at about $1075 per year.

Shopping

Many national and regional chain stores are represented locally, in addition to the local businesses. Most stores are open on Friday evenings.

For wider choices in shopping, Indianapolis is 121 miles to the northeast, Louisville is 106 miles to the east, and St. Louis is 153 miles westward on U.S. 50.

Residential Properties

Homes in every price range can be found in Vincennes. A few typical listings are:

> RETIRING OR STARTING? 2-bedroom, aluminum-sided home with living room, new kitchen, enclosed porch, full bath, carpeting, gas heat and window air, 1-car garage. Only $22,000.
>
> LIKE NEW 3-bedroom cedar-front ranch home on large corner lot, central heat and air, large kitchen and family room. $39,500.
>
> NESTLED IN THE TREES on 1.12 acres, this 4-bedroom home has a swimming pool, appliance-packed kitchen, breakfast room, living room with fireplace, formal dining room, utility room, full carpeting, central air and heat. Includes 2-car garage and 2-car carport. Close to schools. $55,000.
>
> BEAUTIFUL BRICK RANCH home with fireplace, swimming pool, 3 bedrooms, 2 baths, living room, family home, large kitchen and dining area, utility room, 2-car garage, storage shed, patio, full central heat and air. $72,000.

Rentals are available, with one-bedroom apartments renting for $150 to $250 per month. Two-bedroom apartments and condos can be rented for $195 to $425 per month.

Safety

Vincennes has a low FBI Crime Index rating of 50 crimes per thousand of population per year. The police department has 31 uniformed personnel, and the sheriff's office serves the unincorporated area with 12 deputies and 30 reserve officers. The fire department has 42 firemen in four stations and the unincorporated areas outside town are served by a rural department with 2 paid officers and 50 volunteers. The Fire Insurance Rating is Class 4 for commercial properties and Class 5 for residential properties.

There are no nearby manmade hazards. The nearest is Crane Naval Ammunition Depot, 40 miles to the east.

Tornadoes are always a potential hazard in Indiana, which has had 277 tornadoes during the past 43 years. Also, several deaths are caused by lightning each year within the state.

Education

Vincennes has six elementary schools, one junior high school, and one senior high school in the public school system. There are also four parochial school with a total enrollment of 602.

From the standpoint of accessibility to higher education, Vincennes is one of the best locations in the United States. Vincennes

University, founded in 1801, is the oldest junior college in the state, offering a two-year program leading to associate degrees in a variety of subjects. Forty percent of its students are enrolled in vocational-education fields.

Indiana Business College has one of its ten centers in Vincennes. The college annually serves 3000 students statewide and 200 locally in secretarial science, accounting, and business.

Vincennes Beauty College, which has a student capacity of 60, provides education toward a cosmetologist license.

For four-year college programs and graduate programs, there are several excellent universities within easy commuting distance. Indiana State University, 51 miles to the south at Evansville, offers 60 academic programs leading to bachelors' degrees. Indiana University, 73 miles to the northeast at Bloomington, has an enrollment of 35,000 and offers associate, bachelors', masters', and doctoral degree programs. Indiana State University, 59 miles to the north in Terre Haute, has an enrollment of over 12,000 and offers associate, bachelors', masters', and doctoral degrees.

Other nearby colleges include Indiana Vocational Technical College in Evansville; Indiana Vocational Technical College in Terre Haute; Oakland City College, a Baptist church-affiliated college 40 miles to the south in Oakland City; and the University of Evansville, a Methodist-affiliated college in Evansville.

Medical Facilities

Good Samaritan Hospital provides 308 beds and full medical care for the community. In addition, there are 55 physicians and 21 dentists in private practice. More specialized medical attention can be found in Louisville and Indianapolis, both within a couple hours' drive of Vincennes.

Cultural Activities

Two libraries serve the area: the Vincennes Public–Knox County Library, with 89,436 volumes, and the Vincennes University library, with 37,250 volumes. A bookmobile with about 15,000 books serves the outlying areas.

Cultural events, including drama, musicals, and concerts, are scheduled throughout the year at Vincennes University.

A much wider variety of cultural activities is available in Evansville, 51 miles to the north via a good four-lane divided highway. These include the Evansville Philharmonic Orchestra, which performs in Vanderburgh Auditorium, and three community theater organizations that offer drama, summer stock, musicals, children's theater, and dinner-theater performances in Evansville. The Musicians Club of Evansville sponsors performances in dance, drama, and instrumental and vocal music.

Recreation

Sports events are scheduled throughout the year in Vincennes. Vincennes University is active in basketball competition.

Golfers have a choice of two courses, a private course at the Elks club and a public course at Bicknell, about 10 miles northeast of Vincennes. A public swimming pool and several public tennis courts are also available.

Camping facilities abound. The area is dotted with fishing ponds and lakes, many free to the public. An active gun club provides a place to shoot for fun or competition.

Government

Vincennes operates under the Mayor-Council form of government.

Water

The city-provided water supply is alkaline, very soft, and not fluoridated. It is drawn from seven wells by a system that provides 2 million gallons per day more than the highest peak loads, assuring an ample supply for the foreseeable future.

Energy

There are two sources of electrical service in Knox County. Public Service Indiana serves Vincennes and other urban areas of Knox County, while Knox County Rural Electric Member Corporation (REMC), a co-op, serves the rural areas. Indiana has the lowest average monthly industrial electricity costs of all midwestern states, according to the Knox County community audit. The average monthly electric bill per home is about $40, though rates are expected to rise sharply in the near future.

Natural gas, piped in from Texas gas fields, is supplied by the Hoosier Gas Company, and propane is available from three local dealers.

Total utility costs for the average home run about $100 per month.

Television

All major television networks are represented in the area and can be received on home antenna systems. There is also a cable system, as well as a local educational television station.

Newspapers
The local daily newspaper is:

The Vincennes Sun-Commercial
Vincennes, IN 47591

The area is also served by the *Valley Advance,* a local weekly newspaper; the *Vincennes Shopper*; and the *County Daily News.* The *Indianapolis Star* is also available for home delivery.

For Further Information

Knox County Chamber of Commerce
417 Busseron St.
Vincennes, IN 47591

Indiana Department of Commerce
Tourism Division
336 State House
Indianapolis, IN 46204

Wausau, Wisconsin

POPULATION: 30,448 within the city limits
70,434 in the immediate area
111,270 in Marathon County

ELEVATION: 1195 feet above sea level

"Some will see our trees, others our forests." This quote taken from the chamber of commerce brochure on Wausau is probably the most honest appraisal any community has made of its own advantages and disadvantages.

Wausau is located in north-central Wisconsin at the junction of the Wisconsin, Big Rib, and Eau Claire rivers, 96 miles west of Green Bay and 188 miles northwest of Milwaukee. It is an area of lakes and forests, dairy farms and small truck farms. Once called "a faraway place" by the Chippewa Indians, Wausau is now a playground for thousands of tourists and the shopping center for a large rural area.

Climate

Located in the upper Midwest, Wisconsin is bounded on the north by Lake Superior and on the east by Lake Michigan, both of which affect the climate of the state. The Wisconsin climate is typically continental. The cold, snowy winters favor a variety of winter sports, and the warm summers appeal to thousands of vacationers each year.

Winter are long, and there are only about 120 freeze-free days per year. The last frost in spring generally occurs in mid-May and the first frost of fall comes in mid to late September. Snowfall averages around 50 inches per year, beginning in October and continuing to April, with the heaviest snowfalls occurring in January. Winters are variable and unpredictable. Some winters bring temperatures as low as −35°F, mountains of snow, and bitter north winds. Other winters are mild and open, with light snowfall. As the chamber of commerce brochure says, "Robins and cardinals sometimes winter in Wausau, but they worry a lot." But a bitter winter for some is snowmobile and skiing time for others. Winters bring about 8400 heating degree days per year.

Spring and fall are beautiful, with the surrounding forests of pine and hemlock filled with color. Summers are short and pleasant, with seldom more than 18 days per year in which temperatures exceed 90°F. Since there are only about 500 cooling degree days per year, air-conditioning equipment in homes or offices is hardly justified.

Precipitation amounts to about 30 inches per year, more or less evenly spread throughout the year, occurring about 10 days most months and a bit more than that in April through June. Total precipitation amounts to 529 million gallons per square mile per year.

History

The early Chippewa Indians of central Wisconsin camped along the banks of the Wisconsin River and called the site of their camp *Waw-Saw*— "the faraway place." White men began arriving in the 1830s and liked the site. George Stevens built the first sawmill in 1839, and by 1842 enough settlers had arrived to form a small community they called Big Bull Falls.

With four lumber mills in operation and a population of 1500, the community was granted a charter as a city in 1842 under the name of Wausau. The growing village was populated by a mixed group of hardy Yankees, Scots, Englishmen, and French-Canadians. The Germans were the last to arrive, coming in two separate migrations in the mid-1850s. Whereas the early settlers were trappers, hunters, and traders, the Germans were the first real farmers. The second influx of German settlers came from the industrial complex already springing up around Pittsburgh. A group of skilled tradesmen, they established their own community 10 miles west of Wausau near the Big Rib River, at the present town of Marathon.

Economy and Employment

Wausau's economy has gone through a series of phases. Starting as a hunting, trapping, and trading community, it became a farming center and then a booming center for lumbering. A number of massive homes still stand in tribute to the fortunes made by the early lumbermen. Following the lumber boom, Wausau began a steady and sound growth in business and industry, coupled with an increasing tourist trade.

Wausau's growth has been healthy and continuous. Labor unrest is unknown. Employment is steady and the unemployment rate is low. Countywide, there are 172 well-diversified manufacturing firms employing over 15,000 people, with payrolls exceeding $206 million per year. In addition to manufacturing and industry, Wausau has 477 retail businesses with sales totaling $120 million, and 100 wholesalers with sales of over $75 million per year.

The largest single business in Wausau is one of the largest insurance companies in the world, Employers Insurance of Wausau, with 2525 employees. When the lumber companies of the early days had stripped out the huge stands of white pine, they did not merely move on elsewhere but reinvested their fortunes in new enterprises, including the mutual insurance company just mentioned and such businesses as the Mosinee Paper Corporation, which has 580 employees today, and Marathon Electric Manufacturing Corp., which now has 1100 employees.

Other major employers in the area include: Wausau Hospital Center (1138 employees); Marathon County (1010); Wausau Paper Mills Co. (675); Weyerhaeuser Co. (lumber and wood products, 671); American Can Co. (526); Land O'Lakes (cheese, 465); Marathon Cheese Corp. (500); General Telephone Co. of Wisconsin (350); and Wausau Medical Center (264).

Taxes

The income tax in Wisconsin ranges from 3.4% on incomes below $3000 to 10% on incomes above $40,000. The combined state and city sales tax is 5%.

The property tax rate is $2.85 per $100 of assessed value, based on 65% of true market value. Thus a home selling for $65,000 would be taxed about $1204 per year.

Shopping

As a shopping and trading center for a large area, Wausau can meet most of the needs of its residents. For greater variety, Green Bay is 96 miles to the east and Milwaukee is 188 miles to the southeast.

Residential Properties

Because of the cold winters, housing in Wausau must be built more solidly, with better insulation, than housing in the sunbelt cities. On the other hand, the proximity of vast lumber resources tends to bring down the cost of construction. Perhaps it is an even tradeoff.

A few typical listings from the local newspaper are:

> 41-ACRE FARMETTE. Ideal setup for horse lovers or people who like privacy. Well-maintained 3-bedroom ranch with extra-large 2-car garage. Some woodland, some cropland. $84,900.
>
> WELL-MAINTAINED 2-bedroom home on Wausau's east side in convenient location. $42,500.
>
> EXCELLENT home for large family. 6 bedrooms. Located on one acre in northwest side. $46,200.
>
> PERFECT for retired couple. First-floor utility area and 3 bedrooms. Recently redecorated. $29,900.
>
> ENERGY-EFFICIENT 3-bedroom home on beautiful wooded 1.8-acre lot with small trout stream, 2-car garage, separate insulated workshop. $64,900.

Rentals are also available, with one-bedroom apartments renting for $175 to $265 per month and two-bedroom apartments or condos renting for $185 to $350. Three-bedroom homes can be found for $350 per month and up.

Safety

The FBI Crime Index rating for Wausau is low, at only 49 crimes per thousand of population per year. Police protection is supplied by a 57-member department. The fire department has 60 full-time employees operating three stations. The Fire Insurance Rating is Class 4.

The nearest manmade potential hazard is a cluster of nuclear power plants 90 miles away in the Green Bay area. While there are many rivers and lakes around Wausau, the land is well drained and flooding is not considered a hazard.

Education

Wausau offers 29 grade schools, 3 middle schools, 3 senior high schools, 1 vocational school, 13 parochial grade schools, and 1 parochial high school.

The University of Wisconsin, Marathon campus (about 12 miles from Wausau), offers a two-year liberal-arts and preprofessional curriculum. For a full college curriculum, the University of Wisconsin at Madison is 141 miles to the south.

Medical Facilities

Wausau Hospital Center serves the people of north-central Wisconsin. This new center was completed in 1979 and offers 260 beds. Across the street is the Wausau Medical Center, which provides emergency services 24 hours a day.

There are 125 doctors and 54 dentists in the area, as well as a number of clinics specializing in various fields. There is also a fully equipped ambulance service manned by personnel of the Wausau fire department.

Cultural Activities

The Marathon County public library contains more than 249,000 volumes and has a circulation of well over 640,000 per year. In addition, the library of the University of Wisconsin at Marathon is available to area residents during the school year.

The Wausau Area Performing Arts Foundation is active in supporting community arts groups, acting as a public information agency for the arts, sponsoring live performances and workshops, and exploring ideas for a performing-arts center. The Community Theater, an 800-member organization, was founded in 1935 and today gives four performances each season. The Civic Symphony is made up of local musicians and gives three concerts each year, and the Central Wisconsin Ballet Foundation gives performances in the area and offers instruction to residents.

The Children's Theater, the Merry Pipers, a traveling children's theater group, and Artists-in-the-Schools all serve to introduce the children of the community to cultural and artistic activities.

Recreation

Winter sports are important in the Wausau area, with some of the best skiing in the Midwest available at nearby Rib Mountain State Park. Marathon County is laced with ski and snowmobile trails, and a free map of these is available from the Wausau Nordic Ski Club, P.O. Box 423, Wausau, WI 54401.

Other sports facilities are provided at 28 city parks and 5 county parks. There are 6 municipal swimming pools, 6 golf courses, 1 indoor ice rink, 2 roller-skating rinks, 15 tennis courts, and 4 baseball fields.

Water-skiing and boating on scenic Lake Wausau and along the Wisconsin River are becoming increasingly popular.

Extensive hunting and fishing areas are within easy driving distance of Wausau. Deer are plentiful in the county, and Lake Wausau and the Eau Pleine River are popular fishing spots. The Marathon County Fish and Game Club maintains its own privately owned clubhouse, and anyone can join.

A shooting-range park, located 11 miles south of Wausau, offers target ranges plus special bench-rest ranges for hunters who wish to sight-in their rifles before the hunting season.

Government

Wausau has a Mayor-Council form of government, consisting of an elected mayor and 13 aldermen, each elected from a separate district within the city. In addition, the aldermen of Wausau are members of the county board of supervisors. A total of 39 supervisors are elected from the various districts.

Water

There is plenty of water in Wausau, with three rivers converging at its doorstep. The tap water is slightly acid and hard and is supplied by the Wausau Water Utility.

Energy

Heating for the long, cold winters is supplied by coal, oil, and gas. Domestic stoker coal and fuel oil are readily available from local suppliers. Natural gas is distributed by the Wisconsin Fuel and Light Company.

Electricity for more than 275,000 customers is supplied by the

Wisconsin Public Service Corporation from generators using fossil fuels, nuclear power, combustion turbines, and hydroelectric power to generate 1.5 million kilowatts. Utility costs for an average two-bedroom home run about $100 per month.

Television

Cable television provides full-channel coverage, and three local television stations offer both local and network programs.

Newspapers

The local daily newspaper is:

The Daily Herald
P.O. Box 1286
Wausau, WI 54401

Valley View Magazine, a free handout paid for by advertisers, is published weekly. A postcard to them will probably bring a free copy.

Valley View Magazine
P.O. Box 1516
Wausau, WI 54401

For Further Information

Wausau Area Chamber of Commerce
P.O. Box 569
Wausau, WI 54401

Division of Tourism
650 Loraine Building
123 West Washington Ave.
Madison, WI 53702

Wisconsin Dept. of Natural Resources
Parks & Recreation Bureau
Madison, WI 53701

Rib Mountain Ski Corp.
Box 387
Wausau, WI 54401

Rib Mountain Ski Corporation will send information on their ski and resort facilities.

Waycross, Georgia

POPULATION: 19,302 within the city limits
36,000 in Ware County

ELEVATION: 144 feet above sea level

Waycross is an industrial, shipping, and trade center in a rich agricultural area of southeastern Georgia, just north of the Okefenokee Swamp, 103 miles southwest of Savannah, and 76 milcs northwest of Jacksonville, Florida.

In addition to attracting industry and tourism, Waycross also serves as a marketing center for naval stores, livestock, forest products, tobacco, honey, and pecans. It is being discovered by retirees from all over the nation, and new retirement communities are being planned and built. Waycross is also becoming a popular convention center.

Climate

Waycross is located in the coastal plains area of Georgia on land that is low and wooded, with sandy soils well suited to a wide variety of agricultural products. Okefenokee Swamp is only 8 miles south of Waycross. Just north of town the Satilla River runs eastward toward the Atlantic Ocean.

As in all of the southeastern part of the United States, the climate in Waycross is warm, with long, hot summers and mild winters. Winter temperatures normally range between highs of 68°F and lows of 45°F, while summer highs range from the mid-80s in May, to the low 90s in June through August, and back to the 80s in September and October. Low temperatures in summer normally range between the 50s and 70s. There are normally 85 days a year with temperatures above 90°F, and only 15 days per year with temperatures below 32°F. The mild winters account for a low 1300 heating degree days, and summers bring about 2600 cooling degree days.

Precipitation is about 50 inches per year, with rain throughout the year but most frequent in the months of June through September, when it usually comes in the form of cooling thundershowers. Humidity is high throughout the year, averaging 75% annually. Waycross averages 65% of possible sunshine during the year, a figure that would be higher but for the many thunderstorms in summer.

Winds are most often northerly in winter and southerly in summer. Except during storms, winds are normally gentle.

History

Waycross began as a lumbering and farming community and was incorporated in 1874. Progress in Waycross stopped for the Civil War, began again, and then succumbed to the boll weevil. Then once again Waycross began its upward climb.

The name of the town came from the location — where the ways cross. In Colonial days, it was the hub of stagecoach roads and earlier pioneer trails. Later the Plant System railroad and the Brunswick and Western railroad lines crossed here. Indian and pioneer trails, stagecoach and military roads, all passed through Waycross and were transformed into today's highways, many of which follow the old routes.

Waycross survived the Civil War and the boll weevil and is rapidly building a solid economic base of industry, agriculture, and commerce.

Economy and Employment

The per capita income in Waycross is growing faster than the national rate of inflation. The economy is expanding at a healthy rate. Agriculture, still important in Waycross, is today based largely on forest products. Industry includes the manufacture of many products such as shoes, cigars, mobile homes, paper boxes, machinery, industrial gases, brick, burial vaults, and concrete products. Processed materials include meats, pecans, tobacco, animal feeds, honey, naval stores, dairy products, and candy.

Taxable sales in the area exceeded $214 million in 1980, and indications are that retail trade will continue to increase at a steady rate in the future.

A new 2500-acre industrial park with rail sidings, natural gas, electricity, and public services invites light to heavy industry.

Major employers include: Seaboard Coastline Railroad (2200 employees); Guerdon Industries (mobile homes, 375); Scapa Dryers (dryer felts for the paper industry, 239); J. H. Swisher & Son, Inc. (cigars, 186); Champion Building Products (plywood, 176); Rubin Bros. (footwear, 153); Dixie Concrete (151); and United Pioneer (clothing, 150).

In nonmanufacturing occupations there are 5 firms in agricultural production, 2 in mining, 77 in construction, 30 in transportation, 75 in wholesale trade, 285 in retail trade, 65 in finance and insurance, and 222 in various services.

Employment information can be obtained by writing:

Georgia State Department of Labor
Employment Office
809 Elizabeth Street
Waycross, GA 31501

Taxes

The Georgia state income tax is 6% on incomes over $7000 per year. The state sales tax is 3%.

Property taxes are moderate and run about $650 per year on a home selling for $65,000.

Shopping

Because there is no large city or population center within a 75-mile radius, local stores are equipped to provide for most of the shopping needs of residents.

Jacksonville, Florida, about 75 miles away, and Savannah, 103 miles away, can satisfy virtually any shopping requirements.

Residential Properties

Real estate prices have not inflated in Waycross to the extent they have in many other parts of the nation. A few typical offerings are:

> THREE-BEDROOM home with one bath is just outside the city limits. Freshly repainted with completely fenced yard. $22,000.
>
> LIVING IS EASY in this spacious 5-bedroom home with two patios and swimming pool. Good loan assumption. $71,500.
>
> FOUR-BEDROOM brick and wood siding, split-level home, over 2000 square feet. Good loan. $39,900.
>
> RANCH-STYLE brick home, 3 bedrooms, 2 baths, 1600 square feet of living space on a 125′ × 175′ lot. $50,000.

Rentals are relatively scarce but inexpensive. One-bedroom apartments rent for $90 to $150 per month, and two-bedroom condos or apartments rent for $150 to $225.

Safety

Waycross's FBI Crime Index rating is a low 54 crimes per thousand of population per year. Police protection is provided by a 67-member department, and fire protection by a department with 36 full-time paid employees. The Fire Insurance Rating is Class 6.

The nearest potential manmade hazard is the nuclear power plant 47 miles north near Baxley.

Education

The city public school system provides a senior high school, a junior high school, and six elementary schools. The county system provides additional schools for the rural areas.

Waycross Junior College, a part of the state system, provides a two-year degree program.

Waycross/Ware Tech, a vocational-technical school, offers training in business, health services, and technical and skilled occupations.

The nearest four-year universities are Jacksonville University, at Jacksonville, Florida, 76 miles to the southeast; Florida State University, in Tallahassee, Florida, 132 miles to the southwest; and a number of universities in Atlanta, 233 miles to the northwest, including Georgia Institute of Technology, Atlanta University, Georgia State University, and Oglethorpe University.

Medical Facilities

Waycross has a 257-bed hospital, an active Public Health Department, a privately owned radiology center, and the Georgia State Regional Health Office, which serves one-third of the state. In addition there are two nursing homes that provide post-hospital care as well as home nursing.

Cultural Activities

The Waycross public library is the center of a regional library system serving five counties with more than 150,000 volumes. A bookmobile reaches the distant parts of the area with regularly scheduled visits.

Heritage Center offers exhibits depicting the history of the area and provides a home for the community's cultural activities.

Much more cultural activity can be found in Savannah and Jacksonville, both of which are within two hours' driving time of Waycross.

Recreation

Waycross is the northern entrance to the Okefenokee Swamp, "the Land of the Trembling Earth," a 600-square-mile world of freshwater prairies or marshes. It is a haven for many species of wildlife, including alligators, otters, birds of prey, migratory birds, wildcats, bears, deer, turtles, frogs, and many other reptiles. Plant life is unbelievably abundant.

The Okefenokee forms the principal base for recreation in the area. Hunting in the swamp is prohibited, but fishing is encouraged. Okefenokee Swamp Park offers visitors a close-up look at the swamp and its inhabitants. Scenic boat tours into the swamp are offered.

The county parks offer 20 tennis courts in the area. Ten parks have playgrounds and picnic facilities. There are three public swimming pools, and the city offers a variety of sports programs as well as classes in arts, crafts, speech, and drama.

Golfers have access to a public golf course, and there is also an 18-hole course at the private Okefenokee Golf Club.

Laura S. Walker State Park, 10 miles southeast of town, provides camping facilities, an 111-acre lake for boaters, swimmers, and water-skiers, and a swimming pool and picnic area.

Government

The town operates under the Council-Manager plan, with a city commission and a full-time city manager.

Water
The local tap water is neutral, hard, and fluoridated. It is supplied by a joint city-county system with a capacity more than three times the present maximum demand.

Energy
Electricity is supplied by Georgia Power Company and comes from a number of fossil-fuel and nuclear-power plants. Natural gas is delivered to homes by the Atlanta Gas Light Company.

Utility costs average about $100 per month for a typical two-to-three-bedroom home.

Television
Waycross has one local television station, and a cable system provides full-channel coverage for subscribers.

Newspapers
The local newspaper, published daily except Sunday, is:

The Waycross Journal Herald
400 Isabella St.
Waycross, GA 31501

The newspapers from Atlanta, Savannah, and Jacksonville are also available locally.

For Further Information

Waycross–Ware Chamber of Commerce
P.O. Box 137
Waycross, GA 31501

Tourist Division
Department of Industry & Trade
P.O. Box 1776
Atlanta, GA 30301

Finding Your Own Best Town

After reading about the best towns in the preceding pages, you will find you like some better than others. Concentrate on the few you like best. These are the ones to begin gathering the latest information on. Write to the chambers of commerce, the employment offices, the realtors, and any other addresses listed. From the information you receive, learn about *current*

employment opportunities
real estate prices
taxes
utility costs

Using this up-to-date information, pick one town that looks best to you, and then pick a spare — just in case. Subscribe to the local newspapers of these two selected towns. Ask your local telephone office to get you a telephone directory for each one.

Read everything you receive from all of the sources you contact. A lot of it will be chamber of commerce propaganda, but some of it will be valuable information.

After reading the want ads and real estate listings in the newspapers, and looking over everything, do you still think your first choice is really the best? It is much easier to change your mind and start concentrating on your second-choice town now than later. But if your first choice is still number one, if it still looks like your own best town, there is still one more step you should take before moving to it.

Visit the town!

A visit is insurance against making a mistake. Nothing you can learn from reading will give you the true feel of a town. Only a visit can do that.

There are two ways to take a look at your selected town. The quick, easy, and expensive way is to fly or drive to the town, rent a motel room for the visit, and eat in restaurants. This may be the easy way, but it is not the best way. A better way is called "Home Exchange" and is simply the temporary trading of homes with someone in a place you want to visit who, in turn, wants to visit the area in which you now live. The advantages are many. First of all, it is a way to save money, since the only cost above your normal living expenses at home is the cost of the trip to and from the town you want to look at.

The greatest advantage of trading homes for a week or two is that it gives you a chance actually to experience living in the town. There is a huge difference between staying in a motel and eating restaurant meals, and living in a home and doing the same things you would do in your own home — cooking your own meals, making your own beds, and meeting your neighbors over the back fence. As a resident, though temporary, you can learn more about a town in a week than you could learn in two months as a visitor.

There is an organization that lists people interested in exchanging homes:

Vacation Exchange Club
350 Broadway
New York, NY 10013

Get in touch with them. Get their catalog. Look for the place or places you are most interested in. And, if they do not list anyone in that particular town, look for somebody in the nearest city or large town. After all, an hour's drive to and from a home in a nearby city is still better than living in a motel.

And don't worry about somebody not taking care of your home while they are in it. Remember, you are in their home just as they are in yours. It tends to make people very, very careful of the home they are visiting.

This visit to your selected town is the time to look for work. If you have a skill or experience that a local employer wants, it is quite possible to get a job before you end your stay. It is even possible, sometimes, to have the new employer pay for some or all of your moving expenses. If you are currently employed, do not quit your present job or leave your present home until you are sure you have both in the place you want to go to.

Of course, it may turn out that despite careful research, one visit will tell you that the town you picked is not the right one after all. What then?

Try again! It is better to find out that you've chosen the wrong town during a brief visit than after a permanent move.

Whether you're visiting your first town or an alternate, talk to everyone you can. Talk to prospective employers, realtors, clerks in the supermarkets, the police officer watching downtown traffic, the waitress who serves you coffee. Find out what they think about their town. If they all like it, you can be pretty sure you will like it too.

If at this point you have found the job you want and have decided that this is the right town, your own best town, you must focus on the last but surely not the least important problem of all — finding your new home! There are basically only two alternatives — rent or buy.

When I talk of renting a home, I refer to any means of paying for the use of a residence without obtaining a title or equity. When I talk of buying, I mean any arrangement by which you occupy a premises and obtain any sort of equity or ownership of the property while doing so.

At the time this book goes to press, interest rates are high and money is scarce, making "ordinary" financing too expensive for most of us. But in times when property is difficult to sell, because of high interest rates or any other reason, it is often possible to negotiate special financing arrangements with some of the owners who want to sell.

On the other hand, at the present time most houses are renting for about one-third of what they should rent for, if the time-tested formula of 1% of market value per month is followed.

Briefly, let's look at a few of the major points to consider when deciding whether to rent or buy.

Income Tax

The decision to rent or buy has a direct effect on a family's income taxes. Interest payments are tax-deductible. Since a large part of the monthly payment on any home purchase is interest, a major portion of these payments is deductible from taxable income.

Renters, on the other hand, are not able to deduct anything for the rent they pay. But if the rent is only one-third of true-value rental, as it generally is today, this may mean that a renter would be paying so little in relation to the cost of buying a home that there would be no tax advantage in home ownership.

Inflation

Prices of everything have shot up as the government has created more money and given us continuing inflation as our reward for letting them do it. This is especially true of real estate prices in many parts of the country.

On the other hand, because of today's high interest rates it is increasingly difficult to sell real estate, so the prices in many areas may no longer be rising and may even be beginning to drop. If this drop continues, it may be better to hold off on buying, wait for the market to bottom, and in the meantime rent a home.

Financing

With the high cost of money today in all of our commercial lending institutions, many homeowners are forced to turn to creative financing when they want to sell. This simply means that more and more sellers are forced to carry part or all of the financing on a sale at rates well below commercial or bank rates.

In today's world, no buyer need accept a deal on a home that includes a large down payment and bank-rate interest on the remainder. Talk to the realtor and find out what the owner is willing to do to sweeten the deal.

Store of Value

Perhaps one of the most important reasons to buy a home is to build up an equity. This is particularly true in times of continuing inflation, since the value of the home will continue to climb as the purchasing power of money declines. However, if the real estate market is losing its momentum, as it appears to be doing today, a purchase now may not be as much of a store of value as it would be in another year when prices have dropped.

Special Considerations

Another point to consider, one not often mentioned by realtors, is the very interesting tax shelter allowed for historic buildings. Do you want the government to help you pay for the cost of remodeling your home? It will, if you buy the right one.

A new government subsidy program gives amazing tax benefits for those renovating old structures in "historic areas." Many communities have such areas. All it takes is a telephone call to the local planning official to learn what is classified as a "historic area" in town. If there are old and historic homes still unrehabilitated, this is a chance to save 25% of your investment through tax reductions.

If you buy an old building in a historic area for, say, $50,000, and you borrow another $100,000 to remodel it, you get $25,000 (25% of the cost of remodeling) as a tax credit. This credit can be carried forward for as much as 15 years, to be used against your federal tax obligations.

This is legal, and it is perfectly legitimate. Congress has said that they want people to invest in the rehabilitation of historic buildings, and this is their way of encouraging you to do it. Remember, deducting the $25,000 from taxes is far better than earning another $25,000 that would itself be subject to taxes!

Selling Your Own Home

While a declining real estate market may make it good for you as the buyer of a new home, it can make it tough for you as the seller of your present home. If you are renting, you may actually be better off. But if you own or are presently making payments on your home, most people will tell you that you have to do one of two things with it: rent it or sell it.

There is another possibility, however. Exchange it. There are real estate agents in almost every community who will take on the task of trying to work out an exchange, sometimes a three-way or four-way exchange, to enable a homeowner in one town to trade his home for one in another town. In these times, such an exchange may well be the best possible alternative.

If neither sale nor exchange seems possible at the present time, then put your home in the hands of a real estate agent who handles rentals and plan to rent in your new town.

Conclusions

For those who have yet to own a home, renting may well be the best way to go. Current real estate prices and interest rates have greatly reduced the financial benefits of home ownership. The increase in purchase prices in relation to rents has just about eliminated any cost advantages of owning a home.

When you have decided that you like the town you picked, when you have found employment and a home to live in, it is time to make your move, settle down, and begin to enjoy the many benefits of town life. When that happens, you have found your own best town in America!

Appendix: Climate and How It Works

Further Reading

Appendix: Climate and How It Works

The weather and climatic data used in this book are taken primarily from material published by the National Oceanic and Atmospheric Administration (NOAA), a part of the United States Department of Commerce. Its address is:

NOAA
Environmental Data Service
National Climatic Center
Asheville, NC 18801

The NOAA has climatic data on virtually every city and town in the United States and will provide an information sheet for any place you ask for at no charge. Just write to the above address and ask.

The basic factors that cause changes in weather and climate are the heat of the sun and the rotation of the earth. These set up circulation patterns in the atmosphere and carry heat and moisture from the equator to the poles, across land and sea, and over flat land and mountains. The geographical features of the land and water masses tend to establish more or less permanent patterns of wind, rainfall, cloudiness, and temperature. This is why the weather in any particular spot tends to follow the same pattern year after year.

The factors that cause climatic patterns in any given area are latitude (distance north from the equator), prevailing winds, location on the land mass, ocean currents, elevation (altitude), and any mountain barriers that may deflect prevailing winds.

Land and water surfaces react differently to the rays of the sun. Land masses heat and cool more rapidly than bodies of water, with the result that the surface air over continents is warmer in summer and colder in winter than the surface air over the oceans. Warm air rises. As it does, it is replaced by cooler air. This flows toward land masses in the summers and away from land masses in the winters. The same effect occurs on a daily basis along some seacoasts, such as the California coast, where winds blow in from the ocean when the coastal valleys are warm. This is what keeps the northern California coast cool in the summer.

The differential heating of the earth by the sun is the main cause of wind systems. Equatorial regions receive much more solar heat than do polar regions. Heat from the sun causes the equatorial surface air to rise. As it does, it is replaced by cooler surface air flowing in from the poles.

Because the earth rotates, there is a rotary *coriolis effect* that creates a global circulation of air, a worldwide wind pattern. Surface winds in the northern half of the world move in three broad belts: the northeasterly trade winds in the tropics and subtropics; the prevailing westerlies (from the west or southwest) in the middle latitudes; and the polar easterlies in the polar regions. Since all but the southernmost parts of the United States are in the middle latitudes, most of the climate is affected principally by the prevailing westerlies.

The coriolis effect leads to the formation of large circulations of air called *anticyclones,* or "highs." Highs tend to remain in certain general locations because of the fixed relationships of land and water masses. The highs that have the most effect on our weather in the United States are the Pacific High, which hovers over the North Pacific summer and winter, shifting slightly northward or southward with the seasons, and the North Atlantic High, which does the same in the North Atlantic. However, since the general flow of air is from west to east across the continent, the Pacific High has much more effect on our continental climate than any other.

Other high-pressure air masses form and disperse, as do low-pressure centers, or *cyclones.* Cold, dry air masses move into the United States from Canada, generally traveling southeastward. Cool, moist air masses generally travel eastward across the country from the Pacific Ocean. Warm, moist air masses move in from the Pacific Ocean, the Gulf of Mexico, or the Atlantic Ocean. Each air mass brings its own characteristic weather.

Between the highs and lows, *weather fronts* form, and most of what we consider "weather" occurs along these fronts, with the most active weather occurring around the low-pressure areas.

The air masses that prevail over an area determine its climate. For example, weather in the southeastern United States is dominated in summer by a moist tropical air mass associated with a high-pressure area located offshore. The southerly winds on the west side of this high bring moist air from the Gulf of Mexico into these coastal states. In winter, these same states are sometimes invaded by arctic air masses that bring cold fronts across the area.

Ocean currents have a great effect on the climates of coastal areas. The best-known of these, of course, is the Gulf Stream, which carries warm water northward along the Atlantic coast and thence northeastward and eastward to the British Isles. Without the Gulf Stream, Great Britain, Ireland, and most of Western Europe would have a climate similar to that of Siberia — which is on the same latitude as England. The Japanese Current is the major ocean current affecting the West Coast, leaving its warmth along the coast of British Columbia and arriving at the California coast as a cooling current.

Mountains tend to block the flow of prevailing winds and the movement of storms. Also, air flowing upward on the slopes of a mountain barrier tends to condense and lose much of its moisture. Thus there are deserts east of the Coast Ranges and the Cascade and Sierra Nevada ranges of California because the winds from the Pacific have dropped their moisture on the western slopes of the mountains and none is left for rain in the desert areas beyond.

Because climate is shaped by the physical features of land masses, a knowledge of the major physical aspects of our geography is helpful in understanding the climate and weather patterns that do so much to shape life in towns of every size. Broadly speaking, the country can be divided into a few generalized physical regions, as shown on the map at the top of page 390.

Each region on the map of Generalized Physical Regions has its own climate. Briefly, let us take a look at these regional climates.

Pacific Coast

This region consists of the coastal plains, the coastal ranges, and the adjacent inland valleys of Washington, Oregon, and California. The climate is of a Mediterranean nature, with dry summers and mild wet winters. The coastal strip remains cool in summer, while the inland valleys are dry and hot wherever they are cut off from the cool ocean air by the coastal ranges.

Cascade–Sierra Nevada

These mountains form a continuous chain extending from Canada to Southern California. As mentioned previously, the westerly winds, loaded with moisture from the ocean, lose almost all of their moisture as they rise along the western slopes of these mountain

GENERALIZED PHYSICAL REGIONS

ranges. Heavy winter rains and snowfalls, and water stored in the snowpack at higher elevations, are the sources of most of the water supply for the region, as well as for the Pacific Coast region. Weather in the Cascade–Sierra Nevada area is dominated by the mild Pacific air. Temperatures are cool because of altitude. Summers are generally fair, sunny, and pleasant. Winters are moderately cold with frequent heavy snowfalls.

Inter-mountain Plateau

This plateau lies between the Cascade and Sierra Nevada ranges and the Rocky Mountains. Many small mountain ranges stretch across this region, and two major river systems cut into the plateau — the Columbia–Snake system in the north, and the Colorado River in the east-central and southwestern portions. This is the driest region of the United States. Most of its scant moisture comes as snowfall. Winters are quite cold, and summers are mostly fair, dry, and sunny, but also sometimes arid and very hot.

Rocky Mountains

The high ranges of the Rocky Mountains extend southward from Canada into New Mexico. The crest of the Rockies forms the Continental Divide, the division between the Pacific Drainage Basin and the Atlantic–Gulf of Mexico Drainage Basin.

The rain and snow that fall in the Rocky Mountains provide most of the water supplies for both the region itself and for the adjacent semiarid areas. Most of the water used for irrigation, industry, and residential needs in western Arizona and Southern California (including Los Angeles) comes from the Colorado River, which is fed by rain and the melting snowpack of the Rocky Mountains.

Winters in the Rockies are very cold, particularly along the eastern slopes. Summers are cool, though valleys and canyons occasionally become quite hot during summer.

Great Interior Plains and Lowlands

This huge region extends west to east from the Rocky Mountains to the Appalachian Mountains, and north to south from Canada to the Southern Coast region. Because there are no climatic barriers, changes in climate across the region are gradual. Differences in climate in the area are controlled primarily by latitude, large air masses and storm movements, elevation, and distance from the ocean.

The climate is predominantly continental, with cold winters, warm to hot summers, and great extremes in temperature. The northern and central portions of this interior region are frequently invaded by cold dry arctic air masses in winter and sometimes even in summer, and these occasionally reach as far south as the Gulf Coast. The contrast between the warm continent and the cooler oceans during the summer months causes moisture-laden air to flow northward over the region, sometimes resulting in violent local storms in the form of tornadoes, severe thunderstorms, and hailstorms.

The western part of the area is considerably drier, because the Rocky Mountains block rain clouds coming from the west.

Appalachian Mountains

These mountains extend from northern Georgia to northwestern Maine and range between 2000 and 4000 feet above sea level. As they are only about one-third the height of the Rockies, they do not form as much of a bar to the passage of weather systems. Cold fronts and storms moving in from the west are forced upward, causing a considerable amount of rainfall during the warm months and heavy snowfall in winter. A similar effect occurs on the eastern slopes when fronts or storms move northward or westward from the Atlantic Ocean. Weather in this region varies greatly from place to place because of the irregular terrain.

Atlantic Lowlands

This region lies between the Appalachian Range to the west and the Atlantic Ocean to the east, and extends southward from Maine to the northern tip of South Carolina. These coastal lowlands vary in width from about 200 miles in the South to 40 miles in the New York–Connecticut area, then broaden again to about 150 miles in Maine. The climate is very similar to, but less severe than, that of the adjacent interior areas. The winters are somewhat warmer near the coast, and the summers are cooler than inland. Storm systems moving northward from the Gulf or along the Atlantic coast, and cold fronts and storms moving over the mountains from the west, bring most of the precipitation in the region. In winter, arctic air masses follow cold fronts into the region from the west, bringing snow showers and very low temperatures. Storms along the Atlantic coastline can also bring heavy snowfall.

Southern Coast

The Southern Coast is the strip of land that follows the coast from Cape Hatteras south to the tip of Florida and then around west to Corpus Christi, Texas, on the Gulf of Mexico. Though adjacent to the southern Interior Plains and Lowlands region, this area has a climate that is controlled for the most part by the Atlantic and the Gulf of Mexico. This contributes to the relatively mild and humid winters and the very warm and very humid summers. Southern Florida has a subtropical climate, its weather being dominated by the trade winds from the Atlantic. The Gulf Coast section is primarily affected by the moist air off the Gulf of Mexico.

The cold dry arctic air masses that frequently invade the interior of the continent sometimes reach as far as this coastal region, bringing a few days of chilling weather. The Gulf and South Atlantic coasts are subject to the destructive forces of hurricanes, which bring high tides, strong winds, and heavy rains.

General

In general, winters are coldest in the extreme northern interior and in the higher elevations of the mountains. Winters are warmest in the southern areas, particularly along the Southern California coast and the Gulf and South Atlantic coasts, and in southern Florida.

In summers the warmest sections of the country are the interior valleys and desert areas of the Southwest, the southern Great Plains, and the Deep South, while the coolest areas are the extreme northern interior areas, the mountains, and the northern coastal areas.

Charles Dudley Warner wrote in an editorial in the *Hartford Courant*, in 1897, that "Everybody talks about the weather, but nobody does anything about it." Since then, heating and air conditioning engineers have not only developed ways of doing something about interior climate, making our homes, offices, and factories more comfortable, but have also developed terms with which we can talk about climate and weather — terms more precise than *hot, cold, muggy,* or *balmy*. Some of their terms must be used if we are to say precisely what we mean, and a few of these terms are covered in the following paragraphs.

Heating Degree Days

Heating engineers have given us a way of measuring the heating required for a given day. The term they use is *heating degree day*, which may be defined as the number of degrees the average temperature for the day is below 65°F. For example, a day with an *average* temperature of 50°F is rated as a 15 heating degree day (65 − 50 = 15). A day with an average temperature above 65°F would rate zero heating degrees. The scores for the separate days are then added for the entire winter season to derive the total heating degree days per year for the area.

The amount of heating required at lower temperatures is directly proportional to the heating degree day value. Thus the fuel bill for a season with 2000 heating degree days will be approximately twice as high as that for a season with 1000 heating degree days.

Cooling Degree Days

Summers may require air conditioning, and the measure used to indicate required cooling is *cooling degree days*. The cooling degree day is defined as the number of degrees the average temperature for the day exceeds 65°F. The amount of cooling required for a building is also proportional to the degree-day value. A season with 2000 cooling degree days would require about twice the energy for cooling that a season with only 1000 cooling degree days would require.

There is, however, one very important point to remember when considering heating degree days and cooling degree days. The point from which both are measured is 65°F. Many of us are quite comfortable at temperatures considerably above and below that figure, if there is good ventilation and movement of air in the summer and there are no drafts in the winter.

Effective Temperature

Humidity also plays an important part in determining the amount of discomfort one feels on a hot day. Thus cooling degree days should be taken only as a general indication and not as an absolute measure of energy required for cooling.

Effective temperature (ET) is an index of the degree of warmth experienced by the human body when exposed to different combinations of temperature, humidity, and air movement. This measurement was developed in a series of studies in 1923 at the laboratories of the American Society of Heating and Air Conditioning Engineers. Most people are comfortable indoors in winter in an effective temperature of 66°F and in summer in an effective temperature of 71° or higher. The Effective Temperature chart shows the relationship of two of the ET factors, temperature and humidity, as they affect human comfort.

EFFECTIVE TEMPERATURE (ET)

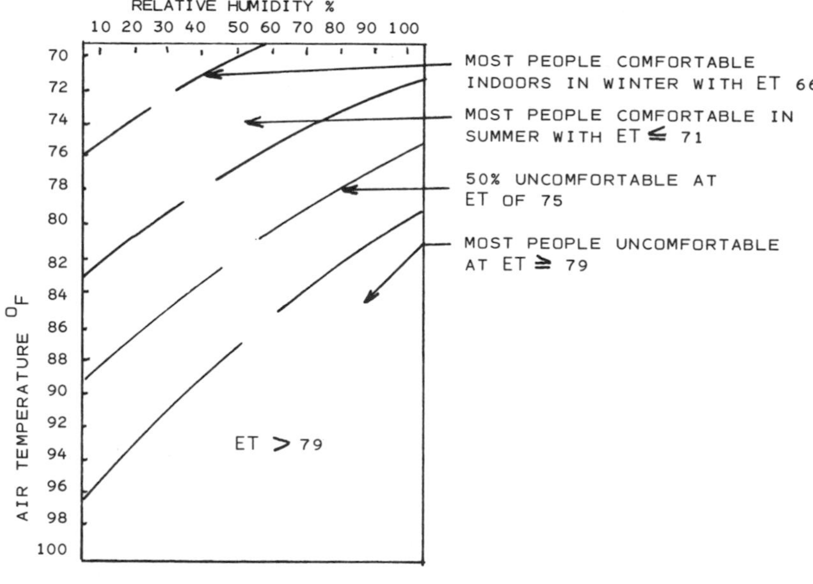

EFFECTIVE TEMPERATURE (ET)

Precipitation

Statistics given for *total precipitation* throughout this book are for the *water content* of all precipitation that falls on an area, including rain, hail, sleet, and snow. Because snow is a loose deposit of tiny ice crystals, the depth of a snowfall can be ten to one hundred times the amount of measurable precipitation contained in it. This accounts for the perhaps puzzling situation where an area can have a total of 40 inches of precipitation a year and 60 inches of snow. Snow piled in high drifts and covering the countryside waist-deep may represent no more than a couple of inches of precipitation.

According to climatologists, we are entering a period of climatic change. Our climate will be increasingly variable, with new highs, new lows, new records in precipitation, droughts, big storms, and high tides. We are probably entering a period of slight cooling over the coming 50 to 60 years, during which an average decrease in worldwide temperature of 1°F to 1.5°F is expected. If this prediction is correct, the southerly shift of population will continue as the northernmost areas come to have shorter and shorter growing seasons. Climate will play an increasingly important part in shaping our lives, whether we experience an overall cooling or not, simply because of the increasing costs of energy to heat our homes in winter and cool them in summer.

Further Reading

A number of good books and interesting articles are available on subjects related to the search for the best place to live. Some are old and some are current, but all are worth looking at. Most should be available at or through your local public library.

Books

Climates of the States

U.S. Department of Commerce, NOAA
Water Information Center, New York, 1974

This is a large book that gives detailed climatic information on all areas of the United States.

The Complete Retirement Planning Book

Peter A. Dickinson
E. P. Dutton, New York, 1976

Like many retirement books, this has useful information for anyone who plans to move to a new home.

Finding and Buying Your Place in the Country

Les Scher
Macmillan, New York, 1974

An excellent guide to the purchase of rural real estate that tells how to cope with the problems involved.

Fodor's USA 1976

Chapter entitled "America Today" by Ben J. Wattenberg
David McKay, New York, 1976

Even though this article is a few years old, it is still an excellent statement about our country.

Good Shelter

Judith and Bernard Rabb
Quadrangle/New York Times, New York, 1975

A guide to mobile, modular, and prefabricated houses, including domes. A must for anyone planning to buy a prefabricated home or build a home. Worthwhile reading for anyone interested in livability in a home.

Goode's World Atlas

Rand McNally, Chicago, 1974

Aside from its many excellent maps, this atlas has a wealth of information on climate, soil, vegetation, natural resources, and crops, and it provides much more about our country that is useful to anyone interested in finding out what some other home might be like.

How I Found Freedom in an Unfree World

Harry Browne
Macmillan, New York, 1973

A provocative examination of the traps we allow ourselves to live in and how to free ourselves from them. Recommended reading for anyone considering a major change in lifestyle.

How to Prosper During the Coming Bad Years

Howard J. Ruff
Times Books, New York, 1979

Howard Ruff presents some very convincing arguments in favor of small-town living, in light of what he sees in our future. Highly recommended.

Instant Weather Forecasting

Alan Watts
Dodd, Mead & Co., New York, 1976

In cities, weather is not really a part of everyday living. In a town it is. Alan Watts has written one of the clearest and most complete books on weather available today. Highly recommended for anyone moving to a small town.

Life After Doomsday

Bruce D. Clayton, Ph.D.
Paladin Press, Boulder, Colo., 1981

A frightening book that discusses potential military hazards in the United States. Worth reading for anyone desiring to explore the reasons behind why some towns are not included among the best towns in this book.

Living on a Few Acres: Yearbook of Agriculture 1978

U.S. Department of Agriculture
Government Printing Office, 1978

A well-done compilation of articles dealing with rural living, for those who are not trying to make a livelihood from the land.

Mobil Travel Guides

Mobil Oil Company

These are a set of regional travel guides covering the entire United States. They will give some information on the towns you are interested in, but their primary value will be apparent on your trip to evaluate your new home. They can save you their price at the first overnight stop by helping you locate the best hotel/motel value. We never travel without them. Available at most bookstores and some libraries.

Move Yourself and Save

Robert Hullinger and Robert Grosch
Clayton Publishing House, St. Louis, 1980

This $3.50 paperback is well worth the modest cost. A useful guide to do-it-yourself moving.

The Nine Nations of North America

Joel Garreau
Houghton Mifflin, Boston, 1981

A remarkable and penetrating analysis of the United States, how it works, and why. It explains with unusual clarity the reasons behind some of the problems certain areas have, and explains the good things about other areas. Highly recommended.

Other Homes and Garbage, Designs for Self-Sufficient Living

Jim Leckie and others
Sierra Club Books, San Francisco, 1975

A comprehensive and readable book on house design and livability, with some very good material on climate.

The Places Rated Almanac

Richard Boyer and David Savageau
Rand McNally, Chicago, 1981

An encyclopedic compilation of data on all the SMSAs in the United States. While few of our best towns are large enough to be included, there is a wealth of information that will apply to towns. Highly recommended.

Safe Places (East and West)

David and Holly Franke
Warner Paperbacks, New York, 1973

An ambitious book (two volumes in paperback) that explores safe living areas throughout the United States.

Shopper's Guide: Yearbook of Agriculture 1974

U.S. Department of Agriculture
Government Printing Office, 1974

A useful compilation of articles on shopping for almost everything. It includes a good chapter on how to move.

Sunbelt Retirement

Peter A. Dickinson
E. P. Dutton, New York, 1978

While written for the retiree, this is worthwhile reading for anyone who is thinking of moving to the sunbelt.

What Color Is Your Parachute?

Richard N. Bolles
Ten Speed Press, Berkeley, 1981

A manual for job hunters and career changers. Well done. Highly recommended for anyone doing either.

Where the Jobs Are

William J. McBurney, Jr.
Video Applications
Chilton Book Co., Radnor, Pa., 1980 and later

A detailed discussion of where jobs are in the United States.

Where You Live May Be Hazardous to Your Health

Robert A. Shakman, M.D., M.P.H.
Stein & Day, New York, 1979

A sometimes-frightening but always-entertaining book on the health hazards of picking the wrong place to live.

The World Almanac & Book of Facts

Newspaper Enterprise Association, New York, current year

An invaluable compilation of data on everything, including current tax information on every state, location of colleges and universities, and much, much more. Available at most supermarkets around the first of each year.

Other Publications

Articles

"America's Small Town Boom," *Newsweek*, July 6, 1981.
"The Best Cities in the West," by Leonard Gross, *New West*, December 5, 1977.
"Big Futures in Small Cities," *Money*, October 1980.
"Bright Futures in the West," *Money*, November 1981.
"If You're Looking for a Great Place to Live," *U.S. News & World Report*, July 12, 1982.

Homes for Living Catalogs

This is a collection of monthly illustrated bulletins from a nationwide network of realtors with offices in all 50 states. Look in the yellow pages of your local directory for a local realtor representing the "Homes for Living Network." Your local agent will put you in touch with an agent in any place you are interested in, at no charge and no obligation. In fact, your local agent may already have a booklet on the town you are interested in. The local representative in my own town has a rack filled with booklets from towns all over the country.

The Mother Earth News

P.O. Box 70
Hendersonville, NC 28791

A bimonthly publication for people interested in alternative energy and lifestyles, ecology, working with nature, and doing more with less. A fun magazine for anyone, but invaluable for people who want to grow their own food and live away from cities.

Strout Catalog

Strout Realty, Inc.
Plaza Towers
Springfield, MO 65804

This gives the same type of coverage as the *United Farm Catalog*. Strout Realty will send you a free copy of their real estate catalog if you write and ask for one. This and the United Farm Agency are the two big agencies dealing in nationwide real estate, most of it rural.

United Farm Catalog

United Farm Agency
612 West 47th Street
Kansas City, MO 64112

Separate catalogs are published quarterly for different regions of the United States. These are comprehensive catalogs of rural and semirural real estate, including real estate in and near many of the best towns listed in this book. Catalogs are free. Write, or call 800-821-2599, to receive the catalog for your area of interest.

Vacation Exchange Catalog

Vacation Exchange Club
350 Broadway
New York, NY 10013

This is one of the best ways to explore a potential new home. Write for their catalog. You will save the $14.00 the first night you don't stay in a motel.